# URBAN POLITICS
## and PUBLIC POLICY

# URBAN
# and PUBLIC

**HARPER & ROW, PUBLISHERS**
New York, Evanston, San Francisco, London

# POLITICS
# POLICY

**ROBERT L. LINEBERRY**
University of Texas
**IRA SHARKANSKY**
University of Wisconsin

For our wives
**NITA LINEBERRY**
**INA G. SHARKANSKY**

# contents

# preface

In the vernacular of contemporary political science, this text is a "behavioral" analysis of politics and public policies in American cities. By that we mean that it asks what people in politics do, why they do it, and what differences result from their activities. This book is more concerned with the realities of political behavior than with legal and structural features of local governments.

This is not to say that we avoid matters of governmental structure and legal processes. Rather, we view them in political and economic contexts. We ask why some forms develop and not others and what impacts on policies come from these forms of local government. By comparing the forms and legal processes of local governments with local economic, political, and policy traits we can then offer some answers to these questions.

Our treatment differs from some behavioral work that follows a style called "value free." Our book is "value relevant." We mention our own priorities at several places. In doing so, we hope that we have not distorted the findings of careful research but, instead, have placed the research into clearer perspective.

We have not hesitated to introduce data and quantitative analysis where relevant. That turns out to be rather frequently. But, on the other hand, we face some questions that have not proved amenable to precise measurement. Perhaps we have covered too much in a brief text on an increasingly complex subject. We prefer to risk criticism for such extensiveness than to undertake too little, raising only the easy questions and letting students fend for themselves with the harder ones.

We are indebted to David Perry and David Danelski for reviewing the entire manuscript and offering constructive suggestions. Robert MacDonald and Charles M. Bonjean read and commented upon parts of the text. Walter Lippincott, Jr., and Firth Fabend of Harper & Row performed indispensable editorial tasks. Our greatest debts, however, are to our wives. It will take more than a mere mention to repay our obligations to Nita and Ina.

R. L. L.
I. S.

# URBAN POLITICS
## and PUBLIC POLICY

# prologue
## The urban setting

The 1920 Census revealed that a majority of Americans lived in urban areas; the 1970 Census demonstrated that a majority of Americans are not merely urbanites but suburbanites as well. Louis Wirth wrote the classic definition of urbanism in 1938: "On the basis of three variables, number, density of settlement, and heterogeneity of the urban population, it appears possible to explain the characteristics of urban life and to account for the differences between cities of various types and sizes."[1]

In terms of *size,* cities range from the community of 2,500 people to a metropolis the size of New York City, with 8 million people. In actuality, the legal entity called a "municipality" is hardly ever coterminous with the social and economic city. In large urban complexes, the borders between one city and a neighboring city are imperceptible, and only signs separate one municipality from another. A "standard metropolitan statistical area" (SMSA)—defined by the Census Bureau as consisting of a central city or contiguous twin cities with a population of at least 50,000, together with its county and contiguous counties of a metropolitan character—contains a multiplicity of local governments.[2] Usually an SMSA includes a dominant central city plus a number of suburban governments, special districts, and school districts. The area described by the Census Bureau as the "New York–North-

[1] Louis Wirth, "Urbanism as a Way of Life," *American Journal of Sociology,* 44 (July, 1938), 18.

[2] According to the 1967 Census of Governments, there are 227 SMSAs in the United States, containing within them 20,703 units of local government.

eastern New Jersey Standard Consolidated Area" is not governmentally consolidated at all and contains twice as many people as does New York City itself.

*Density* also varies between and within cities, ranging from the single-family dwelling units of suburbia to the tightly packed tenements of the central city. The number of persons per square mile (a common measure of density) in the suburban city of New Rochelle, New York, is 7,500. On the other hand, the population density of Harlem's densest blocks, only a few miles south of New Rochelle, is so high that the United States Civil Rights Commission estimates that, if densities in the rest of the city were comparable, the entire American population could live in three of the city's five boroughs.

*Heterogeneity* is the third dimension of urbanism. Heterogeneity of class, occupational, religious, and ethnic interests generates conflicts that spill over into politics, and the spatial proximity arising from higher population densities exacerbates the conflicts that reflect these diverse interests.

Technically, about three-fourths of the American population now lives in areas the Census Bureau defines as "urban." It is easy to argue, as Senator Abraham Ribicoff has done, that because "seventy percent of all Americans now live in or close to cities . . . the fate of the city and the future of our country are one and the same thing."[3] There is something to be said for this line of reasoning, but it can also be seriously misleading. In the first place, the United States is not so overwhelmingly urban as Census Bureau figures imply. Figures depicting three-quarters of the population as urban are a statistical artifact of the Census Bureau standard—first adopted in 1790—that designates all places of 2,500 or more persons urban. Unless we want to think of Tyler, Texas, and Pekin, Illinois, as urban in the same way that St. Louis and Boston are urban, then we shall want to take all claims that urbanization is nearly complete with considerable skepticism. In fact, the 1960 Census revealed that only about 10 percent of the American population lived in cities with populations of 1 million or more and only a third lived in cities with populations of 50,000 or more. Many more lived in metropolitan areas, but in smaller communities, which guarded jealously their own autonomy against encroachment of urban giants. Air travelers flying over "megalopolis" see both forest and farmland between the cities.[4] A balanced view

3 Statement before the Subcommittee on Executive Reorganization of the Committee on Government Operations, United States Senate, *Federal Role in Urban Affairs* (Washington, D.C., Government Printing Office, 1966), part 1, p. 1.

4 In *Megalopolis*, Jean Gottman's exhaustive study of the urbanized eastern seaboard from Boston to Washington, D.C., two chapters are devoted to agriculture and natural resources. (New York, Twentieth Century Fund, 1961, chaps. 6–7.)

of urbanization recognizes that, although most Americans *are* urbanites, there are many kinds of urban places.

In the second place, Americans have never been characterized by the psychological and philosophical traits of an urban people. Even contemporary Americans share much of Thomas Jefferson's aversion to urbanism. A Gallup poll in 1966 revealed that only 22 percent of the population preferred to live in cities, 28 percent wanted to live in suburbia, 18 percent preferred farms, and a plurality, 31 percent, preferred small towns.[5] Americans may be urbanites, but their clear preference is for smaller rather than larger urban communities.

Recently a profusion of books and articles with ominous titles have decried the state of urban life. *Sick Cities, Cities in a Race with Time, The Death and Life of Great American Cities,* and *The Metropolitan Enigma* suggest the widely held view that life in the city is increasingly inhospitable.[6] Some observers, however, take a more optimistic view and argue that life in the city today is better than it ever has been.[7] They see a fallacy in lumping together everything from automotive fumes to gouging by ghetto merchants in a single overarching "urban crisis." Our book is not about the urban crisis and its components. Our subject is urban politics and the policy choices of urban governments, and our discussion bears upon such urban ills as pollution, crime, racial strife, poverty, the transportation problem, and fiscal inequities only insofar as they confront policy-makers and only insofar as their existence is recognized in public policies designed to deal with them.

By narrowing our focus to urban politics and public policy, we shall be dealing with an important range of questions, but we shall not feel obliged to explore the whole gamut of problems shaping the future of the city. Although not all the problems of the city are "political" ones, many of them come into sharper focus when they are viewed in relation to the public policies designed to cope with them. Still, in the final analysis, there may be no more important issue in the future of the city than the capacity of public authority to transform the urban condition.

[5] Cited in Daniel J. Elazar, "Are We a Nation of Cities?" in Robert A. Goldwin, ed., *A Nation of Cities* (Skokie, Ill., Rand McNally, 1966), p. 97. It is worth contrasting Elazar's discussion of the nonurban character of the American population with any argument that the urbanization of the United States is virtually complete.

[6] Mitchell Gorden, *Sick Cities* (Baltimore, Penguin, 1963); Jeanne Lowe, *Cities in a Race with Time* (New York, Random House, 1967); Jane Jacobs, *The Death and Life of Great American Cities* (New York, Random House, 1961); and James Q. Wilson, ed., *The Metropolitan Enigma* (Cambridge, Mass., Harvard University Press, 1969).

[7] Edward C. Banfield, *The Unheavenly City* (Boston, Little, Brown, 1970).

# 1

# The urban political system

## WHAT IS AN URBAN POLITICAL SYSTEM?

In this book we shall use the concept or model of the urban political
system to clarify our description of politics and policy-making. According to David Easton,

*The very idea of a system suggests that we can separate political life from the
rest of social activity, at least for analytical purposes, and examine it as though
for a moment it were a self-contained entity surrounded by, but clearly distinguishable from, the environment or setting in which it operates.*[1]

Easton's model of a political system, which emphasizes environmental
influences on political activity, begins with the premise that it is
possible to separate things political from their environment. Using
this notion as our point of departure in this book, we shall separate
political processes from elements that are neither urban nor political
and shall place such factors as economic, social, religious, and ethnic
attitudes and behavior in the environment of our system. The environment also includes the decisions, policies, rules, and expenditures of
states and the federal government.

In addition to the environment, the basic analytic elements of an
urban political system include the *inputs,* or demands and resources
from the environment; the actors and agencies in the *conversion* process who respond to inputs; the *outputs,* or policies formulated by

[1] David Easton, "An Approach to the Analysis of Political Systems," *World
Politics, 9* (April, 1957), 384.

**Figure 1.1**    *The urban political system*

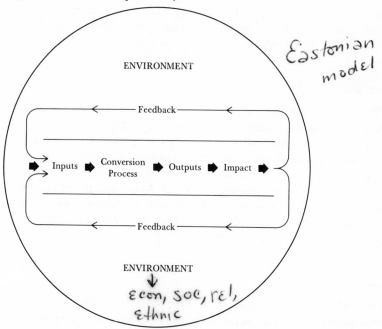

decision-makers in the conversion process; the *impact* of policies on the environment; and the *feedback* of subsequent inputs to decision-makers in response to policy impacts. A diagram of our model of the urban political system is presented in Figure 1.1.

We have taken this systematic approach because it has the advantage of directing attention to the myriad ways in which environment influences political activities. It is through the input process that environmental characteristics directly affect politics, but the environment also *indirectly* affects the other elements of the system by imposing constraints upon decision-makers, policies, and impacts of policies.

**Inputs**

Inputs may be viewed as demands or commitments of resources by individuals, groups, or the community as a whole that are intended to influence the choices of decision-makers and thereby to alter public policies. In a very simple political system, such as a very small town, the input process is informal and interpersonal.[2] The only political

[2] Arthur Vidich and Joseph Bensman, *Small Town in Mass Society* (Princeton, N.J., Princeton University Press, 1958).

resources needed are friendship, access, and a little time. In larger political systems, the input process is impersonal and institutional. Political parties, elections, interest groups, and even mass demonstrations dominate the process.

## Conversion

Decision-makers convert inputs into *outputs*. They take the raw materials presented to them in the form of demands and resources and use them to determine public policy. Decision-makers, however, are not neutral computers, automatically summing up resources and constraints. Rather, they are human beings who set limitations on their decisions, as do the institutions in which they operate. Urban decision-makers may be limited to elected and appointed officials and bureaucrats, or they may include members of a relatively concealed "power structure" of private citizens.

## Outputs, impact, and feedback

It is tempting to view policies as the end-product of the urban political system, insofar as they are the culmination of the inputs that are processed by the decision-makers. But politics does not really end with the enunciation and implementation of policies. Policies have impacts, sometimes intended, sometimes unintended. They may accomplish precisely what decision-makers desire, no more and no less, but more commonly there is slippage between the goals of a policy and its actual impact. Moreover, policies generally have side effects or unintended consequences. The impact of and feedback from a particular policy can be positive or negative, depending upon the announced goals of the policy and one's own views of the announced goals.

As Richard E. Dawson and James A. Robinson have pointed out, many political scientists view public policy as "the major dependent variable which political science seeks to explain. The task of political science, then, is to find and explain the independent and intervening variables which account for policy differences."[3] We concur in this statement of objectives, because we know that different urban political systems pursue different policies, spend more or less money, and tax more or less heavily. A major goal of this book, then, is to explain and understand such variations. But we must also understand the *impact* of policies upon urban populations.

3 Richard E. Dawson and James A. Robinson, "Inter-Party Competition, Economic Variables, and Welfare Policies in the American States," *Journal of Politics*, 25 (May, 1963), 266.

Along these lines, Edward C. Banfield has identified a series of research goals for the student of urban politics:

*One would like to be able to show how particular causes produce particular effects. If one could trace out several links in a causal sequence, that would be especially satisfying. Thus, one might begin by showing how certain "starting place" [environmental] characteristics of a city, such as its size, rate of growth, economic function, rate of home ownership, or the class or ethnic composition of its population exert a causal influence on the form and style of its government. (By "form and style" is meant whether the electoral system is partisan or nonpartisan, whether the office of mayor is strong or weak, whether the city council is elected on a ward basis or at large, whether the system is centralized or decentralized, and so on.) A second link might be established by showing the causal connections between form and style on the one hand and the content of the city government's policy on the other. . . . A third link might be established by showing a causal connection between the content of city government policy and the quality of life in the city.*[4]

Banfield's formulation would link the analysis of urban politics and policy with the "quality of life in the city." In the most complete sense, however, this goal is unattainable, because there is neither wide agreement upon nor any reliable measure of the "quality" of urban life. We have, at best, an idea of some things that are not desirable: pollution, poverty, crime, and the like. But neither policy-makers nor political scientists are fully able to design policies to rid society of its unwanted urban problems—and guarantee their success. We are even farther away from being able to prescribe policies that will guarantee a beneficent urban environment.

## Feedback

The feedback that comes to decision-makers in response to the impacts of earlier policies is an imperfect guide to future policy. There are two broad kinds of feedback, one a "when-the-shoe-pinches" feedback and the other a feedback from technical research on policy impact. The "when-the-shoe-pinches" type most often takes the form of public complaints. Elected officials are particularly sensitive to this kind of feedback, especially if it comes from groups whose votes they need. Feedback from technical research into policy questions is relatively new. If technical analysis of policy impacts becomes more common, it may be possible to evaluate them in a systematic and continuous way, without having to wait for grievances to build to a boiling point.

---

[4] Edward C. Banfield, *Big City Politics* (New York, Random House, 1965), p. 7.

## MACROANALYSIS AND MICROANALYSIS

The distinction between macro- and microanalysis, long familiar to economists and biologists, has only recently begun to penetrate political science.[5] The significance of the macro-micro distinction is its usefulness in explaining behavior both of communities and of subcommunity actors.

Macroanalysis deals with the behavior or properties of communities. When we explain variations in the level of public expenditures or segregation in housing, we are explaining differences between communities. When we discuss why municipalities within a metropolis have or have not coalesced into a metropolitan government, we are explaining the interactions of communities. Macroanalysis deals with the community as a whole.

Microanalysis examines the behaviors and interactions of individuals and other subcommunity units, like groups, parties, councils, power structures, and bureaucracies. To explain who participates in riots, how budgetary decisions are arrived at, and what social and psychological traits affect individual participation in municipal elections is to utilize microanalysis.

The macro-micro distinction enables us to examine any particular behavior from either or both perspectives. Political participation, for example, may vary both from city to city and from individual to individual. Quite often, some additional insights can be gained by examining political participation as a function of both macro (community-level) and micro (individual-level) attributes.[6]

For example, one of the most common characteristics of participation in politics is its strong relationship to indicators of social status. Individuals with higher levels of income and education are more likely than the average to vote and otherwise to participate. Interestingly, however, when we take a macro perspective and examine the levels of turnout from community to community, we find that one measure of social status, education, is actually negatively related to the turnout rates.[7] This finding is puzzling unless we use macroanalysis to explore how a community and its social structure can influence individual

5 An abstract, but provocative, treatment of the macro-micro distinction is contained in Amitai Etzioni, *The Active Society* (New York, Free Press, 1968), pp. 43–56.

6 See Robert L. Lineberry, "Approaches to the Study of Community Politics," in Charles M. Bonjean *et al.*, eds., *Community Politics: A Behavioral Approach* (New York, Free Press, 1971), chap. 2.

7 See Robert R. Alford and Eugene C. Lee, "Voting Turnout in American Cities," *American Political Science Review, 62* (September, 1968), 796–813.

voters. Then we discover that the communities with generally high educational attainments are often culturally homogeneous—as is the prototypical dormitory suburb, for example—and have fewer bases of social conflict. Homogeneous communities generate fewer of the political issues that impel people to vote. It is the mixture of social and economic traits in a community that produces political conflict. In local elections citizens in well-educated communities may thus simply have fewer incentives to participate. Many political phenomena other than political participation can also best be understood by examining both their micro and macro dimensions.

The combined use of macro- and microanalysis also directs our attention to the *discrete* (individual) and *contextual* (environmental) factors in political behavior. Microanalysis without attention to macro-level properties may produce serious distortions by leading to a personalistic and voluntaristic view of local politics. Such a perspective, for instance, might attribute policy-making to the values of the policy-makers without taking account of the environmental constraints upon their behavior. We emphasize throughout this book the myriad ways in which the environment impinges upon and constrains individual choices. For example, the economic base of a community is particularly important in determining the availability of resources. In deciding upon spending and taxing levels, city officials are not free to choose any level of spending they desire, because numerous community factors, not the least of which is the availability of resources, place limits on their discretion. Indeed, a major theme of this book (and of Chapter 2 in particular) is the stringent limitations imposed on urban decision-makers by factors outside their control.

On the other hand, macroanalysis, without the corrective provided by microanalysis, may promote a deterministic view of local politics. To view economic forces, social structures, and other macro properties as the only explanations for social change implies that "forces" and "processes," rather than men, are the prime movers in such change. In sum, balanced assessment of urban politics emphasizes both macroscopic and microscopic explanations.

## A MODEL OF THE URBAN POLITICAL SYSTEM

If we combine the elements in the system model with the micro-macro distinction, we can construct the more elaborate model of an urban political system shown in Figure 1.2. Each element in the political system—inputs, conversion process, outputs, impact, and feedback—can be identified at the macro (community) level, and each has an analogue at the micro (subcommunity) level.

**Figure 1.2**   *Micro and macro elements of the urban political system*

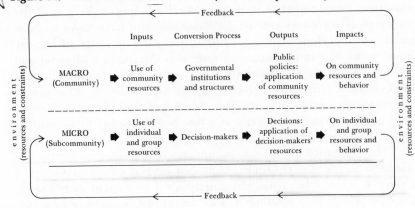

⟶ = flow of the policy process

Figure 1.2 emphasizes the environment as the source of *resources* and *constraints*. (These two elements will be discussed in the next section.) Availability of resources to individuals and groups depends in part, though not entirely, upon the magnitude of community resources. The availability of micro-level resources will enable individuals and groups to make demands on decision-makers, and the availability of macro-level resources will enable decision-makers to respond to these demands.[8]

The conversion process also has macro and micro aspects. Decision-makers, whether they are lower-level bureaucrats or elected city officials, operate within the context of governmental institutions. It is obvious that the attitudes, roles, and preferences of individual policy-makers have some effects on policy. If a liberal mayor ousts a conservative, then policies will probably change in the direction of more spending. But government institutions also affect the degree of change. For example, change from a conservative to a liberal mayor should produce more genuine difference in the strong-mayor form of government than in the council-manager form, in which the mayor's powers are minimal. Other characteristics of governmental institutions—the structure and rules of the budgetary process, rules and regulations of state and federal governments, the degree of centralization of power—impose their own constraints upon policy-makers.

At the micro level, the outputs of individual decision-makers are *decisions*. At the macro level, the outputs of governmental institutions

---

[8] The term "demand" is used so commonly by political scientists who follow Easton that it is worth noting that it need not imply table pounding. A demand may be articulated as forcibly as rioting in the streets or as subtly as diplomatic discourse.

are *policies*. Outputs apply the resources of the political system as a whole or the individual decision-makers in it to produce certain changes in the urban environment. Any specific policy may be analyzed in terms of its impact upon the community and upon subcommunity units. Education, for example, performs both macro and micro functions. On the micro level, it may increase an individual's earning power and expand his respect for cultural affairs. On the macro level, the educational system may increase the community's attractiveness to industry and thereby alter its economic and tax base.

It is possible that the impact of a policy may be beneficial at one level yet detrimental at another. For example, critics of urban renewal allege that it has benefited communities by increasing tax bases of cities and slowing urban decay but that it has imposed micro-level costs on individuals with lower incomes who have been forced to relocate (see pp. 339–342).

## THE URBAN SYSTEMS MODEL: A GUIDE FOR THE READER

We have introduced the systems model of urban politics and the distinction between macro- and microanalysis to guide the reader through the following chapters.

Our model is not a precise theory of local politics or a concrete mold into which all of our analysis must fit. It is designed only to guide ourselves and our readers. As yet, we do not know enough about urban affairs to account for all the political manifestations we shall describe, much less to predict what will happen under a given set of circumstances. We propose this model only as a framework for coding information.

The systems model guides us to an appreciation of the relations among political phenomena. It emphasizes that politics does not occur in a vacuum. By focusing on policy, we hope to convey some notions about political relations that will help our readers as political scientists and as citizens. Although our model cannot—and does not claim to—account for all that is relevant in the urban scene, it does, we think, combine relevance with rigor. A model should not obscure the real people, their real problems, and the constraints upon their behavior within the urban system. It should, rather, make it possible to organize the fragments of available information so that we get a complete and very *real* picture of the urban scene.

Within each chapter we deal with many issues that are not directly related to the components of the model. This does not mean that we abandon the model. It means, rather, that it is more a framework for assembling information than a rigorous theory. Models are necessarily abstract and deliberately simplified. Their utility lies in their capacity to organize disparate bits of data into some pattern. Indeed, by using one model to the exclusion of others, we may distort research findings that were formulated from different intellectual perspectives. Sometimes we are prepared to pay this cost; sometimes we prefer to break with our model and examine a question of interest to us on its own terms. Our model guides our discussion of diverse subjects, but it does not commit us to mental rigidity. And, although it guides, it does not always govern our treatment of urban politics and public policy.

## SOME ECONOMIC PERSPECTIVES ON URBAN POLITICS

One of the issues we deal with throughout the book is the role of the economic environment in the urban political system. The argument that economic factors are the primary motivating forces in human behavior unites such otherwise diverse figures as Karl Marx and James Madison. Although their political theories diverge sharply, each begins with an assumption that the seeds of political conflict are sown in the economic differences among men and among classes. Twentieth-century thinkers, realizing that psychological, social, and political phenomena cannot be fully explained by economic differences, have challenged the philosophical underpinnings of such "economic determinism." Indeed, today it seems clear that no single principle like economic determinism could explain such complex phenomena as racial prejudice, poverty, and criminality. Granted, then, that the economic perspective is only one of several alternative (and not altogether mutually exclusive) ways of viewing the urban political system, we nonetheless believe that certain economic categories are essential to our understanding of this system. We emphasize four particular economic concepts: resources, constraints, interests, and stakes.

### Resources and constraints

At the macro level of analysis, urban politics is in many respects a politics of economics. Cities are dependent upon their economic resources to a far greater extent than are either the states or the federal government.[9] This dependence is greater because most communities depend upon the relatively narrow economic bases that lie within their borders.

The economic bases of some communities depend upon the con-

---

[9] Ira Sharkansky, *The Politics of Taxing and Spending* (Indianapolis, Bobbs-Merrill, 1969), chaps. 4–5.

tinuance of federal programs. San Antonio and El Paso, for example, depend heavily for their existence on the presence of large military bases. Cities also are vulnerable to location choices made in the private (and nonlocal public) sector, over which they have little control. Although location choices are based upon numerous grounds, many city governments mount expensive campaigns to attract or retain industries by offering lower taxes, free or cheap land, zoning manipulations, relocation assistance, and free training of industrial workers. Although larger and more diverse communities are less affected by location decisions, many of the largest cities have lost residents and tax bases because of industrial out-migration.

American cities have enormous resources theoretically available to them, but much of this wealth is locked away from their decision-makers by private and public constraints (see Chapter 2). Urban policy-making can be seen as the search for strategies to overcome the constraints upon resource use. Policies of attracting industry and the continued search for intergovernmental aids are two devices used by policy-makers to cope with limitations on their access to resources. The pursuit of these strategies, however, imposes its own set of constraints. The need to attract industry may make a community wary of industrial taxes, and the existence of intergovernmental grants for specific programs forecloses options in other areas.

In analysis at the individual and group levels, the concepts of resources and constraints are useful. An economist uses the term *resource* for money or things readily convertible into money. A political scientist, however, uses the term *political resource* in a somewhat broader sense, to refer, as Robert A. Dahl has done, to "anything which can be utilized to sway the specific choice or strategies of another individual." From the micro perspective, political resources, Dahl goes on,

> might include an individual's own time; access to money, credit, or wealth; control over jobs; control over information; esteem or social standing; the possession of charisma, popularity, legitimacy, or legality . . . the rights pertaining to public office . . . solidarity . . . the right to vote, intelligence, education, and perhaps even one's energy level.[10]

The typical condition of resource use—at both macro and micro levels—is "slack," rather than "tight," to use Dahl's terminology again.[11] Resources are slack when less than the full supply of an individual's or community's political resources is actually employed. We have already noted, and shall explore more fully in Chapter 2, that

[10] Robert A. Dahl, *Who Governs?* (New Haven, Conn., Yale University Press, 1961), p. 225.
[11] *Ibid.*, chap. 25; and Roscoe C. Martin *et al.*, *Decisions in Syracuse* (Garden City, N.Y., Doubleday Anchor, 1965), pp. 8–10.

communities use only a fraction of the resources potentially available to them. The same is true of individuals and groups. Very low levels of political participation and electoral turnout, for instance, indicate slack in voters' resource application.

Every political resource is to some degree substitutable for others. Communities short on economic resources can attempt to pirate industry from other communities or can rely upon federal grants. Money can purchase information, time, and political organization for individuals and groups. But even groups without money are not completely without resources: The rich may have money, but the poor have both the franchise and strength in numbers. Groups that have low financial resources often resort to such other resources as protests, charisma, ethnic solidarity, and the manipulation of political symbols. Not all are equally endowed with political resources, but each has slack in some kind of resource. The trick is often to generate the motivation needed to apply available resources. The importance of resources lies less in their potential availability than in the actual extent of their application and in the skills with which they are applied.

### Interests and stakes

Political man (close cousin to "rational economic man") operates to maximize his own self-interest. No economist, of course, wants to be taken literally when he uses a model of human beings as essentially rational (identifying a hierarchy of goals and seeking the most efficient way to attain them) and self-interested (acting only to increase their incomes). In fact, both economists and political scientists emphasize that some people behave, at least part of the time, in a "public regarding" fashion, setting aside their own interests to further those of the "community as a whole." Wilson and Banfield, for example, find that some voters, particularly higher-income WASPs and Jews, vote against their own "self-interest narrowly conceived" and support referenda that cost them higher taxes to benefit other social groups.[12] Indeed, it would be difficult to explain the behavior of high-income groups in supporting all kinds of municipal referenda without introducing a concept like "public-regardingness."[13]

12 James Q. Wilson and Edward C. Banfield, "Public Regardingness as a Value Premise in Voting Behavior," *American Political Science Review*, 58 (December, 1964), 876–887.

13 *Ibid.*; see also Eugene S. Uyeki, "Patterns of Voting in a Metropolitan Area: 1938–1962," *Urban Affairs Quarterly*, 1 (June, 1966), 65–77; and Alvin Boskoff and Harmon Zeigler, *Voting Patterns in Local Election* (Philadelphia, Lippincott, 1964), chap. 3.

The stakes in local politics are the perceived gains and losses from the political system that may affect one's interests. Sayre and Kaufman list four main kinds of "stakes and prizes" in city politics: (1) public office or public employment, (2) money, (3) governmental services and policies, and (4) ideological and intangible rewards.[14] We expect that persons who perceive high stakes in urban political life will participate heavily, commit their resources to political ends, and be conscious of policy impacts. There is some evidence, for example, that labor unions —active participants in state and national politics—see fewer stakes in local politics and therefore participate less actively at that level (see pp. 68–69). Although both home owners and renters pay local property taxes (renters pay them through rents high enough to cover their share of the taxes), the home owners ordinarily perceive higher stakes in city tax policies, probably because the actual payments are more visible to them. Each may have a corresponding "interest" in lower taxes, but the home owner sees the "stakes" more clearly.

## SUMMARY

We have outlined in this chapter some perspectives useful for understanding the rest of the book. We use the model of a political system to analyze urban politics and public policy. The political system is embedded in its environment, which is the source of both resources and constraints. The task of urban decision-makers is to convert inputs from the environment into public policies designed to have an impact upon problems of the environment. Feedback from that policy impact affects future inputs and shapes new demands upon the political system.

By combining the systems model with macro and micro perspectives, we can gain a fuller understanding of the urban political process. The macro level of analysis helps to provide the big picture, and micro analysis enables us to sketch in some of the details. Any particular activity—participation, budget-making, the impact of urban renewal —may be seen from either perspective.

In our analysis of the political system and its outputs, we do not pretend to have the final answers to most of the issues; in some cases, we have only hypotheses. But on the basis of the arguments in this chapter, we hope that the reader will have the tools to follow our analysis and to challenge us when our arguments do not fit the realities of urban political life.

[14] Wallace S. Sayre and Herbert Kaufman, *Governing New York City* (New York, Russell Sage Foundation, 1960), chap. 2.

# part one

# THE ENVIRONMENT
# OF URBAN POLICY

ENVIRONMENT is our term for the major features that underlie
urban policy-making. These features produce both the resources
and the constraints, as well as the human and economic energies
that face the urban decision-maker. In keeping with our model
of the urban political system, we consider in Part One both macro-
and microscopic views of the urban environment: the characteristics and resources of whole communities and those of individuals and groups.

In Chapter 2, "The Socioeconomic Context," we discuss the *irony of
urban wealth:* that the vast economic resources of urban America are, for
many reasons, virtually inaccessible to urban governments. Factors of distribution, as well as social, political, and legal features of the urban system,
keep that wealth from meeting the policy demands of urbanites. In Chapter
3, "The Political Context," we move to a microanalytic perspective, dealing
with inputs from individuals and groups. Beginning with the proposition
that all political systems must discover something about the interests and
needs of their citizens, we examine participation, interest groups, parties, and
elections as devices to facilitate the transmission of citizens' demands. We
devote particular attention to the timely and multifaceted topic of black
politics. Our theme in that chapter is the imperfection of the input process,
which makes obtaining information about citizens' needs very costly for decision-makers.

# 2

# The socioeconomic context

The irony of urban wealth is that the tremendous human and economic capital in our cities lies tantalizingly just beyond the reach of urban policy-makers. Observers differ in their estimates of our cities' future, but there is wide agreement about the current situation of urban areas—especially about the congestion, pollution, and tensions of the cities and about the inability of local politicians to alleviate these problems because they do not command enough resources to do so. We discuss in this chapter three key aspects of the policy environment of the urban political system: (1) the great economic and human resources of urban areas, (2) the distribution of those resources within the metropolitan area, and (3) the impediments to the use of those resources by urban governments.

It is difficult for urban governments to use these resources because of the distribution of wealth within the metropolis (and the corresponding distribution of problems) and because of legal, political, and economic barriers. In Greek mythology Tantalus, from whose name the verb "tantalize" is derived, is condemned to have fruit and water recede beyond his reach whenever he tries to grasp them. The irony of urban wealth is not that simple, but the inability of cities to use what lies just beyond their reach is at the core of the American urban crisis.

## THE WEALTH OF CITIES

Cities are the major producers of wealth in the contemporary United States, primarily because they have the personnel and facilities that process the raw materials of the fields and mines into finished commodities. Almost as important, cities have those specialists in medicine, law, theater, the arts, fashion, and entertainment whose work is highly prized in a culture of increasingly sophisticated tastes. Money flows to the cities to pay for the services of these specialists, and prospective specialists flow to the cities to complete their own training and to compete for employment.

The population growth of urban areas is one sign of their economic prosperity, but this growth is also a source of problems for urban authorities, because prosperity also attracts many untrained segments of the population who want better opportunities for themselves and their families. The cost to the city of providing some newcomers with services is substantially greater than the value of these newcomers' skills to the city's economy. Urban slums, to which many of these immigrants flock, represent a combination of the attractions of the city for poor people and the inability of many immigrants to succeed in the urban environment. Here, again, is an irony of the urban economy: an abundance of wealth that begets poverty even while it reproduces itself, and local authorities who do not have adequate access to the resources to satisfy the intense demands made upon them.

### Indicators of urban wealth

Although the economic resources of urban areas are many, ranging from industrial capital, commercial facilities, transportation arteries, and financial institutions to the human "capital" of citizens' training and skills, state constitutions and statutes generally limit local governments to only one source of revenue: taxes on real property. Local governments determine the "value" of each taxpayer's property.

Because of wide divergences in assessment standards, market conditions in each community, and the location of one piece of property in relation to others of greater or lesser value, no compilation of property values has the same meaning from one city to another. Therefore, to ascertain the relative levels of wealth in various kinds of local governmental jurisdictions, we must use indirect measures of the kind of wealth that is subject to taxation.

We shall use population growth, income levels, and education as our indicators of the wealth of urban areas,[1] because these features help us to distinguish urban and rural residents and give us some ideas about the kinds of urban areas that are most likely to be wealthy. We assume that population growth signals a dynamic economy that is expanding

[1] For a discussion of the usefulness of various measures of economic resources, see Harvey S. Perloff et al., Regions, Resources, and Economic Growth (Baltimore, Johns Hopkins, 1960).

rapidly enough to attract immigrants in search of improved living conditions. Levels of personal income indicate the amounts of resources available to "average" families and should affect the revenues available from residential property taxes. Similarly, levels of education indicate the kinds of people who live in various communities—in terms of both their demands for services and their likely contributions to local taxes. Urban areas tend to score higher than do rural areas on all these measures of wealth, and larger urban areas tend to score higher than do smaller urban areas.

POPULATION GROWTH    The patterns of urban growth indicate the concentration of economic opportunities in urban, as opposed to rural, areas. Figure 2.1 depicts the population growth in the twentieth century of the United States as a whole, together with the growth in SMSA and non-SMSA areas. In 1900 approximately 42 percent of the American population resided in SMSAs, a proportion that will increase to an estimated 69 percent by 1975. Table 2.1 shows population growth in urban and rural areas between 1950 and 1960.

**Figure 2.1**    *The growth of U.S. population between 1900 and 1975*

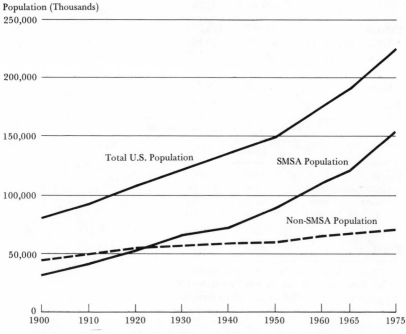

SOURCE: Advisory Commission on Intergovernmental Relations, *Fiscal Balance in the American Federal System,* vol. 2 (Washington, D.C., Government Printing Office, 1967), p. 29.

Rural areas lost population in absolute as well as in percentage terms during this period: from approximately 54.5 million to 54.1 million. Most of the population growth in metropolitan areas is accounted for by the natural increase of the population. Indeed, the "population explosion" is a reality in metropolitan areas; three-quarters of the population increase there has resulted from the propensity to reproduce rather than the propensity to migrate. Rural areas, on the other hand, do not produce enough offspring to replace the migrants to the cities.

INCOME AND EDUCATION    Median family incomes are consistently higher in metropolitan than in nonmetropolitan areas, as Table 2.2 indicates. Indeed, rural farm residents who live on the fringes of metropolitan areas often find it profitable to commute to jobs in the city, or they profit from truck farming that serves the big-city market.

**Table 2.1**  *Population growth, by type of area, 1950–1960*

|  | Population (in 1,000s) | |
| --- | --- | --- |
|  | 1950 | 1960 |
| Urbanª | 96,847 | 125,269 |
| Urbanized areasᵇ | 69,249 | 95,848 |
| Central cities | 48,377 | 57,975 |
| Urban fringe | 20,872 | 37,873 |
| Other | 27,598 | 29,420 |
| Ruralᶜ | 54,479 | 54,054 |

|  | Percentage of total population | |
| --- | --- | --- |
|  | 1950 | 1960 |
| Urban | 64.0 | 69.9 |
| Urbanized areas | 45.8 | 53.5 |
| Central cities | 32.0 | 32.2 |
| Urban fringe | 13.8 | 21.1 |
| Other | 18.2 | 16.4 |
| Rural | 36.0 | 30.1 |

a Communities of at least 2,500 population.

b At least one city of 50,000 (central city) plus contiguous closely settled areas (urban fringe).

c Communities of less than 2,500 population and the countryside.

SOURCE: U.S. Bureau of the Census, *Statistical Abstract of the United States, 1968* (Washington, D.C., Government Printing Office. 1968).

THE SOCIOECONOMIC CONTEXT

The distribution of educational attainments shown in Table 2.3 mirrors the distribution of personal wealth and population growth. The urbanite is generally better educated than is his rural cousin, indicating that cities possess greater reservoirs of skills and human resources on which to draw.

In short, the great economic and human energies of the United States are concentrated in its metropolitan areas. Metropolitan areas, containing two-thirds of the nation's population, also account for

1    more than four-fifths (82 percent) of savings-and-loan deposits;
2    four-fifths (80 percent) of all banks deposits;
3    more than three-fourths (77 percent) of value added by manufacturing;

**Table 2.2**  *Median family income in metropolitan and nonmetropolitan areas, 1959*

|  | SMSAa | Non-SMSA |
|---|---|---|
| Central city | $5,940 | — |
| Urban fringe | 7,114 | — |
| Other urban | 7,002 | $5,296 |
| Rural nonfarm | 5,830 | 4,303 |
| Rural farm | 4,543 | 3,061 |

a Standard Metropolitan Statistical Area.

SOURCE: U.S. Bureau of the Census, *U.S. Census of Population, 1960. General Social and Economic Characteristics: U.S. Summary.* Final Report PC (1)–1C, reprinted from Alan K. Campbell and Seymour Sacks, *Metropolitan America: Fiscal Patterns and Governmental Systems* (New York, Free Press, 1967), p. 21.

**Table 2.3**  *Distribution of educational attainments in urban and rural areas*

| Educational characteristic | SMSA | Non-SMSA |
|---|---|---|
| Median school years completed | 11.1 | 9.5 |
| Percentage completing fewer than 5 years of school | 7.0 | 10.7 |
| Percent completing 4 years of college or more | 8.8 | 5.6 |

SOURCE: U.S. Bureau of the Census, *U.S. Census of Population, 1960*, (Washington, D.C., Government Printing Office, 1961).

**Figure 2.2** The St. Louis urbanized area in 1960, one example of the "governmentally crowded" modern metropolis

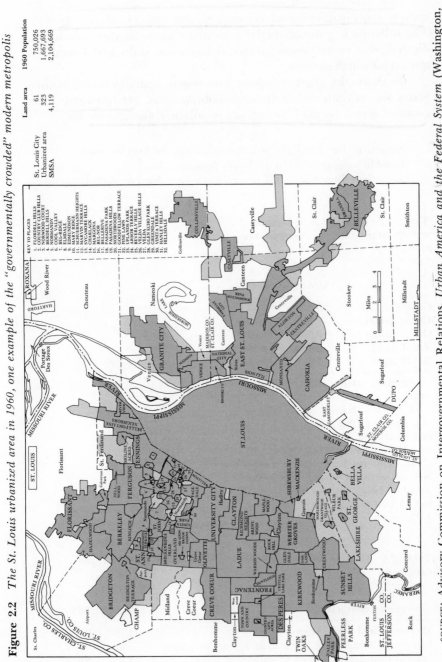

| | Land area | 1960 Population |
|---|---|---|
| St. Louis City | 61 | 750,026 |
| Urbanized area | 323 | 1,667,693 |
| SMSA | 4,119 | 2,104,669 |

KEY TO PLACES
1. FLORDELL HILLS
2. NORWOOD HILLS
3. NORWOOD COURT
4. BERDELL HILLS
5. KINLOCH
6. COOL VALLEY
7. BEL-RIDGE
8. ELMDALE
9. EDMUNDSON
10. MARY RIDGE
11. SCHUERMANN HEIGHTS
12. MARVIN TERRACE
13. SYCAMORE HILLS
14. CHARLACK
15. MARGINA
16. BEL-NOR
17. BELLERIVE
18. PASADENA PARK
19. PASADENA HILLS
20. NORTHWOODS
21. GOODFELLOW TERRACE
22. PINE LAWN
23. UPLANDS PARK
24. ARBOR TERRACE
25. BEVERLY HILLS
26. VELDA VILLAGE HILLS
27. VELDA CITY
28. GLEN ECHO PARK
29. GREENDALE
30. VINITA TERRACE
31. HANLEY HILLS
32. HILLSDALE

SOURCE: Advisory Commission on Intergovernmental Relations, *Urban America and the Federal System* (Washington, D.C., Government Printing Office, 1969), p. 85.

*4*   three-fourths (75 percent) of the nation's personal income;
*5*   more than seven-tenths (71 percent) of all retail sales;
*6*   seven-tenths (70 percent) of assessed property value.

## THE DISTRIBUTION OF PEOPLE, PRODUCTION, AND PROBLEMS

### Double migration

Two simultaneous migrations—of the poor to the central cities and of the well-to-do to the suburbs—have characterized metropolitan growth in the twentieth century. These migrations are not yet completed, but they have progressed to the point where now the vast majority of urban population results more from natural increases rather than from the continuing movement of people to and within the metropolis. Metropolitan areas include the greatest concentrations of human and economic wealth in our society. As we see in this section, however, these resources are not distributed evenly within metropolitan areas.

The fundamental distinction in this section is between the *central city* (CC) and the areas *outside central city* (OCC). A metropolitan area is a combination of one large central city and an outer area, sometimes also called the "urban fringe" or "suburbia."

The most prominent political characteristic of the metropolitan area is the fragmentation of its governments. If a cartographer were to color every municipality in each metropolitan area a different color, he would need 474 different colors for the St. Louis SMSA, 268 for the Seattle SMSA, and 191 for the Syracuse SMSA. The enormously fragmented St. Louis area, shown in Figure 2.2, is not atypical. As a matter of comparison, there are approximately four times as many local governments in the St. Louis area alone as there are nation-states in the world. The consequences of this fragmentation of urban governments are discussed in this chapter and again in Chapter 4.

Central cities have attracted and held particular kinds of persons and production. The migration to the central city has included disproportionate numbers of blacks, Puerto Ricans, Cubans, Mexican-Americans, and poor whites. From 1940 to 1966 3.5 million blacks left the South, mostly for the CCs of the north. Fifty-six percent of all American blacks now live in the CCs of metropolitan areas, north and south, whereas only twenty-five percent of white Americans live in CCs. In Florida, Cuban refugees populate the CCs; in the Southwest, Mexican-Americans and a small population of American Indians are concentrated in CCs. By far the largest proportion of growth in CCs is accounted for by increases in minority-group populations. The white population in CCs of all SMSAs rose only 5 percent between 1950 and 1960, whereas the black population alone grew 50 percent. In the five largest metropolitan areas, white population declined 7 percent, and black population increased 56 percent. When the 1970 Census is finally tabulated, it is likely that a dozen of the largest central cities will contain 40 percent or more blacks each. Washington, D.C., and Newark, New Jersey, now have black majorities, and other cities are rapidly approaching this mark.

A parallel migration, the effects of which are equally significant, has been the movement from CCs. Today _almost all the population growth of the United States is concentrated in the OCCs of the metropolis_. The populations of rural areas, small towns, and central cities are virtually stagnant. The population advantage of OCC areas, compared with CC areas, is shown in Figure 2.3. In the 1960 Census there was near equality in populations of CCs and OCCs. Since then growth has been concentrated in the OCCs, and projections indicate that this

**Figure 2.3**  *The trend in distribution of SMSA population between central cities and outside between 1900 and 1975*

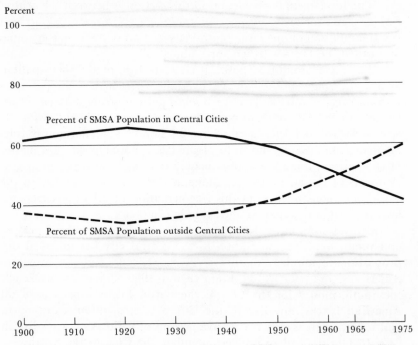

SOURCE: Advisory Commission on Intergovernmental Relations, *Fiscal Balance in the American Federal System,* vol. 2 (Washington, D.C., Government Printing Office, 1967), p. 30.

trend will continue. Such growth does not result from larger families in OCCs; it reflects, rather, the net balance of out-migration from CCs by those who can afford it and in-migration into the CCs by the less well-to-do. The Cleveland SMSA as a whole grew 25 percent between 1950 and 1960. But because out-migration and natural increases in the OCCs more than counterbalanced in-migration and natural increases in the CC, the latter suffered a net loss of 4 percent during the decade.

At the time that this book went to press, there were only preliminary figures from the 1970 Census. From these figures, it appears that several trends of the 1960s repeated those of earlier periods. Metropolitan growth exceeded that of the countryside, and within metropolitan areas most of the growth occurred in the suburbs, as the following statistics indicate.

(1)    More than three-fourths of the growth in national population occurred in metropolitan areas, with most of this growth occurring in suburban areas. People living in OCCs now outnumber people living in CCs.

(2)    From 1960 to 1970, the farm population declined from about 15 million to about 10 million.

(3)    Of the 25 largest central cities, 13 lost population between 1960 and 1970. The largest losses—in terms of percentage—occurred in St. Louis, Cleveland, and Pittsburgh. Each of them lost at least 15 percent of their population. The most startling cases of population growth of central cities were Phoenix, Houston, and Dallas, which grew because of population migration to their regions, and Indianapolis and Jacksonville, which grew primarily because of *city-county consolidation*.

## The migration of production

Production has also been moving to the OCCs. The movement of industries and commercial establishments has both followed and encouraged the movement of families, and most economic growth is now concentrated in OCCs. The Advisory Commission on Intergovernmental Relations notes that in 1960–1965 62 percent of the valuation of new construction permits was issued to OCCs within the metropolis.[2] The proportions for the largest SMSAs are even higher. In the Washington, D.C., area, 96 percent of construction value was being undertaken in suburban areas between 1960 and 1965.

The flight of industry and commerce from the CCs exacerbates the already high unemployment rates in those areas. As for families, there are many explanations for industrial movement. Hoover and

[2] Advisory Commission on Intergovernmental Relations, *Fiscal Balance in the American Federal System*, vol. 2 (Washington, D.C., Government Printing Office, 1967), p. 53.

*Hoover* &

Vernon identify five major reasons for choosing to relocate within the metropolis: (1) the search for space, (2) changes in transportation technology, (3) movement of labor, (4) the availability of external economies, and (5) the flight from taxes.[3] Perhaps the paramount reason for both family and business movement is the sheer need for space. The cost of relocating a growing plant in the CC is many times more than that of moving it to the suburbs. Moreover, plants now located in areas zoned for residential purposes often cannot obtain permission to expand.

As rails displace waterways and roads displace rails, there is even less reason to concentrate production in small core areas. Indeed, intermetropolitan movement is facilitated by location outside the congested downtown areas, as are a firm's chances of obtaining a labor supply. The majority of skilled personnel now live in OCCs, and three-quarters of union members under age forty live in the suburbs.

What Hoover and Vernon mean by "external economies" is the input factors and the tertiary services necessary to produce commodities. These elements are more essential to smaller than to larger and more autonomous firms, which have found it relatively easy to locate outside the CC. The smaller (and often less profitable) operations are left in the central city, where they benefit from close contact with suppliers and distributors. The small garment manufacturer is typical of the kind of firm that still benefits from a central-city location. Equally typical, unfortunately, are the low wages and unpromising futures that the garment industry offers its employees.

The pursuit of low taxes, though often exaggerated by businessmen and families seeking new locations, has been a determining factor in some movement to OCC. We discuss the "attractions"—and problems—of CC and OCC taxes below.

### Disparities between CCs and OCCs

The result of the dual migrations is a series of socioeconomic disparities between CCs and OCCs, reinforced by the fragmentation of metropolitan government. These disparities are illustrated by the personal-income data in Table 2.4. Incomes reflect both demand and supply aspects of the urban political economy. Viewed as reflecting demand, they indicate certain needs associated with poor housing, inadequate health care, and other aspects of poverty, plus the various demands that are made by middle- and upper-income taxpayers; viewed as reflecting supply, they indicate the resources potentially available to

3 Edgar M. Hoover and Raymond Vernon, *Anatomy of a Metropolis* (Garden City, N.Y., Doubleday Anchor, 1962), chap. 2.

**Table 2.4**  *The ratio of number of families with incomes over $10,000 to those with incomes under $3,000 per 100 families, by SMSA size, 1959*

| Population of SMSA | Entire SMSA | Central City (CC) | Outside Central City (OCC) | Difference in Ratio (OCC–CC) |
|---|---|---|---|---|
| United States | 124.2% | 93.9% | 169.4% | 75.5 |
| Over 3,000,000 | 183.0 | 126.7 | 311.5 | 184.8 |
| 1,000,000 to 3,000,000 | 160.5 | 97.3 | 238.9 | 141.6 |
| 500,000 to 1,000,000 | 95.6 | 73.8 | 129.3 | 55.5 |
| 250,000 to 500,000 | 82.8 | 78.6 | 87.4 | 8.8 |
| 100,000 to 250,000 | 70.3 | 73.1 | 66.6 | − 6.5 |
| Less than 100,000 | 67.0 | 76.3 | 44.0 | −32.3 |

SOURCE: U.S. Bureau of the Census *U.S. Census of Population, 1960. Selected Area Reports: Standard Metropolitan Statistical Areas.* Fund Report PC(3)–1D, reprinted from Alan Campbell and Seymour Sacks, *Metropolitan America: Fiscal Patterns and Governmental Systems* (New York, Free Press, 1967), p. 23.

policymakers. To be sure, income levels are only imperfect measures of supply and demand, and anyway urban governments rely not on income taxes but on property taxes. The income figures in Table 2.4 must therefore stand as a rough approximation of the disparities in needs and resources within the metropolis. As we can see from those figures, central cities have a larger share—though by no means a monopoly—of poor people, while the suburbs contain a larger proportion of the well-to-do. The ratio of well-to-do (those with incomes in excess of $10,000) to poor (those with incomes below $3000) people is 93.9 in CCs and 169.4 in OCCs. That is, in CCs the poor outnumber the well-to-do, whereas OCCs have more than half again as many well-to-do as poor persons. To the extent that the poor have more "need" for government services and the affluent have more "ability to pay," it is clear that CCs have a disproportionate share of problems and that suburbs have a considerable advantage in resources. In the words of the Advisory Commission on Intergovernmental Relations, "one set of jurisdictions (usually the central city) has the problems and the other set of jurisdictions (usually the suburbs) has the resources."[4] The most important qualification to this generalization, as indicated by Table 2.4, is related to the size of the metropolitan area. The larger the metropolitan area, the sharper the resource gap favoring the suburbs. In the smaller SMSAs, the pattern of suburban affluence and central-city poverty reverses itself: The central cities contain more

[4] Advisory Commission on Intergovernmental Relations, *op. cit.*, p. 6.

affluent populations in metropolitan areas with populations of fewer than 250,000.

In the larger metropolitan areas, therefore, the central city bears a disproportionate number of problems necessitating government action, whereas the suburbs have a disproportionate share of the resources. The central city, for example, contains:

1    more crime, necessitating heavier expenditures on law enforcement;
2    older buildings and housing, necessitating more costly fire protection;
3    more poverty and more unemployment, necessitating higher welfare expenditures;
4    more aged persons, necessitating greater public assistance to the aged;
5    more substandard housing units, necessitating more public housing;
6    higher traffic counts, necessitating more highway expenditures and traffic control;
7    more students from culturally disadvantaged backgrounds, necessitating more compensatory-education programs in schools.

The principal disparity that tends to produce higher public expenditures in the suburbs is the larger proportion of school-age children there (see Table 2.5). The economic resources represented by well-educated adults also translate themselves into demands for expensive children's schooling. Suburbs also have one additional characteristic that strains their political economy: high growth rates. Central cities are called upon to provide programs to compensate for a decline in their private sectors, but suburban governments must serve the demands resulting from their own growth.

The socioeconomic disparities between CCs and OCCs are reflected in the public expenditures and taxation patterns of urban governments (for further discussion of spending and taxation, see Chapter 7). OCC residents are able to escape not only many problems but also much of the tax burden of CC residents. The average suburbanite pays local taxes amounting to about 5.4 percent of his

**Table 2.5** *Proportion of school-age children in public schools within SMSAs, 1960*

|  | SMSA | Central City | Other Urban | Rural Nonfarm | Rural Farm |
|---|---|---|---|---|---|
| Kindergarten | 85.1% | 83.4% | 86.1% | 88.7% | 91.8% |
| Elementary | 81.1 | 78.3 | 80.9 | 91.3 | 90.1 |
| High school | 84.7 | 81.2 | 86.3 | 92.4 | 94.1 |

SOURCE: Alan K. Campbell and Seymour Sacks, *Metropolitan America: Fiscal Patterns and Governmental Systems* (New York, Free Press, 1967), p. 28.

**Figure 2.4**  *Per-capita local educational and noneducational expenditures in the thirty-six largest SMSAs and the remainder of the nation in 1965*

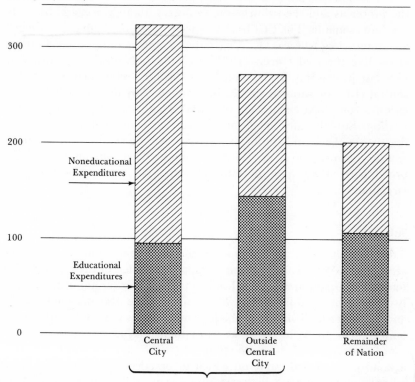

Per Capita (Dollars)

SOURCE: Advisory Commission on Intergovernmental Relations, *Fiscal Balance in the American Federal System,* vol. 2 (Washington, D.C., Government Printing Office, 1967), p. 72.

income, whereas the average central-city resident contributes about 7 percent of his income to municipal coffers. On the other hand, Figure 2.4 illustrates that central cities in the largest SMSAs spend much more per capita on such noneducational functions as police, fire protection, urban renewal, public housing, streets and roads, public health, and welfare than do the suburbs. Suburban areas spend a great deal more money on education than central cities do. In thirty-two of the thirty-six largest SMSAs, suburban educational expenditures were larger than central-city school spending, often by as much as $100 per capita.[5] It is not surprising, in light of these findings, that the most common

[5] *Ibid.,* p. 65.

explanations for a move to the suburbs include "lower taxes" and "better schools."

This analysis suggests that the judgment that the central city has the problems and the suburbs the resources, though oversimplified, is not unreasonable. The CCs have a concentration of "high-cost citizens" and enterprises, whereas OCCs have the advantage of resources. Central cities, like the Red Queen in *Through the Looking Glass,* must run very fast just to stay in the same place. Still, extreme images of either central cities or suburbs should be avoided. Any depiction of central cities as composed exclusively of huddled and starving masses is misleading. Equally, any image of suburbia as composed exclusively of doctors, bankers, and junior executives is, as we shall see in the next section, seriously in error. What we can see from our analysis is the broad pattern common to most metropolitan areas, especially the larger ones.

## Suburbia

Suburbanization became a massive social phenomenon in the years after World War II. It has been a response to some of the major social tensions in urban areas and is itself responsible for several of the major issues of urban public policy. The suburbs have also spawned myths, and to understand urban problems and policies it is necessary to examine these myths to see what truth there may be in them.[6]

In suburbia, according to myth, one will find a home of one's own, a small piece of real estate on which to practice yeoman's skills, good schools, plenty of land for recreation, clean and traffic-free neighborhoods, a small-town atmosphere, a local government with whose members one is on first-name terms, rural mailboxes, low taxes, Christmas lights, a Fourth of July parade, a homogeneous community without social tension, young neighbors, and an open leadership unstratified by age or social class. In many suburban areas, this myth is a reality. When compared to those of metropolitan central cities, suburban homes are far less often judged "dilapidated" or "crowded" by the Census Bureau. Many suburbs also tend to show higher levels of family income and adult education, spend proportionately more of the local budgets on education, and have younger and almost entirely white populations.

These features make the suburbs attractive to many young families, who choose to move there also because of crowding and the lack of

6 Suburban myths have been explored in a number of careful studies, including Robert C. Wood, *Suburbia* (Boston, Houghton Mifflin, 1959); Bennett Berger, *Working Class Suburb* (Berkeley, University of California Press, 1960); William Dobriner, *Class in Suburbia* (Englewood Cliffs, N.J., Prentice-Hall, 1963); and Herbert Gans, *The Levittowners* (New York, Basic Books, 1967).

suitable dwellings within their financial means in the central city; easy commuting from the suburbs to work or shopping; increasing availability of jobs, shopping, and service facilities in the suburbs themselves; the aesthetic appeal of middle-class neighborhoods with private homes and yards; the fear of central-city crime; and reluctance to send their children to central-city schools. Increasingly, young families do not have to face the question of *moving* from the central city to the suburbs. The "war babies" of the 1940s who have now advanced into parenthood have the simpler decision to remain in the type of community they have known since birth.

Not all the elements of the suburban myth are true. Some appear to be rather gross distortions, whereas others are oversimplifications that hide significant exceptions. For one thing, the surplus land in a new suburb is characteristically taken up by private home sites and commercial developments, with the result that there is often a smaller proportion of park land in a mature suburb than in the central city. Suburbs may grow more rapidly than their leaders' taste for—or skill in—controlling land use. One frequent result is a proliferation of filling stations and tawdry drive-ins alongside a main road that had been tree-lined and free of litter; another may be failure to control unsanitary alignments of private wells and septic tanks. Taxes may be low when the first new families migrate to an established small town, but when the migration increases to flood proportions the demand for more schools and teachers produces a sudden bulge in the local budget that may send property taxes above their levels in the central city. The social homogeneity of many suburbs may be attractive to members of the local "tribe," but, if it is uniformly of the working class and if there is no large tax revenue from industry or shopping centers, it may be impossible to support a level of education that is better than or even as good as that in the city.

The myth also emphasizes high participation in and personal familiarity with suburban government, but studies indicate that the rates of organizational participation are no higher in the suburbs than in central-city neighborhoods of comparable class levels, and voting turnouts in suburban local elections are frequently lower.[7] Finally, although conflicts in the suburbs may not have their origins in class or ethnic tensions, there are antagonisms. Old-timers and newcomers, Main Street merchants and commuters tend to clash.

TYPES OF SUBURBS    Leo F. Schnore, a specialist in demography and urban growth patterns, has made a useful distinction between two basic

---

[7] John C. Bollens *et al., Exploring the Metropolitan Community* (Berkeley, University of California Press, 1961), pp. 87–88.

**Table 2.6**  *Population characteristics of 300 employing, intermediate, and residential suburbs of the 25 largest metropolitan areas, 1960*

|  | Employing | Intermediate | Residential |
|---|---|---|---|
| Percentage of foreign-born | 10.5% | 8.5% | 7.7% |
| Percentage of nonwhite | 7.0 | 6.2 | 2.4 |
| Percentage of white-collar occupations | 44.6 | 49.8 | 58.8 |
| Median family income | $6,869 | $7,510 | $8,210 |
| Percentage of owner occupancy | 57.7 | 63.1 | 71.4 |
| Growth rate, 1950–1960 | 6.0 | 18.1 | 26.9 |

SOURCE: Leo F. Schnore, *The Urban Scene* (New York, Free Press, 1965), p. 178.

suburban types, *employing* suburbs and *residential* suburbs; there is also an *intermediate* type.[8] An employing (or satellite) suburb is characterized by a net excess of daytime over nighttime population. It is a manufacturing or wholesale- or retail-trade center, producing goods and services for a larger area within the metropolis. Whereas large numbers of suburbanites commute to jobs in the central city, even larger numbers commute from all over the metropolis to jobs in the employing suburbs.[9] A residential (or dormitory) suburb, on the other hand, has a net excess of nighttime over daytime population. Functionally it is a consumer of commodities and a supplier of labor. The economic enterprises found in such a suburb are almost entirely in retail trade.

Table 2.6 shows the population characteristics of residential, employing, and intermediate suburbs in 1960. Residents of dormitory suburbs are considerably more affluent than are residents of employing suburbs. The growth rates of the two polar suburban types also show wide disparities: Employing suburbs experienced a much slower population growth than did the United States as a whole between 1950 and 1960, while residential suburbs grew faster than did the nation as a whole; the 1970 Census confirms these trends.

SOME CONSEQUENCES OF SUBURBANIZATION  Suburbanization produces governmental fragmentation in the metropolitan area. Indeed, suburbanites claim that such fragmentation is a virtue. By leaving the central city, a young family can escape a political system in which its taxes and its children's education are subject to influence by alien forces. Yet fragmentation also precludes coordination of policies that affect a whole region.

[8] Leo F. Schnore, *The Urban Scene* (New York, Free Press, 1965), chaps. 7–9.
[9] Hoover and Vernon, *op. cit.*, p. 139, divide the New York metropolitan region into three zones, the *core*, the *inner ring*, and the *outer ring*. More than 80 percent of the metropolitan work force lives and works in single zones. Only 14 percent lives in the inner or outer ring and commutes to the core.

In the suburbs, resources are frequently isolated from need. One suburb may enjoy the tax payments of a shopping center or an electric utility, but others must exist solely on the property taxes of home owners. The separation of service demands and economic resources by legal boundaries between the central city and each of its suburbs complicates the translation of private wealth in the urban area into fiscal resources for needed public services. The distinctions between city and suburbs also generate cleavages in the state legislature that may work against the interest of the entire metropolis. If metropolitan legislators were unified, they could more effectively influence the formulas used to apportion state aid. But with city set against suburb, there may be a stalemate of efforts to use the state's taxing powers to overcome local revenue shortages.

It is not true that the suburbs have destroyed the central city. Antisuburbanites have also produced myths. They claim that suburbanites weaken the central city by withdrawing their full contributions as citizens and taxpayers, but it is difficult to evaluate to what extent the suburbs actually deprive the city's policy-making process of needed talent or resources. Commuters can serve the central city as employees of its government or business agencies and even as members of its civic commissions. Moreover, it is not clear that a more heavily middle-class electorate would alter the kinds of policies made by central-city councils or executives. The problems of grime, social tension, and high crime rates result from persistent social and economic factors, and not solely from the removal of a segment of the population to the suburbs.

The revenue problem in the central city, which deprives local governments of sufficient funds to meet the demands for service, is also composed of numerous elements, including state constitutions that inhibit reliance on anything but local property taxes; state redistribution of aid funds paid by central cities to the suburbs and rural areas; local government boundaries within the metropolis that permit industrial and commercial properties to enjoy the low rates of "tax islands"; high land prices in the central city that prohibit the construction of low-cost single-family homes; and the physical and aesthetic deterioration of the central city. These elements are not easily changed, and it would take more than a greater sense of urban commitment among the suburban middle classes to tip the fiscal balance in favor of central cities.

### The underside of the urban economy: Poverty amid plenty

Completing the irony of the urban economy are the unskilled migrants from rural areas who have come to the city for a better life. Today this migration comes largely from the black-belt counties of the South, from the all-white counties of the southern Appalachians and the Ozarks, from Puerto Rico and other Caribbean islands, from Mexico, and to some extent from Indian reservations.

At the present time, cities all over the country are attracting these unskilled rural folk. New York, Newark, Washington, D.C., Detroit, Chicago, and Los Angeles have received the most attention from the popular media, but there are also streams of migrants to Atlanta, Jacksonville, Miami, Birmingham, Memphis, Denver, and other places. The common attraction is the city's dynamic economy. The migrants no longer anticipate streets paved with gold, but they still come in order to share in the city's wealth, and they look forward to better opportunities than they have had at home.

Today's unskilled migrants encounter frustrations unknown to their predecessors.[10] The urban economy used to have lots of room for unskilled workers. Factories and construction were more dependent upon hand labor than they are today, and the municipal government employed large numbers of menial laborers. There are still many such opportunities, but their proportion of the urban economy has diminished markedly. Literacy is increasingly required for even the lowest-paid and least permanent jobs. The spread of the labor movement and union control of apprenticeship programs mean that today's ethnic newcomers suffer from institutionalized discrimination by fellow workers as well as by prospective employers.

GHETTO PROBLEMS    The deep and complex economic needs of the communities of rural migrants in the central cities are described in the report of the National Advisory Commission on Civil Disorders. This report—assembled by a committee headed by Governor Otto Kerner of Illinois after the urban riots of 1967—describes the inability of many urban residents to share in the economic wealth of their communities and the ramifications of their poverty in such problems as family disorganization, illegitimacy, crime, sanitation, public health, and welfare dependency. The importance of the Commission's *Report* in the recent discourse about urban problems warrants an extensive quotation. The commission summarized its findings as follows:

*Although there have been gains in Negro income nationally, and a decline in the number of Negroes below the "poverty level," the condition of Negroes in the central city remains in a state of crisis. Between 2 and 2.5 million Negroes—16 to 20 percent of the total Negro population of all central cities— live in squalor and deprivation in ghetto neighborhoods.*

*Employment is a key problem. It not only controls the present for the*

10 A classic work on European immigrants in American cities is Oscar Handlin, *The Uprooted* (Boston, Little, Brown, 1951).

*Negro American but, in a most profound way, it is creating the future as well. Yet, despite continuing economic growth and declining national unemployment rates, the unemployment rate for Negroes in 1967 was more than double that for whites.*

*Equally important is the undesirable nature of many jobs open to Negroes and other minorities. Negro men are more than three times as likely as white men to be in low-paying, unskilled or service jobs. This concentration of male Negro employment at the lowest end of the occupational scale is the single most important cause of poverty among Negroes.*

*In one study of low-income neighborhoods, the "subemployment rate," including both unemployment and underemployment, was about 33 percent, or 8.8 times greater than the overall unemployment rate for all United States workers.*

*Employment problems, aggravated by the constant arrival of new unemployed migrants, many of them from depressed rural areas, create persistent poverty in the ghetto. In 1966, about 11.9 percent of the nation's whites and 40.6 percent of its nonwhites were below the "poverty level" defined by the Social Security Administration (in 1966, $3,335 per year for an urban family of four). Over 40 percent of the nonwhites below the poverty level live in the central cities.*

*Employment problems have drastic social impact in the ghetto. Men who are chronically unemployed or employed in the lowest status jobs are often unable or unwilling to remain with their families. The handicap imposed on children growing up without fathers in an atmosphere of poverty and deprivation is increased as mothers are forced to work to provide support.*

*The culture of poverty that results from unemployment and family breakup generates a system of ruthless, exploitative relationships within the ghetto. Prostitution, dope addiction, and crime create an environmental "jungle" characterized by personal insecurity and tension. Children growing up under such conditions are likely participants in civil disorder.*

*A striking difference in environment from that of white, middle-class Americans profoundly influences the lives of residents of the ghetto.*

*Crime rates, consistently higher than in other areas, create a pronounced sense of insecurity. For example, in one city one low-income Negro district had 35 times as many serious crimes against persons as a high-income white district. Unless drastic steps are taken, the crime problems in poverty areas are likely to continue to multiply as the growing youth and rapid urbanization of the population outstrip police resources.*

*Poor health and sanitation conditions in the ghetto result in higher mortality rates, a higher incidence of major diseases, and lower availability and utilization of medical services. The infant mortality rate for nonwhite babies under the age of one month is 58 percent higher than for whites; for one to 12 months it is almost three times as high. The level of sanitation in the ghetto is far below that in high-income areas. Garbage collection is often inadequate. Of an estimated 14,000 cases of rat bite in the United States in 1965, most were in ghetto neighborhoods.*

*Ghetto residents believe they are exploited by local merchants; and evidence substantiates some of these beliefs. A study conducted in one city by the Federal Trade Commission showed that higher prices were charged for goods sold in ghetto stores than in other areas.*

*Lack of knowledge regarding credit purchasing creates special pitfalls for the disadvantaged. In many states garnishment practices compound these difficulties by allowing creditors to deprive individuals of their wages without hearing or trial.*

*We address ourselves to a fundamental question that many white Americans are asking: why have so many Negroes, unlike the European immigrants, been unable to escape from the ghetto and from poverty. We believe the following factors play a part:*

*The Maturing Economy: When the European immigrants arrived, they gained an economic foothold by providing the unskilled labor needed by industry. Unlike the immigrant, the Negro migrant found little opportunity in the city. The economy, by then matured, had little use for the unskilled labor he had to offer.*

*The Disability of Race: The structure of discrimination has stringently narrowed opportunities for the Negro and restricted his prospects. European immigrants suffered from discrimination, but never so pervasively.*

*Entry into the Political System: The immigrants usually settled in rapidly growing cities with powerful and expanding political machines, which traded economic advantages for political support. Ward-level grievance machinery, as well as personal representation, enabled the immigrant to make his voice heard and his power felt. By the time the Negro arrived, these political machines were no longer so powerful or so well equipped to provide jobs or other favors, and in many cases were unwilling to share their influence with Negroes.*

*Cultural Factors: Coming from societies with a low standard of living and at a time when job aspirations were low, the immigrants sensed little deprivation in being forced to take the less desirable and poorer-paying jobs. Their large and cohesive families contributed to total income. Their vision of the future—one that led to a life outside the ghetto—provided the incentive necessary to endure the present. Although Negro men worked as hard as the immigrants, they were unable to support their families. The entrepreneurial opportunities had vanished. As a result of slavery and long periods of unemployment, the Negro family structure had become matriarchal; the males played a secondary and marginal family role—one which offered little compensation for their hard and unrewarding labor. Above all, segregation denied Negroes access to good jobs and the opportunity to leave the ghetto. For them, the future seemed to lead only to a dead end.*[11]

GHETTOS AND GOVERNMENTS    The poverty in central cities makes their plight worse than that of other communities within metropolitan areas. It provokes the exodus of middle- and upper-middle-class resi-

---

[11] National Advisory Commission on Civil Disorders, *Report* (Washington, D.C., Government Printing Office, 1967), pp. 6–7.

dents, as well as of merchants, industry, and office buildings to the suburbs, and this exodus reduces the tax bases and leaves the central cities with high concentrations of costly social problems. Local governments, formerly called upon to supply traditional services of public education, welfare, and health, are now asked to support massive programs—including new ventures in adult and "preschool" education, counseling, job training, housing, and "community" control of local services—to alleviate the distress of the poor and to attack the basic social problems underlying poverty.

The dissatisfaction the urban poor express at the nature of their public services seems justified when it is viewed in relation to the high level of taxes that they pay to local and state governments. The major state and local taxes (on retail sales and real property) are regressive: They take larger percentages from the incomes of low-income groups than from those of high-income groups. A 1961 study found that sales and excise taxes took 4.8 percent of the annual income from families earning less than $2,000 but only 2.1 percent from families earning more than $15,000; property taxes were even more sharply regressive, taking 5.9 percent from the lowest income group and 2.1 percent from the highest.[12]

These findings may seem odd at first glance, for sales taxes are charged at the same rates on everyone's purchases, and there is no overt discrimination against low-income groups. By the same token, property taxes are not levied directly against the urban poor; they are charged to home owners, not renters. Yet some not-so-subtle economic mechanisms work to the disadvantage of low-income taxpayers. First, the poor must spend most of their current income on retail purchases, even dipping into whatever savings they have or going into debt to make further retail purchases, all of which are, of course, taxable. Higher-income taxpayers, in contrast, use much of their income for investments or other purposes that are not subject to sales taxes. The result is that a relatively large portion of the resources of the poor are subject to sales taxes each year.

A similar principle operates with property taxes. The poor do not pay them directly, but they pay them indirectly as part of their rent. There is little in the ethos of the slum landlord to suggest that he pays his property taxes out of his own profits; rather, he passes the tax on to the tenants, and each increase in the tax rate produces a proportionate increase in rents. Again, the poor pay larger portions of their incomes in property taxes than do the wealthy because they spend a higher portion of their income for housing.

The poor recognize the disadvantages in the local tax system. A

[12] George A. Bishop, "The Tax Burden by Income Class, 1958," *National Tax Journal, 14* (March, 1961), 41–58.

survey taken during a gubernatorial campaign in Wisconsin revealed a high degree of awareness among low-income residents that sales and property taxes operate to their disadvantage. They were most in favor of increases in the state income tax, which was progressive and would take the greatest percentage from higher-income families.[13] Other surveys find that low-income urban residents with little education are most resentful about local taxes, whereas the upper-income and professional-managerial-proprietor classes show the most acceptance of current local taxes.[14] Still other studies find that low-income residents express the "illogical" views that welfare, health, and educational services should be improved but that taxes should be reduced.[15] These views are illogical only to the person who pays his fair share of taxes and no more. To the low-income person who needs improved services but who also pays a disproportionately high share of taxes, they make a great deal of sense.

### Other service demands growing out of the urban economy

It is not only the urban poor who perceive a need for public policies. Commercial, industrial, and financial groups demand of local governments that public investments be made to enhance their own private investments. Often they justify these demands in terms of micro- and macroeconomics: claiming that what is good for their private investments will "spill over" to benefit the public sector. If they prosper, so will other residents.

Each kind of economic interest has its own special demands, and the result is competition over urban public policies. Downtown merchants typically fear the competition of suburban shopping centers. They want publicly subsidized mass transportation, traffic control, expressways, and parking facilities that permit convenient access to their stores. They consider the "central business district" the heart of the community, the single most important feature distinguishing an important city from a rural crossroads. Merchants ally themselves with other occupants of the central business district—the .owners of office buildings, theaters, and restaurants—who want to maintain the commercial value of their high-priced and highly taxed properties. Professional, service, and industrial interests value the close interaction possible in a central location, and law firms, accountants, investment counselors, publishers, and advertising agencies share with the opera-

13 Ira Sharkansky, *The Politics of Taxing and Spending* (New York, Bobbs-Merrill, 1969), pp. 17–19.
14 Bollens *et al., op. cit.,* p. 277.
15 V. O. Key, Jr., *Public Opinion and American Democracy* (New York, Knopf, 1961), p. 167.

tors of manufacturing plants a desire to preserve the appeal of the central area.

Local officials must often cope with the conflicting demands of these various industrial and commercial interests, each of which claims special privileges because of its present—or potential—contributions to the local economy. Those downtown merchants who are not inclined to open branches in the suburbs oppose zoning variations that will permit large tracts of land to be turned into new shopping plazas; the owners of existing apartment houses oppose zoning variations that will permit massive new apartment developments, especially when they are already having some trouble keeping their own units filled to capacity; the operators of a suburban shopping center may oppose a zoning variation for a nearby industrial development if they fear that a smoky or unsightly manufacturing plant will deter shoppers.

An urban-renewal program raises a whole series of economic opportunities and problems for the makers of public policy, for there is frequently sharp antagonism between those who want prime land for development and those who speak for the present occupants of the land. The occupants are typically the poorest residents of the community and often members of an ethnic minority. It is frequently alleged—with some accuracy—that they are to be moved for the benefit of well-to-do businessmen or the prospective occupants of the new middle- and upper-class dwellings.[16] Spokesmen for the poor charge that they are being shunted to other depressed neighborhoods and forced to break whatever community ties they have established in their present locale. To exacerbate matters, the residents of the neighborhoods destined to receive the displaced families often charge that this move will bring the slums to them and expose them to the problems of poor schools, crime, and general social decay.

Public policy-makers must also deal with those issues of code enforcement related to housing and urban renewal. Housing codes specify the kinds of features to be provided in each dwelling unit, like the number and types of entrances and exits, plumbing, heat and hot water, fire escapes, trash removal, and general upkeep. If these provisions are enforced rigorously, the problems of physical decay and intense overcrowding that generate slums are not likely to develop. It is the policy-makers' task, however, to remind those who want tight enforcement of housing codes that some people need cheap housing. A large and dynamic urban area may need its slums to provide homes for the poor, unskilled immigrants who are attracted by the "better

16 See Herbert Gans, "The Failure of Urban Renewal: A Critique and Some Proposals," *Commentary* (April, 1965), pp. 29–37. See also our discussion of urban renewal in Chapter 10.

life" that they believe the city offers or who have been born in the city but lack the training and the good fortune necessary to live outside the slums. In Chapter 10 we shall turn to a more detailed examination of housing and urban renewal.

Local governments are often faced with demands from industrial and commercial interests for concessions. Businessmen insist that they are willing to "pay their share," but they object to being the principal source of support for such services as education, health care, and recreation. Some firms—particularly those that can choose freely where they will locate within a metropolitan area—seek special tax concessions in exchange for settling in a specific community. Not all members of the community favor this kind of deal. Industries already located there, for example, object to concessions to competitors that are not matched for themselves. Others object on the principle of equity, claiming that no taxpayer should receive concessions not given equally to all. Such debates are clouded further by ambiguities inherent in the standards of value applied in assessing different categories of land, buildings, and other facilities. We shall see in the discussion of urban taxing and spending in Chapter 7 that tax equity is a subject of great dispute among experts.

Besides tax concessions some firms are interested in service improvements and use their tax payments, payrolls, and local purchases to bargain for higher levels of local services. They want schools and recreational facilities to make the community attractive to their own managers and executives, and they want shipping facilities, electric power, and clean water sufficient for plant needs. They also expect local governments to help them obtain benefits from other authorities. Local shippers seek favorable decisions on transportation rates from the Interstate Commerce Commission and ask political support from municipal officials. Industries seek location of new highways and interchanges convenient to their plants and ask for the support of local authorities in their petitions to state or federal highway officials. When management is caught up in intense negotiations with labor unions, it may ask local officials to urge rapid settlement upon the unions. Companies located in a low-wage area sometimes pressure local authorities to maintain the wage structure by indicating that any major change may force them to relocate.

In this section we have examined a number of key demands on government that arise from the urban environment. Many, though by no means all, are products of conflict of economic interests. Some emerge from conflict among the already well-to-do, others from conflicts between the latter and those who want larger shares of the community's wealth. It is the responsibility of the decision-makers to take these problems and apply resources to their solution. Yet the resources at their disposal are not unlimited. One of the most serious constraints on officials' efforts to meet demands is the inaccessibility of urban wealth.

## THE ACCESS OF URBAN OFFICIALS TO URBAN WEALTH

The inaccessibility of urban wealth to urban policy makers is a function of several problems: (1) an unequal distribution of needs and resources throughout urban areas; (2) legal limits on the kinds and amounts of revenue that local authorities may collect; (3) the "monopoly" of income taxes and sales taxes by federal and state governments; and (4) the failure of local officials to tax or borrow up to the legal limits.

### The unequal distribution of needs and resources

The unequal distribution of needs and resources results from the fragmentation of governments throughout the metropolitan area. Local governments vary greatly in the resources that their residents provide, as well as in the residents' demands for public services. The suburb that is thick with industrial and commercial properties has high tax revenues for its local government but minimal demands for schools and other social services. The purely residential suburb, however, faces high demands for school expenditures but has no source of revenue beside private home owners. Residential suburbs that are predominantly working class in composition are often characterized by many children and low incomes and property values. When such communities are new and rapidly growing, they must bear the burden of adding new school buildings and facilities, as well as the operating costs of established programs. Some working-class communities adjoin municipalities with a high incidence of industrial or commercial properties. The industrial complex is likely to draw its labor force from the working-class town, yet the industries' property taxes support only the schools that lie within their own municipality.

In jurisdictions that have more resources than their services demand, some remain untapped. In fact, because metropolitan areas are not governed by integrated institutions, abundant resources lie unused within short distances of unmet service needs.[17]

[17] Many of the arguments in this section are explored more fully in Robert C. Wood, *1400 Governments* (Garden City, N.Y., Doubleday Anchor, 1964).

### Legal limits on kinds and amounts of taxation and indebtedness

State constitutions and statutes restrict local authorities to certain kinds of revenues and to certain levels of taxation and indebtedness. Local governments in most states are restricted to taxes on property; charges for city-operated services like water, trash removal, sewage, gas, and electricity; and limited borrowing for capital improvements (for example, construction of buildings and highways or the purchase of major equipment). In several states local governments also tax their residents' incomes, the retail sales of local merchants, or both. But these taxes are typically low: 1 percent is a common upper limit on local income and sales taxes. Some cities also collect revenues from local "wheel taxes" (on automobiles) or levies on motel and hotel rooms. These taxes, too, typically make only small total contributions to local government revenues. The property tax is the single major source of support.

Property taxes may apply to "real" property (land and buildings); "personal" property (clothes, furniture, and other such possessions); and "intangible" property (stocks, bonds, bank accounts). The reluctance of both citizens and officials to reveal their resources in full detail precludes thorough assessment of personal and intangible property, however, and these taxes are widely evaded. It is common for the amount of a local government's debt and the level of its property taxes to be limited to a certain proportion of the assessed value of real property in the jurisdiction. "Assessed value" is flexible, however, and can be increased to permit more revenues either from taxation or borrowing when the need arises. Nevertheless, legal limits are important in the minds of many officials and citizens, who may keep city budgets low when the limits are approached, even if there are still some options to increase total valuation.

The set of taxes that is legally available to a local government may not be adequate for its revenue potential. Some resort communities could raise significant funds through local amusement or restaurant taxes, and some jurisdictions with large upper-income populations might benefit significantly from local progressive income taxes. The state legislatures, however, decide which taxes can be raised by local authorities, and the individual communities are often left with revenue possibilities not suited to their resources.

### The monopoly of income and sales taxes by federal and state governments

One reason for the restrictions on local governments' use of income and sales taxes is the heavy use of these same taxes by federal and state governments. It is said that the latter governments "use up" almost all the revenues that are potentially available from these sources. Although this allegation is neither clear nor even established as fact, a number of authorities do believe that two levels of government cannot make simultaneous heavy use of the same form of taxation.

Through a series of tacit understandings—as well as through the legal restrictions that state governments have imposed on their municipalities—the federal government has become the chief user of the personal and corporate income taxes, state governments rely heavily on the general sales tax, and local governments are left with the tax on real property. In 1967, personal and corporate income taxes accounted for 44 percent of federal tax revenue, general sales taxes accounted for 29 percent of tax revenues collected by state governments, and property taxes accounted for 45 percent of tax revenues collected by municipalities.

It has not always been so. Tax "specialization" came after the Depression of the 1930s and may reflect the overall increase in taxes that characterized this period. During the 1930s and through World War II the states' income-tax receipts leveled off while those of the federal government increased greatly. Before the Depression both state and local governments were major users of the property tax, but the states left that revenue source to municipalities during the 1930s, and they themselves became increasingly dependent upon retail sales taxes. State governments earned almost 45 percent of their revenues from property taxes in 1902. By 1940, however, this percentage had dropped to only 5, and by 1968 it was only 1.3 percent.

As most local governments are left without a major source of tax revenue other that real-property taxes, they find themselves unable to tap large segments of the local economy for support. Much of the wealth in the local community takes the form of profits from retail sales and personal and corporate incomes, but in most places this wealth is not subject to local taxation. Moreover, many earners and retail spenders live outside the community in which they earn or spend their incomes, and their property taxes are paid to their communities of residence. The burden lies especially heavily on central cities. As noted, it is the city that faces heavy demands for social services, transportation, fire and police protection, and housing, yet the incomes of its wealthiest business and professional people are not (in most cases) subject to local taxation, and the purchases made in the central business district are (in most cases) taxed only by the state government. The tax options of most central cities do not match their economic resources, and so there may be starvation of public services in the presence of enormous private resources.

### The failure of local officials to tax or borrow to the legal limits

Officials in some communities do not tax or borrow to their legal limits, yet they fail to satisfy some prominent demands for service. Also some officials "compete" with other jurisdictions for the location of industrial or commercial establishments by offering the incentive of low taxes. The reason given is that high taxes will discourage a firm from locating in a jurisdiction or even prompt an established firm to move elsewhere. Actually, the availability of manpower, transportation facilities, electric power, and clean water—plus recreational and educational opportunities for the staff—often have more to do with management's decisions about location than does the simple factor of the tax rate. Yet local authorities are tempted to compete for industries by means of their tax rates. When different communities in the same urban area do compete over tax rates, an occasional firm may be induced to choose a low-rate community or even to leave a community whose taxes rise significantly above those in a neighboring jurisdiction. In this case, the firm can still recruit its labor force from the surrounding towns, and its officers can live in those surrounding communities with the most attractive amenities. Also if a large firm is persuaded to settle—or stay —in a community because of a low tax rate, the taxes from that firm alone may nevertheless be sufficient in their total magnitude to permit a low tax rate for the community's home owners.

The failure of local governments to tax or borrow up to their legal limits does not result solely from the preferences of municipal officials. Sometimes community leaders may urge tax increases or bond issues to pay for needed services, only to run up against intense popular opposition. Forty-two of the fifty states require that local governments obtain the consent of their citizens in referenda before issuing bonds for improvements in streets, sewers, schools, and other public facilities. Twelve states require consent by extraordinarily high majorities, ranging from 55 percent to two-thirds of the electorate, before capital investments may be undertaken. The proportion of referenda in which local electorates reject such investments has increased in recent years. The voters of Youngstown, Ohio, who may hold the record for negative referenda, defeated proposals for school taxes on six consecutive occasions before the fall of 1968, when the schools ran out of money and shut down for most of the term.

### The auxiliary devices of intergovernmental aid
### and special districts

Although officials face severe problems arising from the inaccessibility of urban wealth, two major devices, the *special district* and *intergov-*

*ernmental grants and loans,* offer partial solutions to their problems.

THE SPECIAL DISTRICT    The special district broadens the tax base that can be used to support public services in an urban area by joining together an extensive area for the purpose of providing a particular service. Special districts are—as the name implies—created for special purposes. They do not provide the full range of local services. Rather, each provides one basic service or a group of closely related services.[18] The most common special districts are school districts; others include districts for water, sewage, or both; trash collection; police, fire protection, or both; parks; libraries; hospitals; and transportation, bridges, and port facilities.

Most metropolitan areas have several of these districts. The largest and best known that deals in transportation is the Port of New York Authority. Each district may have its own borders, not necessarily coterminous with the borders of others. A school district, for example, may include one set of municipalities (or some whole municipalities and parts of others) and may partly but not entirely overlap a water-and-sewer district that covers a different part of the metropolitan region. Where special districts have proliferated in this manner, they can provide individual services on the basis of the resources that lie within their extensive boundaries. They appeal to those who prefer that financial support for services be tied directly to the receipt of those services.[19]

Because of the confusion that arises from a variety of separate jurisdictions, however, citizens cannot easily determine which districts provide which services to their homes, much less how they may influence the policies made by the authorities of each district. The governing bodies of many special districts are boards appointed jointly by the councils or mayors of several municipalities, by the state governor, or both, and the indirect lines of responsibility, as well as the confused geographical boundaries, help to isolate special districts from voter control.

INTERGOVERNMENTAL AID    Intergovernmental aid permits urban governments to receive some of the revenues raised within their jurisdictions by the income and sales taxes of the federal and state governments.[20] One of the advantages of this scheme is that federal

[18] John C. Bollens, *Special District Governments in the United States* (Berkeley, University of California Press, 1957).

[19] *Ibid.*, p. 81.

[20] See Deil S. Wright, *Federal Grants-in-Aid: Perspectives and Alternatives* (Washington, D.C., American Enterprise Institute for Public Policy Research, 1968).

and state authorities can raise revenues from urban areas without imposing differential tax rates that might drive away industry from these
jurisdictions. Since they are not troubled by the unequal distribution
of needs and resources throughout a metropolitan area, they can use
a wider variety of taxing and borrowing mechanisms than can local
authorities. Admittedly, only a portion of the revenues raised from an
urban area is returned to that area by state and federal governments,
because much of this wealth must be used to support a variety of federal and state programs, including national defense and financial aid
to small-town and rural citizens.

The nature of intergovernmental aid varies considerably from
one program to another.[21] Some programs are designed to redistribute
resources from "have" to "have not" areas; others substitute the resources raised by superordinate governments for those raised locally;
others are provided with only portions of the funds needed and are
designed to stimulate local authorities to put more effort into raising
money through their own taxes or service charges; and others are
meant to add resources to those that the municipalities have raised for
certain programs from their own resources.

There are systematic variations in intergovernmental aids among
states. Some state governments assume a large part of the responsibility
for financing public services and use aids to municipalities in order to
accomplish their objectives.[22] Others provide only minimal state aids,
and leave to the local communities the task of supporting whatever
services their citizens desire. Not all local officials, however, feel that
the disbursement of state money is equitable, even in the former
case.

One of the most common complaints of CC officials is that state
and federal aids have failed to equalize the resource disparities between CCs and OCCs. CC officials claim that the suburbs have more
wealth and fewer problems than do the central cities. As of 1965, however, total per-capita aid to central cities and outside areas was nearly
identical ($78 per capita).[23] Federal grants-in-aid support programs
that are used more by central cities than by suburbs (for example,
public housing and urban renewal), and state aid supports programs,
especially education, that are more important to suburbs than to central cities. In 1965, the central-city orientation of federal aid was just
enough to counterbalance the suburban orientation of state aid. In
light of such evidence, the Advisory Commission on Intergovernmental

---

21 See, for example, Richard A. Musgrave, *Essays in Fiscal Federalism* (Washington, D.C., Brookings Institution, 1965).

22 Sharkansky, *op. cit.*, chap. 4.

23 Advisory Commission on Intergovernmental Relations, *op. cit.*, p. 84.

Relations concluded that "total Federal and State aid scores rather low marks from an equalization standpoint."[24]

## Toward flexibility

Although special districts and intergovernmental aid are important sources of revenue for local governments, they are not the only tools available. Successful officials can demonstrate creative use of the various resources at their disposal and perhaps invent some new ones. Although some local authorities see their property taxes as already at the uppermost feasible limit, for others such taxes are not exhausted as a source of funds. If the statutes or constitution of the state place an upper limit on the tax rate (the proportion of assessed value that an owner can be taxed in one year), local officials might increase the assessments. By increasing such assessments across the board they can spread the tax increase to all kinds of property owners; they can also increase assessments selectively—on those kinds of properties least likely to react negatively to the increase or on those that have enjoyed several years of inordinately low assessments.[25]

In some municipalities officials actively solicit business investments in industrial or commercial developments, because they add to the value of real property and tax revenues. Such campaigns are, of course, likely to be more effective in some communities than in others, for geographical location in relation to the sources of supply and labor and to markets is important to industrialists, as is the availability of water, electric power, and transportation facilities. In many cases these tangible needs of a prospective investor outweigh any arguments—or even temporary tax concessions—that local authorities can provide.

Local authorities are not prohibited from trying to alter provisions of the state constitution or statutes that keep their fiscal position weak. Debt and tax limitations, for example, as well as the formulas for distributing state aid, are subject to change. Recent increases in the representation of urban areas in state legislatures may also aid the city's efforts to reduce its fiscal impediments. Yet in some states reapportionment has only heightened city-suburb conflicts in the legislatures; it may even have ousted certain rural legislators who were allies of the cities. The process of reapportionment is complex and cannot be said to have uniform influence on city-state relations across the country.[26]

24 *Ibid.*

25 Wood, *1400 Governments*, pp. 76ff.

26 See Ira Sharkansky, "Reapportionment and Roll Call Voting: The Case of the Georgia Legislature," *Social Science Quarterly, 51* (June, 1970), 129–137 and the references cited.

It is dangerous to oversimplify our notions of the economic problems and opportunities that face urban governments. Economic and political features vary from one state to another, and within certain states they vary from one metropolis to another. The fortunes of a city may be shaped by something as intangible as a tacit agreement between its representatives and other members of the state legislature. There is plenty of opportunity for the creative local official, and he should not be discouraged by a pessimistic general evaluation of the plight of cities in the 1970s.

## SUMMARY

In this chapter we have described part of the context in which urban governments formulate their policies, focusing on economic and social conditions in urban areas. These conditions determine the resources and demands that in turn shape the services provided by local governments.

America's cities have most of our material wealth: most of our industry, professional and technical skills, financial and commercial activity. On three indirect measures of this wealth—population growth, personal income, and education—the large urban areas demonstrate consistently higher scores than do rural and small town areas. Metropolitan areas are not homogeneous in the internal distribution of their wealth, however, and their populations are diverse and distributed unequally among various neighborhoods and legally autonomous jurisdictions. The resulting unequal distribution of economic needs and resources presents some of the most complex policy problems facing local officials.

Demands on local governments include help in maintaining or enhancing the economic positions of commerce and industry, as well as social services for people attracted to cities but unable to benefit fully from their economic opportunities. Many services that local governments provide are new since the Depression of the 1930s, and some are new since the surge of welfare legislation in the mid-1960s. Now there are programs for housing, slum clearance and urban renewal, welfare payments, job training, personal and family counseling, and mass transportation. Other services lie within the traditional responsibilities of local governments: education, streets, traffic control, zoning, police and fire protection, public health, and sanitation. Even in these fields, however, the nature of policies is shaped by recent escalations in the demands of clients and innovations in social technologies.

With all these demands for economic and social services, there are also demands by individuals and corporations for tax stability or concessions. There is also a host of legal and political impediments that keep local authorities from taking full advantage of the economic resources that lie within their boundaries. These barriers include the unequal distribution of needs and resources throughout extensive urban areas, the failure of local authorities to tax or borrow up to the limits permitted by state constitutions or statutes, limitations on the kinds or amounts of local government taxation or indebtedness, and the control of lucrative income and sales taxes by federal and state governments. Auxiliary devices help local authorities to maximize their economic opportunities. Special districts broaden both the geographic and economic bases of units providing certain kinds of public services, and federal and state aid funnels some of the money raised in urban areas by those governments back to local officials. Creative local officials have numerous opportunities to provide leadership that may allow their municipalities to make the most of their fiscal opportunities, even though their prospects may appear bleak.

# 3
# The political context

Every political system provides channels—more or less imperfect—through which individual and group interests flow as "input" into the political system. In Iran, which is characterized by a "politics of informality," groups as we know them do not play very significant political roles, but there are other ways of expressing political preferences. One observer described a visit by the provincial governor to a small village: Residents' petitions were given to the governor's driver, butler, secretary, and guests in hopes that they would be transmitted to the governor himself. A more direct way to secure community improvements was apparent when the governor's entourage drove through a small village on an inspection tour, for which local crowds were duly assembled to shout: "Long live the Shah! Hurrah! Long live the Governor! Hurrah! We need another doctor in this town! Hurrah!"[1]

In American cities, resources are applied to affect public policy when voters troop to the polls, when rioters "trash," when interest groups talk to councilmen, when parties tout their candidates. The input process, whether in the Soviet Union, Iran, or American cities, encompasses all activities in which individuals and groups use time, information, money, skills, votes, and other resources to secure favorable policy outcomes. The process in American cities in particular is the subject of this chapter.

1 James A. Bill, "The Plasticity of Informal Politics: The Case of Iran" (Pape delivered at the Conference on the Structure of Power in Islamic Iran, University of California, Los Angeles, June 26–28, 1969), p. 7.

We shall discuss participation in local politics, interest groups, political parties, nonpartisanship, municipal elections, and the unique aspects of black politics.[2]

## PARTICIPATION IN LOCAL POLITICS

"You can't fight city hall" is a hallowed cliché in American politics. Judging by the available evidence, relatively few urbanites take advantage of routine opportunities to change things at city hall. Participation in local voting rites is much lower than in either state or national election contests. In 1968, more than 60 percent of the adult population voted for its presidential favorite; in the typical state election, about 50 percent of the eligible electorate turns out to vote. In city elections that are not held concurrently with state or national contests, however, only about 31 percent of the adult population appears at the polls.

To be sure, voting is not the only device through which people participate in politics. Participation also includes a variety of such activities as discussing politics, campaigning for candidates, running for office, and contributing money to political causes or candidates. Still, for most Americans, voting is the most vigorous participation they are likely to undertake, and the level of apathy in local politics is quite high relative to interest in state and national politics in the United States.

Participation in community politics may be seen as a function of both "macro" (community) and "micro" (individual or subcommunity) factors. The probability of participation will vary both from individual to individual and from community to community. Unless participation is viewed from both perspectives, a one-sided picture results. Even if two people resemble each other in social characteristics, they may participate differently, depending upon whether factors in the political environment operate to facilitate or to hinder political activism.

The aggregate level of participation in any given community is a product both of the kinds of individuals found in the community and of the characteristics of the community and its socioeconomic and governmental systems. A listing of some of the more significant correlates

---

2 The special character and context of black politics, even more than its newsworthiness, argue for singling it out and giving it separate treatment in our study of urban politics. The black American does participate, of course, through conventional channels, but he merits our particular attention because he is, far more than businessmen, labor unionists, and members of the more politically established ethnic groups, seeking an "identity." How this "identity crisis" will ultimately be resolved is a matter of profound importance for the future of the American city.

**Table 3.1**  *Correlates of participation in community politics*[a]

| Macro factors | | Micro factors | |
|---|---|---|---|
| *1.* Form of government | | *1.* Social class | |
| Mayor-council or | | Higher | + |
| commission | + | Lower | − |
| Manager | − | | |
| *2.* Form of election | | *2.* Stakes in policies | |
| Partisan | + | High | + |
| Nonpartisan | − | Low | − |
| *3.* Type of constituency | | *3.* Ethnicity | |
| Ward | + | Ethnic | + |
| At large | − | Non-ethnic | − |
| *4.* Party system | | *4.* Mobility | |
| Strong | + | High | − |
| Weak | − | Low | + |
| *5.* Community stability | | | |
| Stable | + | | |
| Unstable | − | | |
| *6.* Intensity of conflict | | | |
| High | + | | |
| Low | − | | |

[a] A + sign indicates that the characteristic identified is usually associated with higher participation rates; a − sign indicates that the characteristic is ordinarily associated with lower participation in community politics.

of participation in community politics, divided into macro and micro categories, appears in Table 3.1. It is important to note that this list conceals the interaction and interrelations among the various factors. It is difficult to isolate the effect of any one of these elements from the others, and it is the sum of various factors that produces a higher or lower level of participation, rather than any one factor taken independently.

## Macro variables and participation

Robert R. Alford and Eugene C. Lee have gathered the most complete data ever assembled on electoral turnouts in American cities.[3] Drawing upon the resources of the International City Management Association, they conducted a survey of city clerks in all American cities whose populations in 1960 were greater than 25,000 and collected data on the turnouts for the city elections immediately preceding their ques-

3 Robert R. Alford and Eugene C. Lee, "Voter Turnout in American Cities," *American Political Science Review, 62* (September, 1968), 796–813.

tionnaire in 1962. Table 3.2 reports correlations between four categories of characteristics and the levels of community turnout. These categories are political structure, social structure, community stability and continuity, and regional location.

**Table 3.2**  *Correlates of local voting turnouts in American cities with nonconcurrent elections, 1961–1962 (N= 294)*[a]

| Characteristic | Correlation with percentage of adults voting |
|---|---|
| Political structure | |
| Council-manager | |
| versus *non-council-manager* | .50 |
| *Partisan* versus nonpartisan elections | .29 |
| Social structure | |
| Ethnicity (percentage of population of foreign birth or foreign or mixed parentage, 1960) | .51 |
| Education (percentage of those 25 or more years old who had completed 4 years of high school, 1960) | —.15 |
| Community stability and continuity | |
| Mobility (percentage migrant from different counties, 1955–1960) | —.40 |
| Age of city (decade in which the city had reached 25,000 population) | .28 |
| Regional location | |
| *East* | .45 |
| *Midwest* | .21 |
| *South* | —.44 |
| *Far West* | —.10 |

[a] Each entry is a product-moment correlation of the actual percentage of eligible adults voting in the last local election held in the given city. The data were derived from Alford and Lee's study of municipal elections, undertaken with the cooperation of the International City Management Association.

The italicized characteristics indicate the directions of the correlations. For example, we may say that the correlation between a non-council-manager form of city government and its turnout is .50; that is, non-council-manager governments are relatively strongly and positively associated with higher turnouts. Similarly, the "easternness" of a city is also rather strongly and positively associated with its turnout, whereas the opposite is true of the "southernness" of a city, which is strongly and negatively associated with its turnout.

SOURCE: Robert R. Alford and Eugene C. Lee, "Voting Turnout in American Cities," *American Political Science Review, 62* (September, 1968), 803, Table 1.

The variables categorized under *political structure* indicate that voting in cities with "reformed" institutions is lower than that in cities with "unreformed" institutions. Council-manager governments and nonpartisan elections (and, by implication, elections at large) are found in cities with lower turnouts; mayor-council governments and partisan elections (and, by implication, ward elections) are found in cities with higher turnouts. Even when other factors related to social and economic characteristics are taken into account, the presence of "reformed" institutions was still significantly associated with lower voting rates. (Chapter 4 provides a more extensive discussion of "reformed" and "unreformed" government structures and their political consequences.)

What features of "reformed" and "unreformed" political institutions are responsible for this relationship? "Reformed" institutions, to borrow a medical analogy, operate to make the local political system more sterile and antiseptic. In a "reformed" city the mayoral office, once the center of political controversy and contention, is largely a ceremonial position, chiefly involved in ribbon clipping and Rotary luncheons. Nonpartisanship weakens political parties and removes party identification as a valuable voters' guide to candidates and issues. Elections at large have eliminated "personalized," neighborhood ward leaders and have produced incumbents who enjoy little personal contact with voters. The "reform" movement emphasizes professional management rather than the kind of political accountability that arises out of hotly contested political campaigns.

In terms of the *social structure* of the community, Alford and Lee have shown that turnout decreases when there are larger proportions of well-educated people in the community. In terms of *community stability* and *continuity,* turnouts are lower in cities with high mobility, partly because mobile individuals are disfranchised in the American electoral system; communities whose institutions have long continuity also have more active electorates. Communities with little residential mobility and with long-standing institutions are characterized by regular channels of communications between leaders and public, political patterns familiar to the electorate, and readily obtainable information about local affairs. The electorates of unstable communities, in contrast, find information less readily obtainable and have fewer ties with established community leaders and groups. There are also sharp regional differences in turnout; eastern and southern cities show the most and the least voting participation among electorates respectively. Eastern cities show the traits of stability, continuity, and European ethnicity that contribute to turnout. The low turnout in southern cities reflects the features that have long tended to depress political participation in that region. Cities in the west and midwest have a mixture of traits, especially of stability and continuity, that makes them indistinctive as regions for political participation.

Other macro characteristics of communities may affect participation but are difficult to assess. One is the nature of the party system. A few cities possess vigorous party organizations, whereas others are nonpartisan in fact as well as in name. A strong party need not "vote headstones" in order to increase political participation. Parties can frame issues, engage in personal contact, and link candidates with voters through the medium of party identification. Katz and Eldersfeld found that an active party can produce up to a 10 percent change in the division of the vote—certainly enough to capture a close election.[4] In American politics, as a general rule, competition between parties increases participation in elections. The competitiveness of local parties can add significantly to the size of the electorate.

The level and intensity of social conflict should also affect local political activity. Political conflict reflects racial, ethnic, class, and cultural differences among urbanites. A homogeneous community, whether it is composed of white-collar junior executives or of blue-collar union members, generates fewer political conflicts and thus fewer incentives to participate in politics. Superficial homogeneity may, of course, conceal important conflict. The Hatfields and the McCoys, the famed feuding West Virginia hillbillies, would look pretty much alike to a casual observer.

## Micro variables and participation

Lester Milbrath divided the American public into four groups with respect to political participation: *apathetics, spectators, transitionals,* and *gladiators.*[5] Apathetics engage in no political activities, not even opening their awarenesses to political stimuli. One example is a woman who responded to a Survey Research Center interviewer during the 1956 election campaign:

*(Is there anything you like about the Democratic party?)* I'm a Democrat.
   *(Is there anything you like about the Democratic party?)* I don't know.

*(Is there anything you dislike about the Democrats?)* I'm a Democrat, that's all I know. My husband's dead now—he was a Democrat. *(Is there anything you don't like about the party?)* I don't know.

[4] Daniel Katz and Samuel J. Eldersfeld, "The Impact of Local Party Activity upon the Electorate," *Public Opinion Quarterly,* 25 (Spring, 1961), 1–24.
   [5] Lester Milbrath, *Political Participation* (Skokie, Ill., Rand McNally, 1965), pp. 16–18.

*(Is there anything you like about the Republicans?)* I don't know.

*(Is there anything you dislike about the Republicans?)* I don't know.

*(Anything you like about Mr. Stevenson?)* Stevenson is a good Democrat.
*(Is there anything about him that might make you want to vote for him?)*
No, nothing. *(Is there anything you dislike about Mr. Stevenson?)* I
don't know. *(Is there anything about him that might make you want to
vote against him?)* No.[6]

"Spectators" constitute a majority of the American population.
They engage in political conversation from time to time and usually
vote (though less often in local than in national elections). "Transitionals" sometimes proselytize for particular candidates or issues but
fall short of the political activity exhibited by "gladiators," a group
for whom politics is a vocation or at least a major activity. Gladiators
contribute heavily in time and money, they campaign for candidates
and issues, they may seek office themselves, and they provide the political leadership cadres of their communities.

The precise proportions of the public found in these four categories vary from election to election, from one level of government
to another, and from community to community. Milbrath estimates
that "about one-third of the American adult population can be characterized as politically apathetic or passive; in most cases, they are
unaware, literally, of the political part of the world around them.
Another 60 percent play largely spectator roles in the political
process."[7] Approximately 5 percent consists of transitionals and an
estimated 1–2 percent of gladiators. When we consider the very low
overall rate of participation in local elections, it is likely that the proportion of apathetics may be even larger in local than in national
politics.

What factors are associated with an individual's position on this
continuum of participation? One of the most universally identified
observations about political participation is the strong positive correlation between social class and political participation. People with
higher class position are generally more likely to participate in politics.
(For an explanation of the apparent contradiction between Alford
and Lee's finding that voter turnout is lower in communities of well-
educated people and the micro-level finding that well-to-do people participate more heavily, see the discussion on pages 8 and 9 in Chapter
1.) One study of local political involvement, using data from four Wisconsin cities, revealed that two measures of social class (educational
attainment and occupation) were among the three most important fac-

[6] Angus Campbell *et al., The American Voter: An Abridgment* (New York,
Wiley, 1964), p. 142.
[7] Milbrath, *op. cit.,* p. 21.

tors associated with political activity, and Robert A. Dahl's study of New Haven found a 34 percent difference in the proportions of high- and low-income people who were "highly active" in local politics.[8] Other studies have confirmed the positive relationship between social class and participation but have found social status much less important. A study of voting on bond referenda in Atlanta revealed a positive, but not very strong, relationship between indicators of socioeconomic status and turnout, and investigators of the St. Louis metropolitan area did not find class significant in differentiating between high and low participators.[9] At the urban level there is thus some variability in the relationship between class status and voting turnout. Variations may reflect peculiarities of election campaigns, the community itself, or the measurements of both class and participation used.

The stakes perceived in local public policies are another factor that seems to affect participation. By "stakes," we mean the material or ideological gains and losses that the voter perceives as likely to result from the activities of local government. The fact is that for most Americans city hall is more distant, politically speaking, than is Washington, D.C., despite American rhetoric about "government close to the people." But for some urbanites local public policy can be calculated in a profit-and-loss column. Businessmen, realtors, contractors, developers, and municipal employees are far more likely than is the average man to see local politics as relevant to their pocketbooks. Developers, realtors, and landowners are affected by decisions about urban renewal, zoning, and economic development. Contractors and suppliers are affected by nearly every capital-outlay decision, and municipal employees have obvious economic interests in municipal decisions. As most local taxes are tied to property values, home owners may see greater stakes in local politics than others do (though they probably see lower stakes than street contractors do). Alford and Scoble have noted that "home ownership is apparently a form of politically-relevant group membership, vesting the individual with tangible interests perceived as impinged upon by local politics quite apart from more conventional interests of high social status."[10]

Mobility, race, and ethnic affiliation also relate to local participation. Mobile people are less active participants for two principal reasons. First, legal residence qualifications for voting in most Ameri-

[8] Robert R. Alford and Harry Scoble, "Sources of Local Political Involvement," *American Political Science Review*, 62 (December, 1968), 1192–1206; and Robert A. Dahl, *Who Governs?* (New Haven, Yale University Press, 1961), p. 283.

[9] Alvin Boskoff and Harmon Zeigler, *Voting Patterns in a Local Election* (Philadelphia, Lippincott, 1964), pp. 130–131; and John C. Bollens *et al.*, *Exploring the Metropolitan Community* (Berkeley, University of California Press, 1961), chap. 11.

[10] Alford and Scoble, *op. cit.*, p. 1203.

can elections disfranchise people who have recently moved. Second, highly mobile people also have fewer roots in the community, fewer social ties, and less information about local political affairs.

The ethnic affiliation, or identification, of an individual seems also to be indicative of his political activism. "Ethnics" ("an ethnic," for our purposes, means either an immigrant or, more commonly nowadays, the son or daughter of immigrants) are more likely to participate than are native Americans. A study of St. Louis found that 77 percent of the German community in the city and 80 percent of residents of southern and eastern European ancestry had voted at least once in municipal elections, whereas only 61 percent of "old stock" Americans and 62 percent of blacks reported having ever voted in such an election.[11] Robert E. Lane, in discussing the "way of the ethnic in politics," has noted:

*In a real sense, the seat of ethnic politics is the local community, not the national capital. This is evidenced by the fact that although ethnic groups often vote no more frequently than native white Protestants in national elections (with the Jews excepted) and sometimes less frequently, they usually vote more frequently in local elections.*[12]

In the heyday of the political machine, ethnic groups were critical elements in the party leaders' victory package. "Ticket balancing" still occurs in cities with large ethnic populations, and politicians often woo ethnic voters with promises of symbolic group-related rewards.

## Low participation and its consequences

The evidence demonstrates very low participation in American urban politics. Voting—which is the most active form of participation undertaken by most Americans—typically involves no more than 35 percent of the eligible local electorates in city elections. Turnouts of 5–10 percent of the adult population are common in referenda, in urban special-district elections, in county and other nonmunicipal elections, and in some city elections. In terms of participation beyond voting— talking to councilmen, campaigning, pressing for specific policies, and so on—the proportion of activists is even smaller. Dahl once observed that politics is just a "sideshow on the great circus of life." This observation is doubly true at the local level.

Few subjects have invoked more conflict among political thinkers of varying ideological bents than has the subject of participation and its role in a democratic system. We propose here only to raise, not to

11 Bollens *et al.*, *op. cit.*, chap. 11.
12 Robert E. Lane, *Political Life* (New York, Free Press, 1959), p. 239.

resolve, the philosophical and political questions associated with the "optimum" level of participation in a democratic system, but such issues cannot be completely ignored in an examination of participation in the urban political system.

Some thinkers, like John Stuart Mill, have believed in the legitimacy of mass participation yet have feared a "tyranny of the majority." Some early American democrats viewed the ordinary man as the repository of innate common sense and virtue and therefore had few fears of a system permitting high participation. More recently, political scientists have debated among themselves about the "desirable" level of participation needed to maintain both stability and democracy. Some have emphasized that a political system that permits "too much" participation suffers strains so severe that its effectiveness may be in doubt. Proponents of this view often argue that high participation usually implies the activation of less-educated and less-tolerant groups, whose views are generally hostile to the very preservation of a democratic order. In Herbert McClosky's words, "democratic viability is, to begin with, saved by the fact that those who are most confused about democratic ideas are also likely to be politically apathetic and without significant influence."[13]

The issue in this "revolt from the masses"[14] is whether the mass public is less supportive of democratic values, more susceptible to demagogic manipulation, and more irrational in politics.

The critics of this "elitist theory of democracy" reply that a purportedly democratic system that tolerates only minimal participation inevitably involves costs in representation.[15] Groups that do not participate very much are, of course, those whose interests will be less adequately represented in the policy process. Presumably such groups will enjoy fewer policy outputs relevant to their needs and interests. The "price" of maintaining an electorate composed mainly of people steeped in democratic values is thus a decrease in benefits for non-participant groups.

The most significant consequence of minimal participation in most communities is a decrease in the possibility of political accountability and an increase in the degree to which professional management premises dominate local decision-making. (For a discussion of political accountability and professional management, see pp. 110–116.) The resource of information includes two basic types: technical know-how (for example, is concrete or asphalt superior for city streets, within

[13] Herbert McClosky, "Consensus and Ideology in American Politics," *American Political Science Review*, 58 (June, 1964), 376.

[14] Peter Bachrach, *The Theory of Democratic Elitism* (Boston, Little, Brown, 1967), chap. 3.

[15] Jack L. Walker, "A Critique of the Elitist Theory of Democracy," *American Political Science Review*, 60 (June, 1966), 285–295.

the bounds of cost?) and political knowledge (for example, what are the preferences of the citizens or of particular groups regarding public policy options?). A high degree of apathy means that costs of decision-makers' obtaining information about group and individual needs increase substantially. For this reason, decision-makers may substitute technical information for "political" information as a basis for their decisions.

## Participation and the costs of information

TECHNICAL INFORMATION    In most developed political systems, technical information is considerably less costly to decision-makers than is political information. The principal explanation is the ease with which urban governments can employ specialists—planners, engineers, public administrators, city managers, school administrators—who can generate, assimilate, and analyze untold quantities of data on any policy option and can provide the skills essential to implementing many policy alternatives. Municipal bureaucrats and specialists are in daily contact with mayors, managers, and councilmen and ready to provide technical information. In a literal sense, the proximity of technical experts and policy-makers is close. Technical information is available for the asking.

POLITICAL INFORMATION    Political information on individual and group needs, aspirations, and perceptions comes largely from two sources: elections and activities of interest groups. The party in urban politics, from its machine days to its present somnolent state, has never provided a particularly effective information-transmission system. In most areas the parties do not even offer their traditional minimum choice between Tweedledee and Tweedledum. This leaves elections and groups, subjects we examine in the following sections, as the institutional sources of input information.

Elections, however, have a number of very serious limitations as devices for registering interests. First, participation in elections is uniformly low in most urban systems. Only a comparatively small number of people exert their political weight through the electoral process. Second, because of the unevenness of participation from group to group, elections do not provide random samples of public opinion. Third, except in the special case of referenda, elections do not present choices among policy options; they present choices among candidates, whose public views on policy questions may be deliberately vague, in order to attract a large number of potential supporters. Fourth, even if particular issue positions can be pinned unambiguously on contending candidates, voters have only one vote each and may agree with candidate Jones on urban-renewal policy but with candidate Smith on taxation. When there is a multiplicity of issues—usually none too clearly articulated by the candidates—it is well-nigh impossible to estimate the collective sentiment of the electorate through an election. And, fifth, most voters have rather limited information about possible policy options, as well as about the probabilities that their candidates, if elected, will in fact pursue voters' policy choices.

Given all of these considerations, we may agree with Dahl's observation that

a good deal of traditional democratic theory leads us to expect more from national [or local] elections than they can possibly provide. We expect elections to reveal the "will" or preference of a majority on a set of issues. This is one thing elections rarely do, except in an almost trivial fashion.[16]

The information that decision-makers glean from the electoral process is likely, therefore, to be sketchy at best and utterly inexplicable at worst. This leaves political interest groups as the major source of information on group preferences and needs, a subject that we treat in the next section.

What we have called "political information" is thus more difficult to obtain—at least through the electoral process—than is technical information of the kind provided by public bureaucracies. Technical experts are there on the spot, whereas groups are, at best, imperfectly organized and integrated into the communication apparatus of the decision-makers. Minimal local participation tends to shift policy-makers' search for information from the mass public to professional bureaucrats. Low participation also reduces the representation of those groups that participate least. To be sure, a group or an interest need not be represented literally in the mayor's office or the council's chambers to have its needs and preferences considered, especially if leaders are oriented toward the public in their approach to policy-making. The poverty legislation that created the Office of Economic Opportunity, for example, was spurred, not by the demands of the poor, but by a group of "professional reformers" occupying important executive positions in the federal government. But, in the last analysis, low participation exacts a heavy loss in representation.

## INTEREST GROUPS IN URBAN POLITICS

Arthur Bentley was the first proponent of the "group theory of politics" in modern political science. So convinced was he that all political

---

[16] Robert A. Dahl, A Preface to Democratic Theory (Chicago, University of Chicago Press, 1956), p. 131.

life could be explained by the interaction of groups that he claimed: ". . . when the groups are adequately stated, everything is stated. And when I say everything I mean everything."[17]

According to Bentley, an individual is merely the sum of his group interests, and government constitutes merely the equilibrium of group interests at a given time. Numerous political scientists have expanded, qualified, or elaborated on Bentley's formulation, but the original outline of the major tenets of analysis of groups and political life was his. Bentley himself despised "definition-mongers," sneering that "he who likes may snip verbal definitions in his old age, when his world has gone crackly and dry."

Part of the difficulty with definitions that may have troubled Bentley is that the words "interest" and "group" seem either redundant or, from another perspective, contradictory. If we conceive of a political group as an organized body of people designed to influence public policy, "interest" becomes a meaningless adjective, for it is hard to imagine such a group without shared interests. On the other hand, if we emphasize the adjective "interest," then it is equally clear that not all interests are organized into groups or, at least, that some clearly are better organized than others. A consumer, a poor man, and a commuter each has an "interest" in common with fellow consumers, poor people, and commuters, but no group—or at least not a very effective one—represents this interest. The term "interest group," therefore, subsumes two somewhat distinct ideas. The degree to which a particular interest is in fact organized as a group to influence public policy is an empirical question.

More specifically, we conceive of a political group as an organization attempting to influence public policies through application of political resources. From either an individual or group perspective, an interest encompasses a set of preferences about the direction of public policy. The essential difference between groups and interests is that interests are psychological, whereas groups are sociological, phenomena. Interests may be more or less organized into groups; groups may share more than one interest.

In this section, we shall treat the interest groups of business, labor, ethnics, reformers, municipal employees, and neighborhoods. We shall discuss briefly some major interests of each group, while recognizing their high variability from community to community; describe some of their major resources and stakes in urban politics; and assess the ways in which groups contribute to policy formation.

[17] Arthur Bentley, *The Process of Government* (Cambridge, Mass., Harvard University Press, 1967; originally published in 1908), p. 208.

## Businessmen

Generalizing about the role of businessmen in the 80,000 units of local government in the United States is hazardous, for the term "businessman" subsumes a range from the owner of a local nightspot to a half-million-dollar-a-year Detroit automobile executive.

"Businessmen" constitute a large proportion of interest-group membership in local politics. Charles Adrian and Charles Press have observed that "so many business groups exert pressure upon government that they would probably overshadow and overpower all the others if it were not that they spend so much of their time opposing one another."[18] Economic interests unite most businessmen some of the time (as in the desire to reduce the tax burden on local business), some businessmen all of the time, but rarely all businessmen for very long. Downtown merchants are interested in policies on mass transportation, urban renewal, and economic development that would infuse new life into the central city. Businessmen in the outlying areas tend to oppose such costly undertakings. Small businessmen, especially those who are downwardly mobile in the status system, are often hostile to "downtown interests" like department-store owners. Realtors are more concerned with zoning and subdivision regulation than with revitalizing sagging downtown areas. Businessmen who provide services over a wide area within the community—major wholesalers and producers, for example—are more interested in community growth, regardless of the direction that it takes.

BUSINESS INTERESTS    The two interests most likely to be shared by most businessmen are the quest for lower taxes and the desire to secure economic growth for the community. The first interest is hardly monopolized by businessmen and may be overstated in any case. Charles Gilbert, in a study of government in the Philadelphia area, noted that "in interviews, industrialists commonly aver that local and county taxes are a small part of the cost of doing business." Moreover, he reminds us that local taxes, because they are deductible from federal taxes, cost industry only fifty-two cents on the dollar.[19] We do not mean to suggest that businessmen are enthusiastic about high taxes, but they may be no more antagonistic to higher taxes than are, say, home owners. Moreover, businessmen, especially those in larger firms, see a need to make local communities as attractive as possible, in public serv-

[18] Charles Adrian and Charles Press, *Governing Urban America*, 3rd ed. (New York, McGraw-Hill, 1968), p. 125.

[19] Charles Gilbert, *Governing the Suburbs* (Bloomington, University of Indiana Press, 1967), p. 145.

ices, as a means of increasing livability both for them and for their prospective employees.

Businessmen are perhaps most unified and vocal in their support for public policies promoting economic growth. More economic growth not only means more sales; it is also a visible and measurable sign of "progress," especially to those accustomed to measuring progress in economic terms. Although not all businessmen share the economic-growth orientation toward local government, it appears to be a dominant theme of policy, especially in small and medium-sized cities.[20] Several years ago, one of the authors interviewed the mayor of a tiny southern town. During the conversation, the mayor, who was also a businessman, used a ream of charts and graphs to support his claim that his town was really "the hub of the South."

POLITICAL RESOURCES   Local businessmen are usually organized in chapters of the Chamber of Commerce. One of the key political resources of the chamber is its inclusiveness, but this factor can also work to its disadvantage. For one thing, in a large group with no power to compel its members to action or even to maintain membership, individual members are inclined to let other members do the work, for all policy gains can thus be shared by all members at no cost to most individual members.[21] Second, groups with large and somewhat diverse memberships will usually be unable to formulate group positions on issues likely to divide the groups.[22] Chambers of commerce harbor numbers of conflicting interest behind the façade of a few unifying interests. Among the conflicting interests typically found in a business association are downtown versus suburbs; wholesalers versus retailers; small versus large business; and absentee- versus locally owned businesses. Such internal differences tend to blunt the effectiveness of this or any relatively large and diverse organization.

Still, businessmen are a significant element in most local political systems. Businessmen are mostly from the upper and middle classes and participate in politics beyond merely voting; most local leaders, formal and informal, are recruited from the business and professional community.[23] Business interests are virtually guaranteed a hearing by

[20] Oliver Williams and Charles Adrian, *Four Cities* (Philadelphia, University of Pennsylvania Press, 1963).

[21] This point is a major theme of the penetrating analysis of groups in Mancur Olson, *The Logic of Collective Action* (New York, Schocken, 1968).

[22] Raymond A. Bauer, Ithiel de Sola Pool, and Lewis A. Dexter, *American Business and Public Policy* (New York, Atherton, 1964), chap. 22.

[23] In the four communities studied by Robert Agger, Daniel Goldrich, and Bert E. Swanson, the proportion of community leaders who came from managerial-professional-proprietorial occupations ranged from a low of 79 percent to a high of

local policy-makers, and businessmen tend to be well educated, to have the social and verbal skills necessary to communicate effectively with bureaucrats and politicians, and to perceive higher than average stakes in community decisions.

## Labor unions

Given the visibility and alleged importance of labor unions in national politics, it is surprising to discover the variability in their political influence at the urban level. Detroit is a one-industry city dominated by automotive manufacturers and the United Auto Workers. The UAW has played a fairly active role in local politics through its Committee on Political Education. But it appears to be much less effective in local affairs than in influencing Michigan state politics.

Kenneth E. Gray and David Greenstone, in their penetrating study of labor influence in Detroit, St. Louis, and Houston, concluded that "despite its power, COPE has had relatively little success in [Detroit] politics."[24] This study indicated that voters and politicians alike tend to view COPE as a self-interested group that does not represent the city as a whole. Also, and perhaps more significantly, Detroit's nonpartisan electoral system weakens the hold of union leaders on their followers. Even when the rank and file do know the union's candidates, many are reluctant to support leader-endorsed liberals for fear of increased property taxation and the possibility that such candidates will enact housing-integration ordinances.

Labor's experience in Toledo, Ohio, demonstrates the difficulty that unions have in securing rank-and-file backing for their endorsements. Some members, particularly the older and less well-educated unionists followed fairly closely the choices of the labor leaders, but for most members, "union involvement in local politics was remote and unimportant."[25] Party identification, rather than leadership endorsement, was the most important element in the voting choices of the members. Since 1953, Toledo's United Labor Committee has endorsed forty-three candidates in local contests, only twenty-three of whom have been elected. This batting average is only slightly better than chance alone would predict.

In Houston, whose population is relatively young and heavily white-collar, labor unions constitute the backbone of the liberal

100 percent. See Agger, Goldrich, and Swanson, *The Rulers and the Ruled* (New York, Wiley, 1964), pp. 332–333.

[24] Kenneth E. Gray and David Greenstone, "Organized Labor in City Politics," in Edward C. Banfield, ed., *Urban Government* (New York, Free Press, 1961), p. 372.

[25] Schley R. Lyons, "Labor in City Politics: The Case of the Toledo United Auto Workers," *Social Science Quarterly, 49* (March, 1969), 827.

faction in the Democratic Party. Union attention is, however, directed much more to state than to city politics. One Houston AFL–CIO official claimed that "the closer politics is to the local level, the more we stay out of it."[26] If union attempts to wield influence in Detroit, Toledo, and Houston are typical, it seems reasonable to conclude that unions are much less effective in city than in state or national politics.

The interests and stakes of trade unions, as well as their political resources, help to account for their minimal (or variable) influence on local policy. As organizations unions have relatively low stakes in local public policy. The key decisions, which are of concern to *all* union members, are those related to wages and hours, safety requirements, right-to-work laws, and purchasing power. These decisions are made not in city halls but by states and the federal government. Said a leader of one union in Toledo:

*City government is not as important for us. We've got to think about state and national issues. The state is in many ways the most important, I think, since it handles workmen's compensation, unemployment, and such things.*[27]

During an earlier era when local police broke up strikes and jailed picketers, unions were more concerned about local politics. Today the overriding concerns of unions as a whole are focused on higher levels of the American federal system. Many significant local political issues tend to divide rank-and-file unionists in ways that would permit no clear leadership position to prevail. Race relations, integration of schools and neighborhoods, and taxation are especially divisive issues. As these issues involve no direct threats to the position of the union as an organization, local leaders commonly avoid taking sides.

To a much greater degree than the local chamber of commerce, unions harbor multiple conflicting interests among their members, which impel them to steer fairly clear of local politics, particularly when their stakes are at higher levels of government anyway. As in all interest groups, limitations on political resources—votes, money, and organization, in particular—require that they be spent where they will have the greatest impact; for trade unions, local government is not that point.

One particular feature of the government structure of "reformed" cities—the nonpartisan ballot—also contributes to the weakening of trade-union influence. Nonpartisanship permits candidates to be more flexible in their issue positions, and it is therefore more difficult to

26 Gray and Greenstone, *op. cit.*, p. 378.

27 Jean L. Stinchcombe, *Reform and Reaction* (Belmont, Calif., Wadsworth, 1968), p. 156.

identify a candidate as either pro- or antilabor. Voters in a non-partisan system do not have the valuable cues of party identification to help them sort out candidates. Psychologically, therefore, it is easier for a rank-and-file member to vote for a candidate of somewhat conservative ideological bent, especially on race and tax questions, even though he might not vote for the same candidate if the Republican label were affixed to the ballot. Nonpartisanship thus weakens the potential influence of labor in city politics.

## Ethnic groups

THE ASSIMILATION THESIS  Mark Twain is said to have grumbled, upon reading his own obituary, that "the rumors of my death are greatly exaggerated." The same may be said about the widely espoused theory of the "assimilation" of European ethnic groups. According to the assimilationist theory, second- and third-generation European immigrants have become so thoroughly socialized in the culture of middle-class America that their political attitudes and behavior are scarcely distinguishable from those of direct descendants of arrivals on the *Mayflower*.

Dahl has suggested that ethnic politics passes through three stages.[28] In the first stage, group members are "almost exclusively proletarian," few indigenous group leaders exist, and social homogeneity within the group produces great similarity in voting habits. In the second stage, group members become socially differentiated, as some members attain white-collar positions and status. People in such roles have different views from those in the first phase of assimilation, but there is still a high degree of ethnic consciousness among these upwardly mobile individuals. In the third stage, considerable heterogeneity develops, as large segments are assimilated into the nonproletarian classes. To these people, ethnic identification becomes a source of embarrassment. Socioeconomic class, rather than ethnic identification, begins to determine individual behavior patterns, and ethnic solidarity becomes a subject for historians. By the late 1950s Dahl had concluded that ethnic politics in New Haven was on the wane and that any politician who pitched his appeal solely to ethnic groups would probably lose.

Superficially at least, assimilation now appears to be extensive. Although 19 percent of the American population consists of either first- or second-generation immigrants, the once-prominent European ghetto within the central city has almost disappeared. No longer are European and Asian ethnic groups crowded into city tenements as

28 Dahl, *Who Governs?*, pp. 34–36.

they once were. As have other Americans, these ethnic populations have moved to the suburbs and home ownership is extensive among them. In Chicago, Detroit, Los Angeles, and Philadelphia, the proportion of home ownership is higher among first- and second-generation immigrants than among Americans of native-born parentage.[29] According to the 1960 Census, there were as many ethnics residing outside central cities as in them.

Although New York City has more Italians than has Naples, more Greeks than has Sparta, and more Puerto Ricans than has San Juan, the salience of most of these groups as communities has declined. There were an estimated 1,300 foreign-language newspapers in the United States in 1914. Today there are fewer than 400. There is also less political cohesion in the ethnic vote than in the past. John Lindsay, whose fellow white Protestants constitute only 5 percent of New York City's population (which prompts Lindsay to quip about being able to understand the problems of minority groups), defeated two Italian-Americans—John Marchi and Mario Procaccino—in his reelection bid in 1969.

THE LIMITS OF ASSIMILATION    On the other hand, there is much evidence against too-hasty acceptance of the assimilation thesis. Ethnic politics has a tenacity that defies academic arguments about assimilation, absorption, and homogenization. Raymond Wolfinger reinvestigated the patterns of ethnic politics in New Haven and found that Italian-Americans gave equally vigorous support to the Connecticut Republican Party in the 1940s and the 1950s.[30] Polish-American voters in urban and rural areas of Illinois will still cross party lines to vote for Polish names.[31] In nonpartisan local elections, ethnic identification takes on added importance, for it is one of the few available cues for voters.[32]

With the growth of civil-rights and Black Power movements among urban blacks, European ethnic groups have produced counter-organizations, particularly in opposition to neighborhood and school integration. Chicago Congressman Roman Pucinski, of Polish extraction, has claimed that "The rise of Negro militancy has brought a revival of ethnic orientation in all the other groups."[33] That many

[29] Stanley Lieberson, *Ethnic Patterns in American Cities* (New York, Free Press, 1963), pp. 98–99.

[30] Raymond Wolfinger, "The Development and Persistence of Ethnic Voting," *American Political Science Review*, 59 (December, 1965), 896–908.

[31] Robert A. Lorinskas *et al.*, "The Persistence of Ethnic Voting in Rural and Urban Areas," *Social Science Quarterly*, 49 (March, 1969), 871–899.

[32] Gerald Pomper, "Ethnic and Group Voting in Nonpartisan Elections," *Public Opinion Quarterly*, 30 (Spring, 1966), 79–97.

[33] Quoted in *Newsweek*, October 6, 1969, p. 33.

police departments in cities with heavily ethnic populations include large numbers of Italians, Irish, Polish, and other ethnics heightens the frictions between the police and blacks.

Considering the evidence against overemphasis on the assimilation theory, Wolfinger has formulated an alternative model of ethnic politics, which he calls "the mobilization theory" of ethnic political life. He argues that "the strength of ethnic voting depends on both the intensity of ethnic identification and the level of ethnic relevance in the election." The most important expression of ethnic relevance is the presence of an ethnic name on the ticket. But, because "middle-class status is a virtual prerequisite for candidacy for major office" and because "an ethnic group's development of sufficient political skill and influence to secure such a nomination also requires the develop-ment of a middle class,"[34] ethnic voting solidarity will not appear until some members of the group become candidates for middle-class status. The peak of ethnic solidarity in elections thus will come not during the first generation—when the group is uniformly of the lower class and subject to manipulation and cross pressures from competing factions—but during the second and third generations. This theory seems better to explain why, in New Haven at least, there was an increasing solidarity of ethnic groups behind their parties over time. It also embodies recognition of political-leadership skills as a crucial ingredient in ethnic politics.

At least in the early years of ethnic solidarity, the ethnic group pursues mostly status goals, as distinct from ideological or material goals. The most important element of the collective mentality of an ethnic group is its uncertainty about its own status in the social sys-tem. The placement of a group leader at the top of a political ticket provides vicarious status mobility to all members of the group. The hiring of policemen or civil servants from the group, the awarding of contracts, the election to party posts, and the "Columbus Day appeal" of ethnic celebrations are all measures of a group's political status. Such matters as taxation, urban renewal, zoning, and crime prevention are also relevant to members of ethnic groups, but they do not benefit the groups per se. In identifying with his national group—although we must recognize that he may also play a number of other politically relevant roles—the ethnic voter will be most concerned with status rewards for his group. The conflict over status will be more intense if the community contains two or more ethnic groups vying with one another for outputs. The vigor of competition among ethnic groups is one explanation for the higher-than-average participation of such groups in local politics. As we noted earlier, European ethnic voters

[34] Wolfinger, *op. cit.*, p. 905.

tend to vote more in local politics than do more traditional Americans. Moreover, where there is considerable political activism among ethnic groups, traditional Americans may also participate more, simply in response to this vigor.

Politics has long provided an avenue of upward mobility for ethnic minorities, even when opportunities in other parts of the social system have been limited. In a system of universal suffrage ethnics have votes and a ready-made basis for group loyalty. The leaders of urban party machines, which dominated politics in many cities during the early years of urbanization, took full advantage of the new immigrants potential. For decades ethnics constituted the hard core of support for the machines, which explains, at least partly, why the reformers, who have been mostly more established white Protestants, have been so outspoken in their criticism of the machines. Through the exchange of status and service for votes and support, the machine and the ethnic groups forged a solid and mutually productive alliance. Most machines, like most ethnic groups, were Democratic (a curious exception is the Italians in New Haven), and the Democratic parties of eastern cities still draw consistent support from ethnic voters.

James Q. Wilson and Edward C. Banfield have emphasized that most European ethnic groups hold a set of attitudes toward government and policy that separates them from the views held by traditional Amercans. They describe these two attitudinal syndromes as *"private-regarding"* and *"public-regarding."*[35] "Private-regarding" attitudes emphasize personal politics, oriented toward the family, group, or subculture— involving a political style not unlike that provided by the machines for many decades. This conception of politics includes bargaining, trading off, and the material satisfaction of group interests, with heavy emphasis on political accountability. The "public-regarding" style, a view associated with a more traditional American value system, encompasses principles of abstract morality, honesty, efficiency, and the value of professional management. The "public-regarding" perspective on local politics is one basis for the reform movement in local politics.

## Reformers

Nearly every major city and most minor ones (assuming that any city admits to being "minor") has its reform group. Where reformers are not organized in groups, there is still widely shared interest in the goals of the reform movement. Oklahoma City has its Association for

[35] James Q. Wilson and Edward C. Banfield, "Public-Regardingness as a Value Premise in Voting Behavior," *American Political Science Review, 58* (December, 1964), 876–887.

Responsible Government, New York City has the Citizen's Union, and Seattle has the Municipal League, each of which seeks to institutionalize the virtues of "good government." (Because of these perennial cries for "good government," critics of the early reformers sometimes called them the "goo-goos.") Virtually every city has a chapter of the League of Women Voters, although the League is not always as influential as its spokeswomen believe. Not all the reformers have identical views about their goals, but most seem to share the following predispositions about local government:

1    an aversion to "politics" as a means of arriving at public-policy decisions and specifically to political parties and organized interest groups;
2    a holistic conception of the community, a belief that there is a single interest of the "community as a whole" to which "special interests" should be clearly subordinated;
3    a strong preference for professional management of community affairs, implying preference for public policy-making by technical experts like the city manager;
4    a strong faith in the efficacy of structural reform.

The goal of the early reformers was to "rationalize" and "democratize" city government by substituting "community-oriented" leadership for the pernicious politics of the machine. They rejected the personal kind of political accountability associated with the machine, patronage, ward leaders, and demands for ethnic recognition. Instead, they stressed a political accountability modeled upon that of the business corporation (or their image of it), which would have a small policy-making body, the council ("board of directors"), directly responsible to the electorate ("stockholders"), without the intervention of parties and groups, and administration by professional experts. A manager ("corporation president") would serve at the discretion of the council. Although a number of structural reforms were advocated by the reformers, the most lasting in their effects have been manager government, nonpartisan elections, and at-large constituencies.

The reformers became prominent in the latter years of the nineteenth century. They have remained so ever since, although there are some differences between the early and latter-day reformers. Businessmen, traditional groups, local chambers of commerce, and upper-class people were in the forefront of the early battles for reform. Harold Stone, in his survey of early adoptions of the council-manager plan, found in Jackson, Michigan, that "most of the campaign work [for the plan] was done through the Chamber of Commerce, which enlisted the support of all the Protestant reform agencies in the city." In Rochester, the campaign for manager government was "supported by the leading industrialist of the city, George Eastman, by the Bureau of Municipal Research which he financed, and by most of the civic, reform, and business associations of the city."[36] (One leader of the Rochester Communist Party also supported the manager plan, believing that it was one stage through which politics would have to pass before the dictatorship of the proletariat could be achieved.) Almost as surely as the manager plan was supported by traditional and business interests in the city, it was opposed by trade unions and ethnic groups.

Many contemporary studies of city politics have revealed the major role played by reformers or by those who share reformist attitudes. Wilson and Banfield have portrayed the reformers as "public-regarding" voters, actors, and thinkers who seek the good of the "community as a whole," rather than benefits to particular interests.[37] Robert Agger, Daniel Goldrich, and Bert E. Swanson have described the rise of "community conservationists," a group that sees the "values of community life maximized when political leadership is exercised by men representing the public at large, rather than 'special interests.' "[38] Robert C. Wood has described a similar set of attitudes in the "no-party politics of suburbia." Suburbanites seem to be characterized by

*an outright reaction against partisan activity, a refusal to recognize that there may be persistent cleavages in the electorate, and an ethical disapproval of permanent group collaboration as an appropriate means of settling disputes.*[39]

The terms "reformism," "community conservationism," and "public-regardingness" all describe the attitudes that pervade American communities among upper- and middle-class citizens in particular. The structure of local politics has been heavily influenced by these attitudes, particularly the emphasis on professional management and the choice of managerial government, nonpartisan elections, and at-large constituencies as models of political accountability.

## Municipal employees

The 4.5 million employees of urban government in the United States are important subjects of inquiry. They have higher stakes than do most citizens in the municipal political system; they form interest groups that press for group benefits, particularly wage and salary improvements; and they are themselves decision-makers who shape the

[36] Harold Stone *et al.*, *City Manager Government in the United States* (Chicago, Public Administration Service, 1940), pp. 25, 35.

[37] Wilson and Banfield, *op. cit.*

[38] Agger, Goldrich, and Swanson, *op. cit.*, p. 21.

[39] Robert C. Wood, *Suburbia* (Boston, Houghton Mifflin, 1959), p. 155.

policies of municipalities, school districts, counties, and other local governments.[40] We are less concerned here with their roles as decision-makers (a subject that we shall cover in Chapter 5) than with their roles as citizens and interest groups.

As the recipients of nearly $2 billion in wages and salaries (by far the largest proportion of city expenditures) city employees have obvious stakes in the wage and salary decisions of municipal government. Many skilled, unskilled, and professional city employees have joined unions. As in the private sector, unionization is less extensive among the white-collar employees of municipal governments, (for example, teachers) than among the blue-collar and the unskilled, but white-collar unionism is growing. Many of these unionized city employees are members of the American Federation of State, County and Municipal Employees, an affiliate of the AFL–CIO. (Most unionized teachers belong to the American Federation of Teachers, also an AFL–CIO affiliate.) Many city employees who are not members of national unions are members of local organizations that attempt to secure collective benefits, and many large and medium-sized cities have organizations of policemen, modeled after New York City's Patrolmen's Benevolent Association.

It is a commonplace of American law that government employees are not permitted to strike. In recent years, however, cities have suffered sudden "epidemics" among employees involved in wage negotiations. (Among policemen, this phenomenon is commonly known as the "blue flu.") New York City has experienced more difficulties with its employees than has perhaps any other city, having endured prolonged "strikes" of both teachers and sanitation workers. New York City's "finest" have also developed to a high art the strategy of variable law enforcement. From time to time, enforcement of parking and traffic regulations slows to a snail's pace under advice from the leaders of the PBA, whereas at other times they instruct patrolmen to "enforce the law 100%."[41]

Even in the absence of these uncommon tactics of negotiation, city employees are a very attentive public. They possess more information about city politics than do most other citizens, and they are more likely to vote than are most other citizens. These resources weld city employees into an interest well worth courting in municipal elections. One of the first considerations in normal municipal budgeting is, if resources permit, to figure in wage and salary increases for municipal employees.

Most professional employees of city government are affiliated with

[40] Edward C. Banfield and James Q. Wilson, *City Politics* (Cambridge, Mass., Harvard University Press, 1963), chap. 15.
[41] See, for example, *The New York Times*, August 13, 1968, p. 1.

professional associations, most of which maintain staffs in Washington, D.C., to press for legislation oriented toward the particular policy concerns of the organizations. Housing administrators are vigorous in their support of public-housing legislation, planners support federal assistance for urban-planning activities, and other professional organizations attempt to secure federal legislation to further their professional interests.

In addition to support for federal and state legislation, these associations provide guidelines and cues to their members. Through newsletters, periodicals, conferences, and conventions, organizations provide channels through which members are kept abreast of one another's thinking. Organizations thus disseminate professional standards that influence members' behavior, whatever the particular ordinances and rules provided by city administrators and councilmen. To a librarian, there are right and wrong ways to operate a library regardless of the position taken by the city council. A planner relies on his training and professional standards for planning criteria, whatever views the manager or mayor may hold.

### Neighborhood groups

Neighborhoods take on particular importance in cities with ward elections, but under certain circumstances neighborhood groups may be important in any city. There is a well-known tendency for people to sort themselves—or to be sorted by others—into relatively homogeneous areas. Because of this tendency neighborhood interests overlap social and economic interests somewhat. Neighborhood-based political organizations are found most often in working-class and lower-middle-class areas, rather than in lower-class or upper-middle-class areas. The lowest-status areas in a city usually lack the stability and the leadership skills to organize viable groups. For other reasons, the neighborhood is not commonly a basis for social organization in more cosmopolitan upper-middle-class areas; organization there is based more often on occupational, professional, or city-wide considerations.

Some neighborhood groups persist for years, are effectively led, and present cogent statements of their interests to the council, mayor, or bureaucracy. But the more typical pattern is the ad hoc neighborhood association organized in response to some perceived external "threat." One of the most frequent spurs to sporadic neighborhood organization is the threat of a change in zoning ordinances, especially one that would change a neighborhood's status from single-family residential to multifamily residential or, occasionally, to commercial. Such ad hoc groups differ widely in the quality of their leadership, their staying power, and the resources they bring to bear on decision-makers. Because of these differences, it is difficult to predict the outcome of their confrontations with planning boards or city councils.

Zoning is not the only public policy that stimulates formation of neighborhood groups. Joint federal-urban programs like model cities, the war on poverty, and urban renewal focus on certain neighborhoods. Federal legislation requires that each program involve some degree of citizen participation. Opposition by neighborhood groups has been one of the most significant obstacles to local urban-renewal agencies. Studies by James C. Davies in New York City have shown that an effective neighborhood organization led by articulate, politically sophisticated people can hamstring major renewal projects.[42] But, because renewal agencies rarely tackle neighborhoods where there are reservoirs of middle-class leadership skills, the relevant neighborhood groups are often ineffective.

The antipoverty and model-cities programs are also obliged to encourage citizen participation in program formation. The early experience of the war on poverty demonstrated that neighborhood participation is highly variable: Some neighborhoods oppose the program, others are basically apathetic, and still others are supportive. (See, for example, our discussion of the antipoverty program in San Francisco, pp. 292–295.) Partly because the antipoverty program had given neighborhood groups some experience in influencing decision-makers, such groups have been more effective in shaping the direction of the model-cities program.[43]

There has recently been a renaissance of the neighborhood organization. As we have just noted it arises partly from public policies that take particular neighborhoods as their "target areas." Some cities have deliberately facilitated this neighborhood resurgence by attempting to decentralize public administration and policy-making, particularly in education. Another contributing factor is the resurgence of ethnic consciousness among racial and national groups, each of which seeks to assert its identity and viability as a community.

## A final note on interest groups

Political scientists are far from agreeing about the power of groups to influence public policy. But there is good reason, we think, to reject literal acceptance of Bentley's observation that, "when the groups are adequately explained, everything is explained." This statement is true only in the somewhat trivial, in fact, tautological, sense

[42] James C. Davies III, *Neighborhood Groups and Urban Renewal* (New York, Columbia University Press, 1966).

[43] Roland Warren, "Model Cities' First Round: Politics, Planning and Participation," *Journal of the American Institute of Planners, 34* (July, 1969), 245–253.

that, if attitudes, values, political parties, electoral mechanisms, bureaucratic premises, and the like are defined as "groups" or "group-determined," then everything can indeed be explained by explaining groups. If "everything" is a "group," then the concept "group" can "explain" everything.

If we restrict ourselves to a more narrow and common-sense formulation of the term "interest group" to denote formal organizations, however, we do not find that interest groups are all-powerful. One of the most penetrating studies of policy-making at the national level examined the influence of such associations as the National Association of Manufacturers, the League of Women Voters, the duPont company, the Chamber of Commerce, and the AFL–CIO and concluded that such groups were surprisingly ineffectual.[44] A study of budgeting at the urban level revealed that decision-makers rarely experienced much "pressure" from specific groups for particular financial requests. When groups did attempt to argue for particular expenditures, decision-makers tended to believe that most requests were reasonable but that "you can't do everything everybody wants."[45] These findings do not invalidate the assumption that groups are significant elements in the policy-making process, but they cast doubt on any theory of urban politics that assumes the primacy of interest groups in determining the use of community resources.

## POLITICAL PARTIES AND ELECTIONS

### The Nineteenth Ward

In the 1890s Chicago's Nineteenth Ward, where Jane Addams and her associates established the famed Hull House, contained 50,000 people of twenty different nationalities, crammed together in a few square miles of dingy tenements.[46] Most were immigrants, and, because of universal manhood suffrage, most of the men were voters.

The political "boss" of the Nineteenth Ward was Johnny Powers, a short, stocky Irishman and one of the most powerful figures in Chicago city politics. He was chairman of the finance committee of the Chicago City Council and used his position to manipulate public-utility franchises and the jobs of thousands of city employees. Powers ran for office on a year-round basis: bailing a son or husband out of jail, fixing matters with a judge, buying funerals through his standing

44 Bauer, Pool, and Dexter, op. cit.

45 John P. Crecine, Governmental Problem-Solving: A Computer Simulation of Municipal Budgeting (Skokie, Ill., Rand McNally, 1969).

46 Our discussion of the Nineteenth Ward is based upon the account in Allen F. Davis, Spearheads for Reform (New York, Oxford University Press, 1967), chap. 8.

account at the undertakers, buying turkeys at Christmas, and keeping 2,600 residents of his ward on the city payroll. Public policy under the Powers machine was "personalized." There was no commitment to alter the conditions that had produced the need for his patronage and favors and little concern for the niceties of honest and efficient municipal government.

This whole system was disturbing to the women of Hull House. They tried to defeat Powers in the elections of 1895, 1896, and 1898. But Powers and his associates survived every challenge from Hull House and its reformist allies. Following the second unsuccessful attempt in 1896, Powers gave a municipal position to nearly every man who had campaigned actively against him. He appointed a printer who was also an opposition leader to a clerkship at city hall, a driver from the opposition camp to the city police barns at a lucrative salary, and the opposing candidate himself to a comfortable position in the city construction department. It was difficult to defeat a man with such political resources. Reform of the Nineteenth Ward had to wait for forces stronger than Miss Addams and her colleagues.

## The rise and demise of the machine

Johnny Powers' operation in the Nineteenth Ward was one example of the urban party machines that dominated many American cities during the years of rapid immigration. The party machine is both the best-known and the least-understood aspect of urban political life. Banfield and Wilson have defined it as a "party organization that depends crucially upon inducements that are both specific and material."[47] Specific inducements are those (like jobs in city government) that can be given to some and withheld from others; material inducements are those that are monetary or readily convertible into money. This definition, however, understates the importance of nonmaterial inducements in generating support for the machine. Banfield and Wilson themselves have noted that one very important resource of the ward captain was "friendship."

Fred I. Greenstein has offered the following more general definition of the machine from a structural and functional point of view:

1    There is a disciplined party hierarchy led by a single executive or board of directors.
2    The party exercises effective control over nomination to public office, and, through this, it controls the public officials of the municipality.
3    The party leadership—which quite often is of lower-class social origins —usually does not hold public office and sometimes does not even hold

[47] Banfield and Wilson, op. cit., p. 115.

formal party office. At any rate, official position is not the primary source
of the leadership's strength.

4    Rather, a cadre of loyal party officials and workers, as well as a core of
voters, is maintained by a mixture of material rewards and nonideo-
logical psychic rewards—such as personal and ethnic recognition,
camaraderie, and the like.[48]

The political machine is treated by reformers as an object of
moral opprobrium, chiefly because of its presumably shady operations
with the public tax dollar. Certainly many machine leaders have
converted public funds to more or less private use, though there have
been machines that were scrupulously honest and even puritanical.
The difficulty with any assessment of the political machine that does
not go beyond its shady dealings is that it ignores what Robert Merton
has described as the "latent functions" of the machine.[49] Merton has
distinguished between "manifest" and "latent" functions of an activity,
the former being those that are intended and recognized and the latter
those that are unintended and unrecognized. Even though the machine
engaged in "honest graft"[50] at best and "dishonest graft" at worst, it
nonetheless facilitated the government of urban America during a
period of severe social tension. It functioned in an era when the
official structures of local governments were inadequate to accommodate the strains of rapid urbanization and immigration. The machine
filled a vacuum created by the fragmentation of legal power and responsibility in urban government. Edward M. Sait observed bluntly that
"leadership is necessary; and since it does not develop readily within
the constitutional framework, the boss provides it in a crude and
irresponsible way from the outside."[51] At a time when the urban
population was skyrocketing, when service needs occasioned by industrialization and immigration were expanding significantly, and when
human relations were unusually tense, the machine provided a
semblance of government in the city.

48 Fred I. Greenstein, "The Changing Pattern of Urban Party Politics," *The
Annals of the American Academy of Political and Social Science, 353* (May, 1964),
3.

49 Robert K. Merton, *Social Theory and Social Structure,* rev. ed. (New York,
Free Press, 1957), chap. 1, especially pp. 60–82.

50 The old "boss" of Tammany Hall, George Washington Plunkett, distinguished between "honest" and "dishonest" graft. Honest graft occurred when "I
seen my opportunities and I took 'em," whereas dishonest graft was "carrying
things to excess." Plunkett's example of dishonest graft was a case in which "the
Republican superintendent of the Philadelphia almshouse stole the zinc roof off
the buildin' and sold it for junk." See William L. Riorden, *Plunkett of Tammany
Hall* (New York, Dutton, 1963; originally published, 1904), especially pp. 29–32.

51 Edward M. Sait, "Machine, Political," *Encyclopedia of the Social Sciences,*
vol. 9 (New York, Macmillan, 1933), p. 659.

The machine also provided a welfare function for the dispossessed and did so with a "personalism" and intimacy that welfare bureaucracies have never equaled. Fires, unemployment, illness, and other human misfortunes were purely personal problems in the days before the welfare state. The political machines softened many of these misfortunes. They also provided an avenue of upward mobility for ethnic groups, helped them to become socialized in American culture, found jobs, and courted favors by providing a measure of status. Partly because of a strong strain of American "nativism," much of the private sector of society was closed to European ethnics. But the machine made mobility a reality. Politics was one of the most certain ways for Irishmen, Italians, and other ethnics to obtain acceptable positions. Although the party leaders themselves (in the early days of the machines) were almost all white and native Americans, they knew that ethnics had critical resources to offer to the parties. Bosses offered jobs, favors, and status in exchange for votes. The machines thus performed certain latent functions, which were performed by no other social institution before the days of legal aid, unemployment compensation, and social security.

The urban party machine survives today as an anachronism; the largest and most powerful is Richard J. Daley's Chicago Democratic machine. There are a number of reasons why the machine has declined as an agency of government almost everywhere. The reasons fall into four somewhat overlapping categories: affluence, the welfare state, technology, and the impact of reform on municipal politics.

AFFLUENCE   Affluence has meant a general decline in the relative values of the rewards available through the machines. Whereas the old machine could dispense jobs as city sanitation worker, census taker, and the like to eager recipients, today unskilled jobs in the public sector do not bring the status they once did. Affluence also means that people need not rely upon party-sponsored activities for social life. Television has replaced the party clambake or barbecue.

THE WELFARE STATE   The welfare state now provides as a matter of right those services that were once provided by the party as favors. Unemployment compensation, social security, and other benefits are more certain and more generous in amount than were the occasional turkeys, hods of coal, and small favors handed out by the machine. Perhaps ironically, the Democratic Party's New Deal undermined the power of dozens of Democratic machines in American cities by introducing elements of the welfare state. The Depression itself was a major blow to machines, because it created a magnitude of poverty and personal distress much too great for the machines' food baskets, jobs, and loans of rent money to assuage. In the long run, the Depression led to federally organized, financed, and supervised old-age insurance, unemployment compensation, and public assistance, which provided a level and consistency of benefits that no machine could match and preempted a principal device that the machines had used to attract large blocs of voters.

TECHNOLOGY    While the machines were losing their "welfare" role, local government units were also beginning to provide ranges of services requiring skilled technicians and professionals. City hospitals, universities, welfare organizations, plus increased concern for quality in the public schools raised demands for employees who could not be recruited from among ward and precinct workers. In a technologically advancing society, the complex decisions of urban government—matters of intricate finance, computerized police protection, and the like—simply could not be made by ward hacks.

IMPACT OF REFORM    The influence of the reformers, and more particularly the institutions they advocated, also dealt a heavy blow to the political machine. Nonpartisanship made it more difficult for voters to know who was behind the names on the ballot and for the machines to keep unwanted candidates off the ballot. Elections at large organized politics around whole constituencies, rather than neighborhoods whose precinct captains could know voters by name. They also raised the costs of machine campaigning.

Furthermore, the advent of manager governments and the professionalization of city bureaucracies through the civil-service system removed the office of mayor from the arena of public choice, lessened the importance of political premises in decision-making, and substituted the trained skills and judgments of professional managers. Civil-service reforms, as they took hold at the local level, increasingly removed middle- and low-level jobs from patronage.

Today there are few big-city or state parties that merit the designation "machine." To be sure, some parties unite many individuals in their support for certain candidates or policies. But the interlocking machine with its "boss," mass electorate, and tangible benefits for voters and precinct workers is more a feature of American history than a contemporary reality.

## Nonpartisanship and elections at large

The political machine was anathema to municipal reformers. Not only did it affront their ethical values, but it also violated their conceptions of policy-making by professional management ("There is no Democratic or Republican way to pave a street"). The machine was an institution that capitalized on social cleavages within the electorate and was therefore also at variance with the reformers' belief in the interest of the "community as a whole."

The institutional choices that reformers advocated to eliminate the pernicious effects of the machine were the *nonpartisan election* and the *constituency at large*. In a nonpartisan election candidates are not identified on the ballot by party affiliations.[52] A constituency at large includes the whole city, and candidates run in the entire city rather than as representatives of geographically bounded wards or districts. Today, among cities with populations greater than 50,000 in 1960, 63 percent use elections at large, and 67 percent use nonpartisan ballots. Only a minority of cities of this size retain the "unreformed" structures of partisan elections and ward constituencies.

Nonpartisan, at-large systems are likelier to be found in some kinds of cities than in others. Council-manager cities are more likely to use nonpartisan and at-large elections, whereas mayor-council cities are more likely to retain the ward and partisan systems. About 85 percent of manager cities use the nonpartisan ballot, whereas only about 50 percent of mayor-council cities are nonpartisan. Region seems to be another differentiating factor. Cities in the Northeast are much more likely to use partisan and ward systems, those in the South and West lean toward nonpartisan, at-large ballots, and those in the Midwest are more evenly split.[53]

Table 3.3 presents data on the social and economic characteristics of cities using reformed and unreformed election and constituency types. The most obvious differences are

1    Reformed cities tend to be smaller in size and to grow more rapidly than do their unreformed counterparts.
2    Although there is a slight tendency for the reformed cities to contain more educated populations and more white-collar people, income variables do not appear as an important correlate of election and constituency type.
3    Racial composition does not show a consistent effect.
4    There is a slight tendency for unreformed cities to have larger proportions of European ethnics.

Despite these tendencies, it is reasonable to conclude that the socioeconomic compositions of partisan versus nonpartisan and at-large versus ward cities are not markedly different. Although popular wisdom holds that nonpartisanship is a special property of small, upper-

[52] Banfield and Wilson, *op. cit.*, p. 151.
[53] Raymond Wolfinger and John O. Field, "Political Ethos and the Structure of City Government," *American Political Science Review, 60* (June, 1966), 312.

**Table 3.3**  *Social and economic characteristics of election and constituency types in American cities with more than 50,000 population in 1960*

| Characteristic | Election type | | Constituency type | |
|---|---|---|---|---|
| | Partisan | Nonpartisan | Ward | At large |
| Population, 1960 | 270,800 | 155,800 | 246,900 | 153,000 |
| Percentage population increase, 1950–60 | 17.1 | 58.3 | 23.1 | 59.1 |
| Median income of families, 1959 | $5,996 | $6,074 | $6,297 | $5,942 |
| Median education, in years | 10.6 | 11.2 | 10.9 | 11.2 |
| Percentage of white-collar workers | 43.5 | 46.7 | 45.2 | 46.3 |
| Percentage of non-white population | 13.0 | 11.5 | 9.8 | 13.0 |
| Percentage of children of foreign-born or mixed parentage | 17.5 | 16.9 | 18.9 | 13.4 |

SOURCE: Adapted from data in Robert L. Lineberry and Edmund P. Fowler, "Reformism and Public Policies in American Cities," *American Political Science Review, 61* (September, 1967), 701–716. All figures are mean values of the particular characteristic. A few cities use combinations of ward and at-large elections; in this table such cities are classified as using ward constituencies.

middle-class, WASP suburbs, it is difficult to differentiate between partisan and nonpartisan cities on the basis of socioeconomic composition alone.[54]

The introduction of nonpartisanship, especially when coupled with elections at large, has a number of consequences for urban politics.[55] To a significant degree, the nonpartisan ballot fulfills the expectations of its designers. It weakens the traditional party structure and isolates local politics from national political tides. There are only a few exceptions (for example, Chicago) to the rule that strong local party

[54] This conclusion is suggested both in *ibid.* and in Robert L. Lineberry and Edmund P. Fowler, "Reformism and Public Policies in American Cities," *American Political Science Review, 61* (September, 1967), 701–716.

[55] There are a number of excellent treatments of the effects of nonpartisanship, written from varying perspectives. Among them are Banfield and Wilson, *op. cit.*, chap. 12; Eugene C. Lee, *The Politics of Nonpartisanship* (Berkeley: University of California Press, 1960); Oliver Williams and Charles Adrian, "The Insulation of Local Politics Under the Nonpartisan Ballot," *American Political Science Review, 53* (1959), 1052–1063; Robert Salisbury and Gordon Black, "Class and Party in Non-Partisan Elections: The Case of Des Moines," *American Political Science Review, 57* (1963), 584–592; and Pomper, *op. cit.*

organization does not coexist with the nonpartisan ballot. In Newark, for example, the political party plays an active role in partisan contests for the state legislature but is dormant in nonpartisan municipal elections.[56] Nonpartisanship also tends to split the systems of campaign finance and candidate recruitment, with one set of funds and candidates for local nonpartisan office and another for partisan political posts.[57] This split has reduced the grass-roots organizational capacities of the political party and has made it difficult for the parties to permit aspiring politicians to "get their feet wet" in local office, thus retarding the development of a national party system. On the other hand, it was not until the local party strongholds were finally broken, in part through the influence of nonpartisanship, that a nationally organized party system could have much meaning, a fact less frequently recognized by critics of nonpartisanship. The dominance of parochial machines was a major impediment to the national organization of the party. Until recent decades the national conventions were largely congresses of fiefdoms, without much genuine power, and even today machines play a major role at conventions. Somewhat ironically, therefore, nonpartisanship has had a mixed effect on the national party system. It has helped to create the conditions (the demise of the local machine) under which national party government could in fact develop, but it has made it difficult for a national party to organize itself at the grass roots.

At the voter level, the nonpartisan ballot at large has increased the information cost to the voter, increased the financial cost of elections, and altered the structure of participation in local elections. The political party in the American system is a great economizer for most voters, because party labels tell something (though certainly not everything) about the candidates and their policy goals. When those party labels are unavailable, voters' information declines and their frustration increases. Kenneth S. Sherrill studied the levels of political information about local candidates in two Ohio cities, one with a partisan ballot and one with a nonpartisan ballot. Even though the nonpartisan city (Oberlin) had a very well-educated electorate and the partisan city (Amherst) a much less well-educated electorate, Amherst voters knew as much about candidates and local affairs as did Oberlin voters.[58]

It is not only the party label that supplies information; contacts

[56] Pomper, *op. cit.*

[57] Charles Adrian, "Some General Characteristics of Nonpartisan Elections," *American Political Science Review,* 46 (September, 1952), 766–776.

[58] Kenneth S. Sherrill, "The Electoral Decision in Partisan and Non-Partisan Settings" (Paper delivered at the Annual Meeting of the Midwest Conference of Political Science, April 27–29, 1967).

with party workers, party efforts to propagandize for causes and candidates, and the tendency of parties to organize issues more clearly than does a nonpartisan system also contribute. In the absence of party labels, voters must rely upon other cues, and familiarity with names and ethnic identification become critical. In Newark voters relied primarily upon party identification in picking candidates in partisan races and primarily upon ethnic identification in nonpartisan races.[59] Because familiarity with names alone is a significant factor in reducing information costs, nonpartisanship favors incumbents in local races.

Electoral turnout is significantly lower in nonpartisan cities than in partisan cities. Reduction in the size of the electorate in the nonpartisan city is not across the board or random but is concentrated particularly in lower-income groups and among those voters who would normally vote Democratic.[60] This group of voters relies most heavily upon partisan affiliation as a cue to voting and has fewest alternative sources of political information (like press reports, personal knowledge of the candidates, civic-club ties, and so on). Nonpartisan elections therefore attract larger proportions of middle- and upper-class citizens and a relatively smaller proportion of working-class citizens than do partisan elections. Another consequence is that the combination of nonpartisanship with elections at large lessens the ability of minority groups to engage in "bloc voting."

These factors suggest that nonpartisanship probably increases the representation of middle-class interests in urban politics. Lee described the "composite councilman" in a California nonpartisan city as Republican, of the middle class, a veteran, a member of a civic club, engaged in business or professional pursuits, and having little or no previous political experience.[61] The typical councilman tended to be Republican by a 3–2 margin in a state that was Democratic by a comparable margin. Unfortunately, Lee's picture does not compare the pattern of incumbency in cities with partisan elections. Even so, it is reasonable to suppose that the nonpartisan, at-large system gives an edge to better-off candidates, if for no other reason than the increased expense of running in a whole constituency.

### The electoral process

Having one's name put on a ballot for President of the United States is a task so difficult that even the mighty shrink from it. Having one's name put on a ballot for city councilman or mayor, the most common elective offices in American cities, is often as easy as dropping into a city clerk's office and paying a small "filing fee." The varying ways in which

59 Pomper, *op. cit.*
60 Banfield and Wilson, *op. cit.*, p. 159; and Salisbury and Black, *op. cit.*
61 Lee, *op. cit.*, pp. 50–56.

candidates have their names put on ballots are detailed in Table 3.4. The most common method of nomination, especially in non-partisan cities, is the simple device of filing by individual candidates; next is the voter petition, in which a specified number of registered voters (usually a proportion of the turnout in the previous election) sign petitions in support of each would-be candidate. These two methods almost exhaust the nominating methods in nonpartisan cities. About half the partisan cities use party primaries, and a lesser number use party conventions to nominate local candidates. Cities that use primaries and conventions have much more "closed" nominating systems than do those using individual filing of petitions. Where individuals can file petitions, "dark horses" can enter a race, and, given the limited information available to the local electorate, sometimes a very dark horse wins.

Urban election campaigns can have four possible effects on the voter: conversion, activation, reinforcement, and minor change. Some voters will be converted, that is, will change their preferences from one candidate or party to another during the campaign; others will be reinforced in their support for their initial choices; still others will become activated to take more supportive roles in work for candidates or parties; and some will modify their views, but not to the point

Table 3.4    *Methods of nominating candidates in all cities with populations over 25,000, partisan and nonpartisan*

| Method of nomination | All cities[a] over 25,000 | Form of election | |
|---|---|---|---|
| | | Partisan | Nonpartisan |
| Percentage filing by individual candidate | 55 | 31 | 64 |
| Percentage by voter petition | 23 | 13 | 26 |
| Percentage by party primary | 20 | 41 | 8 |
| Percentage by party convention | 3 | 6 | _[b] |
| Percentage by other methods | 6 | 5 | 8 |
| Total number of cities reporting | 574 | 157 | 414 |

[a] Columns may not total 100 percent because some cities failed to report data, whereas others used more than one method.

[b] Less than 0.5 percent.

SOURCE: Eugene C. Lee, "City Elections: A Statistical Profile," *Municipal Year Book* (Chicago, International City Managers' Association, 1963), p. 80, Table 7.

of conversion. Most voters experience reinforcement or minor changes, a few are activated, but only a handful are converted. These categories, however, are more meaningful and useful in partisan cities. Party identification provides the voter with a ready-made cue for choice even before the campaign begins. In nonpartisan elections, in which less is known about the candidates and their positions, the influence of the campaigns is much more variable. In a nonpartisan election, it is often possible for a relatively unknown candidate to pull off a victory through an effective campaign. A common pattern is for familiarity with his name or ethnic affiliation to determine the results.

Adrian has provided a useful typology of nonpartisan cities.[62] In the *nominally nonpartisan* city, nonpartisanship is little more than a façade, more formal than real. Political parties in these cities retain the dominant role in the nomination process and generate resources for candidates; they have no serious competition from other groups. Chicago is the most notable example of the nominally nonpartisan city. Even there, however, cracks appear in Mayor Daley's machine from time to time. In the 1967 aldermanic elections a black leader, Sammy Raynor, rather militant (by Mayor Daley's and Congressman William L. Dawson's standards), successfully challenged the machine's candidate in the dominantly black Sixth Ward.

In other nonpartisan cities, the electoral process is one in which *slates of candidates are put up by both parties and other groups.* In these cities, parties are among several factions competing for public office. A third type of nonpartisan system involves *slating of candidates by groups other than parties.* Dallas is one example; there the Civic Committee, an association of economic leaders in the city, recruits and supports candidates for local office. In such cities, political parties are dormant in local elections, but other associations perform some typical party functions like organizing electoral choices and supporting candidates. In the final type of nonpartisan city, a *"free-for-all"* pattern prevails, and neither parties nor groups endorse or finance slates. No stable coalitions prevail in these cities, and each candidate runs on his own. The single label "nonpartisan" thus conceals a great deal of real variation among American municipal electoral patterns.

### The shape of the local electorate

At the beginning of this chapter, we observed that Americans participate much less frequently in local than in national elections. A con-

---

[62] Charles Adrian, "A Typology of Nonpartisan Elections," *Western Political Quarterly, 12* (June, 1959), 449–458.

siderable proportion of American citizens (like some American youth) "drop out" of the electoral process in local elections. Perhaps this fact makes no significant difference: If the dropout rate is relatively equal among all social groupings, then the local electorate is merely the national electorate in miniature. Our hypothesis, however, is that the dropout rate is not uniform among social and economic groups and, that, therefore the "shape" of the municipal electorate differs markedly from the national electorate. Suppose we take Figure 3.1a as a hypothetical picture of the social class composition of the electorate in a presidential election in either of two hypothetical cities, Alpha or Beta. We have somewhat arbitrarily classified voters into three income groups, a relatively small upper class, a slightly larger middle class, and a large working class. The line separating voters from nonvoters in each class reflects the familiar pattern of higher participation among higher-status groups. On the other hand, as fairly large proportions of the working class turn out, their relatively large numerical representation gives them considerable weight in determining the outcome.

If, however, working-class members drop out in local elections in larger proportions than do the well-to-do, then the local electorate will contain a larger proportion of the latter. The key question, therefore, is, are there reasons to suspect that dropout rates are higher among working-class people? We think there are. First, as we have already seen, labor unions are much less active in local than in state and national politics. Whatever motivational, financial, and organizational resources are provided by unions to working-class citizens are less often found at the local level. Second, the stakes in local politics seem to be less significant for working-class than for higher-status people. Issues like minimum-wage legislation, welfare programs, unemployment insurance, civil-rights questions, and so on, are decided in state capitals and in Washington, D.C., more often than in city halls. The predominantly local problems of zoning, property taxation, levels of public service, and economic growth are, to be sure, of some interest to all voters. But they have more apparent significance for wealthier and better-educated voters. A third reason to suspect a higher dropout rate in working-class groups is related to the relatively dormant role of political parties in local elections, especially in nonpartisan cities. Party identification, as we have emphasized, is a major voting cue for less well-educated voters. Voters with better educational backgrounds and those with wider contacts in the social structure have less need for the cue of party identification.

The presence of "reformed" political institutions—particularly manager government, nonpartisan elections, and constituencies at large—tends to accentuate the higher dropout rate of lower-class

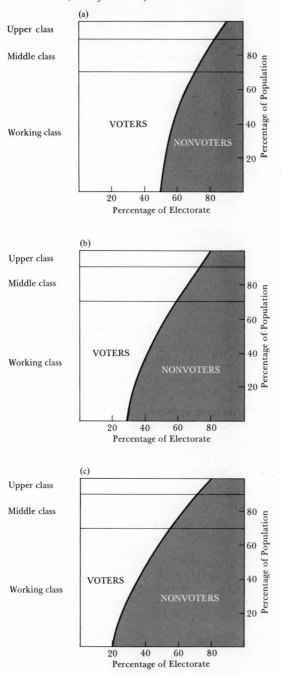

**Figure 3.1** *Some hypothetical differences in the shape of national and local electorates: (a) the electorate in a national election in community Alpha or Beta; (b) the electorate in a noncurrent local election in Alpha, a city with unreformed institutions; (c) the electorate in a noncurrent local election in Beta, a city with reformed institutions*

voters. The fact that nonpartisanship tends to reduce the participation of lower-class groups is well documented by studies of local politics, and the presence of other reformed features probably operates in similar fashion. If our reasoning is correct, the dropout rate between national to local elections should appear in both reformed and unreformed cities but would be more pronounced in reformed cities. Figures 3.1b and 3.1c represent hypothetical shapes of the local electorates in Alpha, a city with unreformed institutions (mayor-council government, partisan elections, and ward constituencies), and in Beta, a city with reformed institutions (manager government, nonpartisan elections, and a constituency at large). They show that in the respective electorates, dropouts are concentrated among the lower-status groups, although the drop is more severe in the reformed city. To some degree, therefore, working-class voters lose the advantage of their numerical preponderance.

We emphasize that this discussion is primarily extrapolated from indirect evidence, rather than from empirical research.[63] To the degree that it reflects actual variation in the shape of the two electorates, national and local, certain consequences follow. Most important, as far as urban decision-makers represent accurately the preferences of their constituents in policy choices,[64] they are representing a more generous proportion of well-to-do people than is present in a presidential constituency. Not, of course, that upper-class interests are represented to the exclusion of all others. First, lower-class voters still retain significant potential power through their numbers alone. Officials must anticipate the reactions even of regularly nonparticipant groups, because nonparticipants can be activated. Second, upper-status groups

[63] One of the few political scientists to examine the implications of the differing compositions of the national and local electorates is Lane, op. cit., pp. 343–344. Lane, however, suspected that it is working-class voters who are "overrepresented" in local electorates, largely because they have more to gain from the rewards of the political machine. Presumably, his views pertain only to those few cities, certainly declining in number, that have strong machines. Our argument that the dropout rate between national and local elections is greater among the lower-income groups seems to us more descriptive of elections in the majority of cities with weak, or nonexistent party organizations.

[64] This qualification is important, for it is clear that no one-to-one relationship exists between constituency opinion and decision-makers' policy choices. In the American Congress there is a high correspondence between congressmen's votes and constituents' opinions on some issues but not on others. In the area of civil rights, there is a very strong relation between the voting behavior of congressmen and what their constituents prefer; on foreign-policy questions there is almost no relation whatever between opinions back home and congressmen's votes. See Warren E. Miller and Donald R. Stokes, "Constituency Influence in Congress," American Political Science Review, 57 (March, 1963), 45–56. No doubt similar studies at the local level would uncover comparable variability in the degrees to which choices mirror constituents' preferences.

are more likely than are others to be "public-regarding" and thus to take account of underrepresented interests. And, third, state and federal programs, designed by decision-makers who are more directly accountable to working-class constituencies, determine many policy options of local officials. In these and other ways groups that are not literally part of the electoral process may nevertheless be represented. The degree to which these indirect bases of representation actually substitute for direct representation in the electoral constituency is an empirical question that we cannot resolve at this time.

## BLACK POLITICS: FROM CONCILIATION TO CONFRONTATION

Wilson has written that "any book on Negroes, particularly on their politics, ought to be published in a loose-leaf binder so that it can be corrected and updated on a monthly basis."[65] Change—its presence, its absence, and expectation of it—is the distinguishing feature of racial politics in American cities. The urbanization of the American black community, or perhaps more precisely its "ghettoization," is the most profound change since the abolition of slavery. In 1910, nine out of ten American blacks lived in the South, primarily in the poor countryside. By 1966, nearly seven out of ten Negroes lived in SMSAs, almost all in the central cities. When the 1970 Census is tabulated, a dozen or more major cities will be more than 40 percent black.

The civil-rights movement secured a number of favorable outputs from the national government—the historic school-desegregation decision, a succession of civil-rights acts, and open-housing and public-accommodations laws. But to some black leaders and their followers, these gains have proved to be chimerical, more symbolic than genuine. Civil-rights decisions heightened aspirations among blacks, but the intended policy gains did not always produce gains for individual blacks. While the black man awaited the fruits of his new legal equality, the income gap between him and the white male narrowed in a fashion more perceptible to statisticians than to wage earners. For many blacks, tension and frustration over the widening gap between aspirations and attainments found an outlet in the summer riots of the 1960s. Racial explosions pockmarked the physical and social landscape of most sizable American cities.

### Political participation of black urbanites

Because of the relatively low status of most black Americans, we expect to find them participating in politics much less than do whites.

[65] James Q. Wilson, *Negro Politics* (New York, Free Press, 1960), p. v.

Yet in many cities blacks vote about as regularly as do whites, at least when there are no other barriers to their participation. Although southern blacks have a record of not voting as a result of a heritage of discrimination, blacks in some northern cities participate at levels that equal or exceed those of whites. Sixty-one percent of the black community in St. Louis reported voting in some local elections; almost exactly the same proportion of whites reporting voting. Blacks were only a small proportion of the total population in New Haven, but their voting participation exceeded that of whites.[66] Despite the evidence of parity in voting participation in these cities, black participation rates lag behind white rates in many, if not most, other cities.

To what degree does voting strength affect urban policies benefiting blacks as a group? The right to vote has been touted as "the most powerful instrument ever devised by man for breaking down injustice and destroying the terrible walls that imprison men because they are different from other men."[67] Such claims make good politics but poor social science. Participation through voting is but one of many means of enunciating political preferences, and public policy is determined by more than occasional elections. The importance of the vote in a scheme of ordered liberty notwithstanding, any claims for the efficacy of the franchise in achieving group goals should be subjected to careful empirical examination.

William R. Keech assessed the strengths and limitations of black voting as a political resource in a study of Durham, North Carolina. Durham blacks have voted for many years and have skilled leadership and vigorous political organization. Still, Keech noted, "the really striking gains of Durham's Negro minority have come through resources other than votes."[68] Some policy decisions are influenced by votes, but

the vote is a far more potent instrument for achieving legal justice than social justice. The gains [that are] most susceptible to Negro voting have consistently been those which most clearly involved fair and just administration of existing laws. Social justice, however, demands more than this.[69]

People have different perceptions of "social justice," but, if the concept includes such things as comparable incomes for comparable jobs, courteous and equal treatment by fellow citizens, and opportunities for

[66] The data on St. Louis are found in Bollens et al., op. cit., p. 226; and those on New Haven in Dahl, Who Governs?, pp. 294–295.

[67] Lyndon B. Johnson, while signing the Voting Rights Act of 1965, quoted in Newsweek, August 16, 1965, p. 15.

[68] William R. Keech, The Impact of Negro Voting (Skokie, Ill., Rand McNally, 1968), p. 105.

[69] Ibid., p. 107.

economic advancement, the vote in urban elections does not win social justice. The vote is much more influential in reducing disparities in treatment in the public sector than it is in changing behavior in the private sector through government action. Other strategies like litigation, boycotts, and demonstrations seem to be more effective than the vote in securing basic social changes.

## Black leadership

If this book had been written two decades ago, the subject of black leadership would have been coupled with the topic of political machines, for most "leaders" of the black community drew their power from their ties with Democratic or (less frequently) Republican machines. The most resilient example of this older style of machine leadership is the organization of the late Congressman William L. Dawson. The hold of this octogenarian on the Chicago black vote can be compared only to Mayor Daley's hold on the Chicago white vote. Wilson described the Dawson machine this way:

*The Dawson machine, like all machines, is an organization whose purpose is the election of men to office and which is sustained mainly through the distribution of tangible incentives to its members. To a greater extent than any other Negro organization which acts in the public or civic areas, it is "issue-free" . . . Negro leaders tend to be conservative, and to share (with the exception of the importance they attach to race) the values of white conservatives. Few feel that there is anything at stake important enough to warrant an attack on the status quo.*[70]

The persistence of the Dawson machine depends upon the survival of the larger Democratic machine in Chicago. Vigorous competition among contending white factions for control of Chicago government would probably fragment the black machine as well, but because such competition has been slow in developing, the Dawson organization has survived both the "moralism" of the civil-rights movement and the militance of the Black Power advocates. Still, attacks upon the Negro organization have increased in vigor in recent years. Dawson's recent death complicates any assessment of the future of the machine.

Philadelphia has exhibited a different type of organization, but it is similar to Chicago in the issueless character of black politics. Philadelphia has vigorous machines in both the Democratic and Republican parties but has never had a Negro machine per se. John H. Strange concluded that black leadership in Philadelphia was weak and relatively unconcerned with racial goals:

[70] Wilson, *op. cit.*, pp. 53, 57.

*There has never been any significant legislation of any kind proposed by a Negro or Negro organization in Philadelphia, nor has the political activity necessary to pass any legislation been conducted under the direction of a Negro organization.*[71]

In fact, the major organizations supporting both the Philadelphia fair-employment practices law and the Philadelphia fair-housing ordinance were dominated by whites. The local chapter of the National Association for the Advancement of Colored People opposed the fair-housing law.

Not all American cities have black organizations like those of Philadelphia or Chicago, which are at times weak and uninterested in racial policies. The Durham black community has been effectively and skillfully organized into the Durham Committee on Negro Affairs and has developed to a high art the strategy of bloc voting for maximum impact on electoral outcomes.[72] Durham blacks have voted with a mean cohesion of 91 percent in recent years. They switch votes from one election to the next, delivering overwhelming majorities for a candidate in one election and against him in the next. This degree of cohesion is significant, although even higher cohesion occurred in the Gary, Indiana, and Cleveland, Ohio, elections of black mayors in 1967 and in the election of Kenneth Gibson in Newark in 1970.[73]

Where blacks have organized to pursue racial ends, they have tried either coalition with liberal or conservative elements or achievement of an independent "balance of power."[74] The Durham experience is an example of "balance of power" strategy. The black leadership in Atlanta has cooperated with the moderately conservative white leadership structure, hoping to capitalize upon the power and "public-regardingness" of the latter. In Houston, on other hand, black leadership has worked with liberals, who have less power than do conservatives in city politics but whose ideological goals are more compatible with black interests. Each strategy has its own costs and advantages, depending upon the history and the context of local politics.

Black Power leadership groups in American cities vigorously oppose "coalition politics." Statements and definitions of Black Power

[71] John H. Strange, "The Negro and Philadelphia Politics," in Edward C. Banfield, ed., *Urban Government*, 2nd ed. (New York, Free Press, 1969), p. 411.

[72] Keech, *op. cit.*, pp. 29–39.

[73] In the election of Carl Stokes in Cleveland, all-black wards produced an average vote for Stokes of 95 percent; in the Gary election of Richard Hatcher, the figure was 93 percent. See Jeffrey Hadden, Louis H. Masotti, and Victor Thiessen, "The Making of the Negro Mayors 1967," *Trans-Action, 5* (January–February, 1968), 21–30.

[74] Harry Holloway, "Negro Political Strategy: Coalition or Independent Power Politics," *Social Science Quarterly, 49* (December, 1968), 534–548.

Table 3.5  *Typology of black leadership styles*

| Characteristic | Leadership style | | |
| --- | --- | --- | --- |
| | *Traditional* | *Moderate* | *Militant* |
| Social position | | | |
| Educational and occupational level | High or Low | High | High or low |
| Economic independence from whites | Low | High | High |
| Goals | Ameliorative action within a segregated system, where few benefit | Improvement of welfare of all blacks; gradual desegregation; legal and political equality | Status goals; symbolic gains for blacks; emphasis on integrity of black community |
| Strategies | Ad hoc, covert, individual approach to influential whites | Continuous, overt, organized effort; voting cohesion; legal attacks on segregation | Mass protest movements and direct action; developing community autonomy first; independence of coalition |
| Sources of influence | | | |
| With whites | Ingratiation; usefulness to white leaders | Control over black votes; legality | Publicity; boycotts; threats of violence |
| With blacks | Access or prestige | Political ability and performance | Agitational, charismatic or forensic abilities |

SOURCE: Slightly adapted from Donald R. Matthews and James W. Prothro, *Negroes and the New Southern Politics* (New York, Harcourt Brace Jovanovich, Inc., 1966), Table 7-4.

are as numerous as are its proponents (multiplied, perhaps, by its critics). One of the most articulate and widely read statements is that of Stokely Carmichael and Charles V. Hamilton. Their fundamental premise is a distinction between "individual" and "institutional" racism. This distinction parallels the difference between micro and macro levels of analysis in city politics.

*When a black family moves into a home in a white neighborhood and is stoned, burned or routed out, they are victims of an overt act of individual racism which many people will condemn—at least in words. But it is institutional racism that keeps black people locked in dilapidated slum tenements, subject to the daily prey of exploitative slumlords, merchants, loan sharks, and discriminatory real estate agents.*[75]

*Individual racism* is direct, specific, and visible; individuals can be singled out and held culpable. *Institutional racism* is covert, indirect, collective, and nonspecific; it is difficult to pin responsibility upon a single group or individual. Carmichael and Hamilton have argued that even achievement of the traditional black goal of integration can deal only with individual racism. They note that it is possible to *assimilate* individuals but that only groups can be *integrated.* Individual assimilation merely siphons off the fortunate few who might otherwise have provided a source of leadership for the black community. Instead of integration, the Black Power philosophy rests upon the "fundamental premise" that "before a group can enter the open society, it must first close ranks."[76] In these authors' view coalitions have failed in the past because blacks have permitted white coalition partners to define the interests of both parties. Black Power rests upon the Machiavellian notion that "a prince ought never to make common cause with one more powerful than himself." Black Power proponents say, "enter coalitions only *after* you are able to stand on your own."[77]

A TYPOLOGY OF BLACK LEADERSHIP    There have been several attempts to construct typologies of black political leadership. Wilson, for example, has drawn a distinction between "status" and "welfare" orientations. Status orientations emphasize class advancement for the black community as a whole, and welfare orientations stress individual material advances that may not improve the status of the whole racial community.[78] Matthews and Prothro provide the most elaborate and useful typology, reproduced in slightly modified form in Table 3.5.

[75] Stokely Carmichael and Charles V. Hamilton, *Black Power* (New York, Vintage, 1967), p. 4.
[76] *Ibid.,* p. 44.
[77] *Ibid.,* p. 81.
[78] Wilson, *op. cit.,* pp. 218–221.

identify three "pure types" based on four dimensions: social background, goals, strategies, and sources of influence.

There are relatively few *traditional* leaders in big cities, although the Chicago machine approaches this type. *Moderate* leadership is most characteristic of groups like the NAACP and the Urban League —the "civil rights" organizations—and seems most appealing to the white middle class. The *militant* style is anathema to most whites, partly because its proponents deny a major role to whites in the quest for equality and partly because they refuse to reject violence as a strategy. There has been an increase in the proportion of militant leaders, but even this term does not capture the essence of some factions of black leadership, like the Black Panthers and other paramilitary groups. The latter, because of their militance (in the literal sense of the term), are as apolitical in terms of the conventional political system and its values as are the "traditional" leaders.

### Race, violence, and politics

Race riots did not begin in the 1960s with Watts, Detroit, Cleveland, and Newark. Racial conflagrations in East St. Louis in 1917 and in Detroit in 1943 matched in deaths and destruction most of the severe riots of the 1960s. Stanley Lieberson and Arnold R. Silverman counted seventy-six major racial disorders between 1913 and 1963.[79] The earlier riots differed from those of more recent vintage, however, in being mostly initiated by whites and involving direct violence against individual blacks or black groups. Most were responses to perceived transgressions of the legal or social taboos of racial segregation. The riots of 1963–1968 (which by one count numbered 283 among cities of over 25,000 population) were more commonly outbursts generated within the ghettos themselves and directed against aspects of white society (particularly the police and ghetto merchants), rather than against whites as individuals or groups.

Whites and blacks, surveyed separately by the National Advisory Commission on Civil Disorders (the Kerner Commission), were sharply divided on the "causes" of the riots. According to Table 3.6, two-thirds of the whites thought that some particular group of "undesirables" —radicals, looters, or communists—had provoked the riots. This micro-level explanation attributes riots to the perniciousness of men. Blacks, on the other hand, almost universally offered macro-level explanations

[79] Stanley Lieberson and Arnold R. Silverman, "The Precipitants and Underlying Conditions of Race Riots," *American Sociological Review, 30* (December, 1965), 887–898.

**Table 3.6**   *Black and white responses to the question "What do you think was the main cause of these disturbances?"*

| Most frequent types of spontaneous response | Blacks | | Whites | |
|---|---|---|---|---|
| | Men | Women | Men | Women |
| Discrimination, unfair treatment | 49% | 48% | 22% | 27% |
| Unemployment | 23 | 22 | 13 | 13 |
| Inferior jobs | 13 | 10 | 5 | 5 |
| Bad housing | 23 | 20 | 15 | 15 |
| Poor education | 10 | 9 | 7 | 7 |
| Poverty | 10 | 8 | 11 | 9 |
| Police brutality | 10 | 4 | 2 | 1 |
| Black Power or other "radicals" | 4 | 5 | 26 | 21 |
| Looters and other undesirables | 11 | 11 | 34 | 34 |
| Communists | 0 | 0 | 8 | 5 |

SOURCE: National Advisory Commission on Civil Disorders, *Supplemental Studies* (Washington, D.C., Government Printing Office, 1968), p. 48, Table V-b. Each reply to the question was coded separately, and, as some people mentioned more than one cause, the percentages do not total 100. Only reasons mentioned by at least 10 percent of a group are presented here, except for the response "communist," which is slightly under this limit.

of the riots, as results of social-structural factors, especially discrimination and unemployment. It thus appears that the premise of "institutional racism" is prominent in black explanations for the riots. It follows from the varying perceptions of "causes" that whites and blacks also favor different policy responses to the riots. When asked what could be done to prevent further rioting, whites most frequently responded that "more police control" is essential, whereas blacks preferred changes in the social and economic structures.[80]

As the data in Table 3.6 suggest, a number of white Americans (and their public officials) pictured the "typical" rioter as part of the "criminal element" or as "radical." This view, sometimes dubbed the "riffraff theory" of riot participation, includes three premises about

[80] See the discussion of white and black perceptions of the riots in Angus Campbell and Howard Schuman, "Racial Attitudes in Fifteen Cities," in National Advisory Commission on Civil Disorders, *Supplementary Studies* (Washington, D.C., Government Printing Office, 1968), chap. 5.

riots: (1) Only a tiny fraction (1–2 percent) of the ghetto community participated in the riots; (2) most rioters were "riffraff"—unattached youths, people with criminal records, the unemployed, disoriented migrants from the rural South who are unable to adjust to an urban environment; (3) the black community as a whole deplores the violence, seeing it as pointless and counterproductive.[81] This theory is "comfortable" for white middle-class Americans and their public officials, but it is not supported by studies of riot participants. Evidence suggests that between a third and a fifth of the ghetto community participates in major riots. And, instead of being drawn largely from the "criminal elements" in the ghetto, the typical rioter is not much different from his fellow ghetto residents. Robert M. Fogelson and Robert B. Hill's study for the Kerner Commission found that the "typical" rioter

1   was slightly better educated than were other ghetto residents;
2   was likely to have been born in the community in which the riot occurred;
3   was usually employed, although at a job requiring little education;
4   had an income about equal to that of other ghetto residents;
5   was no more likely than other ghetto residents to possess a "record."

After an examination of rioters in Newark and Detroit, Nathan S. Kaplan and Jeffrey M. Paige concluded that

the rioters are not the poorest of the poor. They are not the hard-core unemployed. They are not the least educated. They are not unassimilated migrants or newcomers to the city. There is no evidence that they have serious personality disturbances or are deviant in their social behavior. They do not have a different set of values.[82]

The rioter is not an atypical member of the ghetto community.

The third tenet of the riffraff theory is that the riots are condemned by most blacks. Yet, despite the fact that a number of ghetto residents suffered personal or material losses during the riots, a significant minority approved of them, and a majority saw them as protests that would ultimately have positive results. In the aftermath of the Los Angeles riots,

81 Our discussion of the "riffraff theory" is based upon discussion and data in Robert M. Fogelson and Robert B. Hill, "Who Riots?" in National Advisory Commission on Civil Disorders, *Supplementary Studies* (Washington, D.C., Government Printing Office, 1968), chap. 3.

82 Nathan S. Kaplan and Jeffrey M. Paige, "A Study of Ghetto Rioters," *Scientific American*, 219 (August, 1968), 19.

*a large minority (about one-third) approved of the rioting, and most Negro*
*residents of the riot area felt it had been a meaningful protest, and most*
*were optimistic about its effects on their life situation.*[83]

Blacks, whether or not they supported the riots, thought that the riots
had helped their cause by drawing white attention to long-standing
grievances.

This belief on the part of blacks appears to be a very serious
misreading of white attitudes. Whereas blacks thought the riots
dramatized their cause, the overwhelming majority of whites in Los
Angeles thought that Watts had increased the gap between the races.[84]
Polarization, rather than understanding, was a major result of the
riots, in the view of white Americans. This perceived polarization of
racial attitudes supports the Kerner Commission's prediction that
"America is moving toward two separate societies, one black, one
white." The intensity of white sentiment on racial questions is dramatized by the "law and order" movement and the surprising success of
some local office seekers who have expounded it (like Minneapolis'
mayor Charles Sventig). Even more telling is the Gallup Poll's 1969
survey of white Americans with incomes in the $5,000–$15,000 range.
In response to the question "Do Negroes today have a better chance
or worse chance than people like yourself to get well-paying jobs?" 44
percent answered that blacks have a *better* chance, 31 percent saw blacks
as having the same chance, and only 21 percent saw black chances as
worse.[85] Related questions about housing, education, and government
assistance revealed that similar pluralities of whites perceived blacks'
chances as better than their own. For one reason or another—and the
riots are presumably a contributing factor—there is a serious polarization of mass attitudes toward American race relations.

The black aspect of polarization appears in responses by blacks in
fifteen cities surveyed for the National Advisory Commission on Civil
Disorders. Table 3.7 shows these responses to questions dealing with
separatism, willingness to resort to violence, and white attitudes. Most
blacks perceived white attitudes as unfriendly, although only a minority supported separatist sentiments or the use of violence. But there
were clear breaks in patterns of attitude by age and, to a lesser degree,
by education categories. The youngest age group (16–19) was the most

[83] David O. Sears and T. M. Tomlinson, "Riot Ideology in Los Angeles: A
Study of Negro Attitudes," *Social Science Quarterly*, 49 (December, 1968), 502.
Similar findings about black perceptions of riots as helping their cause are pre-
sented in Campbell and Schuman, *op. cit.*, p. 49.

[84] Sears and Tomlinson, *op. cit.*, p. 499; and Campbell and Schuman, *op. cit.*,
p. 49.

[85] This survey is reported in *Newsweek*, October 6, 1969, pp. 34ff.

Table 3.7 Black attitudes toward separatism and use of violence and perceptions of white attitudes

| | Age 16–19[a] | Age 20–39 | | | | | Age 40–69 | | | | |
|---|---|---|---|---|---|---|---|---|---|---|---|
| | | 8th grade or less | Grades 9–11 | Grade 12 | Some college | College graduate | 8th grade or less | Grades 9–11 | Grade 12 | Some college | College graduate |
| **Separatism** | | | | | | | | | | | |
| Believe stores in "a Negro neighborhood should be owned and run by Negroes" | 22 | 19 | 18 | 18 | 20 | 30 | 16 | 13 | 13 | 17 | 13 |
| Believe that schools with mostly Negro children should have mostly Negro teachers | 16 | 8 | 11 | 10 | 10 | 20 | 10 | 4 | 5 | 5 | 3 |
| **Use of violence** | | | | | | | | | | | |
| Negroes should be ready to use violence to gain rights | 22 | 19 | 16 | 17 | 24 | 24 | 9 | 11 | 7 | 14 | 1 |
| Would probably participate in a riot | 13 | 11 | 10 | 8 | 8 | 9 | 7 | 6 | 3 | 4 | 6 |
| **Perceptions of white attitudes** | | | | | | | | | | | |
| Believe few white people dislike Negroes | 38 | 28 | 36 | 33 | 36 | 38 | 39 | 39 | 38 | 49 | 60 |
| Believe many dislike Negroes | 47 | 42 | 45 | 51 | 48 | 53 | 40 | 45 | 47 | 42 | 34 |
| Believe almost all dislike Negroes | 12 | 22 | 11 | 12 | 9 | 6 | 11 | 9 | 8 | 4 | 5 |

a Combines all educational categories.

SOURCE: Angus Campbell and Howard Schuman, "Racial Attitudes in Fifteen American Cities," in National Advisory Commission on Civil Disorders, Supplemental Studies (Washington, D.C., Government Printing Office, 1968), pp. 19, 26, 57.

hostile and the most separatist. Still, the majority of blacks, though not very optimistic about white attitudes, seem to favor integrationist goals, together with nonviolent means of achieving them.

### The community-control issue

The decade of the 1970s will surely see changes as yet unanticipated in race relations. Although a majority of black urbanites still profess integrationist goals, they are pessimistic—or perhaps realistic—about white attitudes toward integration. The new pessimism is bolstered by Black Power emphasis on racial identity and integrity. A significant manifestation of these parallel trends is the new demand for "community control" of political and social institutions.[86]

Although the concept of community control has implications for law enforcement, urban renewal, housing, model cities, public welfare, and other policies, education has so far been the main target. New York City, Detroit, and other cities have experimented with decentralization of public-school systems. Within carefully drawn limits of city and state standards, neighborhood school boards have been granted certain powers to establish programs and to hire and fire teaching personnel. A distinction should be made, however, between purely administrative decentralization and community control. Decentralization may include no more than the geographical reshuffling of administrative personnel and tasks from a central office to field offices. "Store front" city halls may possess real power or may be no more than outposts of the central bureaucracy. Decentralization of administrative organization may or may not imply that power has been redistributed to community groups. Bringing bureaucrats into physical proximity does not bring them under neighborhood control. Many urban police departments are decentralized at the precinct level, but advocates of community control do not have this sort of geographical decentralization in mind. Community-control supporters advocate a measure of actual policy control of city-government operations and decisions that affect themselves, their children, and services that they require. Suburbanites, they argue, have genuine power to shape the policy and direction of their schools, police forces, tax systems and other concerns; central-city neighborhoods should enjoy the same kind of citizen influence over public policy.

Alan Altshuler has identified several major sources of opposition to the community-control movement, and it is a formidable list indeed.[87] Many public officials oppose community control because it

---

[86] For an excellent discussion of the community-control issue, see Alan Altshuler, *Community Control* (New York, Pegasus, 1970).

[87] *Ibid.*, chap. 3.

threatens to undercut their own control over city budgets and policies. The established municipal bureaucracies—teachers, policemen, welfare workers, and others—see neighborhood control of service personnel as threatening their jobs. Municipal employees' unions like the American Federation of Teachers have been active opponents of modest schemes for neighborhood control of schools in New York City. Contractors who do a major portion of their business with city governments fear disruption of their established relations with city hall. Large numbers of whites oppose any program that might contribute to disruption of the status quo in race relations.

Although there is hard-core opposition to black demands for greater neighborhood participation in policy formation, the issue of community control cuts across many conventional political groupings. Liberal whites who favor integrationist goals find themselves in a bind because their long-range commitments to integration are challenged by black separatism. To liberals and black moderates alike, the major unknown is whether the program will promote integration or apartheid in the long run. Many black leaders, pessimistic about the prospects for integration, see community control as the most immediately practical alternative. The late Whitney Young, Executive Director of the National Urban League, argued that "community control is the most crucial issue right now. Institutions have failed because control isn't in the hands of the people who live in the communities."[88] Bayard Rustin, on the other hand, has argued that "black community control is as futile a program as black capitalism. . . . The truth of the matter is that community control as an idea is provincial and as a program is extremely conservative."[89] To white segregationists, the program of black power over neighborhood institutions poses equally difficult issues. Some favor the idea as a diversion from further housing and educational integration, but others fear a new militance arising from black control.

The responses of various groups to an abstract scheme for citizen control depend very largely upon the specific contents of operational proposals. Segregationists might be perfectly content to cut off the ghetto from city-wide policy control, but not if their own taxes were used to fund programs there. Black leaders and white liberals argue that a program relying exclusively upon neighborhood resources would doom the minority community to poverty of public services when compensatory programs are actually needed. Fiscal resources sufficient to maintain only symbolic programs are no substitute for ghetto needs

[88] Quoted in *ibid.*, p. 61.
[89] Bayard Rustin, "The Failure of Black Separatism," *Harper's*, January, 1970, p. 28.

for massive educational programs, extraordinary levels of law enforcement, and a high level of public services. It is the specific content of neighborhood-control schemes that will be most controversial in the cities of the 1970s.

The issue of community control, of course, is predicated upon the assumption that no major dispersal of the ghetto population is likely in the coming years. No public policies designed directly to disperse ghetto populations throughout the city have yet appeared, though some policies may have modest indirect effects (for example, open-housing legislation may permit already comparatively well-off ghetto residents to buy homes they would not otherwise have access to). Indeed, some policies have directly or indirectly contributed to the maintenance of the ghetto (for example, the construction of public-housing units in ghetto areas). We present evidence in Chapter 10 (see pp. 322–323) to demonstrate that the segregation of housing by race is increasing rather than decreasing in major cities. In light of the absence of a ghetto-dispersal policy and the operation of the private-housing market, it appears that the ghetto will be with us for some years to come.[90] The subject of community control of ghetto institutions will, therefore, be a major question of policy.


## SUMMARY

We have reviewed in this chapter the "input process," the mechanisms by which opinions and interests are channeled into the political system. Perhaps the most significant point to emerge from this discussion is how limited the informational input from large numbers of groups and individuals is. Political participation, whether through elections or in more active forms, is much lower in local political life than in state or national politics, for reasons we have tried to indicate. Not only is individual participation somewhat low, but the institutional and organizational devices for presenting interests are also not as well developed at the local level as they are at higher levels of government. Labor unions, for example, though quite active in national politics, play only minor roles in most cities. Because of the influence of non-partisanship and other factors, political parties may be active in national and state elections but may be quite dormant in municipal contests (except in a few cities). Generally, the relatively low participation levels, coupled with the fragmentary channels of interest articulation, make the costs of political information—information about

[90] Anthony Downs carefully outlines some projections in his "Alternative Futures for the American Ghetto," *Daedalus, 97* (Fall, 1968), 1331–1378.

groups and individuals and their policy preferences—quite high. Because of the incompleteness and distortion of information processed through the input mechanisms, municipal decision-makers can rarely obtain more than a fragmentary sense of community preference about public policy.

# part two

# THE CONVERSION
# PROCESS OF URBAN
# POLITICAL SYSTEMS

THE demands and resources of the socioeconomic and political environment do not automatically produce public policy. The process by which these inputs are translated into policies is the subject of Chapters 4 and 5. In Chapter 4 we describe the urban conversion process from a macro perspective, which includes the governmental institutions of the metropolitan area, together with the impact of state and federal governments on urban decision-making. These structures are not neutral features of the urban system. They impose their own constraints upon the choices open to cities.

The formal structures of local government are not all there is to the conversion process. In Chapter 5, we shift to a micro perspective, analyzing the behavior of decision-makers themselves. To some observers, there seems to be a conspiracy of power in local (and perhaps state and national) politics, in which upper-class citizens work in concert to shape public policy in their own interest. Whatever the truth of such allegations, the role of public officials (mayors, councils, managers, and bureaucrats) cannot be discounted. These roles, the resources that individual decision-makers possess, their decision-making strategies, and the ways in which they cope with limited information and resources are the major topics of Chapter 5.

# 4

*thru 116*

# The structure of urban government

The design of government structures is beset with political controversy. Debate surrounds the creation of new municipalities or special districts, development of new departments in existing governments, transfer of programs from one department to another, changes in the structure and authority of a local legislature or executive office, changes in relations between local agencies and the state or federal government, and changes in budgeting and other administrative procedures.

## PREMISES OF URBAN GOVERNMENT

In this chapter we discuss four premises that consistently appear in disputes about the nature of local government structures: (1) the effort to maximize political accountability by keeping policy-makers responsive to the voters, (2) the effort to maximize professional management and the efficient use of public resources, (3) the notion that local governments are properly subordinate to state governments and must be responsible to state authorities, and (4) the effort to maximize local governments' independence from state authorities.[1] The first and second premises are clearly in conflict (between "political" and "profes-

---

[1] This discussion about the roots of local government structures borrows from the work of Herbert Kaufman, especially "Administrative Decentralization and Political Power" (paper delivered at the Annual Meeting of the American Political Science Association, Washington, D.C., 1968). See also Ira Sharkansky, *Public Administration: Policy-Making in Government Agencies* (Chicago, Markham, 1970), chap. 4.

sional" government), and the third and fourth premises are also in conflict (between "state control" and "home rule"). In this chapter we show how a predisposition toward one or another premise influences the development of local institutions, and we illustrate some specific conflicts in local politics that grow out of these contradictory premises.

## Political accountability

A desire to maximize political accountability is evident in many features of national, state, and local governments in the United States. It is the "democratic," or "Jacksonian," strain that runs throughout the political system. Not that political accountability is the dominant theme in governmental structures. At the national and state levels, it competes with the desire to maintain separation of powers and checks and balances (designed to limit the power of popularly inspired movements), as well as with the "professional management" theme. At the local level, political accountability competes not only with the professional-management theme but also with the belief that local governments are properly the subordinates of the state government and should be governed by the legislative and executive branches of the state.

Several devices are built into governments in order to keep policymakers responsive to popular sentiment: Elected legislators and executives establish the legal authority and budgets of administrative departments; elected officials select administrative subordinates who have supported their campaigns and who presumably will administer programs in ways that support the policies of elected officials. Elected officials are reluctant to develop rigid career lines within government departments. Instead of promoting long-time bureaucrats to leading positions, mayors often select businessmen, college professors, and other "outsiders" who may "bring a fresh approach" to local government. Of course, the theme of political accountability is not equally emphasized in all local governments. It must compete with other goals of government organization.

Some manifestations of political accountability are distinctively urban in nature, including selection of aldermen by wards, efforts by suburban communities to maintain their own governments apart from that of the central city, and demands from some neighborhoods within the central city for community control of schools, welfare programs, and the police. Selection of aldermen by wards is common in about one-third of the cities with more than 50,000 population; it is designed to give each neighborhood a separate voice in city hall and thus to facilitate its demands for improvements in streets, playgrounds, schools, garbage collection, police protection, and other services. When a city is governed by a "machine," the ward representatives provide a medium for transmitting local demands to the "boss" and for the machine's mobilization of voters on election day.

The independence of suburban communities is a constant element in the politics of metropolitan areas. We mentioned it in Chapter 2 in connection with the separation of economic resources and service demands. Here we shall view it as a feature that permits urban residents to maintain control of their most immediate government. Suburbanites voice several reasons for keeping their governments apart from that of the central city: to avoid the high taxes necessary to support the welfare, police, health, and educational services of low-income neighborhoods, to keep government small and in the hands of familiar officials, and to facilitate residential exclusiveness—either by keeping out public housing for low-income residents or by zoning restrictions that force up the costs of private-home building.[2]

The desire of ghetto residents in the central city to have "neighborhood control" of municipal services springs from the same roots that cause suburbanites to opt for separation. Of course, the details differ: Whereas suburbanites demand separation in order to free themselves from the costs of public health and welfare and to maintain high-quality education, ghetto residents demand neighborhood control of municipal services in order to ensure that education, health, welfare, and police services are commensurate with their needs. Both suburbanites and ghetto residents, however, identify specific urban areas with relatively homogeneous needs for public services and seek control over those services.

### Professional management

A second influence on the design of local government structures is a management theory that likens government agencies to private firms. Its most prominent features are an insistence on "professional" (as opposed to "political") criteria for selecting personnel, a hierarchical organization based on "efficiency" in provision of public services, and attempts to take local government "out of politics" and to put it on a "business-like" basis. Its hierarchical principles are taken from principles-of-management manuals that were originally developed for private industry:

*1*    Activities should be grouped by purpose, process, clientele, place, or time and made the responsibilities of small units under the direct control of supervisors.[3]

[2] Scott Greer, *Governing the Metropolis* (New York, Wiley, 1962), chaps. 3, 5.

[3] Albert Lepawsky, *Administration: The Art and Science of Organization and Management* (New York, Knopf, 1949), chap. 8.

2    Work units should be organized hierarchically, so that several are grouped under the control of a single supervising unit (or supervisor), which is in turn grouped with other supervising units under the control of a higher supervisor.
3    There should be a narrow "span of control," with a limited number of subordinates under each supervisor, so that supervisory personnel can give sufficient attention to each subordinate unit or person.
4    There should be a clear "chain of command" and "communications through channels," so that superiors will have full information about the activities of subordinates and be assured that their own directives will control their subordinates.
5    Executives should have sufficient authority to appoint and remove their subordinates.
6    Personnel appointments and promotions should be made on the basis of competence without interference from "politicians" seeking to reward fellow partisans.
7    Executives should control the expenditures of administrative units.
8    There should be sufficient staff services to provide the executive with the information necessary to understand and control the activities of subordinates.

Several structural aspects of local government reflect emphasis on professional management: the council-manager form of government; nonpartisan elections; selection of councilmen from the city at large, rather than from separate wards; selection of administrative employees according to merit; and efforts to consolidate the territory of several adjoining communities into one jurisdiction. The appointment of a professional city manager and the use of merit criteria in selecting employees are the most prominent of the businesslike features of local governments. They eliminate partisanship from local administration and restrict political accountability to the elected legislature. Where this body is selected by nonpartisan ballot and from the entire community at large rather than by wards, local policy-making is likely to be even farther removed from partisan politics. The service demands or partisanship associated with particular neighborhoods are not guaranteed hearings in the local legislature, and the interests of the "entire community" are supposed to prevail.

People who advocate the consolidation of several communities into single jurisdictions hope to broaden the tax and service bases for government programs and rationalize their administration. Encompassing a larger territory broadens the financial support available for a service and thus makes it more economical. Where it is not feasible to extend the territory of a municipal government and to offer its full range of services to a larger clientele, then individual services may be separated from a municipality and offered to larger areas. Special districts govern education, libraries, parks, police, hospitals, airports, highways, and sanitation..in extensive areas within metropolitan areas.

The labels that appear frequently in relation to the management root of local government structures reflect the interests and socioeconomic backgrounds of many advocates. "Businesslike," "professional," and "management" describe the occupational groups that most often favor council-manager structures and the merit selection of city employees. "Nonpartisan" takes on defensive connotations when used by middle- and upper-income supporters of these structures. The truth is that the conservative and Republican tendencies of professional-management supporters would not often be satisfied if city elections were conducted on a partisan and overtly political basis. This group is inclined toward low-spending policies, toward "economy." We discussed these and other motivations of reformers in Chapter 3 (see pp. 65–67).

There are latent tensions between the political-accountability and professional-management modes of local government. The first reflects reverence for popular control of local public services, whereas the second reflects faith in objective measures of proficiency and efficiency. The two can exist in some form of accommodation. Local politicians are more often concerned with "getting along" than with pushing a form of governmental organization that has only abstract appeal. Yet the tensions burst into prominence when the advocates of one or the other mode feel their essential demands are threatened. The teachers of New York City struck for most of the fall of 1968 on behalf of professional management; they felt threatened by the actions of neighborhood school boards. On the other side, local boards exerted intense pressure for control over teachers; they viewed the academic approach of many teachers as irrelevant to ghetto children.

## Local control versus state control

The third and fourth premises of local government structures are clearly in conflict. Most of the legal powers are on the side of the state governments, but there are substantial—and perhaps increasing—political resources on the side of the cities. The subordination of local to state governments is shown in the lack of specific provision for local governments in the U.S. Constitution; by the acceptance in many state courts of "Dillon's rule," which limits local government powers to those explicitly provided by state constitutions and statutes; and by the failure of local governments to raise sufficient revenues to meet their citizens' service demands, even when their jurisdictions include abundant private wealth.

THE LEGAL BASIS OF LOCAL GOVERNMENT   The structure of government established by the Constitution recognizes the nation, the states, and "the people"; the Constitution provides certain guarantees to each. There are no provisions for local governments. Municipalities were considered to fall under the umbrellas of their states and to be subject to whatever powers and restrictions the state constitutions and laws provided. The charter of a municipality is the state statute that affects it most directly, but other state actions also apply. They include general laws pertaining to all local governments and numerous "local bills" pertaining to specific municipalities. The standard interpretation of local government powers is "Dillon's rule":

*It is a general and undisputed proposition of law that a municipal corporation possesses and can exercise the following powers, and no others: First, those granted (by the state) in express words; second, those necessarily or fairly implied in or incident to the powers expressly granted; third, those essential to the accomplishment of the declared objects and purposes of the corporation—not simply convenient, but indispensable. Any fair, reasonable, substantial doubt concerning the existence of power is resolved by the courts against the corporation, and the power is denied.[4]*

This severe standard resolves even reasonable doubts against the local government.

Where the state constitution is restrictive in its general grant of power to municipalities, the state legislature is a busy enactor of local laws; it may approve specific sites for local schools and other public facilities, condemn private property, and define local employees' salaries and working conditions. Under this kind of arrangement, the legislators who represent an urban area become an important—if informal—adjunct to the local government; they can modify those items that municipal officials ask them to introduce in the legislature and can select proposals to steer personally through the legislative process.

Even the most permissive state constitution restricts the nature and extent of local government taxation or indebtedness. All typically limit municipalities to property taxes and perhaps to small levies on retail sales and personal incomes. In an era when the most dramatic social demands are made in urban communities, the governments most closely affected by these demands do not have the authority to raise sufficient revenues from local resources. Local officials lack access to the wealth from high personal incomes and lucrative commercial transactions if they cannot tax income or sales. In New Mexico, which does not have home-rule provisions for city governments, it took state laws to

1    permit cities to destroy weapons and narcotics confiscated by police;
2    authorize cities with populations over 100,000 to acquire and operate their own bus systems;

4 Quoted in Duane Lockard, *The Politics of State and Local Government* (New York, Macmillan, 1963), p. 132.

3    allow municipalities to discontinue water service to customers who had
     not paid their bills;
4    permit cities to zone for flood control.


HOME RULE    About half the states have written provisions into their
constitutions that are designed to increase the discretion of local officials. The term "home rule" suggests a large grant of authority to local
governments, but this image is more generous than the actual grant of
authority. The home-rule movement began in Iowa in 1851, and such
provisions were first adopted into a constitution in Missouri in 1875.
By 1960 it had become part of the constitutions of twenty-three states,
and cities in twenty-one of these states had taken advantage of its
provisions. When a city operates under home-rule provisions, it can
change its own powers and operations without first going to the state
legislature for consent. The mechanism for changing local powers is
typically a citizens' referendum. Some home-rule cities can change the
form of their local governments, including the nature of local elections;
can annex fringe areas; and can regulate public health, safety, and
morality.

The practical significance of home rule is not as great as many of
the reformers originally anticipated. State reins on local authorities
remain short and can be tightened at the convenience of the state
legislature. Some local authorities view their narrowly defined home-
rule provisions as disadvantageous in that they preclude some imaginative efforts that would be permitted by more broadly defined provisions. Yet home-rule provisions may raise a psychological deterrent
to state legislators. The broad connotations of the term may benefit
cities, especially during an era when urban problems and reapportionment at the state level may heighten legislative support for local
authorities. At the least, home-rule provisions relieve local officials of
the nuisance of having to go to the state legislature for many detailed
enactments.

To some observers, state control over local authorities seems to
reflect deep-seated features of American politics: distrust of all cities
and urban governments. Our cities are widely viewed as dangerous,
unhealthy, and even "sinful," governed by "bosses" or "party machines," and populated by alien groups. The flight of middle-class
whites (and a few blacks) to the suburbs and the reluctance of state
legislatures to reapportion themselves in accordance with population
changes reflect this antiurban sentiment, as David Danzig and John
Field have noted:

*Great American cities, unlike such European counterparts as London, Paris,
Rome, and Moscow, have not played a dominant part in the history of the*

*nation. American history has not been made by the cities, nor have the cities supplied any of our heroes. European kings and rulers have always been largely urban; in contrast, no American President has been identified with the city. Franklin Delano Roosevelt, whose political power was heavily based on the cities, preferred the image of the Dutchess County gentleman farmer, while John F. Kennedy, instead of being taken for Boston Irish, chose to show his Harvard-Hyannisport profile to the public. Only in the veins of the East Side's defeated Al Smith did the blood of the city course unashamedly. . . . At a recent Washington conference, which was given the neighborly title of "Town and Country" to avoid the unpleasant term city, the Secretary of Agriculture seemed not to offend anyone when he spoke of the "garbage can life in the inner city"; nor, on another occasion, did New York State Senator William E. Adams provoke any public ire when he attributed the growth of welfare cases in the suburbs to the spread of "the welfare rot of the central cities." Obviously, the historic "shame of the cities" is still with us, although the "wicked city" has now become the "asphalt jungle" and what was once the slum is now "the rotting cancer" of the inner city.[5]*

The cities are not without some clout in their competition with state governments. Some of this power is intangible and reflects only the revered position of local control and home rule in American traditions. The cities also benefit from whatever attachments there are to political accountability as a mode of government organization. Insofar as local residents are thought to be most aware of their needs, they are considered to be the most suitable governors of local activities. Much of the time, however, such strengths are not sufficient to free the cities from the hard bonds of law and precedent that subordinate them to the states.

Recently cities have gained some ground in their competition with the states. Their victories—which promise even greater gains in the future—include a series of federal court decisions, since *Baker* v. *Carr* in 1962, that have vastly improved the representation of urban areas in state legislatures and an increasing willingness in Congress to establish grant-in-aid programs that are national-local in character and involve only minimal participation for state governments. Although the impact of legislative reapportionment on state governments' treatment of the cities is yet to be demonstrated,[6] it has at least increased urban representation in the legislatures. Optimists predict increased state sensitivity to urban needs and more permissive legislation pertain-

5 David Danzig and John Field, "The Betrayal of the American City," *Commentary*, June, 1968, pp. 52–59.
6 See Ira Sharkansky, "Reapportionment and Roll Call Voting: The Case of the Georgia Legislature," *Social Science Quarterly*, 51 (June, 1970), 129–137, and the literature cited there.

**Figure 4.1**   *Simplified government structure of a strong mayor-council city*

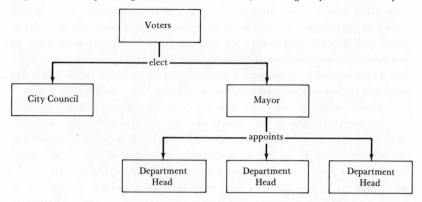

ing to city revenues. The federal government started to provide direct aid to the cities through housing legislation in the 1930s (see pp. 125–132), and more recently there have been substantial increases in federal aid to cities for primary and secondary education, preschool classes, job training, highways, mass transit, and community action.[7]


## STRUCTURES AND CONSEQUENCES

### The structure of city government

The structures of most urban governments reflect the influence of political accountability or professional management or—more typically—a mixture of the two. Here we shall outline the principal institutions of local governments. In Chapter 6 we shall return to this topic and describe the personal traits and decision-making procedures of office holders.

MAYOR-COUNCIL FORMS   The classic model of local government combines an elected mayor with an elected council. Figure 4.1 portrays the relations of a typical mayor and council with the voters and with the departments of the city government. Depending upon the predominant

[7] Deil S. Wright, *Federal Grants-in-Aid: Perspectives and Alternatives* (Washington, D.C., American Enterprise Institute for Public Policy Research, 1968); Andrew T. Cowart, "Anti-Poverty Expenditures in the American States: A Comparative Analysis," *Midwest Journal of Political Science, 13* (May, 1969), 219–236; and J. David Greenstone and Paul E. Peterson, "Reformers, Machines, and the War on Poverty," in James Q. Wilson, *City Politics and Public Policy* (New York, Wiley, 1968), pp. 267–292.

influences at work in the initial design or later modification, these structures may reflect emphasis on political accountability or professional management. Offices may be filled through partisan or nonpartisan ballots; the personnel of administrative departments may be selected by the chief executive according to political criteria or according to professional personnel standards and protected by a merit system; the legislators may be elected at large or from individual wards.

Mayor-council cities may also differ in the formal powers given to the mayor and council. In "weak mayor" governments, the selection of department heads and the responsibility for administrative policies are usually given to boards or commissions, whose members are chosen by direct election or by the mayor and the council. Mayors can also be weakened by being denied a veto over the actions of the council or by being required to share responsibility for preparing the budget with the entire council or a council committee. An individual executive can also be made "stronger" or "weaker" by virtue of the staff he is allowed to hire. Where he is permitted an extensive, well-paid, and professional cadre of assistants, he can use the high-quality information they provide to assert himself in dealings with the council or administrative departments.

A local government reflecting the primary influence of political accountability would tie the mayor and council to the voters and minimize the authority of any local official to make policy on his own initiative. It would have partisan elections for the mayor and council, councilmen elected from wards, selection of administrators according to political criteria, control of departments by the elected chief executive, but budgeting and other policy-making functions shared by the mayor and the council.

THE MANAGER FORM    The extreme expression of the professional-management doctrine is the council-manager form of government. This form is depicted in Figure 4.2. It typically combines a small council, elected at large by nonpartisan ballot, along with a professional administrator who is selected by (and responsible to) the council. There is often also a mayor, who performs ceremonial functions as head of the local government. He may preside at meetings of the council, represent the city on public occasions, and sign legal documents for the city. He may be elected by the voters or selected by the council from among their own members (see Table 5.2 for details). The typical manager has the power to appoint (and remove) the heads of administrative departments, to prepare the budget for the council's consideration and to allocate funds after the budget's approval, and to make investigations, reports, and policy recommendations to the council on his own

**Figure 4.2**  *Simplified government structure in a council-manager city*

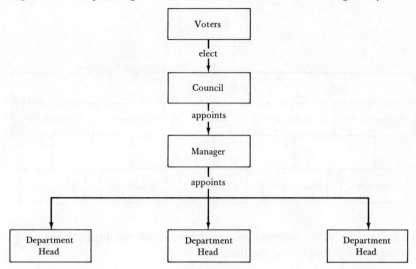

initiative or at its request. ' ..ue professional-management ideal is even more nearly realized when administrative personnel are selected on the basis of professional competence and protected from political dismissal and when the manager has the budget and authority to hire competent staff.

As the council-manager plan was originally designed, the manager was expected to administer but to remain assiduously aloof from "politics" or "policy-making." In recent years, however, it has become evident that the manager is inevitably involved in controversial issues. Even the most careful manager encounters "politics" when he conducts policy-oriented research for the council, formulates a budget for the council's deliberation, interprets the council's preferences in allocating funds to the departments, or seeks to change a department's procedures in rendering service. The manager's role in policy-making is heightened when the council depends upon his professional judgment. Council members are typically part-time officials not professionally trained to make policy decisions or to supervise their implementation. Although most—if not all—managers do involve themselves in politically charged issues, they differ markedly in style. Some shape the basic policies of their governments and enlist the aid of interest groups, private citizens, and councilmen in their efforts. Others work more narrowly through official channels. Managers have no tenure in their positions; they can be dismissed by majorities of their councils or forced to resign by intensely hostile minorities. Some managers define success by their ability

**Figure 4.3**  *Simplified government structure in a commission city*

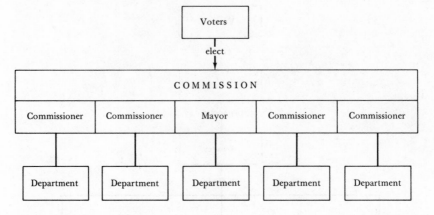

to remain in office, whereas others define it by the innovations they have guided through local politics.[8]

THE COMMISSION FORM   The third form of local government, the city commission, departs radically from the distinctive American pattern of separate legislative and executive branches. This structure is portrayed in Figure 4.3. It consists of a small group of elected commissioners, each heading an administrative department, as well as sitting as a member of the local legislature. There is no strong executive, although one member of the commission is designated the nominal head of government. In some cities, the chairman's position rotates periodically among the commissioners. At one time this form of government was the darling of "good government" reformers. It was first developed in Galveston in 1900 and was in use in 108 cities by 1910. It is said that commission cities suffer from a lack of administrative integration. Separately elected department heads and the absence of a real central authority provide no focus of coordination. Vote trading and "you stay out of my department, and I'll stay out of yours" characterize the style of government. The plan has lost its appeal to reformers, most of whom have switched their allegiance to the council-manager form. The commission is now used by only thirty-seven cities with populations over 50,000 plus a smattering of smaller cities, mostly in the South.

### The absence of hierarchy in American cities

Although the professional-management approach to local government has shown its success in the widespread acceptance of the council-

[8] See Karl Bosworth, "The Manager Is a Politician," *Public Administration Review, 18* (Summer, 1958), 216–222.

manager form of government, it has not been notably successful in implanting principles of hierarchical management. The lack of hierarchy is evident in two ways: First, no chief executive of a major city has sufficient control over personnel and funds to exercise direction of his own administration comparable to that of the national President or most state governors, and, second, the multiplicity of jurisdictions in any metropolitan area limits whatever powers the city executive does possess to the artificial borders of his municipality. President Lyndon B. Johnson is said to have commented in one of his most harried moments that "things could be worse. I could be a mayor."[9] A mayor of Milwaukee once observed that "the central city mayor survives only when he has the psychological capacity to handle at one time three man-eating gorillas of crises and two of the paper tigers that, it seems at times, are thrown upon his back just to test him."[10]

Much of the difficulty in appraising our mayors is that we are influenced by the "myth of hierarchy," which does not describe American city government. Although the President and most governors have at least nominal hierarchical controls working for them, American cities are surrounded and beset by formal pluralism.[11] In the first place, city governments are only one of multiple types of governments in urban areas. Milwaukee County has forty-six taxing units of local government: the City of Milwaukee; eighteen suburban municipalities, "each proudly waving its own flag of suburban independence emblazoned, 'Don't invade me' "; twenty-two suburban school boards; two sewage commissions; two city school boards; as well as the county government.[12] Even if a mayor reigned supreme in his own bailiwick, he would thus be at best a feudal lord in a castle, beset by numerous other claimants to the throne.

Within what we call city government, there is also fractionalization of power, with the mayor being both limited in his powers and compelled to share responsibilities with other decision-making agencies, particularly the council and perhaps also a manager. Also there may be other decision-making officers elected by the public and thus not "beholden" to the mayor. (For further discussion of the mayor's political-leadership role, see Chapter 5, pp. 162–172.)

9 *Newsweek*, March 13, 1967, p. 38.

10 Henry Maier, *Challenge to the Cities: An Approach to a Theory of Urban Leadership* (New York, Random House, 1966), p. 190.

11 For some appropriate qualifications on the hierarchical controls available to the President and governors, see Ira Sharkansky, *Public Administration*, chap. 4. The point is that mayors have even fewer such controls, not that they are the only American chief executives who lack them.

12 Maier, *op. cit.*, p. 23.

## Incidence and significance of government structures

Politicians, journalists, and political scientists have argued the merits of one or another form of local government for many years. There are various allegations about the democratic futures of governments dominated by political accountability, and about the businesslike efficiency to be expected from governments dominated by professional management. As we have noted, however, these elements are generally mixed in the structures of individual municipalities. The best we can do in assessing them is to compare local governments showing traits that have been reformed in the name of professional management with those that have not. Unreformed cities have mayor-council governments, ward selection of councilmen, and partisan ballots for mayor and council. Reformed cities have either manager-council or commission governments, selection of councilmen at large, and possibly nonpartisan ballots. The incidence of each element in cities with populations over 50,000 is shown in Table 4.1.

There has been some research into the kinds of cities that have adopted each form of government. Table 4.2 shows the distributions of various features by size of city over 5,000 population. Unreformed mayor-council forms dominate in both the smallest and largest cities, whereas the council-manager and commission forms together dominate the middle-sized ones. Council-manager forms are by far the most common among reformed institutions. As we have noted, commission forms are a small minority and are concentrated in middle-size cities.

There are two separate explanations for the predominance of mayor-council governments in small and large cities. In the former there is seldom enough revenue—or enough work—to justify employment of a professional manager. Both the mayor and the council in towns under 10,000 are typically part-time officials, receiving little or no salary. In the largest cities there may be too much social and eco-

**Table 4.1**  *The incidence of government forms in 200 cities with over 50,000 populations*

| Institutional form | Reformed | | Unreformed | |
|---|---|---|---|---|
| Form of government | Manager | 45% | Mayor-council | 43% |
| | Commission | 12 | | |
| Type of election | Nonpartisan | 67 | Partisan | 33 |
| Type of constituency | At large | 63 | Ward or mixed[a] | 37 |

[a] Includes a small proportion of cities that use a combination of ward and at-large elections.

SOURCE: Robert L. Lineberry and Edmund P. Fowler, "Reformism and Public Policies in American Cities," *American Political Science Review, 61* (September, 1967), 705–706.

**Table 4.2**  *Distribution of government forms by population of cities over 5,000*

|  | Mayor-council | Manager | Commission | Na |
|---|---|---|---|---|
| 1,000,000+ | 100.0% | – | – | 5 |
| 500,000–1,000,000 | 73.7 | 26.7% | – | 15 |
| 250,000–500,000 | 40.0 | 43.3 | 16.7% | 30 |
| 100,000–250,000 | 37.5 | 48.8 | 13.8 | 80 |
| 50,000–100,000 | 35.3 | 50.5 | 14.2 | 190 |
| 25,000–50,000 | 34.0 | 52.8 | 13.1 | 388 |
| 10,000–25,000 | 49.7 | 40.3 | 10.0 | 1,005 |
| 5,000–10,000 | 66.7 | 28.1 | 5.2 | 1,257 |

a $N$ = Number of cases.

SOURCE: John H. Kessel, "Governmental Structure and Political Environment: A Statistical Note About American Cities," *American Political Science Review*, 56 (September, 1962), 615.

nomic heterogeneity to escape severe political tensions. Political accountability seems most suited to such a community: Major offices go to the coalition of interests that can muster a plurality at the polls. Strong factions are unlikely to accept a professional manager who would take the key offices out of their reach. The rules of the unreformed city keep the most recent winner from collecting his chips and ending the continuing competition of popular democracy.

There is also a regional bias in the selection of local government structures. Mayor-council cities dominate in the Northeast; council-manager cities are found most often in the South and West; the Middle West shows a mixture of the two forms.[13] These differences may reflect the ages and social compositions of cities in each region. Northeastern cities are most likely to be old and to have large European ethnic communities. The mayor-council structure has the legitimacy of tradition, and competition among distinct European ethnic communities (now joined by politically sophisticated black enclaves) ensures that politics remains in local government. In contrast, a number of cities in the South and West have reached substantial size only during this century. They have faced an obvious need to reexamine their government structures because of population increases during the period when reformers were working hardest for council-manager (or commission) forms. In the South, moreover, the ethnic situation favors professional management. Because of sizable black communities in the cities, entrenched whites have regarded the professional manager as a device to isolate local government from the potential black vote.

A number of scholars have examined the formal structures of gov-

[13] Raymond E. Wolfinger and John O. Field, "Political Ethos and the Structure of City Government," *American Political Science Review*, 60 (June, 1966), 206–226.

ernments as they affect the nature of local politics and public policies.[14] To the extent that high (or low) scores on the measures of politics or policy coexist in those municipalities that have certain kinds of government structures, we can infer that structure has something to do with the scores. Yet it is also possible that such findings reflect nothing more than the influence of a peculiar social or economic environment. The coexistence of structural features with particular politics or policy may be a happenstance that does not indicate the influence of government structure. Local political life may affect the choice of government structures, or features of the social or economic environment may be powerful enough to affect a certain kind of politics or policy, as well as to affect the development of government structure. This possibility is recognized in some of the research, in which refined analytic techniques are used to identify the strengths of relationships between structure and policy that are "independent" of influences from social or economic environment. Some findings are ambiguous, however, and generate controversies about the validity of the measurements or about the sensitivity of the analytic techniques used.

There is some evidence that cities with reformed government structures have lower rates of voter turnout[15] and that their officials are less responsive to the demands of social and economic groups.[16] These findings square with the expectations of the reformers themselves. The features of council-manager government, nonpartisan elections, and selection of councilmen at large were expected to put local government on a professional-management basis and to keep it "out of politics." They mask the cleavages that exist within the local electorate and make it difficult for voting blocs to gain control of particular officials in the municipal government. Local politics must develop its own language, with disputes expressed in terms other than the labels of the major national parties. Such debate is difficult to follow for those whose marginal interest in politics leads only to identification as Democrats or Republicans. Reduced voting turnout is a natural result, as is municipal government that operates at some distance from popular demands.

*Partisan electoral systems, when combined with ward representation, increase the access of two kinds of minority groups: those which are residentially*

---

[14] *Ibid;* see also Robert L. Lineberry and Edmund P. Fowler, "Reformism and Public Policies in American Cities," *American Political Science Review, 61* (September, 1967), 701–716, and the literature cited there.

[15] Robert Salisbury and Gordon Black, "Class and Party in Partisan and Nonpartisan Elections: The Case of Des Moines," *American Political Science Review, 57* (September, 1963), 584–592; and Robert R. Alford and Eugene C. Lee, "Voting Turnout in American Cities," *American Political Science Review, 62* (September, 1968), 796–813.

[16] Lineberry and Fowler, *op. cit.*

*segregated, and which may as a consequence of the electoral system demand and obtain preferential consideration from their councilmen; and groups which constitute identifiable voting blocs to which parties and politicians may be beholden in the next election. The introduction of at-large, non-partisan elections has at least five consequences for these groups. First, they remove an important cue-giving agency—the party—from the electoral scene, leaving the voter to make decisions less on the policy commitments (however vague) of the party, and more on irrelevancies such as ethnic identification and name familiarity. Second, by removing the party from the ballot, the reforms eliminate the principal agency of interest aggregation from the political system. Hence, interests are articulated less clearly and are aggregated either by some agency or not at all. Moreover, nonpartisanship has the effect of reducing the turnout in local elections by working class groups, leaving office-holders freer from retaliation by these groups at the polls. Fourth, nonpartisanship may also serve to decrease the salience of "private regarding" demands by increasing the relative political power of "public regarding" agencies like the local press. And when nonpartisanship is combined with election at-large, the impact of residentially segregated groups or groups which obtain their strength from voting as blocs in municipal elections is further reduced. For these reasons, it is clear that political reforms may have a significant impact in minimizing the role which social conflicts play in decision-making. By muting the demands of private-regarding groups, the electoral institutions of reformed governments make public policy less responsive to the demands arising out of social conflicts in the population.*[17]

There are some findings about the substances of policies enacted in cities with reformed and unreformed structures. One study finds lower "expenditure effort" (expenditures as a percentage of aggregate personal income) in communities governed by city managers than in those governed by elected mayors.[18] This finding suggests that the city-manager form of government occurs in "business-minded," conservative communities and that it works against high taxes and expenditures, although a study of school-board expenditures reveals the highest spending in communities governed by city managers.[19]

## VERTICAL INTERGOVERNMENTAL RELATIONS

### Cities and the federal system

The city's relations with national and state governments are a dimension of government structure that has profound implications for the resources and policy options available to local officials. Under the

[17] *Ibid.*, pp. 715–716.
[18] *Ibid.*
[19] Thomas R. Dye, "Governmental Structure, Urban Environment, and Educational Policy," *Midwest Journal of Political Science, 11* (August, 1967), 353–380.

American system of checks and balances, no government unit can make decisions in isolation from other units. National and state governments are protected from each other by the bulwarks of the federal system and can exert only strong pressures and constraints on each other's policies. Local governments enjoy no specific federal protections, however, and are more open to state demands and controls through constitutions, statutes, and administrative acts. Yet the officials of local governments enjoy the extraconstitutional protections of local customs and political institutions. These latter combine with the formal components of federalism to protect the officials of each government against those of other governments, even while each is partially dependent upon the decisions of others. The result is something of a muddle: A "marble cake" is a common and accurate analogy for relations among national, state, and local governments.[20] No understanding of policy-making in local governments can be complete without some comprehension of the links, barriers, assistance, and influence between local authorities and their national and state "superiors."

Every major nation in the world has both central and local units of government. A federal arrangement is peculiar, however, in that it provides certain assurances to both levels of government involved. It is common to speak of the American national and state governments as "superior" and "subordinate" to each other, but this terminology is inaccurate. On some dimensions the national government (often called the "federal" government) has prerogatives reserved to it alone. The states are not the creatures of the national government, however. Some states predate the current national government, and those that postdate Independence enjoy the same guarantees as do the original states.

The federal nature of American politics is supported by a combination of constitutional provisions, laws, extralegal political institutions, and customs. Constitutional guarantees provide for equal representation in the U.S. Senate (which is protected from the normal procedures for amending the Constitution), selection of members of the U.S. House of Representatives by state, a role for the states in the Electoral College and the process of constitutional amendment, and provision in the Tenth Amendment that certain powers are "reserved to the states." Some of these prerogatives provide direct grants of authority to state governments, whereas others protect the states by ensuring their citizens a role in important decisions by the national government. The use of states as the electoral units for the House, Senate, and President permits the leading politicians in each state to exact promises from candidates in exchange for their own campaign

[20] Morton Grodzins, "The Federal System," in The President's Commission on National Goals, Goals for Americans (Englewood Cliffs, N.J., Prentice-Hall, 1960).

support. Candidates are frequently oriented toward the demands of state populations by the need to win elections within state jurisdictions. Insofar as the officials of leading cities have some influence over their states' political parties (Chicago's Mayor Daley is the best example), this consultative role of the states in national politics also serves the interests of the cities.

Whereas the constitutional provisions merely set the stage for the protection of state and local interests within the federal structure, a series of laws, customs, and political institutions provide the detailed bulwarks for these interests. The laws establishing grant-in-aid programs recognize the demands made by state and local officials who testified before Congress, and federal laws may require subsequent hearings about the standards set by the federal agencies.

Prominent, but extralegal bulwarks of state and local governments include the political parties and "civil societies" that use the institutions of state and local government to pursue or protect their own goals. The American party system has its roots within the states, congressional districts, counties, and municipalities and serves to protect state and local interests in national councils.[21] Members of the House and Senate, as well as candidates for the presidency, owe their political obligations to the leaders of state or local party organizations, rather than to national party leaders. The national parties are composed of fifty state parties, which are themselves composites of separate organizations based on counties, municipalities, or legislative districts. Nominations and financial support for candidates come from state or local party organizations, which may be no more than personal organizations focused on the careers of single politicians. The national party offers few tangible incentives for state or local cooperation and exerts no formal sanctions against state or local recalcitrants. Some congressmen, governors, and mayors compaign openly in opposition to the presidential nominee of their party, and some congressmen compile voting records sharply at odds with the program of their party's President.

State populations have shown their loyalty to regional parties in the face of outside pressure.[22] This loyalty is most pronounced in the South but is not limited to that section. Officials of state and local governments in the South have responded in concert with private organizations against federal statutes and administrative "guidelines" that require racial integration. In every state numerous groups seek federal contracts for industries or federal expenditures on military

21 See Morton Grodzins, "American Political Parties and the American System," *Western Political Quarterly, 13* (December, 1960), 974–998.

22 See Daniel J. Elazar, *American Federalism: A View from the States* (New York, Crowell, 1966), chap. 1.

**Table 4.3**  *Federal aid payments in urban areas, 1961, 1966, and 1968 (budget and trust accounts in millions of dollars)*[a]

| Function and program | Actual | | Estimate |
|---|---|---|---|
| | 1961 | 1966 | 1968 |
| National defense (civil-defense and national-guard centers) | $ 10 | $ 20 | $ 26 |
| Agriculture and agricultural resources | 155 | 149 | 235 |
| Natural resources | 54 | 105 | 200 |
| Commerce and transportation | | | |
| Highways | 1,398 | 2,138 | 2,176 |
| Economic development | | 2 | 36 |
| Airports | 36 | 30 | 33 |
| Other | 1 | 52 | 6 |
| Housing and community development | | | |
| Public housing | 105 | 169 | 208 |
| Water and sewer facilities | | | 61 |
| Urban renewal | 106 | 235 | 336 |
| Model cities | | | 132 |
| Urban transportation | | 14 | 98 |
| District of Columbia | 25 | 44 | 71 |
| Other | 2 | 23 | 100 |
| Health, labor, and welfare | | | |
| Office of Economic Opportunity | | 449 | 1,010 |
| School lunches, special milk, food stamps | 131 | 196 | 290 |
| Hospital construction | 48 | 75 | 95 |
| Community health | 33 | 127 | 450 |
| Public assistance (including medical care) | 1,170 | 1,905 | 2,243 |
| Vocational rehabilitation | 37 | 108 | 211 |
| Employment security and manpower training | 303 | 417 | 501 |
| Other | 21 | 47 | 101 |
| Education | | | |
| Elementary and secondary | 222 | 895 | 1,292 |
| Higher | 5 | 37 | 172 |
| Vocational | 28 | 90 | 160 |
| Other | 3 | 27 | 80 |
| Other functions | | _[b] | 6 |
| Total aids to urban areas | $3,893 | $7,354 | $10,329 |

a Excludes loans and repayable advances.
b Less than $0.05 million.
SOURCE: Advisory Commission in Intergovernmental Relations, *Fiscal Balance in the American Federal System*, vol. 1 (Washington, D.C., Government Printing Office, 1967), p. 295.

installations or public works. These efforts involve chambers of commerce, elected officials of state and local governments, congressmen, and individual businessmen.[23]

A feature that heightens the importance of federalism in local politics is the mixture of governmental responsibilities in each field of public service. There is no important domestic activity that is manned or financed solely by federal, state, or local government. The activities that consume most domestic expenditures—education, highways, welfare, health, natural resources, public safety—are funded by combinations of federal grants or loans, state and local taxes, and service charges.

The combination of a viable federal structure, political values that respect home rule and local self-government, and shared responsibilities for major domestic services means that policy-makers at any level of government must be alert to inputs from other levels of government. Federal grants and program requirements provoke state and local officials to action, whereas the demands or unwelcome decisions of state and local officials often provoke federal authorities. It is not simply elected officials who engage in intergovernmental relations. The list of important actors includes administrators at each level of government, plus members of the staff agencies of each chief executive and legislature. For local adminstrators intergovernmental relations may take the form of requests, demands, or appeals to state or federal agencies, legislatures, or executives. These communications may go directly to federal or state administrators or be routed through the political contacts of local authorities in the national or state legislatures.

FEDERAL AIDS TO THE CITIES    Grant-in-aid programs are the single most prominent feature of federal relations with state and local governments. In 1968 they amounted to $17 billion, of which $10 billion was direct federal-local aid and an unknown additional amount was channeled through state governments into the municipalities. Table 4.3 shows how $10.3 billion in federal grants and other aids to urban areas were distributed through numerous programs during 1968. The President's budget for 1971 included $27.6 billion for state and local governments.

Federal grants have several distinct features, each of which has certain implications for the recipient. Each program has a specific purpose; there is no "general support" for local a¢tivities. Recipient agencies must provide some of their own resources to support the program and must administer it according to prescribed standards.

23 Wallace S. Sayre and Herbert Kaufman, *Governing New York City: Politics in the Metropolis* (New York, Norton, 1965), pp. 559–562.

The tying of federal grants to "purposes" and the requirements that go with them are frequent sources of conflict between federal and local administrators. It is alleged that the federal carrot leads recipients to undertake activities that are not in their own best interests and that requirements are frequently inconsistent with the local social or economic problems. Federal money is not "free." Recipients must pay some economic and political costs in order to receive its benefits.

Grants-in-aid are only one of several devices for providing financial and technical assistance to state and local agencies. Federal loans, loan guarantees, tax credits, deductibility of state and local taxes from federally taxable income, and direct federal benefits to urban residents are additional kinds of aid. Some programs mix grants-in-aid with other features to provide different options to recipients. In the public-housing program, for example, federal guarantees of private loans support the bulk of most projects, whereas outright grants cover additional costs. Some programs make available direct loans from the federal Treasury if federal guarantees will not allow recipient agencies to contract commercial loans at desirable interest rates.

Many taxpayers do not recognize the subtle federal aids that are written into the income-tax code. In computing income subject to federal taxation, a citizen can deduct any amounts paid as state or local income or sales, excise, or property taxes. Furthermore, any income received from interest on state or local government bonds is not subject to federal taxation. These provisions lessen the impact of state and local taxes and permit state and local agencies to pay lower than commercial interest rates for the money they borrow.

Several other federal programs provide indirect, or subtle, forms of aid to state or local agencies. The direct provision of federal benefits to institutions or private citizens relieves states and municipalities of demands for services that otherwise would come to them. In this category are federal grants, loans, or loan guarantees to institutions of higher education (both public and private) for the construction of instructional facilities and dormitories; loans and scholarships to the students of these institutions; and federal insurance payments for the aged and disabled.

The Advisory Commission on Intergovernmental Relations (ACIR) is a research agency of the federal government whose purpose is to provide information and technical assistance to state and local governments and to facilitate the administration of federal programs in ways most helpful to states and municipalities.[24] The commission itself includes twenty-three officials of national, state, and local gov-

[24] Deil S. Wright, "The Advisory Commission on Intergovernment Relations," *Public Administration Review*, 25 (September, 1965), 193–202.

ernments and three members representing the "public." A professional staff does detailed analyses and prepares recommendations for review by the commissioners. The statute that established the ACIR outlined its duties:

1    to bring together representatives of the federal, state and local governments for the consideration of common problems;
2    to provide a forum for discussing the administration and coordination of federal grant and other programs requiring intergovernmental cooperation;
3    to give critical attention to the conditions and controls involved in the administration of federal grant programs;
4    to make available technical assistance to the executive and legislative branches of the federal government in the review of proposed legislation to determine its overall effect on the federal system;
5    to encourage discussion and study at an early stage of emerging public problems that are likely to require intergovernmental cooperation;
6    to recommend, within the framework of the Constitution, the most desirable allocation of governmental functions, responsibilities, and revenues among the several levels of government;
7    to recommend methods of coordinating and simplifying tax laws and administrative practices to achieve a more orderly and less competitive fiscal relationship between the levels of government and to reduce the burden of compliance for taxpayers.

FEDERAL URBAN POLICY    One charge made against the urban programs of the federal government is that they are not coordinated among themselves. Frederic N. Cleaveland and his colleagues have written that, "in comparison to established policy fields like agriculture policy, foreign trade policy, or labor policy," the federal structure for making urban policy is "vague and hopelessly diffuse."[25] Wilson sees various federal urban programs as working consistently at cross purposes:

. . . the new Department of Housing and Urban Development stands squarely in this tradition. Under its previous name (the Housing and Home Finance Agency), it subsidized the flight to the suburbs with FHA mortgage insurance, while trying to lure back suburbanites to the central city with subsidies provided by the Urban Renewal Administration. The Public Housing Administration built low-rent units for the poor while urban renewal was tearing them down.[26]

Examples of apparent contradictions in federal urban policy could be multiplied almost indefinitely: While trying to reduce air

25 Frederic N. Cleaveland et al., Congress and Urban Problems (Washington, D.C., Brookings Institution, 1969), p. 375.
26 James Q. Wilson, "The War on Cities," in Robert Goldwin, ed., A Nation of Cities (Skokie, Ill., Rand McNally, 1966), p. 19.

pollution, the federal government nonetheless encourages more auto-mobile traffic by constructing new superhighways; while claiming to improve the housing of the poor through public housing, it benefits the middle classes through tax write-offs on home-loan interest; while funding public-welfare programs, it also subsidizes community-action agencies that attack welfare bureaucracies.

Although these and other contradictions occur in federal urban policy, some of them are the inevitable by-products of politics itself, or of politics in a relatively democratic system. There are, after all, mul-tiple constituencies in each field of policy, and efforts to provide at least some "goodies" for all seem bound to produce inconsistencies in terms of some abstract ideal. Moreover, it is not clear that urban policy is any more fragmented and inconsistent than are other federal policies. Policy-making in foreign trade shows elements of logrolling and "every man for himself" instead of well-ordered consistency. Farm policy shows inconsistent mixtures designed to benefit both commercial enter-prises and less profitable family farms. Federal urban policy may be fragmented and inconsistent. But so, as we saw in the last chapter, are the interests of various groups within the urban area.

STATE AIDS TO THE CITIES    The array of state aids to municipalities includes many patterned after federal aids to state and local govern-ments. But state aids emphasize shared taxes and "bloc" grants (for broadly defined types of programs), rather than grants-in-aid for specified projects. A fixed portion of taxes revert to the local govern-ment in whose jurisdiction they were collected. As bloc grants and shared taxes are used by most states, they provide more freedom to local governments than do federal grants-in-aid. They are awarded not for specified projects or in response to detailed applications but go auto-matically to local governments according to certain criteria and may be used for any programs within generally defined areas (for example, "education," "roads and streets") or even for any local government activities. State aids are generally "free," and no matching by locally raised revenues is required. For the most part, local governments re-ceive state aid as a matter of "right"; there are few application pro-cedures and few limitations on expenditures. The financial relations between state and local governments are not, however, free from dis-putes over local and state control. We have noted the issues involved in these debates on pp. 113–117.

State governments use various criteria to allocate financial aids to each local government. Some redistribute economic resources from "have" to "have-not" communities; some merely return to communities certain proportions of state taxes collected there; some reward com-munities that make some effort to use their own resources in support of certain programs; some award funds "equally" according to arbitrary criteria (like population); and some rely on special considerations of emergency or agreements between state and local agencies. Table 4.4 shows the distribution of funds to city governments according to the

**Table 4.4** *State payments to municipalities by percentages distributed according to various standards, 1962*

| Standard | California | Massachusetts | Pennsylvania |
|---|---|---|---|
| Population of local jurisdiction | 69.9% | 0.4% | 21.5% |
| Sales or licenses in local jurisdiction (for example, sales of alcoholic beverages, tobacco, or other taxed items and the number of auto or drivers' licenses issued locally) | 6.7 | – | 17.1 |
| Road mileage | – | – | 32.3 |
| Amount of state-owned land in local jurisdiction | – | 0.4 | – |
| Equal aid to all jurisdictions | 1.4 | – | – |
| Contractual arrangements with specific cities for services provided to state institutions | 0.2 | – | – |
| Specified rate of aid per unit of service provided (for example, per patient day in city hospital) | 0.1 | 1.8 | – |
| Assessed value of certain types of property (for example, industrial property) | – | 22.6 | – |
| Local fiscal ability | – | 12.6 | – |
| Ratio to local expenditures for aided function | 21.8 | 58.8 | 18.9 |
| Need as determined by state agency | 0.3 | 3.1 | – |
| Criteria undefinable by available data | – | 0.2 | 11.0 |
| Total[a] | 100.4% | 99.9% | 100.8% |

[a] The columns do not add up to exactly 100% because the separate percentages within the table have been rounded.

SOURCE: Ira Sharkansky, *Public Administration: Policy-Making in Government Agencies* (Chicago, Markham, 1970), p. 254.

criteria used in California, Massachusetts, and Pennsylvania during 1962. California and Pennsylvania did not offer great rewards for local effort. California distributed almost 70 percent of its funds on the basis of local sales of taxed items or licenses or in equal amounts to all jurisdictions. Pennsylvania distributes almost 22 percent according to population and another 49 percent according to local sales of taxed items or licenses and local road mileage. California distributes only 22 percent according to criteria that reward local effort (ratio to local expenditures for the aided function) and Pennsylvania only 19 percent. In contrast, Massachusetts awards almost 59 percent of its aid according to local-effort formulas. It also awards almost 13 percent of its aids in a way that redistributes economic resources from "have" to "have-not" areas.

The concept of "state aid" is necessarily loose because of the wide variety of programs and techniques in fifty state governments. In many states, the aid granted to local governments represents only a small portion of the services that state governments provide to local residents. State governments vary in the kinds of services they provide themselves and the kinds they leave to local authorities. In education, for example, some state governments pay the entire cost of supporting public junior colleges, whereas others provide only some of the costs to county or municipal governments. In public welfare, some state governments pay for all aid payments not covered by federal grants, whereas other states share these costs with local governments. The most complete record of state involvement in the support of public services shows the percentage of total state and local government revenues that are raised or spent at the state level. Table 4.5 shows this record for each state during 1966–1967.

There is considerable variation in the role that state governments play in raising revenues for themselves and local governments. The nationwide average is 52.1 percent of total state and local revenues raised by the state government. But the range extends from 78.8 percent in Delaware to 37.5 percent in New Hampshire.

There is a tendency for low-income states to rely heavily on state revenues. In Louisiana, North Carolina, South Carolina, and Vermont, there are numerous local governments (especially rural counties) that are hard-pressed to support mimimum levels of public services with the economic resources available within their borders. Perhaps because many local authorities in these states must rely upon state aid, all local governments are inclined to view the state governments as the prime sources of funds. It is therefore probably easier to pass a state-aid bill when there is something in it for the constituents of most legislators. At the other end of the income scale, local governments in the well-to-do states of New York, New Jersey, Massachusetts, and California carry a larger than average share of state and local financing.

Apparently out of step with the general pattern is Delaware. This state has one of the highest levels of personal income per capita in the nation but is also about the heaviest user of state revenues. It thus reflects the pattern of its southern neighbors. Southern states have been centralized historically, owing partly to colonial experience of dispersed population and a plantation economy that did not nurture the development of strong, autonomous towns. Nebraska is another state that deviates from the normal association between low income and high reliance on state revenues. It ranks below the national average on several measures of economic resources but close to the top in the proportion of revenues raised locally. There a strong local orientation together with fiscal conservatism seems to have retarded the development of sources of state revenue. Nebraska was one of the last state governments to abandon its reliance on locally raised property taxes.

**Table 4.5** *State-government portions of state-local total tax revenues, fiscal 1966–1967*

| United States | 52.1% | | |
|---|---|---|---|
| Alabama | 71.0 | Montana | 44.1 |
| Alaska | 68.5 | Nebraska | 34.9 |
| Arizona | 57.3 | Nevada | 51.5 |
| Arkansas | 72.5 | New Hampshire | 37.5 |
| California | 43.8 | New Jersey | 37.7 |
| Colorado | 49.0 | New Mexico | 74.5 |
| Connecticut | 48.1 | New York | 48.3 |
| Delaware | 78.8 | North Carolina | 74.6 |
| Florida | 53.2 | North Dakota | 50.8 |
| Georgia | 65.8 | Ohio | 44.4 |
| Hawaii | 73.2 | Oklahoma | 62.2 |
| Idaho | 62.5 | Oregon | 51.4 |
| Illinois | 44.6 | Pennsylvania | 54.3 |
| Indiana | 50.0 | Rhode Island | 53.7 |
| Iowa | 50.1 | South Carolina | 77.2 |
| Kansas | 49.6 | South Dakota | 43.1 |
| Kentucky | 68.5 | Tennessee | 62.4 |
| Louisiana | 72.3 | Texas | 53.6 |
| Maine | 51.4 | Utah | 59.5 |
| Maryland | 53.6 | Vermont | 61.3 |
| Massachusetts | 47.7 | Virginia | 58.5 |
| Michigan | 55.2 | Washington | 70.6 |
| Minnesota | 51.6 | West Virginia | 70.0 |
| Mississippi | 66.6 | Wisconsin | 62.0 |
| Missouri | 51.3 | Wyoming | 47.9 |

One service that state governments provide to officials of local governments receives little attention from political scientists, but it has important implications for local policy-makers: the definition of municipal boundaries. This service has special importance on the fringes of urban and metropolitan areas, where a proliferation of autonomous municipalities confounds the matching of taxable resources and service demands (see pp. 25–32). In many states new municipalities are established when voters in unincorporated areas submit petitions to the legislatures and hold elections to determine local sentiment. Several states have taken the lead in giving administrative units a strong role in this process, in the hope of applying well-reasoned standards to applications for new incorporations and defining the borders of new municipalities in ways that will maximize their efficiency in providing services. The Minnesota Municipal Commission reviews incorporation and annexation proposals; Wisconsin divides these responsibilities between the circuit court and the state Director of Regional Planning; and California has an agency-formation commission in each county. Some of these units encourage annexation to existing municipalities rather than creation of new entities; oppose gerrymandering of jurisdictions to include tax-rich areas or to exclude "nuisance" islands; use man-made or natural features (rivers, lakes, highways, railroad tracks) as boundary lines; and oppose boundaries that would divide existing commercial districts or residential areas.[27]

## HORIZONTAL INTERGOVERNMENTAL RELATIONS

### The metropolitan problem

Vertical associations among federal, state, and local administrators and other officials do not exhaust the intergovernmental relations of local officials. The presence of 81,248 local governments produces numerous opportunities for "horizontal" relations among officials of different local governments. Whereas vertical relations center on the provision and receipt of financial aid, there is no single prominent stimulus for horizontal relations. They vary with the incentives that prompt them; they include formal "federations" and "compacts" that permit joint administration of public services, agreements to share information and technical assistance, reciprocal legislation permitting citizens of one jurisdiction to receive the services (or avoid the taxes) of another, and membership of government officials in organizations that seek solutions to common problems.

27 Clarence J. Hein and Thomas F. Hady, "Administrative Control of Municipal Incorporation: The Search for Criteria," *Western Political Quarterly, 19* (December, 1966), 697–704.

Metropolitan areas are the most frequent settings for horizontal relations among local officials, reflecting the high population density and the demands for policy that are thus generated, as well as the proximity of many separate governments with policy problems that depend partly on one another's actions. In Chapter 2 we discussed the social and economic differences between central cities and their suburbs and mentioned some features that hinder the smooth coordination of local activities in metropolitan areas. Here we return to the subject of metropolitan areas, this time to focus on problems and opportunities in governmental integration.

The number and density of governmental units in metropolitan areas (see Table 4.6) are the primary conditions that beg for coordination. In 1967, the Chicago SMSA had the dubious distinction of containing the most units. Its 1,113 jurisdictions were divided among school districts, counties, municipalities, townships, and special districts as shown in Table 4.6.

The "metropolitan problem" has been studied and decried by a generation of urban scholars. The fundamental problem they identify

Table 4.6 Number and types of local governments in United States and in the Chicago SMSA

| | United States | | |
| Type | 1962 | 1967 | Percentage change, 1962–1967 |
|---|---|---|---|
| All local governments | 91,186 | 81,248 | − 10.9 |
| School districts | 34,678 | 21,482 | − 37.2 |
| Other | 56,508 | 59,466 | 5.2 |
| Counties | 3,043 | 3,049 | 0.2 |
| Municipalities | 18,000 | 18,048 | 0.3 |
| Townships | 17,142 | 17,105 | − 0.2 |
| Special districts | 18,323 | 21,264 | 16.1 |

| Chicago SMSA | |
| | 1967 |
|---|---|
| All local governments | 1,113 |
| School districts | 327 |
| Other | |
| Counties | 6 |
| Municipalities | 250 |
| Townships | 113 |
| Special districts | 417 |

SOURCE: U.S. Bureau of the Census, *Census of Governments 1967*: Vol. 1, *Governmental Organization* (Washington, D.C., Government Printing Office, 1968), Tables 1 and 19, pp. 23, 126 ff.

is the *noncongruence of policy-making units and problem units*. Municipal borders follow railroad tracks, creeks and rivers, streets and alleys, and other artificial lines of demarcation, but problems of crime, pollution, poverty, transportation, and so forth, do not respect these boundaries. Lineberry[28] has identified four basic aspects of government fragmentation in the metropolitan area: externalities, fiscal and service inequities, absence of political responsibility, and lack of coordination.

EXTERNALITIES    Because the metropolis is an interdependent system, policies undertaken by "independent" municipal corporations or special districts may produce changes, sometimes unintended, in other parts of the total region. Economists call such consequences "externalities," or, more descriptively, "spillover effects." Land-use and zoning policies are examples. Sophisticated manipulation of zoning requirements is regularly used to produce the most "desirable" mix of residents and commerce, while shifting burdens to other areas in the metropolis, particularly to the central city. The "zoning game" may thus be used to maximize the benefits to one's own community while shifting the costs to other "players," particularly the less fortunate ones.[29] Although zoning decisions especially illustrate the spillover effects of municipal policies, decisions in numerous other functional areas, including crime prevention, transportation policy, pollution control, schooling, and industrial attraction, may also entail externalities for other communities.

FISCAL AND SERVICE INEQUITIES    We noted in Chapter 2 the problems resulting from the segregation of economic needs and resources in the metropolitan area. To reiterate by example, in Detroit, twenty-five suburban school districts spent up to $500 more per child per year to educate their children than did the city of Detroit. In the central city of Detroit, on the other hand, nearly a third of the public-school buildings were built during the administration of President Ulysses S. Grant.[30] One New Jersey community had an assessed valuation of $5.5 million per pupil, and a neighboring community had a valuation of $33,000 per pupil.[31]

---

[28] This discussion is based on Robert L. Lineberry, "Reforming Metropolitan Governance: Requiem or Reality?" *Georgetown Law Journal*, 58 (March–May, 1970), 675–718.

[29] See Seymour Sacks and Alan Campbell, "The Fiscal Zoning Game," *Municipal Finance*, 35 (1964), 140–149; and David Ranney, "Regional Development and the Courts," *Syracuse Law Review*, 16 (Spring, 1965), 600–612.

[30] National Commission on Civil Disorders, *Report* (Washington, D.C., Government Printing Office, 1968), p. 241.

[31] Robert C. Wood, *1400 Governments* (Garden City, N.Y., Doubleday Anchor, 1961), p. 55.

ABSENCE OF POLITICAL RESPONSIBILITY  When there is a plethora of government units, citizen control of decision-makers is diffuse. A citizen of Fridley, Minnesota, a Minneapolis suburb, is expected to exercise informed control over eleven local governments, in addition to the state and national governments. In the absence of an overarching metropolitan government there is no policy-making body to hold accountable for broad metropolitan problems or for failures arising from government action or inaction. Such fragmentation of the citizens' attention can hardly contribute to responsible democratic government.

LACK OF COORDINATION  The construction of public policy requires at least minimum coordination both among functions and among decision-making units. The absence of both types of coordination in the metropolis suggests that it will be unable to realize all the benefits of coherent policy and the consequent economies of scale that larger units should be able to secure. If communities fail to coordinate air-pollution control, for example, a municipality downwind may have the most advanced regulation yet still suffer the effluence of its upwind neighbor.

## The politics of metropolitan reform

There are ten major alternative forms of metropolitan reorganization, ranged here from the least to the most extreme:[32]

1  municipal extraterritorial regulation of real-estate developments in the rural fringe outside municipal borders;
2  intergovernmental agreements;
3  voluntary metropolitan councils;
4  the urban county;
5  transfer of functions to state governments;
6  metropolitan special districts;
7  annexation and intercity consolidation;
8  city-county separation, that is, separation of the urbanized and rural areas;
9  consolidation of the city with the urbanized county surrounding it;
10  federation of several municipalities.

Measured in terms of the oceans of ink used by reform advocates, the reorganization movement has been only modestly successful. Without attempting to construct a theory of metropolitan reform ourselves, we may still cite some propositions showing that metropolitan govern-

[32] Advisory Commission on Intergovernmental Relations, *Alternative Approaches to Governmental Reorganization in Metropolitan Areas* (Washington, D.C., Government Printing Office, 1962).

ment is a volatile and divisive issue and fundamentally political. The following explanations of the overall failure of reorganization schemes are offered.

First, *public officials and the "power structure" of the metropolitan area rarely initiate reform*. Although city officials do sometimes initiate reorganization proposals, more typically a group like the League of Women Voters, a civic-betterment association, a newspaper, or a band of intellectuals initiates the movement. Yet, without the support of elected officials and community power structures, a reform campaign begins with at least one strike against it. If public officials are relatively unconcerned about reorganization, voters will be even less enthusiastic.

Second, *voters are often apathetic about metropolitan organization and place higher values upon other goals (like community autonomy) than upon reform (for efficiency and the like)*. Studies of several metropolitan areas[33] suggest that citizens (except for residents of racial ghettos)[34] are quite satisfied with levels of municipal services. Voters seem to be more impressed by arguments concerning loss of community autonomy and by fear of higher taxes than by abstract arguments in favor of metropolitan consolidation. Moreover, voter information about metropolitan reform tends to be minimal and inaccurate. Evidence from survey data suggest that in one Miami campaign less than a third of the electorate had heard of the reform proposal and "had a sliver of a correct idea about it."[35]

Third, *suburban officials form a hard core of opposition to change*. In the St. Louis consolidation effort, the major source of organized opposition was the Citizen's Committee for Self-Government, dominated by municipal officials and Republican Party leaders from the county. Also, political party leaders, though they have sometimes (as in Cleveland) supported change, tend to be either apathetic or antagonistic to it. It is well known that the central cities of larger metropolitan areas outside the South are dominated by the Democratic Party and that suburban areas are generally Republican. The merging of central cities and fringe areas into a single metropolitan entity would almost certainly decrease predictability for local party leaders. In most areas it would also benefit the Republican Party. As Banfield has concluded,

*Even if the proportion of Republicans declines sharply in the suburbs, metropolitan government north of the Mason-Dixon line would almost every-*

---

[33] See, for example, John C. Bollens *et al.*, *Exploring the Metropolitan Community* (Berkeley, University of California Press, 1963), pp. 188–190; and Metropolitan Community Studies, *Metropolitan Challenge* (Dayton, Ohio, 1959), p. 241.

[34] National Commission on Civil Disorders, *op. cit.*, pp. 79–83.

[35] Edward Sofen, *The Miami Metropolitan Experiment* (Bloomington, University of Indiana Press, 1963), p. 76.

*where be Republican government. In effect, advocates of consolidation
schemes are asking the Democrats to give up their control of the central
cities, or at least to place it in jeopardy.*[36]

In addition to the opposition of party leaders and municipal officials,
labor unions also often oppose metropolitan reform proposals.

Finally, *black leaders and voters are almost always opposed to reorganization.* Given the national policy commitment to betterment for
black Americans and the increasing concentration of blacks in the
central cities of the metropolitan complex, the opposition of black
leaders and voters merits special attention. No study of a proposal for
metropolitan reorganization, successful or not, has found a majority of
black voters on the side of restructuring. The most impressive evidence
of this opposition comes from a study of voting on reorganization proposals in Cleveland-Cuyahoga County. For a succession of ten reorganization proposals over a twenty-five-year period, black support
declined with each election.[37] This increasing opposition was contemporary with a proportional increase in black voting strength in the city
itself, culminating in the 1967 election of Carl Stokes as mayor. Black
resistance to such reform is based on two beliefs about the consequences
of metropolitan merger. First, blacks anticipate dilution of their voting
strength in any larger area government. They also fear redirection of
urban public policy away from the issues of poverty, ghetto rehabilitation, and civil rights.

There are two factors in the socioeconomic structures of metropolitan areas that are especially relevant to metropolitan reform. First,
*the larger the metropolitan area, the smaller is the probability of a
successful reform campaign,* and, second, *the sharper the socioeconomic
differences between suburban and central city areas, the smaller is the
probability of reform.* In the largest metropolitan areas, where there
are distinct social-class differences between central cities and fringe
areas, metropolitan integration would be most difficult. These observations are substantiated by studies of school-district mergers and municipal annexation. Where the central-city and suburban populations
resemble each other, annexation seems more feasible than where the
two populations represent distinct social and economic compositions.[38]
Annexation seems most difficult where the central-city population is

[36] Edward C. Banfield, "The Politics of Metropolitan Area Organization,"
*Midwest Journal of Political Science, 1* (May, 1957), 77–91.

[37] Richard A. Watson and John H. Romani, "Metropolitan Government for
Metropolitan Cleveland," *Midwest Journal of Political Science, 5* (November, 1961),
365–390.

[38] Thomas R. Dye, "Urban Political Integration: Conditions Associated with
Annexation in American Cities," *Midwest Journal of Political Science, 8* (November,
1964), 430–446; and Basil Zimmer and Amos Hawley, *Metropolitan Area Schools*
(Beverly Hills, Calif., Sage, 1968), p. 307.

distinctly less well educated and employed in less attractive occupations than are the suburbanites. Under these conditions suburbanites seem to resist entering the same government unit with central-city residents. Opponents of annexation argue that suburban voters will be forced to pay the high costs of welfare, police, and fire protection required for residents of the central city, especially of its slums. As these problems are the ones that many suburbanites left the city to escape, they are hardly likely to welcome reaffiliation with the central city. In the minds of many suburbanites, the city means undesirable people and the high taxes necessary to provide services for them. Annexations are also impossible in older cities already surrounded by incorporated suburbs. Where all the fringe area is incorporated, the central city may be literally "hemmed in" and blocked from taking new land outside its borders. Very few of the major central cities can take advantage of annexation provisions.

## Metropolitan government in practice

Even though metropolitan government reorganization has been urged upon urban areas by a generation of political scientists, the record of accomplishment has not been impressive. Almost fifty referenda have been held on metropolitan reorganization proposals in the post-World War II years,[39] but only a minority of them have passed. City-county consolidations have succeeded in several areas of Virginia, in Baton Rouge, in Nashville, and in Jacksonville; a federation of several governments was adopted in the Miami area. Most recently a modified city-county consolidation was imposed on Indianapolis-Marion County by the state legislature, one of the rare cases in which a referendum was not required.

Each of these metropolitan governments has taken significant steps toward eliminating fiscal and service disparities, lack of coordination, absence of political responsibility, and the problem of externalities. Yet, as we have seen, adoption of these metropolitan reforms requires overcoming so many legal and political hurdles that it is rare. Williams, a leading student of urban government, has observed that

*through the second quarter of this century many political scientists were writing on why metropolitan areas needed to be politically integrated*

---

[39] Lineberry, *op. cit.* For discussions of the major reforms, see Sofen, *op. cit.;* Brett Hawkins, *Nashville Metro* (Nashville, Tenn., Vanderbilt University Press, 1966); and William C. Havard, Jr., and Floyd Corty, *Rural-Urban Consolidation: The Merger of Governments in the Baton Rouge Area* (Baton Rouge, Louisiana State University Press, 1964).

*through local government consolidation. Thus far, in the third quarter, a major theme has been documentation of how thoroughly this advice has been rejected by the American people.*[40]

## Federal policy and the metropolitan problem

In recent years several federal policies have been directed toward the problems of fragmented government in the metropolis. The substance of federal metropolitan policy has been to encourage metropolitan-wide planning and councils of government. Federal encouragement of area planning may be traced to the "701" assistance program of the Housing Act of 1954, but the most extensive requirements are contained in the Demonstration Cities and Metropolitan Development Act of 1966.

The act requires that all applications for federal grants or loans in nine categories of assistance be submitted for review to an area planning agency, which must be "to the greatest practicable extent, composed of or responsible to elected officials" of the government units of the area. If no such area agency exists, applications must be reviewed by a state planning agency. By August, 1969, the U.S. Bureau of the Budget, charged with designating such review agencies, had approved review agencies for 211 areas. Area agencies were charged with review responsibilities for 198 areas, and state planning agencies were designated for the remaining thirteen. A total of 100 specific federal assistance programs come under the purview of the Demonstration Cities and Intergovernmental Cooperation Acts.

A common result of federal involvement in metropolitan affairs is the "council of government." Examples include the Association of Bay Area Governments (ABAG) in the San Francisco–Oakland Area and the Association of Central Oklahoma Governments (ACOG). The councils of government, or COGs, usually include elected officials from counties, school districts, municipalities, and special districts. Their most important function is to approve or disallow applications for federal grants-in-aid based upon the consistency of the submitted proposals with metropolitan-area objectives. Before any single government unit in the area can receive federal assistance, its application must be reviewed by the COG. Typically the COG has prepared, or is in the process of preparing, an overall plan for metropolitan development (see our discussion of metropolitan planning, pp. 315–318).

Most of the powers of the metropolitan COGs are, therefore, negative, rather than positive. They can reject local grant applications

---

[40] Oliver Williams, "Life Style Values and Political Decentralization in Metropolitan Areas," *Southwestern Social Science Quarterly, 48* (December, 1967), 299.

that are inconsistent with sets of (sometimes vague) metropolitan criteria, but they cannot compel any local government to do anything against its wishes. Practically, their limited powers extend only to matters involving federal money and not to local decisions on zoning, taxation, spending, and other policies that do not commit the federal Treasury. Although they have the organizational potential for effective metropolitan coordination, they are at present little more than metropolitan planning agencies, with no real basis of authority beyond their power to disapprove grant applications. They still lack the effective power actually to coordinate the activities of the numerous local governments in the metropolis. As Banfield has described the difficulty of metropolitan planning agencies, "the catch is that the making of a plan is precluded by the very problem—lack of coordination—that the plan is supposed to solve."[41] Plans are often, in Norton Long's words, little more than "civic New Year's resolutions." Even if metropolitan COGs and planning agencies were truly effective coordinators of local policies, they would still be a long way from solving the deeper problems of the absence of political responsibility and the presence of fiscal and service disparities within the metropolis.

## SUMMARY

In this chapter we have outlined the structural context of urban policy-making. We have not simply described government institutions but have also shown how different kinds of structures grow out of basic notions about government organization and how they interact with local politics and public policy. The premises of local organization include the desire to maintain the political accountability of local officials, the desire for professional management, and the desire to maintain either local or state control of city affairs.

The three prominent models of local government organization are the mayor-council, council-manager, and city-commission types. These basic models can be combined with any number of secondary features, each of which may be the subject of political controversy because of its implications for local policy-making: the use of partisan or non-partisan ballots; selection of legislators at large or by wards; executive veto of legislative actions; assignment of personnel and budgetary controls to the legislature, executive, or semiautonomous boards; and the use of partisan or professional criteria in selecting the heads and employees of administrative departments.

41 Edward C. Banfield, "The Uses and Limitations of Metropolitan Planning in Massachusetts," in H. Wentworth Eldridge, ed., *Taming Megalopolis* (Garden City, N.Y., Doubleday Anchor, 1967), p. 716.

Many issues of local government structure involve the cities' relations with national and state governments: vertical intergovernmental relations. Others involve relations among officials of different local jurisdictions: horizontal intergovernmental relations. Both have enormous relevance for local policy-making. Local officials seldom make important decisions without considering the resources or requirements available from national and state authorities. And, particularly in metropolitan areas, few officials can work for long without having influence on—or feeling the influence of—officials from other local jurisdictions.

# 5

# Decision-making in urban government

Decision-making is a two-sided process, involving both input from the political system and outputs of public policies. Decisions are choices among alternative courses of action that shape the outputs of the urban system. Policy-makers are not free to make whatever decisions suit their fancies, for they are confronted with numerous demands and have only limited resources of time, information, money, and authority with which to meet them. Administrators, legislators, executives, and members of informal power structures must therefore develop various strategies for coping with this complexity. These strategies are the subject of this chapter.

Inevitably, procedures for coping with inputs will represent compromises with a strictly rational model of decision-making, for the strictures of rationality are ordinarily too severe for operating political systems. Before we begin to address the important issues involved in the decision-making process, however, we shall need to clear some difficult preliminary ground. It will be useful if we understand something about the nature of political power, particularly its role in the urban political system. Then we can examine the application of power to decisions. Because a variety of people in a community beside the formal officeholders may hold power, we shall also have to discuss the structure of community power. What may seem at first to be a relatively simple matter—the identification of power holders in an urban area—is really quite complex.

## THE STRUCTURE OF COMMUNITY POWER

Formal decision-makers (those who hold significant public offices) may or may not be the "real" decision-makers in a political system. Sociologist C. Wright Mills won considerable notoriety with his argument that "the power to make decisions of national and international consequence is now so clearly seated in political, military, and economic institutions that other areas of society seem off to the side and, on occasion, readily subordinated to these."[1] Mills argued that elected officeholders are essentially subject to historic decisions made by the "big three" institutions of government bureaucracies, military commanders, and economic elites. Whether Mills was right or wrong need not concern us here, but his implication that power may not always reside with the occupants of formal positions is clearly relevant to the study of urban politics. The degree to which formal officeholders actually exercise power is a most significant empirical matter.

### The concept of power

Power is a commonplace analytical device for political scientists, political activists, and ordinary citizens. It is as ancient as Aristotle and as current as Black Power and student power. It is as ambiguous as it is ubiquitous, as elusive as it is useful. There is much controversy over the definition of power, but most contemporary efforts are based on that of the German sociologist Max Weber, who wrote in 1922, " 'Power' is the probability that one actor within a social relationship will be in a position to carry out his own will despite resistance, regardless of the basis on which this probability rests."[2]

One of the most penetrating students of power in American communities, Dahl, has relied upon Weber's formulation: "My intuitive idea of power, then, is something like this: A has power over B to the extent that he can get B to do *something that B would not otherwise do.*"[3] More recently, Dahl has argued:

*At the most general level, power terms in modern social science refer to* subsets of relations among social units such that the behaviors of one or

[1] C. Wright Mills, *The Power Elite* (New York, Oxford University Press, 1956).

[2] Max Weber, *The Theory of Social and Economic Organization,* ed. by T. Parsons (New York, Free Press, 1957), p. 152.

[3] Robert A. Dahl, "The Concept of Power," *Behavioral Science, 2* (July, 1957), 202.

more units *(the responsive units, R)* depend in some circumstances on the behavior of other units *(the controlling units, C)*.[4]

According to this formulation, power can be a micro (individual) property or a macro (community) property. It is both a capacity of the individual to alter his environment and a capacity of the community itself to manipulate the economic, social, and cultural spheres in which the individual operates.

### Anticipated reactions and nondecisions

There are a number of problems in the analysis of political power. Power cannot be directly observed but can only be inferred from behavior or from reports. The problem of *anticipated reactions* means, however, that B will take account of A's possible reactions, even if A makes no visible effort to apply power, force, or influence. B may respond even when A does not communicate his preferences verbally. In their appointment of Supreme Court justices, for example, Presidents anticipate the reactions of the Senate. In voting municipal budgets, the city council and the manager anticipate the reactions of taxpayers, interest groups, and service personnel.

The problem of *nondecision* reflects the social context of power and directs attention away from A's overt attempt to influence B's behavior. Nondecision occurs when decision-makers choose not to embark upon a program that might offend an important group of the community's residents. These and other problems do not render power a worthless concept, but they suggest that essentially superficial observations like "Smith (or Mayor Daley or Senator So-and-so) has a lot of power" may be so oversimplified as to be misleading.

It is helpful to conceive of power as a relation persisting through time and depending upon the situation. Because power relations do persist through time, A and B usually coexist in a reciprocal relation. A manager depends upon his council to fund the programs he proposes to undertake, but the council depends upon the manager for policy recommendations. Because the power relationship ·persists, the wise strategist will not exhaust all his resources in a single attempt at influence. Although, for analytic purposes, we may be interested in a single decision and a successful application of power by A, it is probable that the specific outcome has been affected by a series of previous interactions between A and B and has implications for future attempts by each to obtain favorable decisions from the other.

4 Robert A. Dahl, "Power," in David Sills, ed., *International Encyclopedia of the Social Sciences*, vol. 12 (New York, Macmillan, 1968), pp. 405–413 (emphasis in the original).

Just as it is difficult to wrench decisions out of the time dimension, so too is it difficult to ignore the situational elements in a power relationship. A few salient situational factors that may influence the success of an attempt by A to influence B include:

1   B's legal, contractual, or political authority to make an agreement with A;
2   the probability that C, D, and E might be activated in a manner unacceptable to A, B, or both;
3   the accuracy with which B perceives the outcome that A seeks;
4   the availability of resources to A and B;
5   the power of other actors over both A and B.

These considerations suggest that the analysis of any single attempt at exercising power is complex and that examination of the myriad influence patterns in an urban system is a staggering enterprise. That is why the proposition "A has a lot of power" is much less useful than is the proposition "A has power over B with respect to Y, under conditions p, q, and r."[5]

## Community power structure

A community power structure may be defined as the power relations among political actors in the community persisting through time. Note that this definition pertains to the community as a whole and not only to the public or political sector. The most important single finding of the research on community power is that power does not reside in the government sector alone. To restrict our definition to government officeholders would be to make an assumption about the power structure that might or might not be accurate.

The initial problem faced by students of community power has been to "operationalize" the concept of power in order to render it amenable to measurement and investigation. Though most researchers have developed their own measures, the major approaches to identification of power holders fall into three types: positional, reputational, and decisional.[6]

THE POSITIONAL APPROACH     The oldest and simplest method of studying community leadership is through the positional approach. Although it

[5] A similar paradigm is suggested by Robert A. Dahl in *Modern Political Analysis* (Englewood Cliffs, N.J., Prentice-Hall, 1963), p. 47.

[6] An excellent overview of these three approaches is found in Charles M. Bonjean and David M. Olson, "Community Leadership: Directions of Research," *Administrative Science Quarterly, 8* (December, 1964), 291–300. This article is reprinted, along with other studies of community power, in Willis D. Hawley and Frederick M. Wirt, eds., *The Search for Community Power* (Englewood Cliffs, N.J., Prentice-Hall, 1968).

has been replaced by more sophisticated techniques in the social sciences, it is still used widely by laymen and journalists. It assumes that leaders perform specified government and organizational roles. When, for example, Samuel Stouffer wanted to know whether community leaders or the public were more tolerant of minority rights, he drew up a list of formal roles, including the mayor, the chairman of the local Parent-Teacher Association, party leaders, the school- and library-board presidents, the newspaper publishers, and others. Each occupant of the designated position was interviewed, on the assumption that he was, in fact, a community leader.[7] Other studies have assumed that occupants of such positions as mayor, councilman, newspaper editor, banker, chamber-of-commerce president, League of Women Voters officer, school-board member, superintendent, and labor-union leader are community leaders.

The positional approach has several advantages: It is simple and economical to apply and it does not presume any particular knowledge about the social and economic structure of the community being investigated. Moreover, it rests upon the probability that holders of governmental and organizational positions will actually exercise influence, which, though not totally justified, is not altogether unrealistic.

The major difficulty with the approach is that it may be both too inclusive and too exclusive. Without independent verification, one never knows whether or not he has included leaders who are merely titular or excluded some who may exercise considerable power. A particular set of positions may encompass the "real" leaders in one community but not in another. The positional approach also assumes that all office holders are approximately equally powerful on every issue. A likelier possibility is that government officeholders may be most influential on some issues (for example, on how much money to spend on road construction) and that nongovernment leaders may dominate on other issues (for example, minority employment opportunities). The positional approach is thus a rough-and-ready technique, useful for some purposes but doubtful as a means of identifying the "real" power holders in a community.

THE REPUTATIONAL APPROACH    The reputational method of identifying community leaders has several labels: the "sociometric approach" (after its technique), the "sociological approach" (after its major academic proponents), and the "elitist," or "power elite," approach (after its major findings).

The earliest and still the most significant reputational study of

7 Samuel A. Stouffer, *Communism, Conformity, and Civil Liberties* (Garden City, N.Y., Doubleday, 1955), pp. 15–19.

**Table 5.1**  *Occupational characteristics of top leaders in Atlanta, Georgia*

| Occupation | Number of leaders | Positions held |
|---|---|---|
| Banking, finance, insurance | 7 | President, executive vice-president, etc. |
| Commercial | 11 | Board chairman, president, editor, etc. |
| Government | 4 | Mayor, superintendents of city and county schools, county treasurer |
| Labor | 2 | Local union presidents |
| Leisure | 5 | Social leaders |
| Manufacturing, industry | 5 | Board chairmen, presidents |
| Professional | 6 | Attorneys, dentist |
| Total | 40 | |

SOURCE: Adapted from Floyd Hunter, *Community Power Structure* (Chapel Hill, University of North Carolina Press, 1953), Table 4.

community power structure is Floyd Hunter's study of Atlanta.[8] Hunter's method, which inspired countless "reputationalists," involved using a panel of informants to identify the most influential men in the community that he studied. The informants might be either a random sample of the population or a specific panel believed to be particularly informed about local decision-making (as newspaper editors or chamber-of-commerce officials would be). By culling newspapers accounts of community decision-making and organizational rosters and minutes, Hunter arrived at a list of 175 possible leaders and then submitted this list to a panel of informants. These informants were told to pare down the list, and forty people were finally identified as the community "influentials" of Atlanta. Once the list of forty had been compiled, Hunter interviewed as many of its members as possible in an effort to identify the "top leaders." The principal question he asked each person on his list was "If a project were before the community that required *decision* by a group of leaders—leaders that nearly everyone would accept—which ten on this list of forty would you choose?" Twelve men were identified consistently enough by the forty "reputational leaders" to convince Hunter that they constituted the top leaders in the community power structure.

The key leaders in the power structure of Atlanta were men from the private rather than the public sector. Table 5.1 shows the occupational composition of this leadership group. Only four of the forty

[8] Floyd Hunter, *Community Power Structure* (Chapel Hill, University of North Carolina Press, 1953).

on the original list had roles in the public sector. Most held positions in commerce, banking, manufacturing, and the professions. Not only were the political officeholders a small proportion of the total leadership, but also, Hunter argued, they were mainly second-level leaders, whose major responsibility was execution of decisions made by economic "dominants." The political and governmental realm was thus secondary to the economic one. In Atlanta, according to Hunter,

*the dominant factor in political life is the personnel of economic interests. It is true that there is no formal tie between the economic interests and the government, but the structure of policy-determining committees and their tie-in with the other powerful institutions and organizations of the community make government subservient to the interests of these combined groups. The government departments and their personnel are acutely aware of the power of key individuals and combinations of citizens' groups in the policy-making realm, and they are loath to act before consulting and "clearing" with these interests.*[9]

The picture of community power painted by Hunter and other "reputationalists" is one in which realities of power are at variance with the democratic theory of political accountability. Instead of decision-making by elected officeholders, power is wielded by economic "dominants" who are relatively invisible to the public and are not subject to electoral control. Rather than a wide distribution of political power among the citizens, power is held by a relatively small upper class.

The reliability of such conclusions depends upon the validity of the reputational method. Its defenders argue that it is relatively efficient and economical to use. The decision method, in contrast, may involve years of observation.[10] Moreover, the reputational approach depends upon study by presumably informed observers of the local decision-making process. Nonetheless, critics of the reputational approach have leveled serious charges against it.

Perhaps the most serious charge is that the approach predetermines its findings by incorporating the a priori assumption of a single power elite. To ask "Who are the top leaders here?" is to assume that some particular group holds top leadership positions. Critics believe that it is no coincidence that the method usually identifies a single cohesive set of leaders. They claim that the existence of a single elite

[9] *Ibid.*, pp. 100–101.

[10] Raymond Wolfinger, in his critique of the reputational approach, has argued that this "advantage" of the reputational over the decisional approach is comparable to that of a TV dinner over a home-cooked one—it does not taste very good, but it is quick to fix. See Raymond Wolfinger, "A Plea for a Decent Burial," *American Sociological Review*, 27 (December, 1962), 841–847.

is an empirical question that must itself be tested, rather than incorporated into the methodology of a study.

Second, ignoring the possibility that power may vary from one policy domain to another, the reputational approach falsely assumes that the power structure identified controls all major issues. Actually, leadership may be specialized, and one group may be influential in one policy area and other groups in other areas.

Third, the reputational approach measures not power per se but rather the reputation for power. Some case studies of decision-making have shown that economic "dominants" are widely perceived as powerful but are not active participants in the decision-making process.[11]

Fourth, there is an inevitable arbitrariness in any particular cutoff point in defining the limits of the "power structure." Why, for example, should Hunter have selected just forty leaders? Why not draw the line at 400 or 4,000 members of the community power structure?

Fifth, the method is primarily subjective, rather than behavioral and empirical. It rests upon the assumption that what informants observe and report accurately reflects what occurs.

THE DECISIONAL APPROACH    The decisional approach has been stimulated by the work of Dahl and his associates at Yale University.[12] It is also called the "event analysis," or "decision-making" approach (after its method), the "political science" approach (after its academic proponents), and "the pluralist alternative" (after its usual findings).

The decisional approach begins with the selection of certain "key issues" in the community and then identifies the people who seem significant in affecting their outcomes. Current decisions may be selected by the researcher from meetings, newspaper accounts, and interviews of participants. Past decisions may be reconstructed through similar procedures and from the minutes of past meetings.

Dahl identified three basic issues in New Haven during the period of his study: school decisions, an urban-renewal decision, and political nominations. His principal conclusions about power in New Haven are, first, that a leader in one issue area was not likely to be influential in another and that, if he was, he was probably a public official and most likely the mayor; and, second, that leaders in different issue areas did not seem to be drawn from a single homogeneous stratum of the community.[13] No identifiable, cohesive elite dominated by economic

11 See, for example, Edward C. Banfield, *Political Influence* (New York, Free Press, 1961).

12 See especially, Robert A. Dahl, *Who Governs?* (New Haven, Yale University Press, 1961); and Nelson Polsby, *Community Power and Political Theory* (New Haven, Yale University Press, 1963).

13 Dahl, *Who Governs?*, p. 183.

and social notables appeared in Dahl's study of New Haven. The power structure included multiple centers. Different sets of decision-makers operated in each arena, and the arenas were bridged only by the mayor. In New Haven, Dahl concluded, economic and social notables had "relatively little direct influence on government decisions."[14] As public officials tended to be the major power brokers, it followed that there was a high degree of mass control over decision-makers. Such political accountability is unlikely when decision-making is controlled by an elite in the private sector.

Dahl's study of New Haven presented a more benign picture of power in an American community than did Hunter's study of Atlanta. But the "reputationalists" have responded with both methodological and substantive criticisms of the decisional approach and its findings. They have claimed that, despite Dahl's criticism of Hunter, the decisional approach still relies upon "reputational" methods: People are asked for reports of their own and others' behavior with regard to particular decisions, the reports of journalists are used, and the reconstruction of past decisions may reflect severe distortions of memory and perception.

Second, the approach rests upon an arbitrary choice of issues. That Dahl identified three major issue areas in New Haven, whereas other "decisionalists" have identified dozens, suggests that standards for a key issue are not well defined. Just as one limitation of the reputational approach involves the initial selection of informants, a critical weakness of the decisional approach involves somewhat arbitrary selection of issues.

Third, by emphasizing the key, or controversial, decisions, the approach ignores the cumulative significance of routine decisions. If the best teachers are continually assigned to schools serving upper-income neighborhoods, lower-income children will study under the worst teachers—a routine decision with potentially significant consequences.

Fourth, the approach ignores leadership ideologies. If there is no ideological divergence among the power structure, it makes little practical difference whether all the leaders participate in every decision or whether there is a "division of labor" among the elite. Accountability to the public depends upon a choice of leaders, and there is no meaningful choice when all leaders share similar ideological perspectives.[15]

Fifth, the decisional approach assumes, rather than demonstrates,

<hr />

14 *Ibid.*, p. 233.

15 See Robert Agger, Daniel Goldrich, and Bert E. Swanson, *The Rulers and the Ruled* (New York, Wiley, 1964), pp. 76–77.

that elections control the nature of public policy. In an earlier statement, Dahl himself argued that elections are severely limited as devices for the registering of public opinion.[16] Our discussion of local elections (pp. 53–63, 86–92) also suggests that they are quite imperfect instruments for insuring political accountability.

### General problems in analysis of power structure

Some additional problems plague both reputational and decisional studies of community power: the *self-fulfilling prophecy,* the *limitations of the case study,* an *absence of longitudinal analysis,* the problem of the *"two faces of power,"* and inattention to *constraints upon power structures.*

Some recent evidence suggests that both the reputational and decisional approaches imply self-fulfilling prophecies. John Walton reviewed analyses of the power structures of fifty-one communities and found that political scientists used the decisional approach just as consistently as their sociological cousins used the reputational approach. The difficulty, however, is that the type of power structure identified, whether pluralist or elitist, was highly correlated with the choice of method. He concluded that "the disciplinary background of the investigator tends to determine the method of investigation he will adopt, which, in turn, tends to determine the image of the power structure that results from the investigation."[17]

The problem of the self-fulfilling prophecy is compounded by the limitations of the case study. It is not clear whether Atlanta, New Haven, or any single city is typical of most American cities. One recent study with a sample of sixty-three American cities concluded that New Haven was an extreme case of decentralized decision-making.[18] There are two ways to cope with the limitations of case studies. The first is to analyze them as sources of data in their own right. Claire Gilbert examined 166 case studies of community power and concluded that "there is very strong evidence that political processes are tending to be more pluralistic" over time.[19] The other solution is to study several communities utilizing a single research design.

[16] Robert A. Dahl, *A Preface to Democratic Theory* (Chicago, University of Chicago Press, 1956), pp. 124–132.

[17] John Walton, "Discipline, Method, and Community Power: A Note on the Sociology of Knowledge," *American Sociological Review, 31* (October, 1966), 688.

[18] Robert L. Crain *et al.,* "The Influence of Reputational, Positional, and Decisional Elites in Northern Cities" (paper presented at the Annual Meeting of the American Sociological Association, Montreal, September, 1969).

[19] Claire Gilbert, "Trends in Community Politics," *Social Science Quarterly, 48* (December, 1967), 378.

Agger, Goldrich, and Swanson studied four communities, two in North Carolina and two in Oregon.[20] The Permanent Community Sample of the National Opinion Research Center has been used to study power structure and decision-making in a large number of cities.[21]

Studies done at a single point in time also suffer from limitations analogous to those of a snapshot. If a power structure is cohesive and truly coercive and entrenched, it should be relatively stable. But without longitudinal analysis we do not know whether the power structure changes from year to year or persists over longer periods of time. The limited evidence from Agger, Goldrich, and Swanson's analysis of four communities over a fifteen-year period suggests that communities may have different power patterns in the space of a single decade.[22] And, until more longitudinal analyses are available, it will be impossible to identify the factors that change the distribution of power.

The problem of the "two faces of power" was first identified by Peter Bachrach and Morton Baratz. They argued that "there are two faces of power, neither of which the sociologists [reputationalists] see and only one of which the political scientists [decisionalists] see."[23] They agree with the "decisionalists" that the reputational approach suffers the fatal defect of confusing potential with actual power. But, they insist, there are serious objections to the "decisionalists" own methodology, because the latter approach "takes no account of the fact that power may be, and often is, exercised by confining the scope of decision-making to relatively 'safe' issues."[24] Those who establish the public agenda may exercise the most important power through their capacity to prevent issues from entering the political system. What the "decisionalists" call "key issues" may actually be minor matters that do not threaten the basic distribution of values in the community. The existence of the private-property system, the legitimacy of wealth, and the validity of the social-incentive system are matters so fundamental that they are missed by the student of the controversial issues facing the city council. Had the decisional approach been used to study community power in a southern town in the 1940s, for example, it might have been discovered that the "key"

20 Agger, Goldrich, and Swanson, op. cit.

21 See Crain et al., op. cit.; and Terry N. Clark, "Community Structure, Decision-Making, Budget Expenditures, and Urban Renewal in 51 American Communities," American Sociological Review, 33 (August, 1968), 576–594.

22 Agger, Goldrich, and Swanson, op. cit., pp. 648ff.

23 Peter Bachrach and Morton Baratz, Power and Poverty (New York, Oxford University Press, 1970), p. 4.

24 Ibid., p. 6.

decisions involved fluoridation, the location of a new high school, and the dismissal of the city manager. The latent yet potentially explosive "issue" of the distribution of values between the races would have been ignored because it was so tightly entwined in the status quo that it was not an issue at all and did not become one until some years later. In sum, the decisional approach ignores the

*values and biases that are built into the political system . . . and the dominant values and the political myths, rituals, and institutions which tend to favor the vested interests of one or more groups, relative to others.*[25]

An examination of the "other" face of power requires a determination of the economic, social, and ideological underpinnings of the status quo.

There are both macro and micro aspects of power relations that add complexity to understanding them. That power is to be located in institutions, as well as in individuals, suggests constraints upon even the most powerful structures. In his analysis of the presidential decision-making process, Theodore Sorensen has emphasized that American Presidents—powerful as they are—are constrained by permissibility, the implications of previous commitments, and the availability of time, resources, and information.[26] If powerful American Presidents are constrained by factors in their environment, then we might expect to find that even monolithic community power structures are limited in their capacities. Urban power structures are no doubt constrained by the same sets of factors that limit all decision-makers, ranging from imperfect information to inadequate resources and including constraints imposed by state and national systems.

### Antecedents and consequences of variations in power structure

ANTECEDENTS    Are certain kinds of communities more likely than others to have monolithic power structures? Does the structure of community power make any difference in the kinds of public policies pursued by local government? These questions have received considerably less attention than have questions of the shape or structure of power and the mere identification of power holders. Nor is either of them easily answered. In some obvious respects, however, there are remarkable similarities between Atlanta and New Haven. Both have recently been governed by mayors nationally regarded as progressive (Ivan Allen and Richard Lee respectively). Both are large central cities

---

[25] *Ibid.*, p. 11.

[26] Theodore Sorensen, *Decision-Making in the White House* (New York, Columbia University Press, 1963), pp. 22–42.

**Figure 5.1**  *Four dimensions of power structure*

| "Pluralist" Structure | DIMENSION | "Monolithic" Structure |
|---|---|---|
| Leaders hold public or associational office | LEGITIMACY ←——→ | Leaders do not hold public or associational office |
| Leaders are recognized by general public | VISIBILITY ←——→ | Leaders are unknown to general public |
| Leaders do not form a cohesive, interacting group | COHESIVENESS ←——→ | Leaders form a cohesive, interacting group |
| Leaders are specialized and exercise power in one or a few policy areas | SCOPE OF INFLUENCE ←——→ | Leaders are general and exercise power in most or all policy areas |

SOURCE: Adapted from Charles M. Bonjean and David M. Olson, "Community Leadership: Directions of Research," *Administrative Science Quarterly, 8* (December, 1964), 291–300

where parks are built, police patrol neighborhoods, fires are fought, and hospitals and public utilities are maintained. Although neither city is usually singled out as an extreme case of discrimination, racial disorders have occurred in both. What are the antecedents and consequences of variations in community power structures, and can they be identified?

This question can be answered more directly if we classify power structures on a continuum ranging from monolithic to pluralistic, as indicated in Figure 5.1. Although several classification schemes have been suggested,[27] the one adapted from Charles M. Bonjean and David M. Olson's analysis of power structures captures the major disagreements among the researchers; it uses the dimensions of *legitimacy, visibility, scope of influence,* and *cohesion*.[28] The two models of pluralistic and monolithic power structures represent extreme points on a continuum. It is doubtful that any existing power structure is completely monolithic or pluralistic. Given the classification scheme, the question then becomes, what variables are associated with power structures that tend toward one or the other extreme? Several antecedents of power structures may be suggested in the form of propositions.[29]

[27] The most extensive and potentially useful ones are found in Agger, Goldrich, and Swanson, *op. cit.*, pp. 73–93.

[28] Bonjean and Olson, *op. cit.*

[29] For a more extensive listing of propositions derived from the literature on community power structure, see Terry N. Clark, "Power and Community Structure: Who Governs, Where, and When?" *The Sociological Quarterly, 8* (Summer, 1967), 291–316.

These propositions are only tentative generalizations rather than absolute laws of social structure. Each community possesses certain features that make it unique and imperfectly comparable to other communities. What is really important may be not the presence of particular factors but their combination and interaction in a particular setting. Moreover, these generalizations are derived from a wide assortment of studies that differ among themselves on the most appropriate methodology for studying community power. The propositions, therefore, are better viewed as tools for analysis than as iron laws of power distribution in the city.

*1*   The larger the number of inhabitants in a community, the more pluralistic is the power structure.

The evidence from case studies is mixed. However, Terry N. Clark's analysis of decision-making structures in fifty-one cities has revealed a moderate relationship $(r = .384)$ between community size and a measure of pluralistic decision-making structures.[30] The smaller the community, the greater is the probability of dominance by a monolithic structure. One study of a tiny upstate New York village has identified a small clique of "influentials" who controlled the village government.[31] On the other hand, the relationship between size and type of power structure is not perfect. Reputational studies of Atlanta and Dallas have concluded that monolithic power structures dominate those communities.[32] Size per se may be less important that certain structural characteristics associated with size. Large cities are ordinarily more socially and economically heterogeneous. It may be this heterogeneity, rather than size alone, that is associated with pluralistic power structures. We can frame this argument in terms of a proposition.

*2*   The more diversified the economic system within a community, the more pluralistic is the power structure.

The evidence for proposition 2 ranges from a slight tendency to strong support.[33] The logic of the proposition suggests that multiple economic centers in the private sector produce alternative resource bases for competition in community decision-making. One particular feature

[30] Clark, "Community Structure, Decision-Making, Budget Expenditures, and Urban Renewal," p. 585.

[31] Arthur Vidich and Joseph Bensman, *Small Town in Mass Society* (Princeton, N.J., Princeton University Press, 1958).

[32] For Atlanta, see Hunter, *op. cit.;* for Dallas, see Carol E. Thometz, *The Decision-Makers* (Dallas, Southern Methodist University Press, 1963).

[33] John Walton, "Substance and Artifact: The Current Status of Research on Community Power Structure," *American Journal of Sociology, 71* (January, 1966), 684–699; Clark, "Community Structure, Decision-Making, Budget Expenditures, and Urban Renewal," p. 586.

of the economic structure that seems relevant to the structure of power
is the degree of industrialization.

3    The more industrialized the community, the more pluralistic is the power
     structure.

Almost by definition, industrialization will broaden the economic
base of a community beyond commercial and service-oriented enterprises and will introduce another potential center of power in the economic system. Moreover, industrialization is usually (at least outside the
South) associated with labor unions, which offer an additional source of
power in community decision-making.[34] The implication can also be
framed as a proposition.

4    The stronger labor unions are in a community, the more pluralistic is
     the power structure.

One other proposition relates community power distribution to the
economic system.

5    The larger the proportion of absentee-owned enterprises in a community,
     the more pluralistic is the power structure.

Perhaps the most monolithic power structure ever identified was that
in "Middletown," where a single local family owned the major source
of livelihood for the town's entire population and dominated nearly
all facets of community life.[35] In cities dominated by absentee ownership, the executives of such nonlocal firms tend to have lower stakes in
community activities and to play less active roles.

Social heterogeneity parallels economic differentiation in its association with more pluralistic forms of power.

6    The more socially heterogeneous the community, the more pluralistic is
     the power structure.

However, a community where elites do not value political equality
and mass participation is unlikely to fit proposition 6. A community
dominated by racists is not a likely candidate for social pluralism. So:

7    Pluralism is promoted by community and, particularly, elite attitudes
     emphasizing widespread participation and political equality.

A well-developed network of secondary associations—civic groups,

34 Note, however, that, as we argued in Chapter 3, labor unions are typically
much less active in local politics than in state and national politics.
35 Robert S. Lynd and Helen M. Lynd, *Middletown in Transition* (New York,
Harcourt Brace Jovanovich, Inc., 1937). Middletown is a pseudonym for Muncie,
Indiana.

social clubs, ethnic and religious organizations, political action groups, and so on—provides multiple channels for expression of opinion, as well as an organizational basis for alternative leadership structures.[36] Another proposition therefore follows.

8    The larger the number of secondary associations in the community, the greater is the probability of pluralism.

There has been too little research on the relation between government structure and power structure to permit confidence in any generalization. Nonetheless, several writers suggest that government reformism, particularly nonpartisanship, is associated with monolithic power structures.

9a    Nonpartisanship is more commonly associated with monolithic structures of power.
9b    Competitive party politics is more commonly associated with pluralistic structures of power.

John Walton found a strong relationship between competition among local parties and pluralism in community power.[37] Clark's study of fifty-one communities went even farther in relating reformism to monolithic structures.[38]

10    The higher the level of reformism of political institutions (form of government, type of elections, and type of constituencies), the more monolithic is the decision-making structure.

The degree of governmental reform was the strongest predictor of power structure in Clark's fifty-one cities. Certain features of the reformist syndrome seem to produce less pluralism in community decision-making. Among them may be the elimination of competition among parties through the nonpartisan ballot, the "depoliticization" of the mayor's office, and the reduction in working-class voting turnout associated with reformed institutions.

A significant consequence of community power structure is its impact upon citizen participation, as several studies have indicated.

11    Competition among different elements of the power structure is a necessary condition for widespread citizen participation.

[36] The importance of secondary associations is emphasized by Agger, Goldrich, and Swanson, *op. cit.*, especially pp. 272ff.

[37] John Walton, "Vertical Axis of Community Organization and the Structure of Power," *Social Science Quarterly,* 48 (December, 1967), 355–357.

[38] Clark, "Community Structure, Decision-Making, Budget Expenditures, and Urban Renewal," p. 586.

Agger, Goldrich, and Swanson concluded that "a competitive political leadership is necessary . . . for the existence of a power structure
of the mass type."[39] If the cohesion dimension of leadership changes
from competitive to consensual, the distribution of political power in
the community will thus change from relatively broad to relatively
narrow. This finding is consistent with much writing by democratic
theorists who stress competition among elites as the sine qua non of
democratic government.[40]

CONSEQUENCES    Although the power structure seems to be strongly and
clearly related to variations in citizen participation, its relation to the
level or distribution of urban public policies is not well established.
In discussing the consequences of power structure, Bonjean and Olson
deplored the fact that "even fewer studies have been concerned with
consequences of leadership structure characteristics than with antecedents."[41] This neglect is particularly unfortunate if, as we believe,
the central task of urban political analysis is the understanding of
policy outcomes.[42]

Perhaps power structures do not make much difference in the outputs of community political systems. Many decisions by local governments are automatic responses to the requirements of state and federal
statutes and prior financial commitments. Regardless of the concentration or dispersion of power, local governments are constrained by
Dillon's rule, by tax rates and municipal indebtedness, and by the laws
and administrative rulings of states and the federal government. Yet
several hypotheses suggest variations in the effects of power structure
on policies. Cities with monolithic power structures may furnish fewer
public services to poor neighborhoods (unless, of course, the power
structure is "public-regarding"), may emphasize economic-development
over social-welfare policies, and may tax and spend at lower than average levels. But, until we have more data, we cannot demonstrate that
policy choices in monolithic cities are notably different from those in
pluralistic cities.

We move now from discussion of informal decision-making struc-

[39] Agger, Goldrich, and Swanson, op. cit., pp. 662ff.

[40] Joseph A. Schumpeter, Capitalism, Socialism, and Democracy (New York,
Harper & Row, 1947), pp. 232ff; and Seymour M. Lipset, Political Man (Garden City,
N.Y., Doubleday, 1960), chap. 2.

[41] Bonjean and Olson, op. cit., p. 299.

[42] For examples of research that attempts to link the structure of community
power with public policies, see Clark, "Community Structure, Decision-Making,
Budget Expenditures, and Urban Renewal"; Agger, Goldrich, and Swanson, op. cit.;
and Amos Hawley, "Community Power and Urban Renewal Success," American
Journal of Sociology, 68 (January, 1963), 422–432.

tures—community power structures—to discussion of formal decision-makers, councils, mayors, managers, and bureaucrats. Regardless of whether a city contains a sub rosa power elite, the formal decision-makers must at least execute decisions made elsewhere. In all cities the formal decision-makers manage the routine decisions. And, in the final analysis, these routine choices—involving as they do spending and taxing, zoning, distribution of services, and the like—may have as much impact as do the allegedly "big decisions" made in a behind-the-scenes "power structure." In the previous chapter we discussed the government structures of urban areas. We shall now deal with the roles, resources, and behavior of occupants of formal decision-making positions.

## FORMAL DECISION-MAKERS: THE COUNCIL

### The councilman

It is difficult to describe a "typical" councilman. Councilmen come from varying income, educational, occupational, and ethnic backgrounds; have different views about municipal government; and, depending upon the particular states and municipalities in which they hold office, exercise different powers and responsibilities. Yet we can gain perspective on the city councilman by positing some characteristics of a "typical" councilman and then suggesting factors responsible for deviations from those characteristics. Typically, a councilman is male, middle-aged, a businessman or professional, relatively well educated and well-to-do, white, active in civic associations, and Republican. A study of councilmen in St. Louis County revealed that 70 percent of the councilmen were at least high-school graduates and that 53 percent had completed college. About half were from managerial, professional, or proprietary occupations, and another 22 percent were from white-collar occupations.

What kinds of community characteristics account for deviations from this typical pattern? Two macro variables, the "social rank" or class composition of the community itself and its electoral institutions, seem particularly significant. Two separate studies, one in the St. Louis area and one in the Philadelphia metropolitan region, have suggested that councilmen tend to reflect—even to exaggerate—the class characteristics of their communities.[43] In communities with well-educated and well-to-do populations, councilmen came from very high-status back-

[43] Bryan T. Downes, "Municipal Social Rank and the Characteristics of Local Political Leaders," *Midwest Journal of Political Science, 12* (November, 1968), 514–537.

grounds; in predominantly working-class communities, councilmen come from working-class occupations.[44]

The use of ward or at-large elections also affects the composition of the council. Ward systems tend to increase the representation of lower socioeconomic groups and minorities. Sloan found that cities using ward systems elected larger proportions of councilmen from minority groups than did cities using at-large elections.[45] The at-large system increases the costs of elections and forces all contenders to run before a constituency of the whole. Minority-group candidates in many cities thus face a white Protestant majority. Even when minority-group candidates are successful, under the at-large system they are usually the more moderate ones.

Factors other than these class and election procedures influence the types of people chosen for the council. Some of these factors are specific to a particular city or even to a particular campaign. But among the more general ones are (1) the degree to which labor unions and ethnic and racial groups are organized and involved in local politics, (2) whether or not the city pays councilmen enough to sustain working-class representation on the council, (3) whether or not the party system facilitates representation of various social groups, and (4) whether or not a covert power structure recruits or prevents recruitment of certain kinds of candidates.

### Roles and resources

RESPONSIBILITIES    *The New York Times Magazine* once entitled a story about a New York councilman "Man in a Wind Tunnel."[46] Its focus was the multiple pressures constantly buffeting an officeholder in the nation's largest city. In smaller and less heterogeneous communities these pressures are less intense. A better analogy is perhaps life in a partial vacuum. Whatever the appropriate model, the council and its members are legally responsible for making all ordinances pursuant to state law and the municipal charter. Yet this statement leaves much unsaid, just as a description of the U.S. Congress solely in terms of its constitutional responsibilities would be incomplete or even misleading.

In the broadest sense, the city council "makes policy" for the city; that is, it chooses among alternative courses for taxing people, spending money, and the like. In a narrower sense, the formal powers of the

44 *Ibid.;* Oliver Williams *et al., Suburban Differences and Metropolitan Policies* (Philadelphia, University of Pennsylvania Press, 1965), p. 228.

45 Lee Sloan, "Good Government and the Politics of Race," *Social Problems, 17* (Fall, 1969), 161–175.

46 M. Arnold, "John Santucci Is a Man in a Wind Tunnel," *The New York Times Magazine,* April 16, 1967, pp. 56–70.

council vary a good deal from one to another form of government. The council operating in the council-manager city is supposed to make policy but to leave questions dealing with administration to the city manager and his administrative agencies.

The council-manager plan enshrines the alleged dichotomy between policy and administration. In the strong mayor-council form of government, the initiative for policy is still more likely to come from the mayor than from the council, although the latter is not confined so narrowly as in the council-manager city. The scope of the council's power is probably greatest in the weak-mayor system. Here the mayor shares his power with other elected officials, and the council itself sometimes appoints officials, prepares the budget, or performs tasks that are considered administrative in other forms of government. A commission government fuses legislative and administrative authority in the council; each councilman is also the administrator of some particular branch or department of the city government. Commissioners are prone to mind their own bailiwicks and to let others do the same, which promotes mutual noninterference at the council level.

As do all legislative bodies, the municipal council performs an important representative function. Yet different councilmen will have different views about the proper role of the representative, and the formal structures of municipal government foster particular styles of representation. In the ward system, "representation" is likely to mean a narrow "bricks and mortar" orientation: ward councilmen tend to look after their constituencies' desires for paved streets, parks, school facilities, and other tangible outputs of municipal government. In one Michigan city using the ward system, one councilman shouted to another at a meeting, "You bastard, you had three more blocks of black-topping in your ward last year than I had, you'll not get another vote from me until I get three extra blocks."[47] One New York City councilman, explaining his approach to the city budget, said:

> . . . the first thing I look for is the budget items involving my district. Are we getting what we're entitled to? Are we being shortchanged on a library or not getting a school we were promised? . . . It's only after I've done all I can for my own area that I look into the rest of the budget.[48]

In the constituency at large, a councilman's political future depends less upon material gains for a small area. A councilman at large can afford to align himself with broad social, economic, or political interests, rather than binding himself to geographical interests.

[47] Oliver Williams and Charles Adrian, *Four Cities* (Philadelphia, University of Pennsylvania Press, 1963), p. 264.

[48] Arnold, *op. cit.*, p. 62.

ROLES   The ways in which a municipal councilman attempts to represent his constituency depend upon his representational role. Political theorists debate the extent to which a representative should be either a trustee or a delegate. The trustee role emphasizes the representative's obligation to vote according to his conscience and best judgment, regardless of whether or not his vote happens to follow his constituents' preferences. The delegate role obligates the representative to vote according to his perception of his constituents' sentiments, regardless of his own views.

Studies of city councilmen suggest overwhelming support for the trustee orientation toward representation.[49] Almost three-quarters of St. Louis area councilmen said that they made decisions on the basis of their own judgment or principles. Councilmen seem to prefer their own to their constituents' thinking on matters of public policy, and Downes has hypothesized that this attitude may reflect councilmen's own belief that "they act as councilmen in their spare time and receive little or no monetary compensation." Therefore they can "ignore the blandishments of neighborhood, ward, or other specialized interests."[50] It may also reflect the very imperfect information on public preferences that councilmen receive. When input institutions like elections, parties, and interest groups provide vague or conflicting intimations of "public opinion," the councilman may find it easier to use his own judgment as a guide to policy.

Partly because most councilmen have trustee orientations, they are relatively free to ignore the sentiments of their constituents. But Kenneth Prewitt finds that councilmen also share an ethic of "volunteerism," which further immunizes them from the necesstiy of responding to constituent attitudes.[51] It is easy for a councilman whose political ambitions are negligible to vote his own policy preferences and to ignore his constituents' wishes. When asked if it was easy or difficult to go against majority preferences in policy-making, one councilman said: "Easy, I am an independent type of individual. I don't feel the weight of voter responsibility. I am not all fired up for a political career." Such councilmen do not fear the ballot, which makes electoral accountability and reprisals difficult. Although "volunteerism" may be more widespread in suburban, middle-class areas than in big-city politics, its prevalence does not make it easier for the electorate to control local government.

[49] Downes, *op. cit.*, p. 528.
[50] *Ibid.*
[51] Kenneth Prewitt, "Political Ambitions, Volunteerism, and Electoral Accountability," *American Political Science Review, 64* (March, 1970), 5–17.

RESOURCES   The city councilman's major political resource is his legal authority to make policy. Whatever influence other elements of the city's political system may have, it is still the legal responsibility of the council to pass ordinances (consistent, of course, with the city's own charter and the laws of the state), to enact the city budget, to hire and fire the manager in a council-manager city, and so forth. Councilmen may also possess as individuals great political skill, some prestige, and experience in the procedures of decision-making. But most councilmen are limited in their resources of time and information, particularly technical information. Serving as a city councilman is a full-time job only in the largest cities. Elsewhere the councilman must divide his time between his private occupation and his public service. Staff assistance is minimal or nonexistent on almost all city councils. What is more, councilmen face increasingly complex and technical policy questions with only their own wits and political wisdom to guide them.

## FORMAL DECISION-MAKERS: THE MAYOR

The mayors of the nation's two largest cities, John Lindsay of New York and Richard Daley of Chicago, illustrate the great differences among mayors.[52] Mayor Daley is one of the most controversial figures in American politics, partly because of his role in the confrontations between police and demonstrators at the 1968 Democratic National Convention in Chicago. He is a product of ethnically heterogeneous Chicago, hailing from an Irish community called Bridgeport. The son of lower-class immigrant parents, Daley, following many ethnic sons of an earlier day, found an avenue of upward mobility in politics. He emerged as a major figure in the nation's largest extant urban political machine in the early 1950s, when he was Clerk of Cook County. In that position he served as a combination "secretary of state" and "chief of staff" for the county machine. Daley's position as Mayor of Chicago, combined with his mastery of the party organization, makes him as powerful a figure as exists in any American city. Unlike some other machine leaders, he has built upon his inheritance of power. Some potential opponents have been absorbed into the party apparatus in positions of political responsibility. Daley and his organization survive precisely because he has used key opportunities for reform. Chicago's merit system for employees coexists with an extensive patronage system;

52 For journalistic portraits of Lindsay and Daley, see the contributions by Larry L. King and David Halberstam, "The New Mayor and the Old," *Harper's*, August, 1968, pp. 25–44.

professional-management techniques are well developed; growth and development policies have won the support of businesmen.[53]

Daley's machine is concerned partly with its own maintenance. Social problems and policies are subordinated to the organizational needs of the party. Aggressive pursuit of social change would, in all probability, threaten the stability of the machine by introducing unpredictable changes in its environment. These factors give Daley and his organization an orientation to the status quo that is reinforced by Daley's own personal values, which center on the home and the faith. According to David Halberstam, Daley

*is deeply religious, but his religion is Pre-Ecumenical, pre-John XXIII, where there is individual sin, but little social sin. He can tolerate small and petty graft, but he cannot excuse adultery, and cannot understand or tolerate a man who fathers a family and then deserts it. He seems unable to understand the forces which create these failings.*[54]

The Mayor of Chicago has great appeal to established second- and third-generation Americans. He is a man of politics but not a man of action or rhetoric. Indeed, he is a master of malaprop. "We must rise," he once said, "to higher and higher platitudes."

There is some irony in finding John Lindsay a more vocal crusader for social reform than is his Chicago counterpart. Daley is a man of the working class, presumably cognizant of its problems, but Lindsay comes from an affluent background. He is a white Anglo-Saxon Protestant who governs a city with even more ethnic diversity than Chicago. The Mayor of New York, unlike the Mayor of Chicago, lacks the backing of a potent political machine. In campaigning for his first term, Lindsay relied on the Republican Party (a minority in Democratic New York City) in coalition with the Liberal Party. The Republican Party denied him renomination for a second term in 1969, and he then relied on the Liberal Party and his hastily forged Urban Party. The city council and board of estimate are solidly Democratic; the municipal bureaucracy has been shaped by a string of Democratic administrations and is composed of relatively autonomous agencies, each of which resists coordination in any form.[55] These factors support the widely held view that New York is "ungovernable." In such a context, any effort at change is difficult. Lindsay possesses no organization

---

[53] One leading Chicago businessman, the president of a major department store, said of Daley and his organization: "Machine? It's just a word. General Motors runs a good machine. So does my store. It's efficient. Good administration makes sense." *The New York Times,* March 5, 1967, p. 78.

[54] Halberstam, *op. cit.,* p. 32.

[55] Wallace Sayre and Herbert Kaufman, *Governing New York City: Politics in the Metropolis* (New York, Russell Sage Foundation, 1960), pp. 711ff.

permeating the interstices of the political system, as does the Chicago machine, and his policy-oriented style is thus blocked by the inertia and sheer weight of a massive public bureaucracy.

## Roles and resources

THE MAYOR'S POLITICAL RESOURCES    Daley and Lindsay illustrate that the personality and political bases of the mayor are important in determining the kinds of influence that he can exercise. But the roles and resources of the mayor are affected by other factors as well. Some of the city-to-city variation in the mayor's office reflects the form of government. The mayor of a council-manager city is normally no more than a titular leader, first among equals on the city council, responsible more for ribbon clipping than policy innovation. The differences between the mayors in a strong-mayor city and in a weak-mayor city are, of course, matters of degree. The weak mayor can rarely be called a "chief executive." He shares administrative power with separately elected officials, with independent boards and commissions, and with the council itself. Often he has no central role in budget-making but shares power equally with other officials. In Milwaukee, for example,

*the mayor does not prepare an executive budget as is done in cities of the "strong mayor" type. Instead, a number of cooks are involved in the making of the budget pie. The Budget Department goes over requests with individual department heads, usually paring their requests sharply. The formal budget is prepared at hearings conducted by the Budget Examining Committee of the Board of Estimates, on which the mayor serves as chairman, together with the council's Finance Committee, the Comptroller, and the Budget Supervisor as secretary.*[56]

In a strong-mayor city, the mayor plays a more crucial role in both policy initiation and administration. He typically dominates the budget-formulation process and key administrative appointments. To be sure, these formal differences do not always predict accurately the power relations at city hall. Sometimes, as in Chicago and New Haven, politically "strong" mayors operate within weak-mayor systems. Still, however, the formal powers of the mayor make it easier or more difficult for him to influence policy-making.

Table 5.2 provides data on three specific features of the formal government structure that may affect the mayor's potential power. It is reasonable to assume that a mayor is most effective when he is directly

[56] Henry W. Maier, *Challenge to the Cities* (New York, Random House, 1966), p. 114.

**Table 5.2**  *Selection, veto powers, and tenure of mayors in American cities with populations of 5,000 or more in 1960, by form of government*

| Form of government | Method of selection[a] | | Veto power[b] | | Term of office | |
|---|---|---|---|---|---|---|
| | Directly elected | Selected by council | No veto | Veto | 1–2 years | 3 or more years |
| Mayor-council | 95.6% | 3.9% | 32.6% | 67.4% | 56.3% | 43.7% |
| Commission | 76.1 | 23.0 | 91.4 | 8.6 | 22.8 | 77.2 |
| Council-manager | 51.1 | 47.8 | 71.4 | 28.6 | 73.3 | 26.7 |

a Percentages do not total 100, for about 1 percent of cities designate the candidates receiving the highest number of votes in city-council elections as "mayors."
b Excluding cities in which mayors are not directly elected.
SOURCE: Orin F. Nolting and David S. Arnold, eds., *The Municipal Year Book 1967* (Chicago, International City Managers' Association, 1967), pp. 104–105.

elected and can claim a popular mandate, when he possesses some veto power, and when he has a longer term of office.

Mayors in mayor-council systems are more likely to benefit from these features than are mayors in either commission or manager cities. Formal structural factors do not exhaust the mayor's resources. Items like political information, experience, strong political organization, ability to bargain, and intelligence cannot be readily measured. But they are no less—and are perhaps more—important than are the structural features of office.

LEADERSHIP ROLES    Some mayors convert limited political resources into significant bases for political leadership; others, perhaps endowed with more generous resources, rarely use them to lead their cities in new directions. We have described the roles of councilmen primarily in terms of their views of representation. As conventional wisdom pictures the mayor as the political leader of the city, his choice of roles reflects his views on policy leadership. Duane Lockard characterized big-city mayors as reformers, program politicians, evaders, and stooges.[57]

The "reformer" rides into office in a campaign against corruption, "bossism," or the "machine." His style is often flamboyant, but he is usually a capable organizer who can weld together an effective following. There is considerable variety among reform mayors, from the dashing and charismatic Fiorello La Guardia (Mayor of New York City from 1934 to 1945), to the blue-blooded Joseph S. Clark and Richardson Dilworth (Mayors of Philadelphia during the 1950s). The policy orientations of reform mayors vary as much as do their social backgrounds. Some mayors are conservative and limit themselves to honest, efficient,

57 Duane Lockard, *The Politics of State and Local Government* (New York, Macmillan, 1963), pp. 413–427.

and businesslike administration of city services. Others are social reformers who try to upgrade services for the poor.

The "program politician" is an activist-entrepreneur, whose political style includes generous doses of public relations and promotional techniques to secure policy changes. Often the program politician dedicates his administration to a miniature urban version of a Great Society or a New Frontier. One example is Carl Stokes' Cleveland Now! Some of the more prominent program politicians include New York's John Lindsay, Cleveland's Stokes, Milwaukee's Henry Maier, New Haven's Richard Lee, and Detroit's Jerry Cavanaugh. Sometimes political fortunes are hard on such innovative mayors. Aggressive advocacy of change alienates certain elements in the municipal electorate. In 1969, New York's Lindsay and Cleveland's Stokes eked out only narrow electoral victories. New Haven's Lee and Detroit's Cavanaugh chose not to seek reelection.

The political style of the "evader" is avoidance of conflict. Sometimes reformers become evaders once they are secure in their posts. A frustrated program politician may find it easier to play an evader's role. To some degree, the fragmented structure of government in American cities (especially in the weak-mayor system) tends to encourage evasion.

The "stooge," who is merely a front man for a political machine or power structure, seems rarer today than in the past. The demise of the machines in most cities, together with the increased presure on and visibility of the mayor's office, has made it more difficult for an informal organization to place a stooge in public office. Yet continuing allegations that some mayors are "owned" by organized crime and the recent actual indictments of some mayors suggest that the role of stooge is still with us.

POLITICAL LEADERSHIP    In examining the current leadership potential of big-city mayors, Alexander L. George has written:

> The nature of the urban political environment makes intense demands on the mayor for special leadership skills of a high order if the need for social change is to be met; at the same time, however, the realities of urban political life make it difficult for him to perform these role requirements effectively and consistently. The root of this paradox lies in the considerable fragmentation of authority and dispersal of power characteristic of the formal governmental structure of American urban areas. In the larger cities, governmental authority is divided and dispersed among federal, state, county, and city jurisdictions; among mayor, council, and various independent officials, boards, and commissions designated by the electorate to deal with specific services and functions.

*In few cities today . . . does the mayor have* formal *authority and resources commensurate with the responsibilities and tasks which face him.*[58]

Above all else, the weakness of the big-city mayor is a function of the limited political resources at his disposal. In the heyday of the political machine, the mayor—assuming that he dominated the machine—could offer material incentives in the form of patronage positions to countless claimants upon the public pocketbook. Even today Mayor Daley of Chicago, the boss of the only major city machine still in operation, has an estimated 35,400 patronage positions (ranging from menial census takers to prestigious judgeships) at his disposal. Daley, however, is the exception. Most mayors have lost to well-developed civil services most of their control over their bureaucracies. Having also lost the support of vigorous political parties, today's mayors must spend much of their time (also a valuable political resource) engaged in generating and maintaining political support for the next elections.

Most contemporary mayors lack the formal powers conferred on both the President of the United States and most state governors. Fully half of all mayors lack veto power of any sort; half are elected to only two-year terms; and nearly half of all cities elect other executive officials (including treasurers, clerks, police chiefs, assessors, and attorneys) who may compete with the mayors for political leadership.

The mayor's powers are circumscribed most sharply in the council-manager system, in which he ordinarily functions as a symbolic leader (having thus about the same amount of political muscle as does the Queen of England). Richard Neustadt has observed that American presidential power is nothing more than the "power to persuade." The central difference, however, is that the President ordinarily has the political resources to add that "extra touch" to his persuasiveness; the mayor merely persuades.

## FORMAL DECISION-MAKERS: THE CITY MANAGER

### The manager plan

The city manager is a professional city administrator who is also chief executive in the council-manager city. The professional organization of city managers is the International City Management Association (formerly the International City Managers' Association). For many years, the ICMA has provided a model city charter, which outlines the

[58] Alexander L. George, "Political Leadership and Social Change in American Cities," *Daedalus, 97* (Fall, 1968), 1196.

ideal relations between the manager and the council and is the basis
of numerous actual city charters and many state enabling statutes.

The city manager is hired by the council and serves at its discretion.
He is subject to removal at any time by a majority vote of the council.
In the early days of the council-manager plan, most managers were
civil engineers by training. Today most city managers have been
trained in graduate programs in public administration. They are
familiar with financial administration, personnel management, municipal law, and planning. Like many professionals in American society,
city managers tend to be highly mobile. Only a minority are "home-
town boys." The career of a typical manager includes work as a staff
assistant to an established manager, then a post as assistant city manager, then appointment as manager in a small town, and, finally, similar
posts in larger or more prestigious communities.

The official responsibilities of a manager are specified in the city
charter. They include (1) overseeing the execution of policy made by
the council, (2) preparing and submitting the budget to the council,
(3) appointing and removing the principal department heads (the police
and fire chiefs, the personnel and budget officers, and so on), and (4)
making recommendations on policy to the council. It is the last point
that receives the most varied interpretations. The underlying philosophy of the manager plan specifies the responsibility of the council to
make policy and of the manager to administer it. The manager is expected to shun interference in the policy choices of the council. The
most egregious violation of the managers' code of ethics is participation
in partisan politics. But, if the manager is expected to make recommendations to the policy-making council, where is the line drawn
between the roles of manager and council?

In practice, of course, there is no clear line between "policy" and
"administration." The manager's persuasiveness in his policy recommendations can make him the most powerful figure in a city's policy-
making process. Matters ordinarily regarded as "administrative" are
laden with policy implications. The cumulative effect of bureaucratic,
or administrative, decisions—many of which are made by the manager's subordinates in the operating units of the city government—may
be as significant as any general policy selected by the mayor or council.
Police treatment of minority groups may have more effect on minority-
group attitudes toward law enforcement than does any policy of equal
treatment enunciated by the city council.

### Roles and resources

In order to define more precisely the roles and behavior of the
city manager, Deil S. Wright conducted a survey of forty-five managers

in cities with populations larger than 100,000. "The behavior of city managers," he wrote, can be "fully and exhaustively characterized by three role categories: managerial, policy, and political."[59] The first managerial role involves his relation with the municipal bureaucracy, including supervision and control of policy administration and personnel. The policy facet of the manager's role includes his relation with the city council, particularly as he is the source of policy recommendations. His political role includes efforts as a community leader and as a representative of community needs and interests before the local council, the community at large, and other units of government. Wright's survey of managers uncovered variations in the ways that they view and perform these three roles.

In his performance of the managerial role, "the capacity of the manager to control the bureaucracy is linked to his abilities to secure information, allocate resources, and impose sanctions (or grant rewards)."[60] The major formal resources available to him in his administrative capacity are his professional staff, his control over the budget, and his power to appoint and remove department heads. Each of these resources may be used to impose constraints and to offer incentives to the municipal bureaucracy. In most council-manager cities, the manager has nearly complete autonomy in his performance of the administrative role. This autonomy is, more than any other factor, at the core of the council-manager system. Many managers guard their administrative autonomy jealously.

The underlying philosophy of the council-manager plan is more ambiguous about the role of the manager in policy initiation and recommendations. Still the manager does play a significant role in initiating policy. Wright has concluded that the manager is the dominant policy initiator in most council-manager cities. More than two-thirds of the managers that he surveyed said they set the agendas of the city councils. This task helped them to control the kinds of questions that were raised and the policy options that were considered. The same proportion of managers reported that most items considered by the council were on the agendas at the behest of managers. The city manager is probably the major source of information for any city council. He bears most of the responsibility for creating the "menu" of policy alternatives to be considered. The council will not accept everything on the menu, but the menu does set forth the policies likely to be considered seriously.

[59] Deil S. Wright, "The City Manager as a Development Administrator," in Robert T. Daland, ed., *Comparative Urban Research* (Beverly Hills, Calif., Sage, 1969), p. 218.
[60] *Ibid.*, p. 219.

Wright has divided the manager's political-leadership role into two components: vertical (extracommunity representation) and horizontal (intracommunity leadership). In dealing with other units of government (particularly the states and the national government), the manager interacts with state or federal bureaucrats. The mayor usually serves as spokesman to elected state or national officials. On the horizontal dimension the manager plays a major role in representing and explaining community policies to the public at large. He ordinarily has no special expertise or information on the political interests of the community, however. His information is technical, not partisan.

The manager is most at home in his administrative role, and he devotes more of his time to administrative tasks. Managers report that they obtain more personal and job satisfaction from their administrative than from their other roles.[61] This attitude reflects their basic professional orientation toward efficient management and delivery of public services and toward detailed financial accounting and personnel administration. Their skills are administrative, and their major resource is technical expertise. Their commitments are, greatest in matters of capital improvements ("bricks and mortar") and established programs. They shoulder responsibility for the formulation of social policy and the burdens of community leadership with less enthusiasm and, perhaps, with less competence. Karl Bosworth wrote some years ago that "the manager is a politician."[62] This view is a useful corrective to myths about "apolitical" managers. As Wright shows, however, managers are primarily administrators; they are more interested in administrative than in political responsibilities.

## FORMAL DECISION-MAKERS: BUREAUCRATS

### Roles and resources

Virtually every policy decision of urban government depends for execution upon the capacities and willingness of the bureaucracy. Few important decisions are "self-executing." But bureaucrats do more than simply implement policy. They are a highly attentive and interested public with unusually high stakes in policy outcomes; they form an interest group that favors certain policy directions.[63] We have pre-

61 *Ibid.,* p. 236.

62 Karl Bosworth, "The Manager Is a Politician," *Public Administration Review, 18* (Summer, 1958), 216–222.

63 Edward C. Banfield and James Q. Wilson, *City Politics* (Cambridge, Mass., Harvard University Press, 1963), pp. 207ff.

viously met the municipal bureaucracy in our discussion of its roles as urban interest group and decision-maker. It is often dominated by two motivations: first, the desire to maintain its autonomy, security, and freedom from "political interference" and, second, an interest in program expansion. These motivations give bureaucrats both conservative and expansionist interests in the policy process. Sayre and Kaufman found that in New York City "bureaucratic groups, especially as they mature in their organization and in their self-awareness as cohesive groups, share with all other groups the aspiration to be self-sufficient and autonomous. In fact, bureaucracies appear to present one of the strongest expressions of this general tendency."[64]

Expertise—knowledge of how to lay out a highway network, how to fight fires, how to organize an educational system—is the major resource of the technical specialist. Bureaucrats resist encroachments on expertise as a premise of decision-making. They also follow strategies that help to maintain autonomy. By insisting on stringent rules for entrance, promotion, and seniority in the bureaucracy, they reduce the opportunities of elected officials to appoint "political" and "nonprofessional" department heads. The appointment of someone other than a "career" public servant is regarded as "political manipulation." Another strategy is the demand for participation in policy formulation. Police administrators seek to impress their own judgments about law enforcement upon the council, school administrators do the same with educational policy, and so forth. As a source of technical information, bureaucracies almost always play some role in policy formulation. It is seldom that policy-makers consciously pursue policies that are opposed by the concerned administrative heads. It seems to be more often that the formal policy-makers seek—and accede to—the advice of administrators on matters of program formulation.

At the same time that bureaucrats resist disruption of their established ways of doing things and seek to "minimize innovation and change,"[65] they often seek to expand their budgets and activities. There is no better spokesman for the interests of policemen than the local Policemen's Benevolent Association or its equivalent. Bureaucrats are their own best lobbyists, although they also commonly align themselves with organized clients and other interest groups. Educational administrators and teachers seek the support of parent-teacher associations, and planners often seek the support of the local Chamber of Commerce. A major source of pressure for expansion comes from the agency itself and its administrative heads.

64 Sayre and Kaufman, *op. cit.*, p. 405.
65 *Ibid.*, p. 407.

## As administrators

By far the most important bureaucratic resource in directing actual policy is its control over the day-to-day execution of programs. Some people think of bureaucrats as neutral automatons who merely carry out policies laid down at higher levels, exercising no choice or discretion. In reality, according to Sayre and Kaufman,

*it is in execution that the bureaucrats have their most nearly complete monopoly and their greatest autonomy in affecting policy. They give shape and meaning to the official decisions, and they do so under conditions favorable to them. Here the initiative and discretion lie in their hands; others must influence them.*[66]

Many bureaucrats—from department heads to the lowest clerks—possess considerable discretion. In fact, studies of traffic-law enforcement and ticketing policies by John A. Gardiner and of local welfare administration by Martha Derthick suggest that top administrators enjoy striking degrees of discretion.[67] Gardiner noted extreme variations in the number of traffic tickets dispensed in cities with nearly identical populations. Boston and Dallas both have populations of about 700,-000, but in one year Dallas policemen wrote twenty-four times as many tickets as did those in Boston! No doubt some of this variation may be attributed to variations in state laws and local traffic ordinances or to different habits of Boston and Dallas drivers, but it is unlikely that such factors account for such a large differential. In fact, between two adjacent Massachusetts cities with similar populations (Cambridge and Somerville) there was a 700 percent differential in ticketing rates. The most important factor accounting for wide differences in law-enforcement policies has proved to be the attitude of the police chief toward traffic ticketing. "In general, the rate of enforcement of traffic laws reflects the organizational norms of a police department—the extent to which superior officers expect and encourage particular policies regarding ticket-writing."[68] Gardiner has reported the change in one New England city from a police chief who viewed detective work as the only really important police function to another who was a zealous advocate of traffic enforcement. During the last year of the first chief's tenure the

---

[66] *Ibid.*, p. 421.

[67] John A. Gardiner, "Police Enforcement of Traffic Laws: A Comparative Analysis," in James Q. Wilson, ed., *City Politics and Public Policy* (New York, Wiley, 1968), pp. 151–172; and Martha Derthick, "Intercity Differences in Administration of the Public Assistance Program: The Case of Massachusetts," in Wilson, ed., *op. cit.*, pp. 243–266.

[68] Gardiner, *op. cit.*, p. 161.

whole force wrote 480 tickets. After the new chief took over, the figure shot up to 4,569, which shows the influence of administrative discretion on the performance of lower-level bureaucrats.

Opportunities for discretion are not monopolized by senior bureaucrats and agency heads. They exist to some degree even at the lower levels of the bureaucracy. Wilson, for instance, has analyzed the discretion of beat patrolmen.[69] He discovered that officers have relatively little discretion when they confront clear transgressions of unambiguous laws: armed robberies, murders, dope peddling, and so on. But, in maintaining "order" and dealing with transgressions against vague standards of public peace and serenity, their discretion increases. In the case of a clear violation, an officer approaches the situation by "enforcing the law"; in other matters, he is free to "handle the situation."

In the final analysis, however, the bureaucrat is not totally free to do whatever he wants. Lower-level bureaucrats—as the traffic-ticketing study indicates—are clearly constrained by the expectations of their superiors, and even their superiors have only finite amounts of discretion. Bureaucrats are not neutral automatons, but neither are they wholly independent in their actions. Certain kinds of policies or circumstances permit greater discretion than do others. When administration can easily be routinized, there is less room for discretion. The maximum welfare payment, the speed that breaks the legal limit, and attendance in school are subject to exact specification. On the other hand, bureaucratic decisions involving determination of what constitutes "undesirable" behavior as grounds for eviction from a housing project or how to handle a scuffle outside a bar do not lend themselves to uniform responses. In much of the administrative process there are continuing attempts at routinization in order to minimize the discretion of subordinates.

### The "new machines"

We have repeatedly mentioned the demise of urban party machines. We have also noted the formal fragmentation of the municipal governments that survive the machines. This fragmentation is characterized by relative decentralization, weakening of the formal and political powers of the mayor's office, and proliferation of independent boards and commissions. The disappearance of the machines left in its wake considerable disorganization of the policy-making process. City government is characterized not by absence of political resources but by their dispersion in countless hands; centralized leadership from

---

[69] James Q. Wilson, *Varieties of Police Behavior* (Cambridge, Mass., Harvard University Press, 1968).

political officials is difficult to obtain. One effect of this dispersion is that the greatest single combination of organized resources now resides in public bureaucracies. They are, according to Theodore Lowi, the "new machines" in urban politics. "The legacy of Reform is the bureaucratic city-state," in which cities "become well-run but ungoverned."[70] The new machines are different from the old machines in their low tolerance for inefficiency and corruption. They also have a resource base of formal authority rather than votes. But, according to Lowi,

> *The New Machines are machines because they are relatively irresponsible structures of power. That is, each agency shapes important public policies, yet the leadership of each is relatively self-perpetuating and not readily subject to the controls of any higher authority.*
>
> *The New Machines are machines in that the power of each, while resting ultimately upon services rendered to the community, depends upon its cohesiveness as a small minority in the midst of the vast dispersion of the multitude.*[71]

New York is a prototype. Sayre and Kaufman describe the public bureaucracies of New York City as relatively autonomous islands of power, in which resistance to innovation is the first operating premise.[72] Many of the old machines were run by the mayors. Now, however, any mayor with an innovative turn of mind must confront the new machine, in which he is permanently denied membership.


## MAKING PUBLIC POLICY: AN OVERVIEW OF THE DECISION PROCESS

The sheer number and variety of inputs that come to decision-makers complicate their task. No simple precedure for making decisions can accommodate all these inputs. In an effort to describe this complex environment of decision-makers, it will be useful to describe a model of "rational" decision-making and then to identify several features that frustrate perfect emulation of this rationality. We shall then be in a position to describe some techniques for coping with complexity and for making decisions when the prescriptions of the purely rational model are too stringent.[73]

[70] Theodore J. Lowi, "Machine Politics—Old and New," *The Public Interest* (Fall, 1967), p. 86.

[71] *Ibid.*, p. 87.

[72] Sayre and Kaufman, *op. cit.*, chap. 11.

[73] Some of the arguments advanced in this section are treated more fully in Ira Sharkansky, *Public Administration: Policy-Making in Government Agencies* (Chicago, Markham, 1970), chap. 3.

## A model of rational decision-making

Rationalism receives wide respect in our social system. The demands of a completely rational decision are severe, however. It is costly to be perfectly rational, and few decision-makers have sufficient resources to meet the costs. According to one formulation, a rational policy-maker would

1    identify his problem;
2    clarify his goals and then rank them according to relative importance;
3    list all possible means—or policies—for achieving each of his goals;
4    assess all the costs of each set of alternatives and the benefits that seem likely to follow from each;
5    select the package of goals and associated policies that would bring the most relative benefits and the fewest relative disadvantages.[74]

Decision-makers who would follow this procedure must inform themselves about all possible opportunities and all possible consequences of each opportunity—an enormous assignment. The model assumes that political systems have vast resources that can be used to gather intelligence and that individual decision-makers are sufficiently uncommitted to—or against—any one set of goals or policies to be able to make their decisions solely on the basis of systematically collected information. There are five major reasons why decisions in public (or private) bodies rarely measure up to the exacting standards of the rational model:

1    the sheer pressures of time;
2    the costs of obtaining adequate information about the various acceptable goals and policies;
3    the mixture of sometimes incompatible or incommensurable goals that are pursued simultaneously within an urban system;
4    structural features of the political system that frustrate coherent and co-ordinated policies;
5    the constraints of "political feasibility."

These five items are not entirely separable in practice, but each does impose its own limitations upon the rational model, and each is worth separate consideration for analytical purposes.

### Limitations on rational policy-making

TIME PRESSURES    Most features of the urban environment that we consider "problems"—high population density, inadequate transportation,

[74] Charles E. Lindblom, *The Policy-Making Process* (Englewood Cliffs, N.J., Prentice-Hall, 1968), p. 13.

pollution, decay—did not appear overnight and will not be eliminated overnight. But policy-makers are pressed for action, for policies, and for solutions. Planners and other bureaucrats may be able to look to the long run and to deal with models covering spans of several decades; politicians, however, must look to the next election. Academicians have time for reflection, but decision-makers are expected to act with dispatch. The press of time is an obvious enough problem, and it is probably the first and paramount reason why public policies cannot be formulated according to the rational model. There simply is not enough time to accumulate the information, survey all the possible alternatives, and select from among them.

COSTS OF INFORMATION    A second factor that makes rational decision-making impossible is the high cost of obtaining information. There are basically two types of information: political (on the needs and preferences of the community and interests within it) and technical (on the most efficient ways of reaching goals). Anthony Downs has listed three conditions that generally prevent bureaucracies and other decision-making bodies from acquiring the types of information required by the rational model:

1    *Information is costly because it takes time, effort, and sometimes money to obtain data and comprehend their meaning.*
2    *Decision-makers have only limited amounts of time to spend making decisions, can consider only a certain number of issues simultaneously, and can absorb only certain amounts of data on any one problem.*
3    *Although some uncertainty can be eliminated by acquiring information, an important degree of unpredictability is usually involved in making decisions.*[75]

Not only is information costly to gather and process, but also different types of information may imply contradictory policy decisions. A common problem is that political information implies different decisions from those implied by technical information. Technical information on access, noise, and similar criteria may suggest the location of a new airport in a particular district, but political information may suggest that it would be wiser to choose another site.

As capacities for obtaining information are limited by the availability of resources, the important questions are When does a decision-maker stop gathering information? And when does he stop assessing what he has gathered? The answer to both these questions may be "never." But, at some point in the formulation of a new policy, the information-search process will have to be replaced by the decision and

[75] Anthony Downs, *Inside Bureaucracy* (Boston, Little, Brown, 1967), p. 3.

action process. Often, decision-makers will cut off their search when they discover a mode of operation that involves the least profound change in their established programs. They do not search all possible alternatives until they find "the one best" mode of operation. Instead they search until they find something that "will work," that will provide some relief from the perceived difficulties without threatening undesirable unrest within the bureaucracy and among other decision-makers and interest groups. In the words of one student of decision-making, the search proceeds until the participants can "satisfice."[76] It is simply too expensive (and the demands for action are too great) to search until the one "optimum" combination of goals and policies has been identified.

INCOMPATIBLE AND INCOMMENSURABLE GOALS    Urban (and other) governments pursue numbers of policies simultaneously, some of which are almost certain to be incompatible with others. This fact is certainly not surprising and is perhaps fortunate when we realize that governments serve multiple interests and respond to numerous demands for service and conflict resolution. At least in the abstract, there is some inconsistency in community policies that encourage the dispersion of population to the urban periphery, while other policies are aimed at salvaging a decaying downtown area. Sometimes, however, such inconsistent goals must be served by a single policy or agency. An example is urban renewal. Among the goals that some people think it should accomplish are such disparate efforts as improving the city's tax base, attracting new industry, reversing suburban migration by providing middle-income housing, and improving the housing plight of low-income families. It is clear that a single urban-renewal program cannot serve each of these goals equally; even if it could, it would fall short of any strict standard of rational policy-making.

Not only are goals served by the community or by particular agencies sometimes inconsistent, but they are even more commonly incommensurable. By "incommensurable," we mean they are difficult or impossible to compare. There is both insufficient consensus on the goals themselves and a highly inefficient system for their measurement. Each of these factors impedes comparability. Decision-makers have little notion of whether or not another dollar invested in urban renewal would reap more "payoffs" than would another dollar invested in education. Even if the goal is supported by a relative consensus, as is the reduction of poverty, there is still incommensurability among policies. There is no very clear evidence that any one strategy for reducing poverty will be more effective than would any other strategy. Because

[76] Herbert Simon, *Administrative Behavior* (New York, Macmillan, 1961).

most goals and policies do not lend themselves to ready measurement, it will be nearly impossible to meet standards of rationality that require comparison between alternative goals and policies.

STRUCTURAL BARRIERS TO RATIONALITY    If rational decisions require the capacity to organize public processes of selection toward certain goals rather than others, the structure of urban government is not geared to maximize rationality. Instead, there are countless local governments in a metropolitan area, as well as the state and federal governments, each of which may be pursuing different policies to achieve the same or different goals. Within the city government itself, fragmentation of legal authority means that various decision-makers can each pursue different strategies and policies, without too much concern for checkmate by superior authority.

POLITICAL FEASIBILITY    In the last analysis, the determination of what to do about a particular problem is made not by what is rational but by what will "sell" to the electorate and to political "influentials." Public attitudes toward taxation are likely to be a major constraint upon any purely rational approach to problem solving. Feasibility depends to a considerable degree upon familiarity. According to Ralph Huitt,

*what is most feasible is what is purely incremental, or can be made to appear so. . . . Paradoxically, it is politically attractive to tout a proposal as "new" so long as it is generally recognized that it is not new at all, but a variation on a familiar theme.*[77]

Elected officials are rarely willing to sacrifice their chances for reelection upon the altar of rationality, especially when justifications abound in democratic theory for adhering to the "voice of the people." Perhaps the most "rational" way to grapple with the problem of poverty in the American system is through a form of guaranteed high-level income for all. Politically, however, such a proposal is likely to generate enough hostility to be considered "unfeasible" by most politicians, even if they might support the notion on other grounds.

### Compromises with the rational model

The failure of decision-makers to follow the rigorous prescriptions of the rational model does not mean that their choices are frenetic, unpatterned, or made without benefit of human reason. In terms of a stringent model of rational behavior urban decision-making should

[77] Ralph Huitt, "Political Feasibility," in Austin Ranney, ed., *Political Science and Public Policy* (Chicago, Markham, 1968), p. 274.

be characterized not as *irrational,* but rather as *nonrational.* Some factors that impede rational behavior are themselves features of the democratic process: politicians' beliefs about voters' preferences, their obligations to constituents, multiple competing interests each of which holds a claim upon government. Other factors characterize private firms, as well as public agencies: the high cost of obtaining information, multiple and sometimes incommensurable goals, time pressures, and so on. Public policy-makers must compromise with the rational model. There are strategies for coping with complexities that permit decisions to be made without the full-scale analysis required by the rational model. Among such resource-saving strategies are the reliance upon tensions between established patterns and unmet needs to signal the need for policy change; conflict avoidance; the use of routine decision-making rules to simplify complex considerations, and the tendency to make "adjustments" to demands, rather than to initiate decision-making processes that seek clear definition of goals or policy. None of these strategies meets the standards of the rational model, but they are all employed by men in search of premises for decision-making in a complex environment involving time pressures and limited information. Common to each of these features is the reluctance of policy-makers to make great departures from customary activities. Policy-makers, as do the rest of us, prefer stability to its opposite. Their shortcut decision-making rules facilitate stability in an environment with a high potential for instability.

"Tensions," for example, are treated by policy-makers as signals of dissatisfaction with current programs and policies. An increase of crime in the downtown area, sudden national attention to poverty, or a sharp increase in pollution may lead councilmen or bureaucrats to rethink policies on police distribution, the welfare system, or pollution control. Tensions are a screening device that decision-makers use to determine when unmet demands are so severe as to require alterations in policy. An administrative system that relies on tensions does not initiate policy change according to any rationally defined set of priorities but waits for changes to be demanded.

A set of procedures for accommodating tensions has been labeled "mutual adjustment," and one of the terms used to identify decision-making by mutual adjustment is "muddling through."[78] Flexibility is a major tenet of the process of mutual adjustment. Decision-makers recognize the impermanence of their choices, and adjustments can accommodate some of the conflicting demands upon them. The term "muddling through" suggests a lethargic organism that would detour around antagonism rather than meeting it head on, implying a strategy

---

[78] Charles E. Lindblom, "The Science of 'Muddling Through,'" *Public Administration Review, 19* (Spring, 1959), 79–88.

of conflict avoidance. Resources are scarce, and there is little to be gained from dissipating them in conflict. Conflict, moreover, is psychologically unpleasant to the contestants. William L. C. Wheaton suggests that conflict avoidance is a common strategy in urban decision-making:

Public officials delay decisions interminably, attempting to appraise the balance of power pro and con. They may defer decision indefinitely if the balance is approximately equal, and will reach decisions only when there is clearly preponderant support for one position. . . . Frequently decisions may be referred to experts or to other levels of government so that local public officials can evade responsibility or place it elsewhere.[79]

Routines are used by all decision-makers to avoid the time-consuming, expensive, and impossible demands of the rational model. Routines specify which of the numerous criteria that might be relevant are actually to be considered in making specific decisions.[80] They simplify the inputs and thus make decisions easier. There are several routines used by local officials in making policy choices. One is the tendency of city councils to rely upon the information presented to them by the executive branch, particularly in the budgetary process, rather than to seek out new sources of information on their own. Several routines are related to the spending process. One of the most commonly employed—and widely researched—is the practice of incremental budgeting (see Chapter 7, pp. 233–237). Another spending routine is the "spending-service cliché," in which administrators who seek to improve their program seek an increase in spending on the assumption that spending and service levels are closely related. If the present level of services is not satisfactory, it is always possible—assuming sufficient resources—to spend more money. The accuracy of this assumption has been questioned,[81] but, in lieu of exacting measures of policy impact, it still constitutes a time-saving routine for decision-makers.

## SUMMARY

In this chapter we have explored a number of subjects, ranging from the structure of community power to the process of decision-making under conditions of limited resources. There is a certain discontinuity between research on formal decision-makers and informal power struc-

---

[79] William L. C. Wheaton, "Integration at the Urban Level: Political Influence and the Decision Process," in Philip Jacob and James V. Toscano, eds., The Integration of Political Communities (Philadelphia, Lippincott, 1964), p. 132.

[80] For a more extensive treatment of decision-making routines, see Ira Sharkansky, The Routines of Politics (New York, Van Nostrand Reinhold, 1970).

[81] Ira Sharkansky, "Government Expenditures and Public Services in the American States," American Political Science Review, 61 (December, 1967), 1066–1077.

tures. One of our working assumptions, however, is that no power structure is so nearly monolithic and completely controlling that the roles of mayors, councils, managers, and bureaucrats become insignificant. In some cities, small and informal groups outside the formal government structures may formulate certain "key" decisions. It is equally true, however, that few decisions implement themselves. Key decisions made by a formal or informal group are not compelling in practice unless applied systematically by administrative heads and middle- and lower-level bureaucrats. Nor can the decisions of even the lower-level bureaucrats be discounted as insignificant; their cumulative impact may be greater than that of a single "major" policy decided by a "power structure." It is important to understand both the informal and the formal sides of community decision-making. Ignorance of either facet will provide only a partial view of the urban political system.

# part three

## PUBLIC POLICIES
## AND THEIR IMPACTS

POLICY is what politics is all about. For many citizens, it is the target
of their willingness to discuss politics, to vote, and to campaign for
the candidates of their choice. For candidates, the opportunity to
shape policy is a major stimulus for the headaches and family de-
privations that their work entails. For political scientists, "policy"
is a term for certain activities that constitute much of what is worth studying
in the urban system.

We devote Chapter 6 to an introductory discussion of public policy and
its relations to other features of the urban political system. The four succeed-
ing chapters deal with the substance of policies: Chapter 7 with taxing and
spending decisions; Chapter 8, with servicing the urban environment, especially in four major areas—law enforcement, education, transportation, and
pollution; Chapter 9 with poverty, race, and public policies of federal, state,
and urban governments; and Chapter 10 with managing urban growth.

In each case, we are concerned not only with what governments do but
also with how they respond to other elements of the political system: the
environment, input mechanisms, and conversion processes. We are also concerned with the effects, or "impacts," of policies on the environmental problems they purport to solve.

By now the reader should be sensitive to community-wide and individual
features of the policy-making process. Policies are shaped in response to
gross aspects of the community's socioeconomic environment and to the demands of citizens and interest groups. Policies also have their impacts on
aggregate features of the community's ecology and economy and on the distribution of benefits among groups and individuals. The aggregate and
individual features of the policy process differ from one sector of policy to
another and from one community to another. We cannot cover all the details
in the chapters that follow. If the argument is successful, however, it should
sensitize the reader to the range of possibilities in the urban policy process,
to general tendencies, and to likely deviations from those tendencies.

# 6

# The analysis of public policy

In the preceding chapters we dealt with certain features of the urban environment, the political input process, and the decision-making process. In the following chapter, we turn our attention to outputs and impacts of the urban political system: the efforts of urban governments to affect their environments.

This chapter introduces the topic of policy as a subject worthy of concentrated attention; it explains how various features of urban culture, economics, and politics interact in the policy-making process; and it lays out the various ways in which political scientists use their skills to determine how certain policies come to be and how they do—or do not—bring about intended improvements in urban conditions.

## DEFINITIONS AND CLASSIFICATIONS

### The nature of public policy

A concern with policies is the common denominator between the writings of Plato and Aristotle, on one hand, and the activities of Richard Daley and John Lindsay, on the other. As political scientists, we recognize that there are disagreements about the kinds of policies governments "should" enact; we also recognize that political scientists use the term "public policy" in different ways. Some restrict it to the basic set of goals or targets that activities are designed to serve, for example, to an approach to housing the poor; they see the activities of condemning and purchasing sites and constructing the housing as program elements handled by officials within policy guidelines.

The question remains, however, do all government programs have identifiable goals? In the case of many housing programs, decisions about site selection and purchase are made with one set of goals in mind (for example, economy), whereas other phases of the project are subject to different goals (for example, preventing "undesirables" from living in housing projects). Moreover, long-range goals are often masked or camouflaged by decision-makers who want to avoid generating opposition from certain elements of the community. Some of the problems in defining policies as goals are relevant to our discussion of incommensurable goals and the difficulties of rational decision-making in Chapter 5.

Some policy analysts broaden the term "policy" to include the *effects* that government actions have upon the populations they are designed to serve. Some of these effects are encompassed by the terms "outputs," "outcomes," "spillover effects," "impacts" or "feedbacks" of policy. As mentioned in Chapter 1, David Easton, one of the progenitors of systems analysis in political science, draws a distinction between "outputs" (roughly, what governments do) and the "outcomes" of these outputs (roughly, what consequences follow from the outputs).[1] Still others use the term "policy" to refer to broadly interrelated government decisions. When we label officials "liberal," "moderate," or "conservative," we use shorthand forms to denote the ways in which specific decisions coalesce into broad policy directions.

The formulation of the main components of public policies presented by Austin Ranney is useful in suggesting major implications of the term:

1    *a particular object or set of objects*—some designated part of the environment (an aspect of the society or physical world) that is to be affected;
2    *a desired course of events*—a particular sequence of behavior desired in the particular object or set of objects;
3    *a selected line of action*—a particular set of actions chosen to bring about the desired course of events; in other words, not merely whatever the society happens to be doing toward the set of objects at the moment, but a deliberate selection of one line of action from among several possible lines;
4    *a declaration of intent*—some statement by the policy-makers, whether broadcast publicly to all who will listen or communicated secretly to a special few, on what they intend to do, how, and why.

[1] David Easton, *A Systems Analysis of Political Life* (New York, Wiley, 1965), pp. 351–352.

5    *an implementation of intent*—the actions actually undertaken vis-à-vis the particular set of objects in pursuance of the choices and declaration.[2]

Note that this listing constitutes a definition of policy per se. It does not speak to the questions of the "effects," "outcomes," or "impacts" of the policies, which we shall discuss later in this chapter.

Various kinds of urban government actions are important enough to have earned the designation "policy." Many of them—for example, public education, welfare, health care, and public hospitals—provide tangible benefits to clearly defined groups of recipients. Other policies prevent or regulate certain behaviors that have been officially designated as obnoxious or dangerous; policemen, jailers, antipollution agencies, and building inspectors implement such policies. Still other policies provide symbolic gratifications to certain groups of citizens.[3] The latter include civic observances of national, religious, and ethnic holidays—perhaps parades, days off from school, or simple proclamations. Presumably they raise the spirits of those who celebrate and also provide some tangible benefits to those who sell the spirits to the celebrants. Some policies involve regulation of the policy-making process itself; recent efforts to alter the apportioning of state legislatures and local councils, as well as to increase the registration of black voters, are primarily procedural but are nonetheless significant policies.

### Classification of policies

The first difficulty in classifying policies is that there may be several ways of describing the same policy. Depending upon the perspective adopted, the same set of actions can be regarded as an example of one form of policy or of another. When we say that public education and welfare provide tangible benefits to clearly defined groups of recipients, for example, we mean the instructional services provided to students and the assistance payments provided to welfare clients. Yet, if we take a macro instead of a micro perspective, these same programs also provide benefits to society as a whole: public education by adding skills and the resulting productivity to the economy, and both education and welfare by providing opportunities for personal advancement to members of low-income families and helping to defuse their social and economic grievances. The Head Start program, to take another example, is both an educational and an antipoverty policy; it

---

[2] Austin Ranney, "The Study of Policy Content: A Framework for Choice," in Austin Ranney, ed., *Political Science and Public Policy* (Chicago, Markham, 1968), p. 7.

[3] For a perceptive study of political symbolism, see Murray Edelman, *The Symbolic Uses of Politics* (Urbana, University of Illinois Press, 1964).

also has implications both for the individual and the community as a whole.

A second difficulty is encountered in attempting to group policies for purposes of analysis. One set of categories simply follows the major administrative departments or budget categories. Policies are thus grouped and described under the headings "education," "welfare," "highways" (or "transportation"), "planning," "urban renewal," and so on. To some writers, these categories are cumbersome and get in the way of meaningful generalizations about policies made in two or more departments or different kinds of policies made in the same department. By confining our attention to the formal classifications, we can miss important functional similarities and differences among policies. Lewis A. Froman, for example, has suggested that we classify policies of local governments into "areal" (that is, affecting the entire population of a city) and "segmental" (affecting only small portions of a city) classes.[4] He has argued that each type of policy tends to be related to a particular kind of community: heterogeneous communities pursue more segmental policies, and homogeneous communities undertake more areal policies.

In a more elaborate classification scheme, Lowi has suggested that we distinguish among policies that are "distributive," "redistributive," and "regulatory."[5] Distributive policies involve minimal ideological conflict and can be applicable to most or all claimants. Such terms as "trade off," "logrolling," and "the pork barrel" describe distributive politics. There are no real winners or losers in the distributive arena, and governments are able to offer something to everybody. The political machine is a classic case of effective use of distributive policies. Redistributive policies, on the other hand, involve relatively clear winners and losers; the conflict is commonly between such large groups as social classes, and rewards are not infinitely divisible. Redistributive politics is, to a large degree, class politics. Regulatory policies, the third type distinguished by Lowi, involve efforts by government to regulate patterns in the private sector in order to achieve certain ends.

Lowi has argued that these three arenas of policy have different kinds of politics associated with them, different patterns of power operating within them, and produce different kinds of environmental alterations. Using Lowi's classification as a starting point, Robert Salisbury has added a "self-regulatory" category and has undertaken

[4] Lewis A. Froman, Jr., "An Analysis of Public Policies in Cities," *Journal of Politics*, 29 (February, 1967), 94–108; and Lewis A. Froman, "The Categorization of Policy Contents," in Ranney, ed., *op. cit.*, pp. 23–40.

[5] Theodore Lowi, "American Business, Public Policy, Case-Studies, and Political Theory," *World Politics*, 6 (July, 1964), 677–715.

some empirical work to illustrate the utility of the typology.[6] Heinz Eulau and Robert Eyestone have offered "adaptive" and "control" as policy categories.[7] Planning is the major example of a control policy, and the provision of amenities is the major kind of adaptive policy.

Williams and Adrian have found four major types of urban policy.[8] In their study of four cities in Michigan, they found city governments pursuing one (or sometimes two) of the following basic policies: economic growth, provision of life's amenities, maintenance of traditional services ("caretaker" government), and arbitration of conflict. Certain kinds of communities emphasized one policy more than the others. Elements of one policy may hinder the pursuit of others. The pursuit of amenities, for instance (including quiet residential streets, parks, and playgrounds), consumes considerable economic resources and is plainly inconsistent with the low-tax, low-service, caretaker orientation of government.

Each set of categories offered by policy theorists is intended to group specific policies that characterize distinct responses to the environment or trigger distinct reponses in the environment. Whereas each of the proposed typologies offers some fascinating insights into the local policy process, each also has certain analytical and methodological difficulties. Some of the typologies operate at such high levels of abstraction that it is difficult to find ways of measuring them in the real world of politics. Others seem to be no more than interesting sets of terminology applied to traditional categories of substantive policy. Williams and Adrian's typology is particularly valuable for its effort to relate actual observations to the categories. But it is not altogether clear how one can ascribe a policy orientation to an entity as complex as a city. Lowi's categories may be the most penetrating and theoretically useful, but they are so abstract as to be difficult to examine empirically. Froman, on the other hand, has applied his categories in some empirical research, but the results are not satisfactory. The areal and segmental categories are not mutually exclusive and discrete, and he has been forced to argue that municipal annexation policies and intermunicipal cooperation are "areal" in affecting the total

[6] Robert H. Salisbury, "The Analysis of Public Policy: A Search for Theories and Roles," in Ranney, ed., op. cit., pp. 151–178; and Robert H. Salisbury and John Heinz, "A Theory of Policy Analysis and Some Preliminary Applications," in Ira Sharkansky, ed., Policy Analysis in Political Science (Chicago, Markham, 1970), pp. 39–60.

[7] Heinz Eulau and Robert Eyestone, "Policy Maps of City Councils and Policy Outcomes," American Political Science Review, 62 (March, 1968), 124–143.

[8] Oliver P. Williams and Charles Adrian, Four Cities (Philadelphia, University of Pennsylvania Press, 1963), pp. 23–26, 272ff.

population of a city, whereas urban renewal is "segmental" in affecting only part of the population. In contrast, annexation seems likely to affect the annexed neighborhood most significantly, whereas urban renewal may affect a whole city through its impact on expenditures, taxes, and political controversy. In an effort to find indicators of areal and segmental policies, Froman has found it necessary to adopt the difficult position that per capita expenditures reflect merely the sum of segmental policies, although he has argued that educational services are primarily areal. On balance, it appears that the underlying logic of Froman's position is more compelling than are his actual findings.

We believe that these and similar ventures into policy classification are necessary for the development of empirically based policy theory. But in the chapters that follow, we rely upon the conventional categories of urban public policy: taxing and spending; traditional urban services (police, transportation, environmental control, and education); antipoverty and civil rights; and planning, urban renewal, and housing policies. We do so for two reasons. First, these traditional categories are most commonly used and understood by citizens and decision-makers in urban politics, and, second, most research by ourselves and our fellow political scientists uses these conventional categories of analysis. We take one lesson from those who theorize about policies of different kinds, however. Within each field of policy, we try to draw meaningful distinctions among various policy manifestations, and we try to relate each kind of manifestation to critical elements in the economic, social, and political surroundings.

## ELEMENTS OF THE POLICY PROCESS

To clarify the discussions of various policies in the following chapters and to relate them to the materials covered in Chapters 1–5, it is helpful to identify several principal elements in the policy process and several of the ways that activities in each phase influence the other phases. In Chapter 1, we offered a general model of the urban political system, but at this point we shall delve more extensively into the components lumped under the rubric "policy." There are several different ways to describe the elements—or phases—in the policy process. Terms differ from one author to another, but the contents of the discussions are generally similar. We have already introduced and discussed in Chapter 2–5 the terms "environment," "inputs," and "conversion process." It is now time to elaborate some additional terminology, specifically, "policy," "impact," and "feedback."

The environment of the urban system includes the social, economic, and cultural surroundings that influence the policy decisions that officials make and also the impact of their decisions upon the policy targets. Inputs include both human and material elements. Requests, claims, or demands for particular public policies and indications that citizens support or do not support the urban political system or its particular policies are human inputs. Program standards laid down by state and federal governments, financial aid from these other levels, and taxes collected from local sources are material elements of the input process.

Policy-making institutions and personnel "convert" inputs from the environment into policies that then produce outputs, impacts, and feedback. The major policy-making actors and processes are found in the formal structures of local government and their occupants (mayors, managers, school boards, the bureaucracy); informal community power structures; the procedures used by officials to make their policy decisions; and the commitments, predispositions, and beliefs that shape these officials' decisions. As we saw in Chapters 3–5, these features are not fixed. They include many varieties of behaviors, which differ with the kind of issue that is introduced and the ways in which inputs flow from the environment. Among the features that may be found in the conversion process are conflicts between formal rules of procedures and the practices followed by officials; clashes among various officials from different agencies or branches of local government; clashes between decision-makers and representatives of interest groups who make innovative demands; and decision-makers' use of routine procedures to simplify complex and numerous demands.

## Dimensions of public policies

Public policies include (1) a particular object or set of objects, (2) a desired course of events, (3) a selected line of action, (4) a declaration of intent, and (5) implementation of intent. Let us say that an urban government (whether confronted by demands from certain citizens or from the courts or motivated by the beliefs of the decision-makers themselves) perceives a problem of racial segregation in the public schools. The particular objects, then, are distributions of pupils by race in public schools; the desired course of events is a redistribution in the direction of more integration. There are, of course, several possible lines of action open: District lines may be redrawn; freedom-of-choice plans may be implemented; or some white children may be transported to formerly all-black schools and vice versa. When a line of action is selected, it may be communicated to the press and to the school administrators who will have the actual responsibility for implementing the policy. The political process does not, however, stop at implementation of the policy because the impact and the feedback from the policies are also relevant components of the policy process.

A number of questions may be raised about public policy: Most politicking centers around policy questions. "Is policy X good or bad?" is the most common question, but it is deceptively simple. Before addressing such questions, we should first examine the policy dimensions of *cost, service output,* and *distribution,* as well as the critical question of *policy impact.*

COST    Few public policies, other than purely symbolic ones, do not involve expenditure of public money. The questions of the total size of the public budget and of desirable tax burdens are among the most critical issues in most urban political systems. Each substantive policy involves the question of finance. Officials pay a great deal of attention to budget-making, and expenditures are widely viewed as a common denominator with respect to items that actually produce service. Although spending does not by itself meet popular demands for service, it does buy many of the things that produce service. We shall examine spending and taxing issues in the next chapter.

SERVICE OUTPUT    Policies may be measured by the level of output attained. Included may be such questions as how much money is spent per capita or per recipient; what service components are in fact purchased by such expenditure; and what mixes of capital investment, personnel costs, and units of service are actually secured. Some writers equate a government's level of services with its level of spending.[9] But the generous provision of funds may have little relation to the quality or quantity of services actually delivered to the public.[10] The correlations between educational expenditures per pupil and various service outputs reported in Table 6.1 clearly suggest that expenditures are not powerful predictors of the level of outputs achieved. It is perhaps not surprising to discover that teachers' salaries and the teacher-pupil ratio are related to expenditures, for salaries are the major item of school spending. But nonmonetary indicators of school outputs—training of teachers, dropout rates, and teacher turnover—are very weakly related to school spending. Money may well be important, but, just as it does not buy happiness, neither does it guarantee a high level of service. In

[9] Robert C. Wood, *1400 Governments* (Garden City, N.Y., Doubleday Anchor, 1961), p. 35; Jesse Burkhead, *Public School Finance* (Syracuse, Syracuse University Press, 1965), p. 50; and Robert H. Salisbury, "State Politics and Education," in Herbert Jacob and Kenneth N. Vines, eds., *Politics in the American States* (Boston, Little, Brown, 1965), p. 331.

[10] Ira Sharkansky, *The Politics of Taxing and Spending* (New York, Bobbs-Merrill, 1969), chap. 6.

**Table 6.1**  *Relation between expenditures per pupil and
selected measures of school services*

| Measure of school service | Correlation with expenditures per pupil |
|---|---|
| Teachers' salaries | .63 |
| Teacher turnover | .02 |
| Teachers without degrees | .19 |
| Teachers with master's degrees | .26 |
| Dropout rate | .02 |
| Teacher-pupil ratio | —.40 |

SOURCE: Thomas R. Dye, "Government Structure, Urban Environment and Educational Policy," *Midwest Journal of Political Science,
11* (August, 1967), 372, Table 2. These data are based upon
Dye's study of sixty-seven big-city school systems.

fact, the actual performance levels in public programs may be influenced by a variety of factors, including the needs of the population
being served and the sources and severity of the problems to be
ameliorated. A service agency may have no control whatever over these
environmental influences.

THE DISTRIBUTION OF PUBLIC POLICY    As Lowi, Froman, and others have
emphasized, policy effects may be distributed differentially within the
city. Froman, for example, has distinguished between areal and segmental policies, suggesting that areal policies affect everyone in the city
equally and that segmental policies affect some people and groups more
than they do others. It is difficult to think of a public policy whose
effects are not distributed differentially from group to group. Perhaps
the only urban policy that affects everyone equally is fluoridation of
water. Because most policy effects are distributed differentially, the
distribution dimension is a critical factor in understanding public
policy.

One important way that policy effects are distributed is among
neighborhoods or social classes. Patricia Cayo Sexton's studies of schools
in a large midwestern city concluded that wealthier neighborhoods
received much higher levels of school services than did poor neighborhoods.[11] In Washington, D.C., neighborhoods with concentrations of
blacks and low-income people received fewer school funds and
facilities of lower quality than did predominantly white and higher-
income neighborhoods. During the 1965–1966 school year the school
system spent a median of $100 more per pupil in white than in black
schools; elementary schools in white areas operated at approximately

[11]Patricia Cayo Sexton, *Education and Income* (New York, Viking, 1961).

77 percent capacity while those in black areas operated at 115 percent capacity.[12] Studies in other cities have documented variability in service consumption from one neighborhood to another. For example, Charles S. Benson and Peter B. Lund examined the distribution of urban public services in Berkeley, California, and discovered wide variations among neighborhoods in their use.[13] Low-income neighborhoods were heavy "consumers" of such services as health clinics, policing, special education programs, and recreation centers. High-income neighborhoods scored high on the "consumption" of libraries, summer schools, and high-school extracurricular activities.

POLICY IMPACTS AND FEEDBACK   The output of a public policy does not necessarily accomplish its goals. Although the elements of a service may be provided by a local agency, they may not have their intended impact on the problem. Impacts represent the effects that a service has on the target population and on other features of the environment. Impacts may be intended or not. Some impacts are planned and anticipated by policy-makers. Others—we call them "spillover effects"—represent the unanticipated products of policy. Unintended impacts arise because the urban system consists of interrelated parts that influence one another and because information about all the potential effects of a policy is unavailable. An elusive hope of policy-makers is to design public policies whose major consequences are intended and whose unintended impacts are either minimal or benign.

An example of unintended consequences may assist in clarifying the concept of impact and spillover. Heavy traffic may prompt city officials to build a second bridge to lessen traffic pressure on an existing span. Yet the expanded access to both sides of the river may encourage more home sites and shopping centers across the river. The net effect may be expanded urbanization that, in turn, produces even more traffic. The spillover effect of building the new bridge is more urban growth and perhaps another wave of traffic congestion.

From the decision-makers' perspective, one classification of impacts is shown in Figure 6.1, which focuses on the dimensions of prediction and control. Cell A identifies the "ideal" policy, one whose effects are predictable and intended. This policy "works," at least in terms of the policy-makers' goals. Ideally, the official would maximize the pre-

[12] *Hobson* v. *Hansen*, 269 F. Supp. 401 (D.D.C., 1967), cited in Gershon M. Ratner, "Inter-Neighborhood Denials of Equal Protection in the Provision of Municipal Services," *Harvard Civil Rights-Civil Liberties Law Review, 4* (Fall, 1968), 1–64.

[13] Charles S. Benson and Peter B. Lund, *Neighborhood Distribution of Local Public Services* (Berkeley, University of California, Institute of Governmental Studies, 1969).

dictability of his policies and limit them to intended consequences. Under these conditions he would know what would happen and would therefore be in control of events. Cells B and C define policies high on either the control or the predictive dimension but low on the other. From the decsion-makers' point of view, the "worst" kinds of policies are those that fall into cell D, for their impacts are both unintended and unanticipated.

There may be no question for the policy-maker that is more important than policy impact. Policies may not accomplish the intended impacts; their spillover effects may be negative and may actually reduce the system's capacity to attain other goals; and there may be no way to measure or evaluate their impacts. Policy-making is problematic at best. Because research on policy impacts has been limited, the information available to decision-makers is scarce. Public policy is at least partially made "in the dark" and based on insufficient information about probable impacts on the environment.

FEEDBACK    Feedback is the influence that policies exert on the subsequent inputs from the environment. Property-tax rates influence the conversion process by regulating the flow of economic resources from the population. Public-service outputs affect the satisfactions and frustrations of citizens and shape their demands for additional services. Programs in planning and industrial promotion may add to the industrial tax base of the community and increase the revenues produced by existing taxes. Economic growth may also increase the loads on public services and stimulate demands to cope with growth. The feedback loop indicates continuous interaction between the policies of one moment and the inputs of the next. To some observers, the policy process appears to be seeking equilibrium, as actors in the conversion process respond to inputs from their environment and strive for a level

**Figure 6.1**  *A two-dimensional scheme for classifying policy impacts*

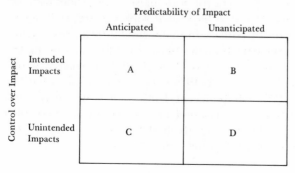

of output that will balance any undesirable future input. Yet, for most of the actors described in this book, equilibrium of policy outputs and inputs is more illusory than real. Few actors remain satisfied with any present state of affairs. Some demand improvements in existing services and policies, expansions of their magnitude, and the addition of new programs. Others demand contraction. There are no final solutions for the major problems of American cities. The dynamism of their economies and their politics defies any attempt to portray them in equilibrium.

## ANALYSIS, MEASUREMENT, EVALUATION

Political scientists and their predecessors have studied public policy for 2,500 years. The earliest writings dealt with the actions of government officials, the conditions that fostered certain kinds of policy, and the implications of policy for other features of politics. We can read through the works of Plato and Aristotle and find a mixture of policy recommendations and policy analysis. Each of these men and countless of their intellectual descendants have combined a willingness to express their preference for certain policies and an obligation to defend their preferences with some assessment of which policy options were available and the likely outputs and impacts of each.

There has been a conscious effort in recent years to improve our analytic capacities to the point at which we can speak with some certainty about the influence that various phases of the policy process have upon one another. There are several dimensions of this new concern with policy analysis: a commitment to explanation before prescription; sophisticated comparisons among the policies of different communities; the search for economic, social, and historical, as well as political and governmental, influences on the policy choices made; and an effort to accumulate different kinds of research in order to build theories about the policy process. In the following chapters we report the findings of scholars (of sociologists and economists, as well as of political scientists) who have used sophisticated techniques to compare measurements of policies in many communities with measurements of other phenomena thought likely to influence—or to be influenced by—the policies. The focus of much of this research is on various "levels," "quantities," or "qualities" of policy, as measured by reasonable surrogates for each policy at issue. These measurements serve the social scientist as the thermometer and barometer serve the meteorologist. It is not the policies themselves that are subject to analysis, but it is indicators of the policies that can be subject to precise measurement.

Not all the information about public policies reported in the following chapters is derived from rigorous analyses using sophisticated statistical techniques. Many important questions about urban politics have not so far proved amenable to precise measurement. Much urban research implicitly denies the applicability of Galileo's dictum to "measure what is measurable and make measurable what is not measurable." Many studies are admittedly "impressionistic" and rely upon the persuasiveness of the author's prose to convince the reader. Some intuitive studies, however, are more convincing than are quantitative studies of comparable policies. The mere presence of statistical computations in a piece of research does not make it reliable. Moreover, there are quarrels among the users of quantitative techniques that open their work to charges of imprecision and unreliability. The quantification of scholarship is less important than are other attributes: the breadth of relevant factors taken into consideration; the use of the most substantial and trustworthy evidence that is relevant and available; and the use of concepts and analytical tools that seem most likely to illuminate the forces important for the policy process under consideration.

In the description of the policy process we present in this and in the following chapters we treat policy sometimes as a dependent variable and sometimes as an independent variable. In the former instance, we are interested in the "dependence" of policy upon features in its environment; we look for evidence on how variations in educational policies, for example, are influenced by variations in its environment. Likely correlates of educational policy are the social characteristics of the community, the economic resources available to the decision-makers, and the policy predispositions of the community elite. When we consider policy as an independent variable, we seek its influence upon the environment. We ignore, for the moment, the influence of environment on policy by abstracting policy elements from their surroundings and considering them "independently" from other sources. We assess as well the impacts that policy has upon its environment by treating certain environmental characteristics as dependent variables.

## Evaluating public policies

Increasingly, policy evaluation depends upon measurement. The rising status of precise measurement and quantitative analysis is evident not only in academic studies of the causes and implications of certain policies—what might be called "basic research"—but also in applied studies that attempt to measure various cost-benefit ratios of public policies. These techniques have been made possible by the advent of high-speed computers that permit multivariate analysis and simulation.[14] Multivariate analysis may indicate the particular mix of environmental characteristics that influence—or are influenced by —a policy. The use of simulation techniques permits experimental variation of a finite number of variables assumed to effect an intended change in the environment. But these techniques require accurate measurement of the factors under consideration. Without precise measurement, the analyst faces—in computing-center shop talk—the "garbage in–garbage out" (GIGO) problem.

Cost-benefit analysis and "planning-programming-budgeting" (PPB) are other techniques currently being touted by some government management specialists. Cost-benefit analysis attempts to estimate the costs of each policy option, including as many spillover costs as can be indentified, and to sum up the benefits of each policy. Decision-makers then use the results in the choice of alternatives.[15] PPB was originally developed as an aid to budgeting in the U.S. Department of Defense and, at President Johnson's order, was then applied to all agencies of the federal government. Under the prompting of management analysts—and with the funding of experimental projects by private foundations—PPB is being adopted by numerous state and local agencies. Its elements include

1    defining the major programs in each area of public service;
2    defining the principal outputs of each program in ways that can be subjected to precise measurement;
3    defining the inputs relevant to each program (for example, various combinations of personnel, facilities, funds, and ways of rendering services);
4    computing the costs of alternative combinations of inputs and the economic value of the various combinations of outputs likely to be produced by each combination of inputs;
5    calculating the cost-benefit ratio associated with each combination of inputs and outputs.

This book is not the place to explore the claims that are made by advocates of PPB or the allegations made by its detractors.[16] Yet the

[14] For a number of points of view on the relations of science, technology, and computers to urban policy-making, see Stephen B. Sweeney and James C. Charlesworth, eds., *Governing Urban Society: New Scientific Approaches* (Philadelphia, American Academy of Political and Social Science, 1967).

[15] An excellent summation of cost-benefit and PPS techniques can be found in Aaron Wildavsky, "The Political Economy of Efficiency," in Ranney, ed., *op. cit.*, pp. 55–82.

[16] The best single-volume compilation of materials is Fremont J. Lyden and Ernest G. Miller, eds., *Planning Programming Budgeting: A Systems Approach to Management* (Chicago, Markham, 1967).

very existence of this technique testifies to the need for careful quantitative evaluation of the policy process.

But techniques for analysis do not solve the complex problems of measuring variables. Among social scientists, economists have claimed some success in surmounting the measurement problem, but then their fundamental unit of analysis, money, readily lends itself to measurement. Other social scientists have found measurement of variables a more difficult problem because such concepts as power, alienation, control, culture, and learning do not lend themselves to precisely measurable formulations that are acceptable to social scientists having different perspectives. In recent years, these social scientists have devoted considerable resources to developing indicators of social phenomena. *Toward a Social Report,* published by the U.S. Department of Health, Education, and Welfare in 1969, represented a major effort to measure and assess the state of American society through the use of social indicators.[17] Because measurement precedes evaluation, developments in the availability and use of social indicators will necessarily precede the full-scale applicability of such techniques as cost-benefit analysis, simulation, and PPB.[18]

## Policy research and application

One attribute of policy-oriented political science is its promise to link the work of scholars with the needs of practitioners. There is some dramatic evidence of this link in the coincidental development of basic and applied research that we have noted. Some of what political scientists design for the purpose of understanding the policy process may be useful for those who toil as policy-makers. Yet the world of the academic and the practitioner are not easily joined. Political scientists who have done part-time duty for government units, either as consultants or as regular employees rotating between campus and government, have reported tensions between the two roles. Whereas the academic researcher strives for a more complete and general understanding of the policy process, the practitioner typically wants specific recommendations for specific problems. The practitioner can rarely afford the academician's luxury of time for reflection and contemplation. The creative academic, it is true, should plot the general tendencies in the activities he observes and should understand the conditions that produce deviations from the norms. Yet his quest and the analytic techniques that he devises will not always coincide with

[17] Department of Health, Education, and Welfare, *Toward a Social Report* (Washington, D.C., Government Printing Office, 1969),

[18] See Bertram M. Gross, ed., *Social Intelligence for America's Future* (Boston, Allyn & Bacon, 1969).

the particular needs of the government official. Academicians are interested in the broad sweep of the policy-making process and its determinants. Public officials, whether presidents, governors, mayors, or bureaucrats, are more concerned with the issue of "political feasibility."[19]

Similarly, the policy research that we are going to treat here is of some use but not totally satisfactory to students of political science who are interested in changing public policies. Indeed, we emphasize in this book the constraints upon decision-makers and upon their power to alter the urban environment. Those who charge policy analysis in political science with irrelevance, however, should first pursue it.[20] But we concede that we have gone only part way toward answers about how policies are shaped and how they exert their influences on target problems. Ours is a slow and perhaps conservative approach to policy change. As scholars we are concerned with the quality of information that supports policy recommendations. At times, we recognize the need to change some policies before all the relevant information is in. (See our discussion of rational decision-making on pp. 180–185.) But someone must speak for obtaining the best information that is feasible. Analytic techniques that emphasize rigorous measurement and careful comparison can become potent tools in the policy process. Government officials and private citizens can enhance their ability to change policies if they can persuade decision-makers that they have identified tangible problems with current policies and if they can identify some alternatives, the resources needed for each, and the impacts that each is likely to have on various features of the environment.

## SUMMARY

In this chapter we returned to our model of the urban political system in order to elaborate the character of urban policy. Policies are the products of the conversion process, which takes demands and resources and translates them into outputs. There have been many efforts to group and categorize policies, and these efforts suggest the importance of looking beyond traditional categories of the budget documents and organization charts of policy-making agencies. Nevertheless, such theoretical policy analysis remains in its infancy. Even when we confine our attention to the traditional classifications of policy, however,

19 The term is Ralph Huitt's, from his article of that title in Ranney, ed., *op. cit.*, pp. 263–275.

20 See, for example, the selections in Ira Sharkansky, ed., *Policy Analysis in Political Science* (Chicago, Markham, 1970).

there are important dimensions common to most or all policies. Among them are cost, service output, and output distribution.

One of the most important aspects of policy analysis is the impact of a policy on the problem it is intended to ameliorate. Impacts may be intended or unintended. We use the term "spillover effects" to characterize unintended impacts. Sometimes, of course, spillover effects are primarily benign, but they can also produce serious problems in other policy areas. We shall have many occasions in the following chapters to assess the spillover effects of various policies.

The absence of information on policy impacts is one reason why it is difficult to evaluate and recommend policy. Successful evaluation often depends upon measurement of results. Although there are now some methods for measuring social policy, for example, cost-benefit analysis and PPB, such techniques have yet to prove their worth to decision-makers confronted with demands for immediate action. Our fundamental assumption, however, is that sensible public policy cannot be made in an information vacuum or solely upon the premises of political feasibility. The next four chapters will reveal some significant areas of ignorance, in which fragmentary data and "informed" guesswork have to substitute for systematic information. But they also indicate our concern for a fuller understanding of urban policies and their impacts.

# 7

# Taxing and spending

There is a lot of money at stake in urban politics. In 1968–1969, the total general revenues of municipal governments in the United States were $24.2 billion. Of this sum, $16.8 billion was raised from local sources, and another $7.3 billion was received from federal, state, and other local governments.

Local governments are the biggest spenders among the three levels of government for the provision of domestic services, although the states are close behind and gaining.[1] These sums are of great interest to the municipal officials who distribute public largesse, to those seeking government contracts, and to those of us who must pay the bills. Builders of roads and schools, countless consultants, and suppliers of equipment and services pay close attention to the decisions of local financial officers. These decisions are never far removed from concern with taxes, for local governments are very close—sometimes perilously close—to their taxpayers. The property tax is the prime source of local revenues, and of all the taxes used by American governments it seems to provoke the sharpest and longest-lasting controversies.

In this chapter we discuss the major choices facing the financial policy-makers of local governments. We also identify the kinds and amounts of taxes and expenditures made by different kinds of cities and the features in the environments of these local governments that seem responsible for their choices. Among the principal features we con-

[1] Ira Sharkansky, *The Politics of Taxing and Spending* (Indianapolis, Bobbs-Merrill, 1969), chap. 5.

sider are the socioeconomic characteristics of the population, the nature of local government institutions, and the procedures by which financial decision-makers arrive at their choices. We look for patterns in the types of taxes and expenditures made by different kinds of communities: large and small, wealthy and poor, WASP and ethnic, and so on, and we try to take account of deviant cases: individual governments whose spending and taxing policies are sharply at odds with the practices of most local governments with similar characteristics.

## LOCAL REVENUE PATTERNS

### Revenue sources of local governments

Urban governments draw upon four major sources of revenue: locally collected taxes, intergovernmental aid, consumer charges for public services, and borrowing. Within each of these major categories the following specific choices must be made: Which kinds of taxes should be collected and how much of each? What services should the municipality provide on a charge basis? How high should service charges be? What federal or state aids can the municipality obtain? And how much and what forms of indebtedness should it incur? Revenue policies provide clear examples of policy outputs that have direct feedback to decision-makers. They reflect not only decisions on tax rates, service charges, and borrowing but also the burden taxpayers are willing to bear.

The data contained in Table 7.1 provide one way of looking at local government revenues. The revenue sources are broken down into two major categories, general and utility revenues.

Although some cities make a profit on utilities, their major income is from general revenues. Local governments are primarily self-supporting. Despite the development of grants-in-aid and the cooperative federal system, a study made in the 1960s found that local governments provide about four-fifths of their own revenues. The growth of intergovernmental transfer payments, moreover, has made "no significant [difference] . . . in the dependence of local governments upon higher levels in the past quarter-century."[2] Although federal and state aids to local governments have increased, revenues from local sources have increased in approximately the same proportion.

The property tax is clearly the most important source of revenue for American local government. In 1968–1969, it accounted for $8.3

[2] Frederick C. Mosher and Orville F. Poland, *The Costs of American Government* (New York, Dodd, Mead, 1964), p. 57.

**Table 7.1**   *Revenues of city governments, 1968–1969*

|  | Millions of dollars | Distribution |
|---|---|---|
| Total revenues | $29,673 | |
| General revenues | 24,153 | 100.0% |
| Intergovernmental | 7,346 | 30.4 |
| State | 5,811 | 24.1 |
| Federal | 1,144 | 4.7 |
| Other local | 391 | 1.6 |
| From own sources | 16,807 | 69.6 |
| Taxes | 12,349 | 51.1 |
| Property | 8,331 | 34.5 |
| Sales | 2,017 | 8.4 |
| Other[a] | 2,002 | 8.3 |
| Charges and miscellaneous | 4,458 | 18.5 |
| Utility revenues | 4,576 | 100.0 |

a Includes new income taxes levied by New York City for the first time in 1966–1967.

SOURCE: U.S. Bureau of the Census, *City Government Finances 1968–1969* (Washington, D.C., Government Printing Office, 1970), Table 1, p. 5.

billion of *municipal governments'* revenues; this sum represented 34.5 percent of total revenues and about two-thirds of all tax revenues. Among all kinds of local governments, the property tax is even more important. When counties, school districts, and other special districts are considered along with municipalities, the property tax accounts for $29.7 billion, 37.4 percent of total revenues and 85.3 percent of tax revenues. Almost all local governments draw heavily upon the property tax, and relatively few of them make significant use of sales or income taxes. In 1967–1968, all local governments combined collected only $2.5 billion from sales taxes and less than $1.5 billion from income taxes. In fact, local government's dependence upon the property tax has not changed much throughout the twentieth century. Cities relied on property taxes to about the same degree in the 1960s that they did in 1900.[3]

State aid is the second most important source of local-government revenue. It takes the form of grants for specific functions (schools, roads, welfare payments), grants to support general local government (the use of which may be determined by local officials), and state tax money that is returned to the jurisdictions where it is collected. In 1968–1969, the total resources transferred to municipal governments from state governments amounted to $5.8 billion. This was 19.5 percent

3 *Ibid.,* p. 70.

of total government revenues and almost half (47.1 percent) the
level of taxes that city governments collected from their own sources.
Direct aids from the federal government are paltry in comparison with
state aids. They amounted to $1.1 billion in 1968–1969, but they do
contribute to significant local programs in education, urban renewal
and public housing, planning, airport construction, health and hospitals, and highway construction.

The third and fourth most prominent forms of city-government
revenue are service charges and borrowing. In 1968–1969, local
governments raised $9 billion in charges and utility revenues and
another $4.2 billion from long-term debt. The most important sources
of charges and fees were utilities, especially water and electric systems.
Other sums come from hospital charges, rents from public housing,
tolls, license fees, and charges for school lunches.

These figures reflect only the general patterns; they do not take
account of the complexity that pervades local revenue policies. The
main source of complexity arises from the position of local governments as creatures of the states.

### The states and local revenues

The powers of cities to tax are heavily circumscribed by the legal
constraints of Dillon's rule (see Chapter 4, pp. 113–117). Cities may
tax only for such purposes and in such manners as are specifically
allowed by state law.[4] Although state legislatures may require cities
to perform a multiplicity of functions, there is no necessary guarantee
that tax resources will match legal responsibilities. Cities cannot determine on their own to adopt a sales tax or an income tax if state law
has not explicitly authorized the levy of such taxes. Even if they are
authorized, their upper limits may be specified. Sometimes the uses
of each tax are also specified in detail by the legislature. These restrictions make local governments the poor stepchildren of American
federalism.

Few municipalities collect sales or income taxes because most
states forbid such levies. The property tax, the only major tax allowed
by all state governments, is the mainstay of local governments. Furthermore, state governments limit the total amounts even of these taxes
that may be raised. They regulate the levels of property taxes, the kinds
of properties that are subject to property taxes, and the amounts that
local authorities can borrow.

Tax and debt limits are typically based upon the amount of

4 One exception to this rule is Pennsylvania's so-called "tax anything" law,
in which cities may, in general, tax anything not already taxed by the state.

"assessed valuation" in a community: the total value of property as local officials have established it for purposes of taxation. The constitution of Alabama, for example, forbids local governments to raise more than 1.25 percent of the total assessed valuation within their jurisdictions in taxes; that of Washington limits taxation to 4 percent; the debt limit of Indiana municipalities is 2 percent of assessed value; and that of Pennsylvania (except for Philadelphia) is 7 percent.[5] Local authorities can exercise some discretion in the face of these limits by simply increasing the assessments on property within their jurisdictions when they reach the current limits of taxes or indebtedness imposed on them.[6] However, such manipulations usually do not escape the notice of tax-wary citizens' groups, and there are high political costs in manipulating assessments in order to increase taxes. State governments also require tax exemptions and deductions for certain kinds of property. Several states give concessions to veterans, the aged, certain kinds of industrial plants, and "homesteads" (single-family homes occupied by their owners). States also exclude from the local tax base or require special tax rates for farm properties, automobiles, and other forms of "personal" property.[7] Certain properties of churches and nonprofit organizations, as well as state and federal properties, are exempt from local taxation. The City of New Haven, the home of Yale University, has only a little more than half the actual property within the city limits on its tax rolls. Tax-exempt properties nevertheless add to the total service burden of the city, for they require transportation arteries, police and fire protection, and other "free" public services. Taxable properties in cities having government, medical, and educational centers thus must bear added burdens.

### Equity, politics, and attitudes toward taxation

Tax *equity* is an issue that often figures in local politics. Equity can be defined as fairness, equality, or distribution of "appropriate" burdens. The issue of equity is complicated by long-standing philosophical disputes about equality, as well as by immediate questions of

---

[5] James A. Maxwell, *Financing State and Local Government* (Washington, D.C., Brookings Institution, 1965), p. 143.

[6] Rarely, if ever, are local property assessments actually based on market value. Properties are typically undervalued, and the limited staffs of assessment offices often permit valuations to remain unchanged over decades. Properties in areas with rapidly rising land values thus may still be assessed at much less than their true values. It may also be noted that in local governments not characterized by pristine integrity, assessments have sometimes been manipulated by local officials.

[7] Real property most commonly subject to property taxes includes land, dwelling units, office buildings, factories, and the like.

whose pocketbook is to be tapped. In principle, an equitable tax is one that distributes the costs of public service in a fair manner among economic groups. But equity is not simply resolved by an *equal* assignment of taxes among citizens or business firms. There is debate over the wisdom of *progressive* versus *regressive* taxation. Those who advocate progressive taxes argue that burdens should be equal only among those with equal economic resources and that people with large incomes should pay not only more taxes than people with small incomes but also higher percentages of their incomes. Some observers favor progressive taxes on incomes, combined with regressive taxes in other areas, because they think that this combination will spread the burden throughout the community most fairly. Regressive taxes, which take larger percentages of the incomes of the poor than of the rich, are defended on the grounds that they leave more resources in the hands of the wealthy, who are likely to promote economic growth with their investments. Regressivity is also supported by those who claim that the poor reap the greatest benefit from domestic spending and should "pay for what they get."

In debates about taxation, the subject of equity cannot be considered apart from the *incidence* and *burdens* of taxation and their subsequent impacts on individuals and the local economy. The incidence of a tax—the ultimate payer—is not apparent in the statute that defines the rates and the items to be taxed. When a property tax is first levied, it falls upon the property owner. If he is a landlord, however, he can shift the tax to his tenants by increasing his rents accordingly. The original justification and still-current defense of property taxes is that higher taxes are placed upon properties of higher values. But, because poor people spend larger than average percentages of their incomes for housing, property taxes take larger shares of the incomes of the poor than of those of the relatively well-to-do. Property taxes generally have a regressive impact, although their regressivity can be modified somewhat if certain low-income groups (for example, the aged) are given special exemptions.

Urban taxation tends to be regressive. Even those local taxes other than property taxes that are commonly used—income and sales taxes—are not progressive in their application at the local level. Sales taxes are generally regressive because they take larger shares of the incomes of poor men, who must spend most of their incomes buying basic necessities that are subject to the tax. At the federal level, of course, income taxes are moderately progressive. Income taxes at the local level, however, tend to take fixed proportions of incomes, typically 1 percent. Considering the whole system of taxation, in which state and local regressivity works against the progressivity of the federal tax structure, the American taxation system is not so progressive as is sometimes supposed. A study of national, state, and local taxes, done several years ago, concluded that people earning more than $15,000 annually paid about 34 percent of their incomes in taxes, whereas those earning $10,000–$15,000 paid about 22 percent of their incomes to various governments. People making less than $2,000, however, suffered tax burdens nearly equal to those of the middle-income group, paying about 21 percent of their incomes in taxes.[8]

Still, the question of tax burdens cannot be dismissed after examination of only the revenue side of government. Although the classic defense of progressive taxation defines the regressive tax as inequitable, certain regressive taxes seem somewhat more equitable because of the expenditures that they support. Local taxes on property and retail sales are regressive in the burdens they impose, but they also help to support such services as public education, health, recreation, and welfare, which provide important benefits to lower-income citizens. Before final answers about tax equity can be determined, we need an analysis of benefits. One such effort has been made by Walter Heller, former chairman of the President's Council of Economic Advisers. Heller estimated that

*the state-local expenditure pattern is strongly [progressive], declining steadily [in the benefits offered] from an estimated 43 percent of income for the poorest families to 6 percent for families with incomes about $10,000.*

He emphasized that "study after study has confirmed the unmistakable pattern of substantially progressive federal taxes and expenditures, strongly regressive state local taxes, and strongly progressive state-local expenditures."[9] The progressive character of the expenditure patterns of state and local governments operates to counterbalance, at least in part, the regressivity of their tax systems.

The issues of incidence, burdens, and equity are important elements in understanding attitudes toward taxation at the local level. The simplest proposition about such attitudes—that self-interest motivates people to oppose any tax increases—contains some elements of truth. Yet people periodically do vote higher taxes upon themselves in local referenda, partly because they perceive taxes as likely to bring improvements in local services. Self-interest does seem to be a major factor in determining attitudes about what *type* of taxes one prefers. A Michigan study found that (1) low-income people preferred income taxes whereas upper-income people preferred other kinds, (2) property

[8] Gabriel Kolko, *Wealth and Power in America* (New York, Praeger, 1964), p. 37.
[9] Walter Heller, *New Dimensions of Political Economy* (New York, Norton, 1967), p. 153.

owners preferred less reliance on property taxes, and (3) people who lived in areas of high property taxes preferred shifts to other forms of taxation.[10] But self-interest does not alone motivate preferences for levels of taxation. For some people a sense of "public-regardingness" supports the belief that taxation may produce collective benefits even if taxes bring no immediate benefits. Upper-income property holders, who bear a disproportionate share of taxes, have sometimes been found to support projects of primary benefit to the poor.[11]

## The future of local revenues

Local governments face both a revenue bind and a crush of demands for public expenditures. As we emphasized in Chapter 2, urban areas are the centers of most concentrations of American wealth, yet most of that wealth is inaccessible to local governments. Such factors as legal limitations upon the objects and levels of taxation, the hostility of tax-payers, debt limitations, and the reluctance of local officials to take advantage of their fiscal options contribute to the "revenue incapacity" of local governments.

Any hints that local governments propose to increase revenues are usually followed by veiled threats from local industries to move else-where and by sharp warnings from business groups that high-tax communities cannot be expected to attract industry and residents. The fact is that a number of studies indicate that the level of state or local taxes is but one of many factors, and often not the most important one, in determining industrial location.[12] One economist has noted the paradox that

*the influence of tax considerations on the location decisions of business is grossly overstated . . . [but] its impact on state and local taxation is not. . . . Fear of losing business to another jurisdiction haunts the mind and stills the pen of the state and local lawmaker, and special pleaders have developed the skill of exploiting this fear to a high art.*[13]

It would not, however, be fair to lay at the doorstep of local business-men the sole responsibility for pressures for low taxes. Also culpable

[10] Elizabeth Likert David, "Public Preferences and State-Local Taxes," in Harvey Brazer, ed., *Essays in State and Local Finance* (Ann Arbor, University of Michigan Institute of Public Administration, 1967), pp. 74–106.

[11] James Q. Wilson and Edward C. Banfield, "Public Regardingness as a Value Premise in Voting Behavior," *American Political Science Review, 58* (December, 1964), 876–887.

[12] See, for example, John F. Due, "Studies of State-Local Tax Influences on Industrial Location," *National Tax Journal, 14* (1961), 163–173.

[13] L. L. Ecker-Racz, quoted in Heller, *op. cit.,* p. 126.

are local electorates, municipal officials reluctant to take political risks, and state legislators unwilling to increase local revenue options.

One of the most frequently advanced solutions to the fiscal difficulties of local governments, as well as to those of state governments, is federal revenue sharing with the states, municipalities, or both. The plan is usually associated with the ideas of Joseph Pechman and Walter W. Heller. Heller has argued that the federal government should provide "no strings attached" block grants to the states in the amount of 2 percent of federal tax receipts.[14] Many critics of his plan cite the reluctance of states to use their financial windfalls for urban needs. They fear that state governments, long dominated by rural forces, will continue to ignore the needs of big cities. To be sure, there is no evidence to support certain predictions, but Lyle C. Fitch has catalogued a number of reasons for skepticism about states' willingness to devote their revenues from a hypothetical revenue-sharing plan to urban redevelopment.[15] Even Heller himself has come to favor a "pass-through" requirement that a certain proportion of state revenues be turned over to local governments for their own use.

Even if a revenue-sharing plan contained a pass-through provision, however, it might not alleviate the financial difficulties of the largest metropolitan areas. If the revenue sharing followed the common practice of weighing assistance to states on the basis of need, usually measured by the per capita income of the state, huge revenues would not go to the cities with the greatest need. The poorest states, which would receive disproportionate largesse under the revenue-sharing plans, do not generally contain those metropolitan areas with the worst urban problems. The dozen states with the lowest incomes contain only five of the fifty-one cities with populations larger than 250,000. No doubt there are substantial advantages to programs to revitalize state governments, but it cannot be assumed that federal-state revenue sharing will "trickle down" to solve the more severe revenue problems of the largest cities as well.

Moreover, the magnitude of the revenue-sharing proposals seems skimpy alongside most projections of urban needs. In August, 1969, President Richard M. Nixon proposed a modest revenue-sharing effort that would have reached a maximum federal contribution of $5 billion in 1975. But, even with a successful revenue-sharing program, it is likely that urban governments will continue to live from hand to mouth. At least in terms of taxing, local governments are close to the people, and the property tax hits—quite literally—very close to home.

[14] See Heller, *op. cit.*
[15] Lyle C. Fitch, "Reflections on the Case for the Heller Plan," in Heller *et al.*, *Revenue Sharing and the City* (Baltimore, Johns Hopkins, 1968).

Revenue limitations by state governments, preemption of taxes on sales and incomes by higher levels of government, perception of industrial opposition to taxes, and the general reluctance of citizens and politicians to explore tax increases all combine to keep the fiscal wolf perennially on the urban doorstep. Later we shall discuss several public policies, including urban redevelopment and zoning, in which efforts to handle revenue needs are paramount. However, there is no sector of urban policy in which revenue questions can be set aside.

## URBAN EXPENDITURE PATTERNS

The other side of the fiscal coin is expenditures. They are of interest to political scientists and citizens for several reasons. First, budgets indicate relative priorities among public choices. Charles A. Beard once wrote that

*in the purposes for which appropriations are made the policies of the city government are given concrete form—the culture of the city is reflected. Indeed, the history of urban civilization could be written in terms of appropriations, for they show what the citizens think is worth doing and worth paying for.*[16]

More recently, Louis H. Masotti and Don R. Bowen have written that "the community budget can be viewed as public policy spelled out in dollars and cents, and that budget decisions represent the allocations of certain kinds of values."[17]

Second, expenditures are of interest because they purchase certain levels of public services through which the municipality can make an impact upon its environment. Educational expenditures buy teachers, schoolbooks, and classrooms in an effort to raise the educational achievement and community aspirations. Police expenditures purchase policemen, cars, paddy wagons, radios, radar equipment, and laboratory devices, all of which are designed to help apprehend transgressors of the law. Expenditures are therefore important as means of procuring certain kinds of output intended to have impact upon the environment.

Third, local expenditures are of interest because they have considerable influence upon the economic system as a whole. That local governments spend about 8 percent of GNP makes them a potent influence on levels of inflation or deflation and on economic growth.

[16] Charles A. Beard, *American Government and Politics*, 4th ed. (New York, Macmillan, 1924), p. 727.
[17] Louis H. Masotti and Don R. Bowen, "Communities and Budgets: The Sociology of Municipal Expenditures," *Urban Affairs Quarterly, 1* (1965), 39.

## Where all that money goes

In 1966–1967, city governments spent a total of $19.2 billion on a wide range of services. Table 7.2 details the distribution of city expenditures by major categories of public function. City governments have a very wide range of expenditure categories. Few separate items require more than 10 percent of the "typical" city budget. Only education, policing, and highways account for as much as 10 percent each of total city expenditures. These major items accounted for $26.81, $17.55, and $17.30 per capita, respectively.

Table 7.2, however, shows only the aggregate patterns of municipal expenditures. The data suffer from several limitations. First, there is wide variation among states in the division of labor. Some state governments perform functions that in others are operated by city governments. In some states, for example, welfare payments are made entirely from state contributions while elsewhere cities contribute to the welfare function. There is also wide variation in responsibilities among different kinds of local government. Education is the major variable. In some states, particularly in the East, city governments are responsible for the operation of public schools and sometimes for colleges and universities. New York City's billion-dollar school budget (which alone accounts for nearly one-third of all municipal governments' spending

**Table 7.2**  *City-government expenditures in 1966–1967*

| Expenditure item | Amount (millions of dollars) | Percentage of total expenditures | Per capita amount |
|---|---|---|---|
| Total general expenditures | $19,172 | 100.0 | $164.75 |
| Education | 3,120 | 16.3 | 26.81 |
| Police and law enforcement | 2,042 | 10.7 | 17.55 |
| Highways | 2,013 | 10.5 | 17.30 |
| Fire protection | 1,294 | 6.7 | 11.12 |
| Public welfare | 1,270 | 6.6 | 10.91 |
| Sewage | 1,124 | 5.9 | 9.66 |
| Health and hospitals | 1,038 | 5.4 | 8.92 |
| Parks and recreation | 913 | 4.8 | 7.85 |
| Housing and urban renewal | 861 | 4.5 | 7.40 |
| Sanitation other than sewage | 797 | 4.2 | 6.85 |
| Interest on debt | 735 | 3.8 | 6.32 |
| General control | 540 | 2.8 | 4.64 |
| Financial administration | 328 | 1.7 | 2.82 |
| General public buildings | 312 | 1.6 | 2.68 |
| All other | 2,784 | 14.5 | 23.93 |

SOURCE: U.S. Bureau of the Census, *City Government Finances in 1966–67* (Washington, D.C., Government Printing Office, 1968), p. 1.

on education) constitutes a very large proportion of its total expenditures. But in cities in the Midwest, South, and West school expenditures are typically made by special school districts. What in one state may be performed by municipal governments is thus performed in other states by counties, special districts, or the state governments themselves. The endless variations in distribution of responsibility among and within states make it risky to generalize about "typical" local expenditure patterns. The expenditure categories listed in Table 7.2 provide only a rough overview of the ways that city governments allocate their budgets.

### Urban expenditures and the federal system

It is increasingly impossible to separate programs into neat categories of federal, state, or local sponsorship. There are very few programs relevant to urban America that do not involve the federal system as a whole. Education is predominantly a local matter, but assistance to public and higher education is the largest single item in state budgeting, and federal aid to local schools has increased significantly in recent years. Quiet residential streets are built mostly with local money, but state and federal assistance is significant in building major traffic arteries, particularly those connected to the interstate-highway program. The federal government helps to build local hospitals and airports and to train policemen. The housing and urban-renewal programs receive federal and local funds, as well as state aid in some states. Because most of these programs are funded by more than one level of government, any neat effort to sort them by layers of the federal system will be misleading. The federal system is deeply embedded in the expenditure options of local governments.

Because the federal system exerts a significant influence on local budgets, the expenditure decisions of local governments are far from independent. The availability of federal and state money for certain programs may "distort" the expenditure choices of local decision-makers. The "distortion" is intended by Congress and state legislators, who hope to orient local governments more toward the performance of aided functions. It becomes "cheaper" for municipalities to engage in aided programs than in unaided ones. To spend $100,000 on an urban-renewal program costs the typical city only $33,333 because the federal contribution is two-thirds of the project cost. But to spend $100,000 on upgrading salaries in the fire or police department will cost close to $100,000, for there are fewer sources of federal assistance.

Grants-in-aid and restrictions on expenditures mean that local governments are not entirely free to make any set of decisions that suit their fancies. State governments require local authorities to perform certain functions in specified ways. Federal aid comes with strings attached. Grants are provided for specific purposes, and local governments that do not conform to requirements find their grants terminated. The rules and legislation of state and federal governments thus establish numerous constraints upon local policy.

## COMMUNITIES AND BUDGETS

Some cities spend more money than do others. In one sense, this difference results merely from financial decision-makers' consciously choosing to spend and tax at certain levels. But, in a broader sense, the level of spending is shaped by the socioeconomic, political, governmental, and legal structures of the community and its environment. In this section, we describe some of the community characteristics most commonly associated with variations in expenditures.

Perhaps the most obvious reason why some city budgets are larger than others is the factor of city size. It surprises no one to learn that New York City spends more money than does Kokomo, Oshkosh, or Ogden. Robert C. Wood, in his study of the New York metropolitan region, discovered that *population* size accounted for the overwhelming proportion of variation in local expenditures.[18] Because of the obvious influence of size, most students of public expenditures "control" their measurements for population size and analyze them in per capita terms.

### Socioeconomic factors and spending levels

Table 7.3 provides a summary statement of the relations between seven key socioeconomic characteristics of cities and the expenditure levels of those cities. Each of these relations will be discussed in the following section.

INCOME    As with families, the richer a community, the more money it can afford to spend. For local governments, income and availability of resources are very important in determining the level of public expenditures.[19] The city with a poor economic base, a large proportion

---

[18] Robert C. Wood, *1400 Governments* (Garden City, N.Y., Doubleday Anchor, 1964), pp. 39–40.

[19] For supporting evidence, see Solomon Fabricant, *The Trend of Government Activity in the United States Since 1900* (New York, National Bureau of Economic Research, 1952), pp. 112–129; Harvey Brazer, *City Expenditures in the United States* (New York, National Bureau of Economic Research, 1959), p. 29; and Otto Davis and George H. Harris, Jr., "A Political Approach to a Theory of Public Expenditures: The Case of Municipalities," *National Tax Journal, 19* (September, 1966), 259–275.

of poor people, or other economic disabilities possesses serious disadvantages in any effort to provide a high level of public services. In Meridian, Mississippi, only 7 percent of the population has incomes of $10,000 or more; in Edina, Minnesota, more than 60 percent of the families earn $10,000 a year.

In some states, state assistance compensates for income gaps among cities, but the deeper problem is that states like Alabama, Mississippi, New Mexico, and West Virginia do not themselves have the revenues to raise expenditures in their cities to levels of minimum support in other states. Dedication, imagination, and political "savvy" of local officials cannot substitute entirely for missing resources.

ECONOMIC BASE   An economic system based upon manufacturing tends to be associated with higher levels of municipal expenditures. In Wood's factor analysis of New Jersey communities, industrialization ac-

Table 7.3   *Summary of relations between socioeconomic variables and municipal spending levels*[a]

| Variable | Relation with municipal spending |
|---|---|
| Income | |
| High | + |
| Low | − |
| Economic base | |
| Manufacturing | + |
| Other | − |
| Density | |
| High | ? |
| Low | ? |
| Growth rate | |
| High | ? |
| Low | ? |
| Owner occupancy | |
| High | − |
| Low | + |
| Ethnic character | |
| Heavy | + |
| Nonethnic | − |
| Metropolitan type | |
| Central city | + |
| Outside central city | − |

[a] A + sign indicates a relationship generally identified as positive. A − sign indicates a relationship generally identified as negative. A ? indicates a variable about which findings are incomplete or mixed.

counted for more of the explainable variation in municipal expenditures than did any other factor except population size. In a study of suburban fiscal policy in the Philadelphia region, Williams and his associates discovered that the largest spenders among communities were suburbs with heavy industrial and commercial activity.[20] Industrialization brings heavy service demands for police and fire protection, roads, and public utilities. Also, as even the most obtuse tax assessor knows, industrial properties provide a lucrative tax base and thus more money for the municipality to spend. In the Detroit area, for example, as much as 95 percent of tax revenues in the industrial suburbs comes from taxes on industrial properties.[21]

DENSITY  Density is commonly measured by number of people per square mile. There are wide variations in this factor not only within cities (ranging from tightly packed ghettos to quarter-acre single-family dwelling units in fringe areas) but also among cities. The mean number of people per square mile in Boston is 15,157, whereas the comparable figure for Houston is 1,293. The impact of population density on city expenditures seems to vary with the particular expenditures being examined.[22] Where population density is high there tend to be low expenditures per capita on streets and highways, which suggests that economies of scale operate in the transportation field. In other fields, however, high densities operate to increase service needs and tend to increase per capita expenditures. Density adds to problems like traffic control, law enforcement, public health, and fire hazards, and it supports high per capita rates of expenditure for police protection, fire fighting, and sanitation.

GROWTH RATES  On strictly a priori grounds, one expects clear and unambiguous positive relationship between spending levels and growth rates: As a community grows it should spend more to meet new service demands. Richard Spangler's careful analysis of growth rates and spending at the state level found strong associations between population and higher expenditures.[23] On the other hand, the spending and debt limits of state governments, the hostility of taxpayers, and the reluctance of politicians to increase taxes suggest that some cities may prefer to "spread themselves thin" and "make do" financially rather than investing substantial resources in coping with urban growth.

[20] Oliver P. Williams et al., Suburban Differences and Metropolitan Policies (Philadelphia, University of Pennsylvania Press, 1965), p. 111.

[21] David, op. cit., p. 86.

[22] See the mixed findings in Brazer, op. cit.; and Davis and Harris, op. cit.

[23] Richard Spangler, "The Effect of Population Growth on State and Local Government Expenditures," National Tax Journal, 16 (June, 1963), 193–196.

In contrast to Spangler's findings, other research has revealed that growth rates bear little relation to increases in public spending.[24]

OWNER OCCUPANCY   The greater the degree of home ownership in a community, the lower municipal expenditures usually are. Lineberry and Fowler have offered two principal explanations for this. First,

> owner occupancy is correlated (almost by definition) with lower urban population density. High density, bringing all manner of men together in the classic urban mosaic, may itself be correlated with factors which produce demands for higher expenditures—slums, increased need for fire and police protection, and so on.

Second,

> no doubt self-interest (perhaps "private-regardingness") on the part of the home owner, whose property is intimately related to the tax structure of most local government, may account for part of this relationship.[25]

Whatever the underlying explanation, the incidence of home ownership in a community is one of the major negative correlates of municipal expenditures.

ETHNICITY AND RELIGIOUS COMPOSITION   Several studies indicate a strong positive relationship between the ethnicity or the religious composition of a community and its spending levels.[26] This relationship may be direct or spurious. For example, it may be that ethnic groups and Roman Catholics prefer high levels of municipal expenditures and support candidates and referenda that increase spending levels. There is some evidence that Roman Catholics are more sympathetic toward increased governmental activity, particularly welfare-state activities, than are other religious groups.[27] But, on the other hand, the relationship may be better explained by factors that are coincidentally associated with the religious composition and the size of the public budget. Ethnic groups and Roman Catholics may be concentrated in areas of high

[24] Amos H. Hawley, "Metropolitan Population and Municipal Government Expenditures in Central Cities," *Journal of Social Issues*, 7 (1951), 100–108; Robert L. Lineberry and Edmund P. Fowler, "Reformism and Public Policies in American Cities," *American Political Science Review*, 61 (September, 1967), 701–716; Brazer, *op. cit.;* and Wood, *op. cit.*

[25] Lineberry and Fowler, *op. cit.*, p. 712.

[26] See *ibid.;* and Terry N. Clark, "Community Structure, Decision-Making, Budget Expenditures, and Urban Renewal in 51 American Communities," *American Sociological Review, 33* (August, 1968), 576–593.

[27] Gerhard Lenski, *The Religious Factor* (Garden City, N.Y., Doubleday Anchor, 1961), pp. 152ff.

density or low owner occupancy; these other factors may explain the relationship between ethnicity and spending.

CC–OCC LOCATION  We saw in Chapter 2 that the location of a city within the metropolitan area may influence the level of its public spending. Central cities are faced with a greater proportion of the burdens—traffic, poverty, poor housing, crime, decay—necessitating public expenditures. Suburban governments, on the other hand, are mercifully free of many of these problems and can keep public budgets lower. OCCs, however, do contain larger proportions of school-age children and thus have higher educational expenditures than do CCs.

OTHER SOCIOECONOMIC FACTORS  There are countless other socioeconomic factors—incidence of poverty in a community, type of industrial activity, general age of buildings, whether or not the climate necessitates snow removal, and so forth—that may affect expenditures of city governments. Any attempt to catalogue all the possible elements that impinge upon the level of spending would stretch the boundaries of an introductory text too far. We have discussed a few of the socioeconomic factors on which the most research has been done. Our listing does not imply lesser significance of an array of unmentioned factors that might influence spending levels.

## Government and political factors and spending

As public officials write budgets, authorize city appropriations, and collect taxes, it might be possible to claim that only government and political factors affect local budgeting. This view is, however, a narrow one that denies the significant relations between community characteristics and municipal spending levels. Numerous community characteristics, from the resource base to the amount of snowfall, may affect public expenditures. But it is inappropriate to attribute all intermunicipal variations in spending levels to socioeconomic forces. There are important factors in the political process and the structure of government that bear upon the level of local spending. Some of these relations are summarized in Table 7.4.

STATE-LOCAL CENTRALIZATION  Different states use different "divisions of labor" among governments. Some states spend very large proportions of total state and local revenues and have broad responsibilities for provision of public services. In other states, local governments are assigned many of these responsibilities. Delaware, North Carolina, and Oklahoma are highly centralized states, making 33, 43, and 47 percent of total state and local expenditures respectively. At the other extreme,

**Table 7.4** *Summary of relations between government variables and municipal spending levels*[a]

| Variable | Relation with municipal spending |
|---|---|
| State-local centralization | |
| State responsibilities greater | − |
| Local responsibilities greater | + |
| Intergovernmental aid | |
| High | + |
| Low | − |
| State debt and expenditure limits | |
| Restrictive | − |
| Unrestrictive | + |
| Previous expenditures | |
| High | + |
| Low | − |
| Degree of government reformism | |
| High | ? |
| Low | ? |
| Participation in local politics | |
| High | ? |
| Low | ? |
| Party competition | |
| High | ? |
| Low | ? |

[a] A + sign indicates a relationship generally identified as positive. A − sign indicates a relationship generally identified as negative. A ? indicates a variable about which findings are either incomplete or mixed.

Wisconsin and Massachusetts are highly decentralized states; the municipalities account for 79 and 67 percent of state and local expenditures respectively. The greater the responsibilities assigned to the local governments, the more cities will spend. Alan Campbell and Seymour Sacks found such arrangements between state and local governments to be the most significant predictor of the level of local expenditures.[28]

INTERGOVERNMENTAL AID   As resources determine the amounts of money available to local governments, the amounts of intergovernmental aid received are positively correlated with expenditures. The most significant question about state and federal assistance is its *substitution effect* on local efforts. Opponents of intergovernmental assistance frequently claim that aid simply reduces local governments' dedication to raising

[28] Alan Campbell and Seymour Sacks, *Metropolitan America* (New York, Free Press, 1967), chap. 2.

money within their own communities and that the net effects of inter-governmental assistance are few. Evidence is, however, that much state and federal aid has a *stimulating effect* on local revenues. Many grant-in-aid programs seem to stimulate local governments to spend more than they otherwise would.

TAX, DEBT, AND EXPENDITURE LIMITS    Although, to our knowledge, no study has ever directly confronted the question and satisfactorily re-solved it, it seems reasonable to expect that cities whose fiscal capacities are under stringent state limitations spend less than do cities in states where such restrictions are looser.

PREVIOUS EXPENDITURE LEVELS AND BUDGET EXPERIENCE    Studies of state expenditure levels have identified the level of previous expenditures as the most significant single predictor of state budgets. Ira Sharkansky found correlations between previous and current expenditure levels for different categories of state-government expenditures ranging from .70 to .96.[29] A similar stable pattern probably prevails in cities. Relevant data for Houston, Texas, appear in Table 7.5. The correlations of expenditures in several budget categories over time suggest that stable "incrementalism" is characteristic of local expenditures. Such findings also suggest

*a conservative element in the political systems of American states and cities. The conservatism may reflect the influence of habit and routine, the practices of incremental budgeting, the problems involved in program expansion and/or the processes of an administration's maturation.*[30]

We shall have more to say later in this chapter about the importance of incremental budgeting.

GOVERNMENT REFORMISM    Much of the rhetorical thunder in support of municipal reforms (manager governments, nonpartisan elections, and at-large constituencies) claims that lower taxes—and by implication lower expenditures—will follow their adoption. What evidence is available, however, is mixed and inconclusive. Lineberry and Fowler's study of taxes and expenditures in cities of over 50,000 population found only slight differences in the expenditure levels of reformed and unreformed cities.[31] Clark found lower spending in reformed

---

29 Ira Sharkansky, "Economic and Political Correlates of State Government Ex-penditures: General Tendencies and Deviant Cases," *Midwest Journal of Political Science,* 11 (May, 1967), 173–192.

30 *Ibid.,* p. 191.

31 Lineberry and Fowler, *op. cit.,* pp. 707–708.

**Table 7.5** *Correlations between per ca-pita budget categories and equivalent items in previous years, Houston, Texas, 1947–1962*

| Budget category | Correlation |
| --- | --- |
| General revenues | .97 |
|   Taxes | .95 |
|   Property taxes | .95 |
|   Intergovernmental revenues | .84 |
|   Charges and miscellaneous | .94 |
| General expenditures | .78 |
|   Capital outlay | .27 |
|   Police | .91 |
|   Fire | .90 |
|   Highways | .85 |
|   Sanitation | .83 |
|   Hospitals | .95 |
|   Interest on debt | .97 |
| Utility revenues | .95 |
| Utility expenditures | .20 |
|   Current expenditures | .92 |
|   Capital outlay | .19 |
|   Interest on debt | .90 |

SOURCE: Adapted from Bernard Brown, "Municipal Finances and Annexation: A Case Study of Post-War Houston," *Social Science Quarterly, 48* (December, 1967), 341, Table 1.

cities.[32] Bernard Booms found that manager cities in Ohio and Michigan had significantly lower expenditures than did mayor-council cities.[33]

LOCAL PARTICIPATION AND PARTY COMPETITION    A well-known hypothesis in political science, originally formulated by V. O. Key, Jr., and Duane Lockard, holds that more vigorous interparty competition and more participation by lower-class groups will produce public policies more attuned to working-class interests.[34] The argument is that single-party systems with low voting turnouts probably tend to favor status quo politics beneficial to upper-income interests. The more competition there is, the more parties seek support among wider circles of the elec-

[32] Clark, *op. cit.*, p. 588.

[33] Bernard Booms, "City Governmental Form and Public Expenditure Levels," *National Tax Journal, 19* (June, 1966), 187–199.

[34] V. O. Key, Jr., *Southern Politics* (New York, Knopf, 1951), pp. 298–314; and Duane Lockard, *New England State Politics* (Princeton, N.J., Princeton University Press, 1959), pp. 320–340.

torate. Participation by lower-income groups increases, and their representatives obtain more benefits for them. Yet there are two difficulties with this argument. First, some careful studies of state spending have concluded that neither the level of voter participation nor the degree of interparty competition makes much difference in state expenditure levels.[35] Although the proposition may be true at the local level, it can hardly be assumed out of hand. Second, it is not at all clear that more effective working-class representation operates to raise or lower public expenditures. Higher government expenditures may aid working-class groups who benefit from numerous local government programs. The evidence suggests, however, that lower-income people are the most dissatisfied with governments and their policies.[36] Some research also suggests that numerous working-class voters are "alienated" and tend to vote against both public expenditures and candidates who advocate increases in public expenditures.[37] Without any direct evidence, we cannot assess the impact of turnout, participation, and party competition on local spending levels.

OTHER POLITICAL VARIABLES    The seven government and political factors that we have described do not, of course, exhaust the wide range of political variables that may influence a community's budget decisions. Besides, all the relations that we have identified are only *tendencies,* which mask numbers of deviant cases. Among other political factors of likely significance are the attitudes of community residents, the nature of the local power structure, and the risk-taking propensities of the local officials called upon to propose budget and tax increases. A community dominated by "public-regarding" people may spend more than one dominated by "private-regarding" people. A monolithic power structure, ruling in the interests of the "upper class," may be less supportive of tax and expenditure increases than would a pluralistic structure.

## Community characteristics, political factors, and spending

In principle, it should be possible to examine any particular city, note its relative standings on scales of the major "determinants" of municipal spending levels, and make some educated guesses about its level of expenditures. Two caveats, are necessary, however. First, as already noted,

[35] Ira Sharkansky, *Spending in the American States* (Skokie, Ill., Rand McNally, 1968).

[36] John C. Bollens et al., *Exploring the Metropolitan Community* (Berkeley, University of California Press, 1961), pp. 258–268.

[37] John E. Horton and Wayne E. Thompson, "Powerlessness and Political Negativism," *American Journal of Sociology 67* (March, 1962), 485–493.

we have so far discussed a collection of mere *tendencies*. Factors unique to a particular community or its political system may account for marked deviations from the patterns predicted by larger studies of numerous communities. Cities may expand or contract their budgets in response to sudden changes in local economic conditions; they may respond to the urgings of strong and powerful political leaders to whittle down or drastically increase local budgets; or they may face particular service problems during single budget periods. A sudden change from a tight-fisted conservative administration to a free-spending liberal one may increase a city's budget expenditures significantly.

Second, we have described factors in isolation from one another. Conceivably, of course, a community could be found to score "high" on all the factors contributing to higher municipal expenditures. More likely, however, any single community will be characterized by some factors that impel it toward lower budgets and others that impel it toward higher ones. In some communities, one factor might take on greater importance than the same factor would in other communities. The particular mix of influences on spending may be more important than the mere presence or absence of individual elements.

These caveats are important, but they should not obscure the general findings that local budgets respond to community socioeconomic and political characteristics. Budget-makers do not simply enter the "fiscal restaurant" and order what they want. The macroeconomic structure of the community provides them with certain kinds of resources and denies them others, and the political structure furnishes additional opportunities and constraints. No amount of zeal on the part of urban officials can eliminate all the strictures imposed by limited resources, political opposition to property taxes, and state spending and taxing limitations. Imagination can be only a partial substitute for resources. Given the macro context of financial decision making that we have described, we can now examine the micro contex of budgeting: the process, the actors, and their strategies in the bu  · geting game.

## THE BUDGETARY PROCESS IN
## URBAN GOVERNMENT

A budget may be viewed from several angles. "In its most literal sense," according to Aaron Wildavsky, "a budget is a document, containing words and figures, which proposes expenditures for certain items and purposes." From a larger social perspective, budgeting is "the translation of financial resources into human purposes . . . [or]

a series of goals with price tags attached."[38] Budgets itemize
public revenues and divide public expenditures into categories by
programs or expenditure items. National, state, and local budgets are
imposing to behold. Some municipal budgets rival the local telephone
directories in sheer bulk (and unreadability).

As an example of budgetary detail, Table 7.6 reproduces the
mayor's budget recommendations for a single agency, the Animal
Regulation Department of the City of Los Angeles. The Los Angeles
council considers requests from thirty-three agencies, most of whose
budgets are far more complex than this one. This level of specificity
is common among national, state, and local budgets. How can such an
array of expenditure claims and decisions be handled by local governments? What strategies are employed by actors in the budgetary
process? What rules govern their behavior and expectations? How do
budget-makers cope with the enormous complexity of the budget?
What implications does the budgeting process have for the larger
policy process in urban government? These questions are addressed
in this section.

## Decision-makers, rules, strategies

There is such a wide variety of organization in local governments that
it is difficult to describe a typical budgetary process, but the general
patterns and major actors identified in studies of national and state
budgeting[39] also seem to hold at local levels. The major actors include
*agencies, chief executives* (in local governments, either mayors or
managers), and *legislative bodies.* Some cities employ such variations
as legislative budget systems, special budgeting boards, or joint committees. In a legislative-budget system, the review of agency requests
occurs within a committee of the city council before the full council
votes on the appropriations. When there is a city budget board, a
group of administrative officers, which may include the treasurer and
controller, as well as the mayor or manager, reviews agency requests.
A joint-committee budget is reviewed by a group that includes both

[38] Aaron Wildavsky, *The Politics of the Budgetary Process* (Boston, Little,
Brown, 1964), pp. 1–3.

[39] On national budgetary politics, see *ibid.* Studies of budget-making at the
state level include Thomas Anton, *The Politics of State Expenditure in Illinois*
(Urbana, University of Illinois Press, 1966); and Ira Sharkansky, *The Politics of Taxing and Spending* (Indianapolis, Bobbs-Merrill, 1969), chap. 4. The most sophisticated
study of budgetary policy-making in urban government is John P. Crecine, *Governmental Problem-Solving: A Computer Simulation of Municipal Budgeting* (Skokie,
Ill., Rand McNally, 1969). Our discussion of the process of determining municipal
expenditures has benefited from Crecine's penetrating treatments of Detroit, Pittsburgh, and Cleveland.

**Table 7.6**  *Mayor's budget recommendations for Animal Regulation Department,*[a] *Los Angeles, California, fiscal 1969–1970*

## EXPENDITURES AND APPROPRIATIONS

| Expenditures 1967–1968 | Estimated expenditures 1968–1969 | | Budget appropriation 1969–1970 |
|---|---|---|---|
| *Salaries* | | | |
| $1,198,181 | $1,261,964 | General | $1,340,524 |
| 5,081 | 7,355 | Overtime | 5,300 |
| $1,203,262 | $1,269,319 | Total salaries | $1,345,824 |
| *Expense* | | | |
| $    9,411 | $   10,950 | Printing and binding | $   10,999 |
| 426 | 548 | Traveling expense | 1,008 |
| – | 8,500 | Contractual services | – |
| 21,031 | 23,000 | Transportation expense | 24,000 |
| 15 | 100 | Governmental meetings | 100 |
| 9,117 | 2,055 | Uniforms | 2,375 |
| 2,984 | 2,966 | Office and administrative expense | 4,167 |
| 21,256 | 24,035 | Operating supplies and expense | 27,300 |
| $   64,240 | $   72,154 | Total expense | $   69,949 |
| *Equipment* | | | |
| $    3,658 | $    5,098 | Furniture, office and technical equipment | $    2,046 |
| 2,580 | 13,810 | Other operating equipment | 1,905 |
| $    6,238 | $   18,908 | Total equipment | $    3,951 |
| $1,273,740 | $ 1,360,381 | *Total animal regulation* | *$1,419,724* |

## SOURCE OF FUNDS

| Actual 1967–1968 | Estimated 1968–1969 | | |
|---|---|---|---|
| $1,273,740 | $1,360,381 | General fund | $1,419,724 |
| $1,273,740 | $1,360,381 | *Total funds* | *$1,419,724* |

[a] This department enforces laws and ordinances regulating the care, custody, control, and prevention of cruelty to all animals within the City. It operates and maintains animal shelters, and issues permits for the operation of animal establishments and makes inspections thereof. The department issues dog licenses and collects dog license fees, and participates in the County's rabies control program. The department enforces the Leash Law, inspects medical research laboratories, and accepts unwanted animals.

legislators and administrators. But, for purposes of simplicity and because the patterns we describe seem to prevail generally, we shall assume that agencies, chief executives, and municipal councils are the
major decision-makers.

A fairly typical sequence of steps in the budgetary process is
presented graphically in Figure 7.1. Although this diagram is only

**Figure 7.1**  *An overview of the municipal budgetary process*

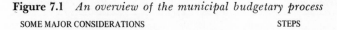

SOME MAJOR CONSIDERATIONS                                         STEPS

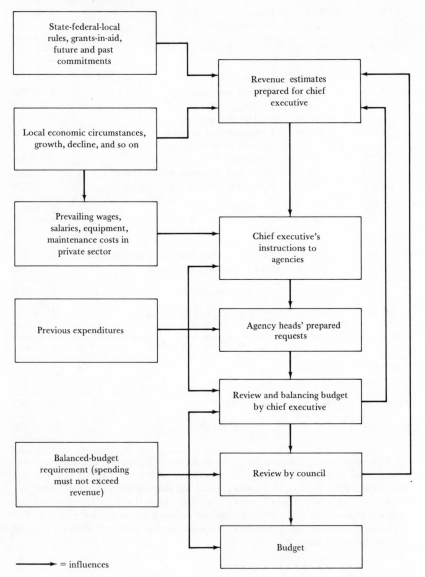

→ = influences

an aid to understanding a complex process, it identifies the major steps and their interrelations. Of enormous importance for actual outcomes is the fact that *revenue decisions are made before expenditure decisions.* One way to construct a public budget might be to identify all the public needs on which money could be spent, add up their probable costs to the government, draw up a budget, and then establish tax rates. But governments do not work this way any more than families decide their needs first and then arrange for their incomes to meet their needs. Rather, revenue estimates for the coming year are made first, and, to a large degree, they determine the expenditure decisions that are made.[40] Estimates of anticipated revenues are submitted to the office of the chief executive and constitute the first significant input in the budgetary process.

In most large cities it is the legal responsibility of the chief executives to present budgets to the municipal councils. In weak-mayor cities, the councils may themselves play more direct roles, or other officials or even the agencies themselves may be charged with budget preparation. In strong-mayor and manager cities, however, the responsibility normally belongs to the chief executives, either mayors or managers. According to John P. Crecine, the problem confronting the executive is

*largely one of recommending a budget which (1) is balanced, (2) at least maintains existing service levels, (3) provides for increases in city employees' wages if at all possible, and (4) avoids tax increases (especially property-tax increases in the belief that increased property taxes cause business and industry to move from the city, reducing its tax base).*[41]

Of these four requirements, the most stringent is that of a balanced budget. In contrast to the federal Constitution, the constitutions of most states do not permit local governments to engage in deficit spending. Revenues and expenditures must match.

Upon receipt of revenue estimates the mayor or manager issues to his department heads a set of budget instructions. He may include guidelines on service increases, levels of salary and wage increments he proposes to grant, and other matters. His instructions are shaped by the revenue estimates, and they guide actions by agency heads.

One of the most significant items included in the mayor's fiscal program and his budgetary instructions is wages and salaries. In an inflationary economy, municipal employees expect wage and salary increases that help them keep up with the cost of living; over the long run, they also expect to better their relative positions. Moreover,

[40] Crecine, *op. cit.,* pp. 32–34, 192.
[41] *Ibid.,* p. 39.

the public sector competes with the private sector for skilled personnel. The municipal government cannot afford to lose large numbers of employees to the private sector as wages become more attractive in business and industry. Thus, the prevailing wage rates in the private sector, plus any inflation that has occurred since the last budget, will almost certainly force increases in the budget.

It is common to expect that public (and private) bureaucracies will seek to expand their own programs by means of increased appropriations. But acquisitive strategies can be pushed too far and backfire. Agencies that consistently ask for much—or for more than their fair shares—will come to be viewed by executives and the council as too aggressive or irresponsible. Such agencies may find their appropriations cut to levels below what they would have received if they had been more reasonable. Many agency heads walk a delicate line between expansion and political feasibility. Their major question "How much shall we ask for?" is answered in part by the question "How much are we likely to get?"[42]

Agency requests are returned to the chief executive, who then prepares the budget proposal. At this point, "the decision process in the (chief executive's) office can usefully be thought of as a search for a solution to the balanced-budget problem."[43] The mayor's or manager's office is not likely to inquire very deeply into an agency's budget if no increase is requested and if the total city budget is close to being in balance. When cuts or increases are necessary, however, there is a well-defined list of priorities:

1    administrative salaries;
2    nonadminstrative salaries and wages;
3    operating expenses, supplies, and materials;
4    equipment;
5    maintenance.[44]

Budget reviewers will cut agencies' requests in maintenance and equipment before cutting supplies and salaries, and they will distribute surplus funds to salaries and wages ahead of other categories. It is only after all other categories have been cut that reductions of salaries and wages are ordered, and it is only after all "higher" categories have received their rewards that any surplus is spent on equipment and supplies. Part of the reasoning behind this hierarchy of priorities is, no doubt, that supplies and equipment do not vote, whereas municipal em-

[42] Wildavsky, *op. cit.*, pp. 18–31.
[43] Crecine, *op. cit.*, p. 67.
[44] *Ibid.*, p. 74.

ployees do. The result of all this juggling, adding, subtracting, and dividing is a balanced budget, which is mimeographed or printed and forwarded to the council. The latter has—within the limits of state law—the legal power either to approve, to disapprove, or to change any allocation of municipal funds or the tax rate.

At the federal level, Congress is generally a budget cutter.[45] The House Appropriations Committee in particular views its major role as "guardian of the public treasury" and takes a jaundiced view of most requests for increased appropriations.[46] The typical city council, on the other hand, operates more as a "rubber stamp" for decisions made by the executive.[47] Councils usually make few changes in the budgets submitted by mayors or managers. The budget is a very complex document, the product of a network of delicate compromises, and to intervene at the final stage would certainly upset this delicate financial balance, for a change in one item would require a compensating change in another, and so on. Moreover, the city council, in contrast to a congressional committee, lacks a staff to assist it in its budgetary review. There are exceptions to the rule of minimum interference, and an unpopular chief executive or one from an opposing political party may find the council in a mood to tinker. Most of the time, however, the executive's budget emerges from the council unscathed.

### Incremental budgeting

One way of constructing a municipal budget would be to follow the tenets of rational problem solving that we described in Chapter 5 (pp. 180–185). Each possible goal of an agency's program might be identified, the goals ranked in a preference hierarchy, and then a series of comparisons made among budget alternatives. The end product would, at some level of abstraction, account for all policy goals served by the government and represent a weighing of every possible budgetary strategy to meet these goals. But, for reasons that we explained in Chapter 5—and for additional reasons that we shall discuss shortly —rational budgeting is virtually impossible to achieve. The more common budgeting model is "incremental": Past experience—and especially past expenditures—is used as a guide to future spending. The nineteenth-century Irish student of public finance, Bastable, wrote:

[45] Wildavsky, *op. cit.*, pp. 47–48.

[46] Richard Fenno, "The House Appropriations Committee as a Political System: The Problem of Integration," *American Political Science Review*, 56 (June, 1962), 310–324.

[47] Crecine, *op. cit.*, p. 207.

*Fortunately the question of expenditure in all its forms does not present itself as a single problem. It would be quite hopeless to prepare a budget of outlay for any country without the aid of the material collected during previous experience. The great mass of expenditure is taken as settled, and it is only the particular changes that have to be anxiously weighed in order to estimate their probable advantage. This method of treatment simplifies issues very much.*[48]

Because "the great mass of expenditure is taken as settled," incrementalism focuses attention mainly on deviations from past behavior. Each agency has an expenditure base below which it is not likely to be cut.[49] It is the increments that are subject to close examination. Agency expenditures, as well as total city expenditures, will be very highly correlated with previous expenditures (see Table 7.5). The tendency toward "incremental decisions" is not the only factor that produces high correlations between present and past expenditures. The stability of local revenue sources and the availability of continuing grants-in-aid for specific programs are two additional factors.

Incrementalism does not, in a strict sense, lead to rational budget making. It rarely raises the broad questions implied by the rational model. Few alternatives are considered, programs are infrequently subjected to rigorous comparisons among themselves, and little evidence is presented to indicate whether or not they are accomplishing their ostensible goals. On the other hand, in a system under severe time pressures ("end poverty now"; "mass transit is essential for the immediate future"; "stop discrimination") and with only fragmentary information, incrementalism is not altogether irrational. It rests upon the fundamental proposition that past experience is the best guide to future policy.

The reasons for incremental budgeting are similar to the reasons why rational models do not adequately describe urban decision-making (see p. 180). But there also are several factors specific to the budgetary process that promote incrementalism and retard "programmatic" decision-making.

COMPLEXITY    As we have emphasized, budgets are complex and detailed documents, and past decisions are the most reliable and handiest tools for grappling with complexity. It is a psychological truism that the human mind tends to respond to similar stimuli in similar ways. That even the largest cities have tiny budget staffs, compared to those of private industry and the federal government, means that there is

[48] Charles Francis Bastable, quoted in Mabel Walker, *Municipal Expenditures* (Baltimore, Johns Hopkins, 1930), p. 37.
[49] Wildavsky, *op. cit.*, pp. 16–18.

very little opportunity for close scrutiny of budgets. The Pittsburgh
mayor's office, responsible for a budget of more than $75 million,
covering scores of accounts and thousands of separate items, has a
budget staff of four people.[50]

IMPERFECT INFORMATION AND INCOMMENSURABLE GOALS   Programmatic,
or rational, budgeting, in which alternatives are successively compared
until an "optimal" complex of expenditures is arrived at, requires
measurements that are seldom available. A programmatic budgeting
process would weigh the marginal utility of a dollar invested in public
health versus that of one invested in education, free school lunches,
street repairs, sewer systems, or the like, but there is no scale of measurement upon which all these categories of public investment can be
evaluated.

THE "UNCONTROLLABLE" BUDGET   A very large proportion of any budget is quite literally "uncontrollable." Support of most local programs
is required by law (maintenance of public safety, education, public
health), and others receive state or federal grants for which the community has undertaken long-term commitments (urban renewal,
public housing, highway construction). Most of the remaining programs have sufficient public support to make reduction politically un-
wise (libraries, parks, snow removal). Most of the costs of municipal
government are absorbed by wages, salaries, and equipment or materials. Changes in the cost of these items is as much a function of the
price system as they are conscious choices of decision-makers. Wages
and salaries must keep pace with the cost of living and with competition from the private sector. Inflation determines the price of
labor and materials to the city government. Viewed in this perspective,
most items in the municipal budget are simply beyond the reach of
decision-makers' control.[51]

CONSTRAINTS OF REVENUES   Because most municipal budgets must be
balanced and because the revenue options of local governments are
resistant to change, revenues operate as a severe constraint on the total
size of the municipal budget. Last year's revenues will be highly correlated with this year's revenues, with perhaps a small increment.
The simplest way to parcel out the additional revenue is to give
agencies whatever new funds may be available as increments over last
year's expenditures.

50 Crecine, *op. cit.*, p. 52.
51 The "uncontrollability" of municipal budgeting (specifically in school
districts) is emphasized as a major perception of decision-makers in James David
Barber, *Government by Committee* (Skokie, Ill., Rand McNally, 1966).

## Decision shortcuts

Because a set of relatively simple rules for decision is followed, it is possible to describe the budgetary process with a limited number of postulates. Although studies of municipal budgeting have been conducted in widely different types of municipalities and in different parts of the country, the findings are sufficiently similar and show sufficient correspondence to studies of government budget-making at other levels to suggest a high degree of reliability. Barber's analysis of local boards of finance in twelve Connecticut towns yielded the following rules:

1   Accept many items as uncontrollable because of previous commitments or the feeling that they support essential programs and therefore do not require careful consideration.
2   Focus on the large budget items, and minimize their growth from one period to the next.
3   Base decisions on concrete aspects of a program familiar to some members of the board, even if they constitute only a small portion of the large budget items.
4   Focus on short-range expectations rather than long-range developments that may occur within each field of service.
5   Focus on the dollars and cents of budget requests, rather than on the elements of programs that the funds will purchase.[52]

Crecine's study of budget-making in three large cities found similar procedures focused on only limited aspects of each agency's budget, seeking to minimize budget growth and concentrating on dollars requested, rather than on programs promised. The primary concern was to keep each agency's budget close to its previous appropriation and to keep the total municipal budget in balance between revenues and expenditures.[53]

Although the incremental model dominates the decision-making process, the future is never a carbon copy of the past, even in an incremental system. Any complete description of the municipal budgetary process must take account of *deviations* from current expenditure patterns. Indeed, the cumulative effect of these deviations over a period of time constitutes a trend that may itself become part of a base for some particular expenditure item. The sources of deviations are many, and they vary from city to city and time to time. The most nearly universal source of deviation from previous expenditure patterns is the addition of new revenues, especially through

[52] *Ibid.*
[53] See Crecine, *op. cit.*

grants-in-aid from the state or federal government. Spurts of expenditures can also be explained by factors like a change in administration, a catastrophic event or emergency, and reorganization of functions within the city administration or between the city government and some other unit.[54]

## Budgeting and the policy process

Students of budgeting have generally used one of three basic perspectives. Crecine has described them as (1) the "optimizing process," (2) "budgeting as an externally determined event," and (3) "budgeting as an internal bureaucratic process."[55] The notion that budgets "optimize" community values reflects the idea that public budgets are a function of public needs and represent decision-makers' efforts to bring public resources into line with overall community goals. The "externally determined" view is that budgets result from economic and political forces. Citizens' demands for service, the power of community elites, the demands of various groups, and responses to economic pressures are some explanations for a budget's final shape. Business groups are said to seek lower taxes; proponents of "law and order" demand more money for law enforcement; and PTAs want more money for schools. These demands or requests for services and expenditures are channeled through mayors, councils, and agencies, and the sum of these pressures determines the level of public expenditures. In the third model, that of budgeting as an internal bureaucratic process, external forces are viewed as unimportant, and instead the budget is explained as the outcome of rules and strategies for decision-making employed by agencies, chief executives, and legislative bodies.

The data presented by Crecine suggest that neither optimization of community values nor externally determined events offer realistic explanations of the budgetary outcomes. "It is quite clear (from interviews) that the decision-makers *do not* see the problem as one of optimally balancing community resources, allocating funds among functions to achieve overall community goals, and the like."[56] Nor was there much evidence that decision-makers perceived great pressures for higher or lower expenditures from groups. When pressures did occur, the common response was, "We just have so much money and we can't do everything."[57]

According to Crecine's findings, budgeting is primarily a bureau-

54 *Ibid.*, chap. 9.
55 *Ibid.*, pp. 9ff.
56 *Ibid.*, p. 38.
57 *Ibid.*, p. 189.

cratic process, operating—once revenue estimates are made—as a relatively closed system. The dominant decision-making method is incrementalism. As we have seen above, however, the local budget-maker operates in a context that is determined partly by the macro-level ·factors of the community's economic resources, social composition, and local government structure, and the constraints imposed upon the city by its state government.

## Incrementalism and innovation

In a nutshell, incremental budgeting permits the human mind to manage complexity. Local authorities limit their discretion over budgeting by the ways in which they make budget decisions. Their procedures facilitate speedy, relatively uncontroversial decisions. These decision-making procedures are highly mechanical in nature, and they narrow the choices available to financial officials. Because they are so widely accepted as proper ways for government officials to make their budget decisions, they serve to inhibit individual officials who would depart from custom in order to innovate. Budget-making procedures thus tend to keep policies of local governments conservative. The budget is a resistant instrument that discourages local policy-makers from seeking large amounts of money for new programs.

The simplistic criteria of decisions that are used by local budget-makers may help them to cope with complexities of political and economic issues, as well as of fragmented institutions, but they provide little encouragement to those who would use the budget process as the vehicle for program planning or those expecting innovations in the use of public money. The budgetary process tends to project past choices into the future. The programmatic reformer, like the proponent of PPB, must be optimistic to approach the budget-maker with a vision of change. The budget system is operated not by officials with compelling sympathies for program but by officials who use their own past decisions as principal criteria for current decisions and who devise nonprogrammatic decision-making rules in order to reduce deficits or to distribute surpluses.

## SUMMARY

In this chapter we have identified the fiscal-policy options available to local government officials and have explained the choices that officials make. Our subject has been one of the most vital resources in urban politics: money. We have identified the major revenue sources of local governments and the major elements of local expenditures. We have found that most revenues come from property taxes, state aids, service charges, and borrowing. The single most important category of local expenditure is education; public utilities, highways, welfare, health, hospitals, police, interest on debt, and other such items take what is left.

We have tried to do more than simply to identify fiscal "intake" and "outgo." We have examined critical differences in the expenditure and revenue patterns of local governments and traced these differences to community social, economic, and political characteristics. From macro perspective, these patterns suggest a lack of individuality or innovation in budgeting. Our discussion of policy-making procedures reinforces this conclusion. Officials do not make policy after a thorough review of all the relevant conditions. They rely instead upon mechanical procedures that "boil down" the potential criteria to very few. Although this tendency is not so strong as to preclude all possibility of innovation, budgeting is a conservative force that militates against introduction of new programs through the local government financial system. Innovations must first be accepted by other officials and must be presented to budget-makers only after they have achieved such wide acceptance as to be considered commitments to be honored by the financial officers.

This treatment of revenues and expenditures does not exhaust our interest in local-government policies. Although it is tempting to assume that levels of spending reflect—or produce—the levels of service that residents of a municipality enjoy, this assumption is not valid. Spending is only one ingredient in determining the level of service provided. After budget-makers have provided an "adequate" amount of money, other officials must allocate their funds to purchase the "right" mixture of skilled personnel, suitable facilities, and supplies and equipment. Some determinants of public-service levels are not subject to the control of local officials. They include the sources and severity of problems in the client population, as well as the attraction of the local community for technical and professional people who must be recruited if certain programs are to succeed.[58] Some policies financed by local expenditures are the subjects of the following chapters.

[58] For an assessment of some factors that limit the capacity of expenditures to ensure the desired level of service, see Ira Sharkansky, *Policy Analysis in Political Science* (Chicago, Markham, 1970), chap. 4.

# 8

# Servicing the urban environment: law enforcement, education, transportation, pollution control

In this chapter we shall examine policy related to four important urban services: law enforcement, education, transportation, and pollution control. These policies are grouped in this chapter because they are relatively "traditional" services of urban governments. Each of these services is of fundamental importance to an urban society. Businesses and families could not operate without a measure of security provided by urban police forces. The skills taught by the educational system are essential for the management and control of a complex urban society. Transportation systems enable urbanites to produce, consume, enjoy leisure activities, and educate themselves. Pollution control, the newest of these four policy areas (having, however, antecedents in garbage removal, street cleaning, and sewer and water provision), may in the long run be the most essential.

Each of these policies has made some impact on the problem it was designed to solve, yet environmental constraints have limited the effectiveness of each as well. It is not clear, for example, whether or not law enforcement can overcome the sources of crime that lie deeply embedded in individual personality and genetics and in the social structure. Educational policies are severely constrained by the home environments of students. Solving a problem in one area may, unfortunately, create more severe problems in another policy area. Construction of bigger and better freeways, for example, may spur additional use of automobiles, which adds to the problem of pollution control. These policies, the environmental problems they are designed to solve, the constraints upon their effectiveness, and their impacts are the subjects of this chapter.

## CRIME IN URBAN SOCIETY

The role of the policeman is much broader than the public image of a "crime fighter" suggests. But the intense emotion evoked by the "crime problem" and "law and order" makes the issue of crime in the urban society a useful point for departure. Evidence from national surveys indicates that Americans consider crime their second most worrisome domestic problem, taking a back seat only to race relations in public concern.[1] About half the women surveyed and about one-fifth of the men hesitate to walk in public places at night for fear of muggings, stabbings, and other acts of violence. The American conviction that the "crime rate" is increasing is "verified" annually by the Federal Bureau of Investigation's *Uniform Crime Report*.

### How much crime?

The President's Commission on Law Enforcement and the Administration of Justice has divided major crimes into two categories: "crimes against the person" and "crimes against property." It discovered that reported instances of both types had indeed increased markedly from 1933 to 1965 and at a pace much exceeding the population increase. Crimes against property (burglary, motor-vehicle theft, and larceny of more than $50) had multiplied much more rapidly, however, than had crimes against the person (homicide, forcible rape, robbery, and aggravated assault). There is also evidence to suggest that "white-collar crime"—for example, frauds, stock manipulations, antitrust violations, and similar transgressions by middle-class businessmen—is increasing.

Actually it is pretty clear that FBI statistics, which are based entirely upon offenses known to or reported to the police, considerably understate the actual incidence of crime. Studies undertaken for the President's Commission used population surveys to uncover actual rates of criminal activity and revealed that the number of crimes against the person reported to interviewers was almost twice as great as FBI reports indicated. The amount of crime against property was more than twice as large. In some areas, the amount of unreported crime was nearly ten times greater than reported crime.

The problem of unreported crime suggests some of the difficulties in determining precisely how much crime there is in the contemporary United States. It is also difficult to ascertain whether or not there has been an increase in the crime *rate* in the last few years. Statistics

---

[1] President's Commission on Law Enforcement and the Administration of Justice, *The Challenge of Crime in a Free Society* (Washington, D.C., Government Printing Office, 1967), p. 49.

have sometimes been used to demonstrate that American society has experienced an increase in "criminality." Several objections can be leveled at this use of crime statistics, however. First, valid comparison of crime rates over time requires a constant relation between reported and unreported crime. Even if the amount of crime were the same today as it was in 1933 and if twice as many crimes were reported today, a purely statistical "crime wave" could be said to have occurred. There is reason to suspect, however, that more crime is being reported today, partly because of improved police efficiency and reporting practices. American police forces have never been particularly good at statistics. For some cities, crime reporting to the FBI has been wildly unrealistic. Chicago for many years reported twice as much robbery as New York, a city twice its size. At one point in the late 1940s, the FBI discontinued reporting New York City's crime statistics because it no longer believed them. Newark and Jersey City, quite comparable in many respects, reported differences as large as 17 to 1 in certain categories of offenses. Crime reporting in New York and elsewhere has improved in recent years. Citizens also seem to be reporting more crime to the police, partly because most people have insurance, and payment of claims requires reports to the police.

In addition to the nature of crime statistics themselves, there are several other reasons for doubting arguments that "criminality" is increasing. They involve changes in the social and economic structure of society. Youth, the most crime-prone age group (more fifteen-year-olds are arrested than are people of any other age, and sixteen-year-olds are close behind), constitutes a larger proportion of the population now than ever before, making an increase in the rate of crime partly an artifact of an increasingly youthful population. Urbanization itself is associated with high crime rates, and Americans are now a thoroughly urban people. Finally, an affluent society provides more temptations to prospective criminals. In the long run, the question of how much crime there is in American society is, in our view, largely unanswerable. Crime rates have probably increased more rapidly than has the population but it is risky to go beyond this rather limited generalization.

We do think that the available evidence offers good reason for discounting some near-hysterical fears about "crime in the streets." Interestingly, although urbanites seem to fear most the possibility of danger from a stranger or group of strangers on the streets, in fact the most serious crimes involving personal violence (aggravated assault, forcible rape, and homicide) are far more likely to be committed by acquaintances, "best friends," or spouses than by strangers. One's chances of falling victim to a homicide are slim in any case (about 5 per 100,000 population, approximately the same probability as for death from fire or drowning and about half as likely as death from a fall), but the chances are *eight times as great* that one will be done in by a "friend," relative, or spouse than by a "perfect stranger." (In a sense, the individual is his own worst enemy, for suicides are twice as common as homicides.)

## The causes of crime

Arguing about the causes of any social phenomenon is tricky in any case, but criminology involves so many complexities and competing perspectives that it is especially susceptible to wrangling. Certainly one confusing factor is the legal definition of crime. Presumably, few would disagree that homicide is a crime, but many disagree about whether or not possession of narcotics, for example, should be classified as a crime. It strikes some as incongruous that selling marijuana is a crime, whereas selling tobacco is not.

The explanations for crime most commonly offered tend to be either a micro type (related to the individual) or a macro type (related to the society). The micro, or individual, explanation rests upon the assumption of moral accountability. Each man is considered sufficiently rational and responsible so that a criminal act can be viewed as a moral dereliction: essentially a "bad man" explanation of criminality. The rise and acceptance of psychology and psychiatry, however, have spread recognition of the psychodynamic aspects of criminal behavior. In this "social science" view, crime is considered a function of psychological disturbances, rather than a function of character defects. More recently, some social and biological scientists have unearthed evidence that proneness to crime may be related to genetic malfunctions.[2]

Macro-level explanations of crime stress socioeconomic circumstances like poverty, deprivation, discrimination, and defects in the socialization process as factors contributing to criminal behavior. Such explanations are buttressed by the fact that there is more crime among the poor than among the wealthy; victimization rates are also eight to ten times higher for ghetto dwellers than for the more affluent. (Interestingly, surveys by Louis Harris and others have consistently revealed that *fear* of crime is inversely related to the *probability* of criminal victimization; middle-class people are thus more anxious about crime than are lower-class people.)

These competing explanations of crime have important implications both for the impact of law-enforcement policy (which we shall discuss later) and for the choice of an appropriate societal response to

[2] See, for example, Ashley Montagu, "Chromosomes and Crime," *Psychology Today, 2* (October, 1968), 43–49; and Kennedy McWhirter, "XYY Chromosomes and Criminal Acts," *Science, 164* (June, 1969), 1117.

crime. If crime is interpreted as the result of moral irresponsibility or as a function of biopsychological forces, the response to crime should be directed at the individual. Depending upon one's assessment of the cause, punishment, reform, or rehabilitation will seem the most appropriate response. This "individualistic" orientation toward crime will encourage selection from among a range of responses, including incarceration (if the individual criminal is held morally culpable) to psychiatric treatment or even, conceivably, genetic manipulation—an issue that may open up a legal and moral quagmire in time to come. If, on the other hand, criminal behavior is viewed as a function of macro factors, caused by problems in the larger social system, responses to crime will take very different forms. One aspect of this view is that society itself is partly responsible for crime, either because it tolerates conditions that engender crime or because it has failed to prevent crime.

## The police

We begin our discussion of the police by reproducing a description, recorded by the President's Commission on Law Enforcement and the Administration of Justice, of an actual tour of duty by two officers, whom the commission called Jones and Smith:

*After receiving routine instructions . . . Officers Jones and Smith located the car to which they were assigned and started out for the area in which they would spend their tour of duty. While en route, they received instructions from the dispatcher to handle a fight in an alley. Upon arrival, they found a group of young men surrounded by their parents, wives, and children.*

*The mother of B was the complainant. She claimed that C had attacked her son with a knife and she demanded that C be arrested and jailed. C readily admitted that he had been fighting with B, but he claimed that he had just tried to protect A. C had been drinking and was very belligerent. He indicated a readiness to take on anyone and everyone, including the police. . . .*

*A attempted to explain the situation. . . . A's mother-in-law interrupted at this time to explain that A was innocent; that the fight was B's fault. B's mother did not stand for this accusation and entered the fray.*

*The confusion spread . . . Officers Jones and Smith decided to take the participants to the station where conditions would make possible a more orderly inquiry. [Finally, at the station] C was formally arrested and charged with disorderly conduct. By charging C with disorderly conduct rather than a more serious crime, the officers observed that they were saving themselves some paperwork. They felt that their action in letting the mother sign a complaint against the "loudmouthed" C had served to pacify her.*

*[After filling out arrest reports on C, Jones and Smith were dispatched to two successive domestic quarrels, in which wives complained that their husbands had beaten them up and then left the houses. After advising each*

*to obtain a warrant or peace bond, they were then dispatched to two noisy parties, advised each host to "hold it down," and stopped for cokes before placing themselves back in service. After breaking up a rowdy crowd at a hot-dog stand, arresting a drunk, and warning instead of ticketing a Vietnam veteran for a traffic violation, the officers requested permission from the dispatcher to eat. Instead, he sent them back to the first party they had quieted. Again denying their request to eat, the dispatcher sent them to a public pool, the scene of a stabbing.]*

*There were three persons present—two lifeguards and a watchman. One of the lifeguards had been knifed. He was placed in a police car and the officers started off to the nearest hospital. . . . [They] later returned to the scene but found no additional information. . . . The reports were turned in for attention by the detectives.*

*The officers then, without asking, took their meal break, after which they reported that they had completed their work on the stabbing. They were dispatched to a party disturbance. . . .[3]*

Without knowing whether Jones and Smith's tour is typical, we can nonetheless deduce from it some useful generalizations, particularly the degree of *ambiguity* and the amount of *discretion* involved in performing the police function. Ambiguity and discretion are mutually reinforcing. Both situations and legal codes (for example, those dealing with "disturbing the peace") are ambiguous, and the more ambiguous the "law" and the immediate situation are, the greater are the discretion and judgment required of the police officer.[4]

POLICE ROLES   Social scientists and experienced policemen seem to agree that the police play three important roles in urban society. Joe Fink, commander of New York City's ninth precinct has enumerated them: "One [role] is law enforcement. Another is keeping the peace. The third is furnishing services."[5] Wilson, one of the leading academic observers of policemen and their departments, has emphasized the same three functions and has provided some systematic data on the relative frequency with which they are performed.[6]

The most common public image of the policeman is that of law enforcer, but, as the Syracuse data in Table 8.1 indicate, only about 10 percent of police calls require exercise of the law-enforcement function. Very few of the calls appear to represent opportunities for

[3] President's Commission, *Task Force Report: The Police* (Washington, D.C., Government Printing Office, 1967), pp. 14–16.

[4] Police discretion is discussed in James Q. Wilson, *Varieties of Police Behavior* (Cambridge, Mass., Harvard University Press, 1968), chap. 4.

[5] Saul Braun, "The Cop as Social Scientist," *The New York Times Magazine,* August 24, 1969, p. 69.

[6] Wilson, *op. cit.*

**Table 8.1** *Citizen complaints radioed to police ve-hicles, Syracuse Police Department, June 3–9, 1966*[a]

| Calls[b] | Number in sample | Percentage |
|---|---|---|
| Information Gathering | 69 | 22.1 |
| Book and check | 2 | |
| Get a report | 67 | |
| Service | 117 | 37.5 |
| Accidents, illnesses, ambulance calls | 42 | |
| Animals | 8 | |
| Assist a person | 1 | |
| Drunk person | 8 | |
| Escort vehicle | 3 | |
| Fire, power line or tree down | 26 | |
| Lost or found person or property | 23 | |
| Property damage | 6 | |
| Maintenance of Order | 94 | 30.1 |
| Gang disturbance | 50 | |
| Family trouble | 23 | |
| Assault, fight | 9 | |
| Investigation | 8 | |
| Neighbor trouble | 4 | |
| Law Enforcement | 32 | 10.3 |
| Burglary in progress | 9 | |
| Check a car | 5 | |
| Open door or window | 8 | |
| Prowler | 6 | |
| Make an arrest | 4 | |
| Totals | 312 | 100.0 |

[a] Based upon a one-fifth sample of the week's calls.

[b] Not included are internal calls: those originating with other police officers or purely administrative calls.

SOURCE: James Q. Wilson, *Varieties of Police Behavior* (Cambridge, Mass., Harvard University Press, 1968), p. 18.

officers to make dramatic "pinches" of hardened criminals, and, in fact, the International Association of Chiefs of Police estimates that only about 10 percent of total police work is related to the traditional enforcement of criminal law.[7]

[7] Cited by Arthur Niederhoffer, *Behind the Shield* (Garden City, N.Y., Double-day, 1967), p. 71.

The role of providing service is far more common. Some police departments, according to Wilson, even emphasize service. For example, those in Nassau County, New York, and Brighton, Massachusetts, provide courteous and efficient, though perhaps low-keyed, law enforcement but also spend enormous amounts of energy and money on community relations. The Nassau County Police Department stands ready to provide articulate speakers at civic or school affairs and maintains a full-time staff of twenty-four officers to operate the department's boys' club program. Departments emphasizing services recruit well-educated men, pay them well, and demand scrupulous honesty from them. This emphasis is most common in homogeneous, upper-middle-class suburban communities. But, regardless of whether or not the department emphasizes service, a considerable part of any policeman's time and energy is devoted to providing it to citizens.

The police role that Wilson has called "order maintenance" and Fink has called "keeping the peace" is both the least recognized and the most controversial. Situations requiring maintenance of order sometimes involve transgressions of the law—especially if the law is sufficiently ambiguous—but more often they involve breaches of public serenity. In most such situations, at least two parties (bickering spouses, feuding neighbors, and people in and outside bars) are involved in disputes in which the fault is not self-evident and is possibly shared equally. (The confrontation of A, B, and C by officers Jones and Smith is a classic example of the exercise of this function, one that happened to lead to an arrest.) These cases involve maximum ambiguity and therefore maximum discretion on the part of the officer. According to Wilson, the policeman "approaches incidents that threaten order *not in terms of enforcing the law but in terms of 'handling the situation.'* "[8] Although it might be possible to turn every such case into a law-enforcement case, strong reasons militate against it: Tempers cool quickly, participants are reluctant to file charges, blame is difficult to determine, and law enforcement involves detailed reports and tedious court appearances. Officers thus tend to handle such incidents informally. When a clear violation of written law occurs—burglary, vandalism, or dope pushing—the police have little discretion, especially if they regard it as a "serious" crime. But the discretion that officers have in maintaining public peace is their greatest opportunity both to inject a "personal element" into the abstract business of law enforcement *and* to exert their personal idiosyncracies, whims, and prejudices. In Wilson's words, maintenance of order involves "sub-professionals, working alone, [exercising] wide

8 Wilson, *op. cit.*, p. 31.

discretion in matters of utmost importance (life and death, honor and dishonor) in an environment that is apprehensive and hostile."[9]

THE POLICEMAN    After the John Birch Society introduced the "Support Your Local Police" bumper sticker (the phrase appeared recently on Alabama's state license plates), New Left critics countered with a bumper sticker of their own, reading "Control Your Local Pigs." A hero to conservatives, who view him as the last bastion of "law and order," the policeman is depicted as bent on violence, authoritarian, and bigoted by the Left and by many blacks. Perhaps the police self-image is equally stereotyped: Most police officers see themselves as performing tough, poorly paid, and unpleasant jobs, risking their lives and receiving either hostility or, at best, grudging tolerance from the public at large. Wilson found from surveys of Chicago police sergeants that policemen believed that (1) most Chicagoans did not respect them or their work, (2) most people gave only minimum cooperation, (3) most people obeyed the law only for fear of getting caught, and (4) even their civilian friends were likely to criticize the department.[10] This image is, however, contradicted by countless studies of public attitudes toward the police indicating that overwhelming proportions of Americans (especially white Americans) think that the police in their communities are doing "excellent" or "pretty good" jobs. Although police see themselves as "downwardly mobile" in the occupational structure, again studies of occupational prestige indicate that their relative position has improved over the years.[11] There is, therefore, a wide gap between *actual* public acclaim for the police and *perceived* public support by the police.

Why, when the general public so widely supports police work, do policemen sense hostility? Part of the answer is provided by Wilson, who has observed that "most police contacts are not with the general public and thus general public opinion is not most relevant."[12] Rather than interacting with a random cross section of the public, the police see much of the "worst kind" of people and the "best people" only at their worst. Police work involves antagonistic contact with a very atypical segment of the public in situations of maximum hos-

9 *Ibid.*, p. 30.

10 James Q. Wilson, "Police Morale, Reform, and Citizen Respect: The Chicago Case," in David Bordua, ed., *The Police* (New York, Wiley, 1967), pp. 137–162.

11 Among ninety occupational groups, the ranking of policeman by the general public went from fifty-fifth in 1947 to forty-seventh (just a notch below the median) in 1963. If anything, therefore, policemen are in an upwardly mobile profession. See Robert W. Hodge *et al.*, "Occupational Prestige in the United States, 1925–1963," in Reinhard Bendix and Seymour Martin Lipset, eds., *Class, Status, and Power* (New York, Free Press, 1966), p. 324, Table 1.

12 Wilson, *Varieties of Police Behavior*, p. 28.

tility. The policeman's lot—the necessity for physical violence, personal danger, low pay, verbal abuse from self-proclaimed "good citizens"—is hardly conducive to an optimistic, "tender-minded" view of human nature. Most policemen, moreover, are recruited from working-class backgrounds; only a handful come from the middle class. "Working class background, high school education or less, average intelligence, cautious personality—these are the typical features of the modern police recruit," Niederhoffer has observed.[13] It thus happens that policemen are recruited from that segment of the population most inclined toward intolerance of unpopular views, racial prejudice, and authoritarian conceptions of family life and public policy.

Recruits bring with them the attitudes and behavior patterns of their backgrounds, including a preference for things physical rather than intellectual, a predisposition toward "toughness," and high regard for established authority and ways. But there is little evidence to suggest that police recruits are any more authoritarian than are other members of the working class.[14] It seems to be the occupational milieu of the force that engenders extremes of authoritarianism, cynicism, and political conservatism among experienced officers. Although police authoritarianism has probably been overemphasized, the police system itself tends to heighten this image by promoting the better educated and least authoritarian officers, leaving behind for patrol work and public contact those with the strongest predispositions toward authoritarianism.

Cynicism about both life in general and the department in particular appears shortly after the rookie has left the police academy, with its "social scientific" emphasis on "professionalism" and has entered the grimy world of the precinct station. General cynicism was expressed by Chief William H. Parker of Los Angeles, who claimed that "this civilization will destroy itself, as others have before it." Cynicism about the force itself is indicated by the widespread belief that "getting ahead" is a result of "whom you know," rather than "what you do." Political conservatism is also a typical police attitude. Chief Parker described the political ideology of the nation's peace officers as "conservative, ultra-conservative, and very right-wing." The dominant political philosophy on the police force is a Goldwater-type conservatism, and such organizations as the John Birch Society harbor generous sprinklings of the "men in blue."[15]

---

13 Niederhoffer, *op. cit.*, p. 38.

14 A Denver survey found that policemen scored no more "authoritarian" on the "F scale," a common measure of authoritarianism, than did the rest of the working class. See David H. Bayley and Harold Mendelsohn, *Minorities and the Police* (New York, Free Press, 1969), pp. 17–18. See also Niederhoffer, *op. cit.*, p. 150.

15 Jerome Skolnick, *Justice Without Trial* (New York, Wiley, 1966), p. 61.

## Police and minority groups

In some respects, the police themselves may be viewed as a minority group—they are physically distinguished from the rest of us by uniforms, they exhibit high in-group loyalty, they view the "outside world" as hostile, and they interact heavily among themselves. Conflict among minority groups is a commonplace in American political annals. Moreover, as the police in some cities are recruited primarily from ethnic groups (for example, the Irish), existing ethnic hostilities spill over into police-citizen relations. In any event, the National Advisory Commission on Civil Disorders' report on ghetto violence in the 1960s observed that "the policeman in the ghetto is the most visible symbol of a society from which many ghetto dwellers are increasingly alienated."[16] It has not been demonstrated that the police are more prejudiced against blacks than are other whites.[17] Yet the commission's surveys indicated that police relations were the leading grievance of ghetto residents, more significant than housing deficiencies, inadequate schools, and unemployment. Incidents involving the police precipitated most of the major race riots of the 1960s, including those in Los Angeles, Detroit, and Newark.

Three major ingredients characterize the hostility between the police and ghetto residents. First is the familiar charge of "police brutality." Whether or not and how much brutality exists depends, of course, upon definitions. But fully half the residents of Watts in Los Angeles believed that some brutality had occurred there. Perhaps more important, more than four-fifths complained of instances not of overt physical force but of "harassment," including "insulting language," "stop and search for no good reason," and the like. In Denver similar proportions of both police and minority-group members (about one-fourth in each case) claimed to have witnessed either harassment or excessive use of police force. The problem of harassment appears to be far more common than that of brutality. The President's Commission on Law Enforcement and the Administration of Justice investigated 5,339 police-citizen contacts and found that only a minuscule proportion had involved excessive force, but that a much larger proportion had involved rude, discriminatory, or abusive verbal behavior.[18] Even though the proportion of police-citizen contacts involv-

[16] National Advisory Commission on Civil Disorders, *Report* (Washington, D.C., Government Printing Office, 1967), p. 157.

[17] Evidence on alleged antiblack attitudes differs. Skolnick, *op. cit.*, pp. 80–88, has argued that most policemen are racially prejudiced. But the Denver study reported in Bayley and Mendelsohn, *op. cit.*, p. 144, found police no more prejudiced than were the rest of the white population.

[18] President's Commission, *Task Force Report*, p. 147.

ing roughness or rudeness may be small, the continual nature of police work enhances the probability that an individual ghetto dweller will at some time experience a hostile confrontation with the police.

The second source of police-ghetto tensions lies in what the ghetto sees as inadequate police protection. Regardless of class or income level, blacks are far more likely than are whites to see the police as ineffectual law enforcers. Ghetto leaders and residents are painfully aware of the crime and delinquency in the ghetto: Black men are six times and black women eight times as likely to be victims of crime as are white men and women respectively. The third ghetto complaint involves the inadequacy of grievance mechanisms. Disputes over "civilian review boards," supported by blacks and white liberals and bitterly opposed by the police, reflect tensions over grievance procedures. Most citizens' complaints against policemen have been handled internally by the departments, in which high "in-group loyalty" and "out-group hostility" have often meant perfunctory treatment of the grievances.

Needless to say, all these police-ghetto tensions have been intensified by racial disorders and police responses. From the police perspective, racial disturbances are clear examples of insurrection against lawful authority; from the black perspective, they are protests against white institutions, including the police themselves. Partly because the police have found it difficult to find a successful response to disorders, they have sometimes vacillated between over- and under-reacting to ghetto violence.[19]

Short of eliminating the ghetto and the conditions associated with it, society is not likely to lessen police-ghetto tensions. The ghetto is a high-crime area, and police are likely to resort to what few techniques they have to reduce the crime rate there: techniques that the police call "aggressive enforcement" and the residents call "harassment." Movement toward centralization of police authority and concurrent reduction of discretion at the patrol level, as well as higher employment standards and salaries may improve the situation marginally.

---

[19] With tongue in cheek, Edward C. Banfield listed some "guidelines" for handling riots, in "Dos and Don'ts of Riots," *Harvard Review*, 4 (1968), 41–44:

| DO | | DON'T | |
|---|---|---|---|
| 1 | Assign black officers to cope with black crowds. | 1 | Don't assign black officers to riot duty, as they are particularly resented by blacks. |
| 2 | Keep uniformed police out of the ghetto as much as possible in order to avoid provocation. | 2 | Don't deprive ghetto dwellers of police protection; this is a major grievance of the ghetto. |
| 3 | Close all bars at once. | 3 | Don't close the bars as this will put scores or even hundreds of half-drunk men on the streets. |

But Wilson has not been optimistic about the impact of changes in personnel on the numerous other factors that influence crime and police-citizen relations:

*. . . If all big-city police departments were filled tomorrow with Negro college graduates and placed under the control of the neighborhoods they are supposed to control, most of the problems that exist today would continue to exist and some in fact might get worse.*[20]

POLICE AND THE "RULE OF LAW"    Through all the policeman's activities —law enforcement, maintenance of order, dealing with minorities, and so forth—he is expected to exhibit respect for individual rights and to provide nonarbitrary treatment for all. In recent years, the U.S. Supreme Court has attempted to spell out the rights of the accused that must be preserved under constitutional guarantees. Beginning in 1957 with the *Mallory* case, in which the Court held that a suspect must be taken before a magistrate for arraignment immediately following his arrest, the Supreme Court has acted to narrow police discretion in the performance of its law-enforcement function. In *Mapp* v. *Ohio* (1961) the Court established the principle that evidence collected in an "unreasonable search and seizure" cannot be used as evidence in either state or federal courts. The most far-reaching decision on suspects' and defendants' rights, that in *Miranda* v. *Arizona* (1966), laid down five principles governing pretrial conduct by law-enforcement officers:

1    A suspect must be informed of his right to remain silent and of his right to have counsel present during interrogation and must be warned that anything he says may be used in evidence against him.
2    Defense counsel must be provided if the suspect desires, but cannot afford, counsel.
3    The prosecution must demonstrate that the suspect knowingly waived his rights if he confessed without benefit of counsel.
4    Prolonged interrogation may be construed as a lack of such waiver.
5    If a suspect indicates "in any manner" that he wishes to remain silent, even after starting to talk, questioning must end.

The impact of *Miranda* and related decisions is unquestionably to increase the rights of the accused. Many police officials and prosecuting attorneys, however, have argued that a corollary impact is a reduction in the effectiveness and certainty of law enforcement. Niederhoffer, however, has provided some compelling evidence to suggest that the major indicators of enforcement success—proportion of crimes

[20] James Q. Wilson, "Dilemmas of Police Administration," *Public Administration Review*, 28 (September–October, 1968), 409.

cleared by arrest and proportion of cases decided in favor of the prosecution—have not declined since 1950, despite the Court's incremental
expansion of defendants' rights.[21] Federal law-enforcement agencies,
notably the FBI, have long been bound by rules that have only recently
been applied to state and local law-enforcement officers, and few people
have accused the FBI of ineffective law enforcement.

## The impact of law-enforcement policy

Measuring the impact of a public policy, as we have already indicated and shall continually reiterate, is complex. Assessing the impact
of police work is especially difficult because the evidence is fragmentary
and its interpretation is subject to ideological debate. But, although it
is difficult to describe the impact of law-enforcement policy, it is next
to impossible to describe that of policy on maintenance of order. We
shall have to confine our discussion to the former.

CRIME, COPS, AND CONVICTIONS    Figure 8.1, though it does not directly
assess the impact of law-enforcement policy, does provide us with some
useful perspectives on the system of criminal justice and the rather narrow role of the police in it. These figures, from 1965, show more than
2.75 million crimes committed and listed in the FBI's "index" of serious
crimes. (Our earlier discussion of underreporting crime suggests that
this figure is lower than the real incidence of crime.) Only 727,000 arrests followed. This figure suggests that the "clearance rate" by arrest is
about 25 percent. About one-third of those "cleared" by arrest were juvenile offenses, and about 40 percent of those arrested were released or
given reduced charges. Of the remaining 177,000, the overwhelming majority (160,000) either pleaded guilty or were convicted and jailed, fined,
imprisoned, or paroled. The most significant facts seem to be, first, that
there is an enormous gap between the "crime rate" and the "clearance
rate" by arrest and, second, that of 727,000 arrests only a fraction (160,-
000) resulted in guilty pleas or convictions in adult courts. Superficially
at least, the sort of data presented in Figure 8.1 inspires pessimism
about the impact of police law-enforcement policies. If only a quarter of
"crimes" are "cleared" by arrest and only a fraction of those arrests
result in convictions, law enforcement cannot be too successful in
affecting the crime rate. This view is buttressed by some fragmentary
evidence on the impact of traffic-law enforcement. A study conducted
at the behest of the International Association of Chiefs of Police concluded, for example, that enforcement rates have little or no effect on

---

[21] The nationwide clearance rate for "index offenses" has remained fairly constant at about 25 percent for the last several years. See Niederhoffer, op. cit., p. 164.

**Figure 8.1** *Flow of people through the criminal-justice system in 1965*

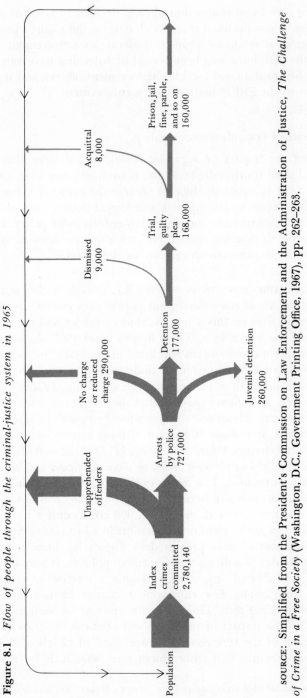

SOURCE: Simplified from the President's Commission on Law Enforcement and the Administration of Justice, *The Challenge of Crime in a Free Society* (Washington, D.C., Government Printing Office, 1967), pp. 262–263.

the rates of either accidents or other violations. A study by the prestigious research firm of Arthur D. Little, Inc., was more cautious in its conclusions but equally dubious about the impact of traffic enforcement: "at present there is no firm evidence to indicate the degree to which enforcement contributes to traffic accident reduction."[22] Unfortunately, however, comparable studies of the impact of enforcement on more serious crimes, such as homicide, rape, and burglary, have never been conducted. Some evidence suggests that government spending for public safety is highest in areas with high incidence of major crimes.[23] Although it does not demonstrate that law-enforcement expenditures help to reduce crime, it does suggest that the money is being spent where the problem is greatest.

CONSTRAINTS ON LAW ENFORCEMENT    All the evidence presented here is best described as "indirect." Direct evidence on police impacts is even more difficult to accumulate, partly because of the "displacement problem." When a vigorous law-enforcement policy is adopted, it may be quite effective in *displacing* crime to other locales but not in reducing the total amount of crime. The displacement problem is a "spillover" effect of vigorous law enforcement in a single community or a single neighborhood.[24] In any event, the displacement problem means that any convincing evidence on the impact of "better," more "professional," or more "vigorous" law-enforcement policies is nearly impossible to obtain.

If we expect law enforcement to result in actual reduction of crime rates, we may be setting unreasonably high standards for our police departments. The President's Commission on Law Enforcement and the Administration of Justice put the argument this way:

*The fact is, of course, that even under the most favorable circumstances the ability of the police to act against crime is limited. The police did not create and cannot resolve the social conditions that stimulate crime. They did not start and cannot stop the convulsive social changes that are taking place in America. They do not enact the laws that they are trying to enforce, nor do they dispose of the criminals they arrest. The police are only one part of the*

22 Robert L. Shumate, *The Long Range Effect of Enforcement on Driving Speeds* (Washington, International Association of Chiefs of Police, 1960), cited in John A. Gardiner, "Police Enforcement of Traffic Laws," in James Q. Wilson, ed., *City Politics and Public Policy* (New York, Wiley, 1968), p. 171; Wilson, *Varieties of Police Behavior*, p. 77.

23 Ira Sharkansky, "Government Expenditures and Public Services in the American States," *American Political Science Review*, 61 (December, 1967), 1066–1077.

24 Although the facts have not yet been firmly established, it is possible that social as well as geographic displacement may exist. Reduction of the opportunities for crime may produce deviant behavior in other forms.

*criminal justice system; the criminal justice system is only one part of the
government; and the government is only one part of society. Insofar as crime
is a social phenomenon, crime prevention is the responsibility of every part
of society. . . . Some "handcuffs" on the police are irremovable.*[25]


## EDUCATING AN URBAN POPULATION

By whatever standard we employ, the largest economic enterprise
in the United States is the Department of Defense. But next in size
and scope is the business of educating an urban population. Defending
the nation against its enemies, real, potential, or (according to some
critics) imaginary, consumed approximately $81 billion in fiscal 1969.
Education was easily the second most expensive public investment,
accounting for $45 billion of local, state, and national expenditures.
But, whereas the Department of Defense is highly centralized, even,
symbolically, housed in the North American continent's largest single
office building, the education of American children is the responsibility
of approximately 22,000 local school districts. Each, though regulated
by state government, has considerable autonomy, buttressed by American insistence upon "local control" of schools. The decentralization of
the public school system parallels the decentralization and fragmentation of municipal governments themselves. In the Chicago SMSA, for
example, there are 327 school districts, in Houston 48, and in Provi-
dence 35.

On balance, the American educational system has contributed
significantly to the nation's economic growth, providing the technological industries with hundreds of thousands of people trained for
occupational roles.[26] Americans have responded with a high regard for
their public school system. Almost 90 percent of the residents of six
metropolitan areas studied by Basil G. Zimmer and Amos H. Hawley
reported that they were "satisfied" with their schools.[27] As we might
expect, the major exception to general public contentment over education is found in the racial ghettos. The Kerner Commission found
that in each of the cities it investigated, the quality of schools was a
major grievance among blacks. At the other extreme are the school systems in upper-status suburban communities, which embody the status-
preserving and status-advancing values of the community.

25 President's Commission, *Task Force Report,* p. 1.

26 See the interesting treatment of the economics of knowledge in Fritz Mach-
lup, *The Production and Distribution of Knowledge in the United States* (Princeton, N.J., Princeton University Press, 1962).

27 Basil G. Zimmer and Amos H. Hawley, *Metropolitan Area Schools* (Beverly
Hills, Calif., Sage, 1968), p. 86.

## Schools and politics

The apolitical and nonpartisan character of education is a fundamental precept of the American credo. But the notion of citizen
control of schools, an equally deep-rooted precept, makes public education an object of citizen concern and, inevitably, of political conflict.
The structure and organization of local school districts partly reflect the tensions between the goals of educational autonomy and
public accountability of the educational system. In important respects,
the organization of the school district parallels the council-manager
system of municipal government. A "lay" school board is given the
responsibility to "make policy," establish budgets, and, most significantly in practice, hire and fire superintendents. Like the city manager,
the superintendent is a professional, mobile, and "nonpolitical" administrator.

About a quarter of the nation's school boards are appointed, but
the great majority are elected. The kinds of people who are elected
or appointed to school boards have been the subject of frequent research. The earliest such study is the now classic report by George S.
Counts, who published the results of his survey of 6,400 board members
in 1927.[28] Counts found that three-fourths of American school-board
members were businessmen or professional men and that only a handful
(about 3 percent) were members of the working class. Over the years
Counts' study has been replicated repeatedly, with similar results: Businessmen dominate, and the working class has little representation.[29]
Most recently, Robert L. Crain, who studied school desegregation in
eight northern cities, found that all but ten of the sixty-nine school-
board members in those cities were from business or professional
backgrounds.[30]

School-board members face not only the tensions between "citizen
control" and "freeing education from politics" but also a conflict between their own legal responsibility for educational policy and educators' "professional" credos. Educators, from the university education
professor to the classroom teacher, generally believe that education is
a professional enterprise, demanding special skills, training, and
expertise. Although the argument is rarely stated so baldly, the professional educator believes that education is too important a matter to be
left to "laymen" like school-board members. Boards are thus caught

[28] George S. Counts, *The Social Composition of Boards of Education* (Chicago,
University of Chicago, 1927).

[29] See, for example, Roy W. Caughran, "School Board Members Today,"
*American School Board Journal, 133* (November, 1958), 39–40.

[30] Robert L. Crain, *The Politics of School Desegregation* (Chicago, Aldine,
1968), p. 180.

between their constitutional and statutory obligations to govern the schools and educators' preferences for noninterference from the board. Given their limited time and lack of expertise in educational questions, boards typically defer all matters that are not plainly "political" to the superintendents. Educators prefer that. The school superintendent thus has the same kinds of political resources as does the city manager: time, training, experience, and a near monopoly of appropriate "technical" information.

Citizens, like school boards, ordinarily defer to the professional judgment of school administrators. But, because education accounts for the largest single portion of the local tax dollar and the educational system is the most potent social institution for molding a new generation, the schools cannot be immunized from political controversy. Educational conflict tends to center on three principal policy issues—taxes and spending, the content of the curriculum, and race—although the relative emphasis on the athletic program sometimes overshadows all these issues.

As a general rule, there is less conflict over education in upper-status communities, where there is broad consensus that education is the avenue to permanent upward mobility. Such communities spend lavishly on school plants and pay teachers generously. The New Trier Township High School District, serving upper-class Chicago suburbs, is such a community, although even it is not wholly free of conflict over school matters.[31] In heterogeneous communities, riddled as they are with racial, class, and ethnic strife, the schools occasionally become political battlegrounds. Youngstown, Ohio, is a case in point. After the defeat of six successive bond referenda, the schools, their operating funds depleted, closed for four months in the fall of 1968. (After the sixth referendum defeat and the subsequent closing of the schools, Rowan and Martin awarded Youngstown voters their "Fickle Finger of Fate" award.) Finally, on May 7, 1969, Youngstown voters passed a bond referendum by a majority of 57.2 percent.

Despite such occasional examples of rancor over schools and their financing, most citizens are willing to translate their abstract support of education into concrete financial support. Public-opinion surveys consistently reveal willingness to spend more on education, even if it means spending less on national defense. That the major correlate of educational spending is the level of community income suggests that the major constraint upon educational support is the availability of resources.

Conflicts over curriculum are rarely as intense as are either racial or

[31] See Louis H. Masotti, *Education and Politics in Suburbia: The New Trier Experience* (Cleveland, The Press of Western Reserve University, 1967).

financial conflicts, but superintendents and boards experience nearly as much public pressure related to what is taught as they do in connection with finance.[32] In recent years, citizen protests relating to the school's emphasis on football or to suspicions that socialism is being taught in the schools have abated somewhat, but sex education has become the focus of bitter controversy in many communities. Some parents have pressured boards to prevent or eliminate sex education in the school curriculum completely, whereas others have urged the superiority of classroom sex education to lovers' lane experimentation. The issue of race will be taken up separately, later in this chapter.

### Bureaucrats and teachers

In some interesting ways, the public-school teacher and the policeman share common role orientations and occupational frustrations. Both perform important public functions, and both see themselves as receiving little pay and relatively little public esteem. Although the political value system stresses the public accountability of both groups, teachers and policemen consider themselves the experts on their own jobs and resent public "interference." Both teachers and policemen tend to be concerned with status and authority, and both are bound by intricate rules and regulations yet faced with actual situations in which their discretion and autonomy are maximal. And, for both, there are wide gulfs between the idealism of the training period and the realities of practice. Just as the patrolman is graduated from the academy filled with the most up-to-date theories of police science, the teacher emerges from the university steeped in the latest theories of curriculum construction. Prepared to forge the best possible teaching program, the teacher discovers that curriculum policy is made "higher up" in an aged and entrenched educational bureaucracy. In New York City, for example, individual teachers play almost no role whatever in the formulation of curriculum policy, a task undertaken by a vast corps of bureaucrats in the city school administration at 110 Livington Street.[33]

The most obvious differences between policemen and teachers are, first, that teachers are more commonly recruited from the middle class and, second, that teachers are overwhelmingly female. Several occupational strains of teachers can be traced to these class and sex characteristics. Teachers suffer some inconsistency in class and status. Although they consider themselves and are considered by the public

---

[32] Neal Gross, *Who Runs Our Schools?* (New York, Wiley, 1958), p. 49.

[33] Marilyn Gittell, *Participants and Participation: A Study of School Policy in New York City* (New York, Center for Urban Education, n.d.), p. 29; and David Rogers, *110 Livingston Street* (New York, Random House, 1968).

to belong to a middle-class occupation, their salaries commonly run below the wages of union members. Although a 1963 study of occupational prestige found that the public ranked teachers twenty-ninth of ninety occupations listed,[34] median salaries for the equally prestigious occupations of "accountant for a large business" and "owner of a factory that employs about a hundred people" range from two to five times higher than that for teachers' salaries. Teachers thus suffer from what sociologists call "status inconsistency."[35]

The social-class position of American teachers is complicated by the high proportion of women in the profession, even though now a much larger proportion of teachers consists of men than in years past. Today almost one-third of all teachers and a majority of secondary-school teachers are male. Most women who enter teaching are from middle-class origins, but most men are from working-class origins and seek upward mobility. Men who enter the formerly feminine domain of teaching, however, do not expect to make long-term careers of it. Most want to use teaching as a stepping-stone to higher positions, particularly in school administration. Few men, however, ever advance beyond the classroom. Most male teachers, Zeigler found, are thus unhappy with their vocational choices, and their unhappiness intensifies with the years. The frustration level of male teachers is high: Their mobility aspirations are unfulfilled, and they are doing "women's work" —and receiving "women's wages" for it. The male teacher is thus, in Zeigler's words, "the underclass of the teaching profession, a rebel in a female system."[36]

Male or female, most teachers' political expressions are implicitly conservative. In the classroom, the teacher rarely addresses controversial subjects. More precisely, controversial subjects are handled, if at all, "noncontroversially." To the degree that teachers cultivate points of view about the American political system, they emphasize a faith in it that borders on chauvinism. In Zeigler's words:

*The classroom operates basically to reinforce a belief in the desirability of maintaining the status quo. It is very doubtful that the classroom experiences of students encourage them toward radical politics. If there is brain washing in the high schools, it is clearly not for indoctrination in socialism; rather, it appears aimed at the production of optimistic, uncritical citizens.*[37]

Almost all American teachers are organized in political-interest groups, the largest of which is the National Education Association.

---

[34] Hodge *et al., op. cit.*
[35] Harmon Zeigler, *The Political Life of American Teachers* (Englewood Cliffs, N.J., Prentice-Hall, 1967), p. 20.
[36] *Ibid.,* p. 30.
[37] *Ibid.,* p. 119.

The state affiliates of the NEA are among the most active and, according to legislators, the most influential legislative lobbies in the state houses. The NEA is an organization that emphasizes a "professional" image of teachers paralleling the professional orientations of such groups as the American Institute of Architects, the American Bar Association, and the American Medical Association. The NEA, however, includes in its ranks—and frequently in its leadership—superintendents, principals, and other administrators. According to its chief rival, the American Federation of Teachers, this inclusion makes the NEA a "company union." The AFT, an affiliate of the AFL-CIO, admits only teachers and emulates labor unions in its tactics. This "teachers' union" makes many upwardly mobile teachers uncomfortable, for union membership is ordinarily incompatible with middle-class status. The AFT thus appeals mainly to urban, male secondary-school teachers, whose frustration levels and status inconsistencies are most marked and whose working-class backgrounds make them most sympathetic to trade unionism.

Although the AFT has been active in many northern cities, nearly one-third of its national membership is drawn from the New York system. There the 35,000 AFT members constitute the majority of the city's 45,000 teachers. The New York affiliate has been willing to use the strike as a bargaining weapon. Its most bitter and widely publicized dispute was that with the city school board over the latter's plan to decentralize New York schools. After the central school board had given neighborhood boards some autonomy in operating community schools, some black and Puerto Rican boards attempted to rid themselves of certain white teachers. The AFT, insisting, as do unions everywhere, that members have a right not to be summarily dismissed from their positions, opposed the local boards. Leaders of the minority groups, particularly in the Ocean Hill–Brownsville area of Brooklyn, insisted upon the right to control their own schools and claimed that many white teachers discriminated against black students. The conflict was long and bitter and resulted in a strike that lasted for many weeks.

### Class, race, and schools

The Ocean Hill–Brownsville confrontation illustrates the intimate links between race and education in urban America. Robert Dentler has argued that "the most urgent urban educational challenge of the day is not curriculum or instruction. It is the challenge of changing race relations."[38]

38 Robert A. Dentler et al., eds., The Urban R's (New York, Praeger, 1967), p. x.

SEGREGATION: DE JURE AND DE FACTO    Segregation by race in public
schools is of two types: de jure (required by law) and de facto (resulting from socioeconomic circumstances). De jure segregation was
declared a violation of the "equal protection" clause of the Fourteenth
Amendment in the Supreme Court's 1954 decision in *Brown* v. *Board
of Education of Topeka*, which theoretically put an end to legally sanctioned segregation in seventeen southern and border states. The Court
ordered school systems in those states to desegregate their schools with
"all deliberate speed." But seven years after the *Brown* decision the percentage of southern black children in schools with whites ranged from
0 in Mississippi, Alabama, and South Carolina, to 1.5 in Texas. Observers calculated that at the rate of integration in 1954–1961 it would
take 3,180 years to desegregate southern schools.[39] The pace quickened
with the passage of the Civil Rights Act of 1964, which required the
U.S. Office of Education to cut off federal funds to schools that
failed to establish and execute desegregation plans. It also authorized
the U.S. Attorney General to initiate legal proceedings to hasten
desegregation. By 1968, 20.3 percent of southern black students were
in school with white students. The proportion continues to increase.

De facto segregation is not overtly a product of law, although it
may be shaped and maintained by policy-makers, and it is by no means
confined to the South. In 1967 the U.S. Civil Rights Commission's
study of seventy-five cities found that three-fourths of black pupils were
in schools that were 90–100 percent black and four-fifths of white
pupils were in schools that were 90–100 percent white. A variety of
social and economic factors have contributed to de facto school segregation, but the two most significant ones are the residential segregation
of minority groups and the practice of assigning pupils to schools according to the principle of "geographical attendance zoning." Some
explanations of patterns of residential segregation will be offered in
Chapter 10, when we explore housing and urban-renewal policies;
here we shall merely note that American cities are sharply segregated
residentially by race. Table 8.2 illustrates how this segregation contributes to public-school segregation in both northern and southern
cities. The practice of geographical attendance zoning, or, in common parlance, "neighborhood schools," means that students living
in black neighborhoods go to black schools and children living in
white neighborhoods go to white schools. Sometimes local school
boards intensify existing school-segregation patterns by deliberate or

---

[39] Donald R. Matthews and James W. Prothro, "Stateways vs. Folkways:
Critical Factors in Southern Reactions to *Brown* v. *Board of Education*," in G.
Dietze, ed., *Essays on the American Constitution* (Englewood Cliffs, N.J.: Prentice-
Hall, 1964), p. 144.

**Table 8.2**  *Extent of elementary-school segregation in selected systems, 1965–1966*

| City | Percentage of blacks in 90–100% black schools | Percentage of blacks in majority black schools | Percentage of whites in 90–100% white schools |
|------|------|------|------|
| Mobile | 99.9 | 99.9 | 100.0 |
| San Francisco | 21.1 | 72.3 | 65.1 |
| Marietta | 94.2 | 94.2 | 100.0 |
| Baltimore | 84.2 | 92.3 | 67.0 |
| St. Louis | 90.9 | 93.7 | 66.0 |
| Cincinatti | 49.4 | 88.0 | 63.3 |
| Providence | 14.6 | 55.5 | 63.3 |
| Houston | 93.0 | 97.6 | 97.3 |

SOURCE: U.S. Commission on Civil Rights, *Racial Isolation in the Public Schools* (Washington, D.C., Government Printing Office, 1967), pp. 4–5, Table 1.

accidental manipulation of educational policy. In Houston, for example, the school board refurbishes and enlarges schools 'in the heart of the ghetto and even builds new schools there, rather than building them on the periphery, which would tend to lessen school segregation. In Milwaukee students were for many years bused from overcrowded schools in black areas to white schools but were segregated within the receiving schools.

The Supreme Court made legal history in the *Brown* decision and stirred enormous legal controversy by departing from strict reliance on legal precedent to cite evidence from social scientists that school segregation is psychologically and educationally harmful to black students. Evidence provided by both the famous "Coleman report"[40] and the Civil Rights Commission emphasizes that de facto segregation is no less serious in its consequences than is de jure segregation. According to the Civil Rights Commission, "racial isolation, whether or not sanctioned by law, damages Negro students by adversely affecting both their attitudes and achievement."[41] Nonetheless, both Congress and the courts have been reluctant to hold de facto segregation based upon the neighborhood-school concept in violation of the Constitution.

SEGREGATION, POLITICS, AND PUBLIC POLICY    Although the incidence of racial segregation in the public schools is high in almost all American

[40] James C. Coleman *et al.*, *Equality of Educational Opportunity* (Washington, D.C., Government Printing Office, 1966).

[41] U.S. Commission on Civil Rights, *Racial Isolation in the Public Schools* (Washington, D.C., Government Printing Office, 1967), p. 190.

cities, certain kinds of cities have higher levels than do others. Thomas R. Dye has explored these differences. Using a sample of fifty-five school systems and indexes of pupil and teacher segregation, he identified the following significant correlates of degree of segregation:

1    The "single most influential variable" affecting segregation levels was regional location. Northern cities had 46 percent of their black pupils in nearly all-black schools, whereas southern cities had 87 percent of their black pupils in nearly all-black schools.
2    Similarly, the larger the percentage of blacks in public schools, the higher was the degree of segregation.
3    In both North and South, socioeconomic characteristics of cities were more strongly correlated with degree of segregation than were political characteristics.
4    In general, "reformed" governments showed greater tendencies toward segregation in both North and South.[42]

These correlations should not be taken as necessarily causal connections, but they do suggest that the pace of school desegregation is strongly related to community structure.

The politics, like the pace, of desegregation varies markedly between North and South.[43] In the South, desegregation has been a slow but relatively simple process. Whether the initial demands have come from within the community or from the federal government, they have been ordinarily met with delays or "tokenism." But as de jure segregation is plainly unconstitutional, most disputes end in the federal courts, which have ultimately ordered desegregation. The issues usually revolve around the degree to which the boards may retain the neighborhood-school system or must arrange the transfer of black pupils to previously white schools.

De facto segregation in the North is more a political than a legal question. Demands for desegregation have come principally from integrated neighborhood groups and from the moderate National Association for the Advancement of Colored People (NAACP), rather than from all-black groups or leaders of the ghetto itself. Although the proposed integration plan for New York City schools evoked bitter backlash from white groups, in most northern communities whites have deferred to the school boards' decisions, as long

---

[42] Thomas R. Dye, "Urban School Segregation: A Comparative Analysis," *Urban Affairs Quarterly, 4* (December, 1968). 141–165. Socioeconomic characteristics of cities examined included size, proportion of Negroes, ethnicity, class characteristics, and regional location.

[43] See Crain, *op. cit.* The materials in this and the next paragraph are taken from Crain's studies of the politics of desegregation.

as those decisions have not appeared to be "capitulations" to militants. The school boards have responded to integration demands more as a result of their initial attitudes toward civil rights than as a response to particular black strategies or pressures. In other words, "liberal" boards have integrated, and "conservative" boards have resisted.

As long as residential patterns remain segregated and the neighborhood-school concept dominates American communities, there will probably be school segregation. Controversies now center mostly on the alternatives of "busing" and "compensatory education" in ghetto schools. Large numbers of both black and white parents and educators are opposed to the elimination of neighborhood schools. Only Massachusetts has enacted legislation specifically limiting the proportion of black students in any school (50 percent), although other states have undertaken policies at the state level to discourage racial concentrations. A coalition of "strange bedfellows"—anti-integration whites, many teachers, and black militants—favors policies of "compensatory education," that is, programs to upgrade the quality of ghetto education in segregated schools. Carmichael and Hamilton, two articulate proponents of Black Power, have argued that "the real need at present is not integration but quality education." The 1965 Elementary and Secondary Education Act was designed primarily to improve the quality of education in schools serving poor areas. The U.S. Civil Rights Commission, on the other hand, has claimed that compensatory education is much less effective than is integration in improving motivation, achievement, and aspirations among black students.

## Class and education

By most standards, what Carmichael and Hamilton call "quality education" has been lacking in ghetto areas and, more generally, in lower-income areas of the city. The caliber of available facilities and teachers varies both between cities and suburbs and within the cities themselves. A great deal of this variation is directly associated with the incomes of the areas served by and supporting the schools. In the Detroit metropolitan area, for example, twenty-five suburban school districts spend an average of $500 more per pupil per year than does the City of Detroit itself. While gleaming school buildings and well-trained teachers serve the residents of many affluent suburbs, in the inner city almost one-third of the school buildings still in use were constructed during the administration of President Grant. James B. Conant, former President of Harvard University and a long-time observer of the public schools, noted that "the contrast in money available to the schools in a wealthy suburb and to the schools in a large city jolt one's notions of the meaning of educational opportunity."[44]

Within the city itself, there are marked differences among the schools, programs, and teachers serving various neighborhoods. Sexton has examined elementary and secondary schools in a place that she labeled "Big City." She used a series of indexes of educational output, including size of classes, teachers' training, availability of special programs, and age and quality of facilities. She found that schools in upper-income areas had (1) newer facilities, (2) more libraries and other special facilities, (3) smaller classes, (4) better-prepared teachers, (5) more extracurricular and special programs, and, surprisingly enough, (6) more frequent provision of free meals and free milk. According to Sexton,

*the problems we describe are principally social class problems, not racial problems. . . . In the long run it may turn out that the educational problems of low-income whites are more stubborn and resistant to treatment than those of Negroes.*[45]

Moreover, the middle-class orientations of teachers probably operate to increase their sympathy and tolerance for middle-class children. A number of studies have demonstrated that teachers have higher expectations for middle-class children and that student performance is positively related to teachers' expectations.

### Correlates of spending and service levels

Of the $45.9 billion spent on public education in 1969, the federal government contributed approximately 10 percent. Most of the remainder came from local school districts, principally through property taxes. Dye has conducted an analysis of sixty-seven big-city school systems in an effort to determine the most important correlates of educational outputs.[46] He identified the significant correlations between "environmental" and "political system" characteristics and "educational outcomes." The most important correlate of variations in school expenditures per pupil is the wealth of the community, a finding confirmed by several other analyses of school expenditures. But, on the other hand, expenditures per pupil were only weakly correlated with indicators of the level of services provided, such as the

[44] James B. Conant, *Slums and Suburbs* (New York, McGraw-Hill, 1961), p. 3.

[45] Patricia Cayo Sexton, *Education and Income* (New York, Viking, 1961), pp. 16–17.

[46] Thomas R. Dye, "Government Structure, Urban Environment, and Educational Policy," *Midwest Journal of Political Science, 11* (August, 1967), 353–370.

teacher-pupil ratios and dropout rates (see Table 6.1). This finding suggests that money does not necessarily buy a certain level of service and is confirmed by recent analyses of state-government expenditures.[47]

## The impact of education

EDUCATION AND POLITICAL BEHAVIOR    There is probably no single variable that accounts for more of the variation in adult political behavior and attitudes than the level of education does. Although we shall emphasize here their contribution to political behavior, educational levels also sharply distinguish consumption patterns, child-rearing practices, family sizes, and a host of other social phenomena. Milbrath identified no fewer than twenty-three studies in the United States and elsewhere that have established a direct connection between educational attainment and political participation. In a study of political cultures in five nations (the United States, Great Britain, Germany, Italy, and Mexico), Gabriel Almond and Sidney Verba found education a more reliable predictor of political attitudes than any other component of social-class position.[48] In addition to being more frequent paticipators, better-educated people have attitudes that distinguish them from less-well-educated people. For example, better-educated people

1    are more tolerant of civil rights and of dissenting opinions and minority groups;
2    have a higher sense of political efficacy, that is, a belief that their activities can affect the outputs of the political system;
3    have a higher sense of civic obligation;
4    have more political awareness and information about politics;
5    have a higher sense of trust in others, in both political and nonpolitical domains.

The importance of education as a predictor of political attitudes and behavior naturally enough directs our attention to the schools as an agency of political socialization.

SCHOOLS AND SOCIALIZATION    Political socialization is the process by which a human being becomes a political being. As Freud discovered about the roots of sexual behavior, so political scientists have discovered that the roots of political life begin at a very early age indeed.

[47] Sharkansky, op. cit.
[48] Lester Milbrath, Political Participation (Skokie, Ill., Rand McNally, 1965); and Gabriel Almond and Sidney Verba, The Civic Culture (Princeton, N.J., Princeton University Press, 1963).

**Table 8.3**   *Median test scores for pupils in 1st and 12th grades, fall, 1965*

| Grade | Racial or ethnic group | | | | | |
|---|---|---|---|---|---|---|
| | Puerto Ricans | American Indian | Mexican- American | Oriental- American | Black | White |
| 1st grade | | | | | | |
| Verbal | 45.8 | 53.0 | 50.0 | 56.6 | 43.4 | 54.1 |
| Nonverbal | 44.9 | 47.8 | 46.5 | 51.6 | 45.4 | 53.2 |
| 12th grade Average of 5 tests | 43.1 | 45.1 | 44.4 | 50.1 | 41.1 | 52.0 |

SOURCE: James S. Coleman *et al., Equality of Educational Opportunity* (Washington, D.C., Government Printing Office, 1966), p. 20.

By the time children enter grade school, some very important facets of their political lives are already deeply embedded, including party identification and basic attitudes toward authority. This fact points to the importance of the family as an agency of political socialization. Observers have described the family as the "foremost," or "dominant," agency of political socialization.[49] The family's dominant role in socialization results from its near monopoly of two critical resources—time and emotional attachment—during the formative years. The critical part played by the family in shaping attitudes toward myriad phenomena, political as well as nonpolitical, is thus a major constraint upon the role of the school as a socializing agency.

The primary role of the family in student achievement and motivation has been observed through the most extensive analysis of American education ever undertaken, the famed Coleman report. This study was commissioned under the Civil Rights Act of 1964 and was designed to investigate educational opportunities available to American children. Prepared under the direction of sociologist James S. Coleman, the report was published by the U.S. Office of Education in 1966.[50] The levels of educational achievement, as Coleman discovered, differ markedly according to race. As Table 8.3 shows, whites scored higher, with only one exception, on achievement tests in both the first and

[49] These descriptions are used, respectively, by Herbert Hyman, *Political Socialization* (New York, Free Press, 1958), p. 69; and Richard Dawson and Kenneth Prewitt, *Political Socialization* (Boston, Little, Brown, 1969), p. 122.

[50] Coleman *et al., op. cit.* See also the commentaries on this report in Daniel P. Moynihan, "Education of the Urban Poor: Reflections on the Coleman Report," *Harvard Graduate School of Education Association Bulletin, 12* (Fall, 1967), 3–13; and in a symposium on policy implications of the report in the *American Sociological Review, 35* (April, 1970), 228–252.

the twelfth grades than did members of any other group. In addition to differences between races in educational achievement, there were also regional differences. Pupils in the metropolitan North were the highest achievers, whereas pupils in the nonmetropolitan South were the lowest achievers, regardless of race.

The single most important factor that Coleman found to explain educational achievement and motivation was the family background of the student. Whatever impact the school has, therefore, is significantly conditioned and constrained by family circumstances. But, taking the child's background as a constant, what factors related to the school itself are most predictive of achievement? A variety of possibilities may be suggested, including the facilities and curriculum of the school, the attitudes of the teachers, the training and skills of the teachers, and the composition of the student body. We might suppose that the most important predictor of student accomplishment would be the competence of teachers. Although teachers' competence is quite significant however, the most important school-related predictor of achievement and motivation was found to be the *composition of the student body*. Particularly for students from minority groups, accomplishment is greatly stimulated by being in class with motivated and able peers. In the words of the report, "attributes of other students account for far more variation in the achievement of minority group children than do any attributes of school facilities and slightly more than do attributes of staff."[51] Coleman summarized his study thus: ". . . the educational resources provided by a child's fellow students are more important for his achievement than are the resources provided by the school board."[52] The importance of peers in either reinforcing or overcoming student attitudes is thus a matter of first importance in assessing the impact of education.

ASSESSING THE IMPACT OF EDUCATIONAL POLICY    It would be a serious oversimplification to read Coleman's report as denying the significance of teachers, curriculum, and facilities. The report examined only measurable factors and could make no determination about the influence of factors that are virtually uniform from school to school, for example, class size. But Coleman did stress constraints upon educational policy, largely those arising out of family background. The formal educational structure is by no means unimportant in producing its intended impact, but the constraints upon it are no less significant.

[51] Coleman *et al., op. cit.,* p. 302.
[52] James S. Coleman, "Toward Open Schools," *The Public Interest* (Fall, 1967), p. 21.

## URBAN TRANSPORTATION POLICY

### Cars and cities

That a few Americans orbit the globe in less time than it takes others to get to work illustrates the urban transportation problem. The provision of a transportation network ranks just after education and policing as a major item of public expenditure. More than any other municipal policy, decisions about transportation are characterized by their permanence. Transportation facilities, whether roads or rails, are costly and long-lasting. This fact is even more significant because the transportation web influences the location of homes, commerce, and industry. Decisions about transportation have an impact upon the shape of the city that extends over generations.

Among other appellations, the twentieth century has been described as the "age of the automobile." Eighty percent of American families—all but a few of the very rich and a number of the very poor—own cars. Many a family owns two, and increasing numbers own three.

If Detroit is the city of the automobile from the point of view of production, Los Angeles is the city of the automobile in consumption terms. In Los Angeles, one-third of the total land area— two-thirds of the downtown area—is devoted to uses related to motor vehicles, principally streets, freeways, parking lots, and facilities to sell, service, and destroy automobiles. In Los Angeles and elsewhere, there is a reciprocal relationship between the decentralization of the metropolitan population and the ubiquity of the car. ("Reciprocal relationship" is a social scientist's term for what laymen might describe as a "chicken and egg" problem.) The automobile has made metropolitan deconcentration possible; deconcentration has made the car essential. Of course, the automobile alone did not cause the suburbanization of the American urban population. Other factors such as central-city land values, deterioration, affluence, and the sheer demand for space abetted population decentralization. Ownership of automobiles by urbanites may not be a "sufficient" condition for suburbanization, but it is almost surely a "necessary" one.

The most frequent use of the automobile is for commuting between residence and job. A significant proportion of such commuting takes place between central cities and their suburbs. Although most urban workers live and work in the same sectors of the city, millions of others commute daily from the suburbs to the central cities, and smaller numbers commute from central cities to the urban fringes. Although a few American cities have systems of mass transportation that are as convenient as private cars, the overwhelming proportion of commuting is by automobile. One study revealed that almost two-thirds of urban journeys to work were by car and only 19 percent by mass transit.[53]

To be sure, the deconcentration of the urban population is not the sole explanation for the dominance of the automobile. This dominance is dependent upon a number of interrelated phenomena, including (1) the increasing affluence of American workers, (2) the role of the automobile as a status symbol, (3) technological innovations that put automobiles within reach even of families with modest means, (4) the deterioration of urban mass-transit systems, (5) the attraction of jobs in the suburbs, and (6) state and federal policies favoring automobiles over mass-transit systems.

### The structure of transportation policy-making

Transportation policies, like most other policies affecting urban America, are intertwined with the federal system. At the federal level, the first assistance-to-highways program was inaugurated in 1916, but it was not until 1944 that the present direction of federal highway policy was made clear. In that year Congress created the skeleton of the now-familiar interstate transportation system, authorizing 41,000 miles of federally assisted interstate highways; no significant funding appeared in the federal budget until the mid-1950s, however. In 1956, Congress (1) established the dominance of the federal government in interstate road financing by providing federal funding for 90 percent of the cost, (2) reoriented the interstate system from a principally rural pattern of roads to an interurban system, (3) gave the Bureau of Public Roads effective power to determine the routes to be taken by the interstate system. By the hoped-for completion date of the system in 1972, 41,000 miles of highways would link the nation's major cities.

Along with education and welfare, the highway program has long been one of the "big three" items in state finance. But for many years states have tended to use highway financing formulas that favor rural over urban areas. This pattern has been common among the states, regardless of the equity of their legislative apportionments. Urban governments have thus been compelled to undertake a larger share of the burden of providing traffic arteries than have their rural counterparts. Within metropolitan areas, the fragmentation of local governments has further complicated the planning of balanced trans-

[53] Lyle C. Fitch *et al.*, *Urban Transportation and Public Policy* (San Francisco, Chandler, 1964), pp. 35–36. The remainder included people who worked at home, walked to work, used other forms of transportation, and failed to report.

portation systems to serve the needs of both suburbanites and central-city interests. Central cities have often made heavier expenditures for transportation facilities for suburbanites, who, in most cases, pay no taxes to the central cities.

### Road versus rail

At all levels—national, state, and local—transportation politics has centered on the conflict between advocates of roads and equally ardent advocates of rail, or mass-transit, systems.[54] At least in the larger metropolitan areas, the essential elements of the "roads coalition" have been officials of state and federal highway departments, truckers, automobile associations, constructions and materials companies, petroleum interests, bus companies, and a number of business interests that would benefit from the expansion of the road network. Their commitment of political resources has been high.

In contrast to the politically potent "road coalition," the "rail coalition" is a shaky alliance at best. Central-city commercial, political, and newspaper interests; commuters; and the railroads themselves have been the main spokesmen for "balanced transportation," but there is considerable disharmony among them. The railroads themselves have often been eager to divest themselves of unprofitable commuter runs, and commuters are often at odds with the railroads over inadequate service.

So far, at least, the policies of national, state, and local governments have clearly favored roads over rails. The amount of federal aid for mass transportation is minuscule compared to that for the interstate highway system, and local governments, faced with a crush of demands for expansion of other services, have been reluctant to invest millions or hundreds of millions of dollars in developing rail transportation. Local governments have stood pat on the status quo—and the status quo means the automobile.

In an effort to persuade Congress to pass a long-term $10 billion mass-transportation-assistance act in 1969, President Nixon recognized that "man does not travel by road alone." Nonetheless, the very reason that the President found it necessary to shore up the rails is that urbanites are increasingly traveling in private cars. According to the President, the number of transit passengers has declined to one-third the 1945 level; transit-company profits have declined from $313

---

[54] See the useful discussions of road-versus-rail interests in Jameson W. Doig, *Metropolitan Transportation Politics in the New York Region* (New York, Columbia University Press, 1966), chap. 2; and Frank C. Colcord, Jr., "Decision-Making and Transportation Policies: A Comparative Analysis," *Social Science Quarterly, 48* (December, 1967), 383–398.

million in 1945 to $25 million in 1967; and, in recent years, 235 bus and subway companies have gone out of business. "The remaining transit companies," he concluded, "have progressively deteriorated. Today they give their riders fewer runs, older cars, and less service,"[55] a fact that riders of most commuter lines knew long before the President told them about it. Although rail-commuting facilities have been developed or modernized in Toronto, Montreal, and Mexico recently, the only major American area developing a new mass-transit system has been San Francisco, which introduced its Bay Area Rapid Transit System (BART) early in 1971.

## POLLUTION AND PUBLIC POLICY

### Air, water, land, and pollution

The resources of the natural environment—land, air, and water—constitute the raw materials for our affluent society. Yet the natural environment is also the receptacle of our economy's waste materials. What engineers call the "law of materials balance" holds that the total weight of materials taken from nature will equal the total weight of wastes discharged into the environment plus any materials recycled. The air, land, and water from which the resources to build a civilization are extracted become the repository for that civilization's solid, liquid, and gaseous waste products. Viewed from the perspective of "material balance," pollutants are the inevitable by-products of the economic system, but to most specialists in public health and environmental engineering, the problem of waste and pollution has become grim indeed.

Air pollution consists primarily of carbon monoxide, hydrocarbons, nitrogen oxides from automobiles and industrial uses, and sulphur dioxide from the burning of oil and coal. Also contained in city air are fragments of solid materials like lead, zinc, and asbestos. Automobiles are responsible for the largest proportion of air pollution—aproximately 60 percent nationally but 88 percent in Los Angeles. In fact, the role of the automobile in producing pollution is one of the major arguments for developing mass-transit systems and a viable alternative to the gasoline-powered engine.[56] By 1970 it was widely believed that air pollution had become a serious health problem.

55 *The New York Times*, August 8, 1969, p. 13.

56 In its 1969 session, the California Senate passed legislation forbidding the sale in California of gasoline-powered engines after 1975. If this legislation were to pass the state House of Representatives, it would effect a most revolutionary change indeed.

Roger Revelle, a specialist on pollution and public health, notes, however, that the effects are not fully understood:

*. . . common sense suggests that pollutants capable of darkening house paint, disintegrating stone statues, corroding metals, dissolving nylon stockings, and embrittling rubber must also be injurious to delicate bronchial and lung tissues, but there is little hard evidence at present.*[57]

It is clear that air pollution is a very serious problem in areas where thermal inversions occur regularly. Such meteorological phenomena, in which layers of warm air settle over layers of cool air and prevent the dispersion of pollutants, have been said to have produced 4,000 deaths in London in 1952 and 200 in New York in 1953. Although there is some disagreement about the causal connection between pollution and various respiratory and pulmonary diseases, few if any scientists doubt that there is a threshold beyond which air pollution becomes a serious public-health problem. The difficulty has been in specifying that threshold.

Like air, water is also used as a receptacle for waste. Lake Erie, the main source of water for 10 million Americans from Detroit to Buffalo, is virtually closed to swimming and fishing; were it not for massive investments in treatment facilities, it would be undrinkable too. The Cuyahoga, Delaware, Potomac, and other rivers are at times unsafe even for boating. In fact, the Cuyahoga has caught fire several times. Although industrial pollution may be more serious than municipal pollution, municipalities have often dumped minimally treated sewage into rivers that are used as water sources by communities farther downstream.

Land is also both a source of raw materials for the economy and a receptacle for waste products. Americans now produce nearly 200 million tons of solid waste annually, about 1 ton per capita, and all of it must either be recycled or disposed of. According to Revelle, "solid wastes can be burned, buried, flushed, reused, or simply thrown away in more or less open country in the hope that they won't be noticed."[58] But each of these options implies certain costs. The first three methods produce air, land, and water pollution respectively. Reusing wastes has so far not been found economical. Simply throwing trash away is a popular but aesthetically unpleasant and increasingly expensive method. In many areas, sanitary land fills are exhausted, and refuse must be either "barged" out to sea (in coastal areas) or hauled to rural areas, at ever higher costs. Technological changes have

[57] Roger Revelle, "Pollution and Cities," in James Q. Wilson, ed., *The Metropolitan Enigma* (Washington, D.C., U.S. Chamber of Commerce, 1967), p. 84.
[58] *Ibid.,* p. 103.

complicated the problem of disposal of solid refuse. The aluminum can, for example, is much more difficult to get rid of than tin cans were, and some plastics are nearly indestructible; others create noxious gases when they are burned, thus adding to air pollution.

## Regulating pollutants and polluters

The most significant constraint upon the public officials who deal with the pollution problem is that, quite literally, pollution cannot be eliminated. At best, public policy can only reduce or eliminate the most serious forms of pollution and then select among several alternatives for distributing the remainder among land, water, and air. The designing of public policies to deal with this problem is also complicated by the familiar problem of an apathetic majority and an intensely concerned minority. Everyone in the urban community shares an interest in improving the quality of the physical environment, but the difficulty is that, in the short run, the general public experiences only minor inconvenience from pollution. Although, in the long run, air pollution may be our most critical social problem, its immediate threat is primarily irritation of the eyes or nose. To the polluter, however, regulations requiring him to install control devices may involve prohibitive expense, perhaps high enough to put his products at a competitive disadvantage with those of other producers, especially if demand is elastic. The cost of some pollution-reduction devices is very high. An open-hearth furnace used in the steel industry costs about $200,000. The electric precipitator used to control its production emissions nearly doubles this cost. Polluters are thus likely to perceive higher stakes in preventing controls or in shifting their costs to the public sector than the electorate perceives in reducing pollution. Not that polluters "favor" pollution, but the short-run costs make their stakes in the pollution-control process high. In much the same sense, the average automobile owner may favor the reduction of noxious ingredients in the air but not if he must give up his car or pay significantly more to buy and maintain it.

Partly because pollution is a long-range problem and because politics, in Lowi's words, "works in the short run," pollution control has been a matter of policy concern for only a decade or two. Sanitation and solid-waste disposal have, of course, been long-standing urban problems, but they seem to be presenting a new order of difficulties now. As with many urban policies, much of the original impetus for pollution control came from supralocal sources, particularly from a few states and the federal government. California passed the first anti-pollution law in 1947, but even as late as 1961 only seventeen states were spending as much as $5,000 each to fight air pollution. The more significant initiatives have come from the federal government. The federal water-pollution control acts of 1954, 1962, and 1965 have expanded federal regulation to include all interstate waterways. Administered by the Secretary of the Interior, these acts permit the federal government, as a last resort, to institute legal action against water polluters. The Clean Air Act of 1963, steered through Congress by Representative Roberts of Alabama and Senator Edmund Muskie of Maine, is partly modeled on the water-control acts. It follows them in authorizing three major regulatory steps. First, the U.S. Public Health Service may call an informal conference of all interested parties, including municipal officials, polluters, and representatives of the public. If the conference does not lead to reduction of air pollution, official public hearings may be called. As a last resort, court action may be initiated against polluters.

Few would claim that such federal efforts have done more than slow the growth of air and water pollution. Surely, this lethargy is significant, but the problem cuts deeper than the contributions of a few flagrant polluters. Wastes and pollution are the by-products of modern life itself, particularly of life in an urban, industrial economy.


## SUMMARY

The four policy areas examined in this chapter—policing, education, transportation, and pollution control—do not exhaust the services that cities attempt to provide their citizens. But they do involve some of the most serious problems of the modern urban environment: safety, knowledge, mobility, and survival, respectively. The environmental problems that these policies attack are themselves complex, and some of their causes are as yet undetermined. The crime rate is a function of numerous factors, including urbanization itself, population density, the social and economic characteristics of the population, and perhaps even its genetic makeup. The constraints upon law-enforcement agencies in their attempts to reduce crime are thus significant; some "handcuffs" on the police, as the President's Commission on Law Enforcement and Administration of Justice has pointed out, cannot be removed.

A similar picture can be painted in connection with educational policy. Although education is a major force in producing both macro-scale and micro-scale changes in society, there are constraints upon its effectiveness. Among the most significant are the families and cultural backgrounds of students. Race and poverty (the subjects of Chapter 9) are thus important considerations in formulating educational policy.

The decentralization of the urban population and the widespread ownership of automobiles are factors in both transportation and pollution-control policies. Most transportation policy has emphasized roads over rails. This emphasis has had significant spillover effects in the arena of pollution control because automobiles are the major source of air pollution. More generally, however, pollution is a product of economic life itself. The "law of materials balance" holds that output into the environment equals intake from the environment, minus whatever materials are recycled. There are a number of ways that an urban society can dispose of its wastes, and cities, individuals, and factories have tried many of them. Only recently have significant efforts —and some doubt their significance and sincerity—been made to reduce the problem of pollution in urban America.

# 9

# Poverty, race, and public policy

Disregarding the biblical warning that "the poor shall never cease out of this land," President Lyndon Baines Johnson, on August 20, 1964, signed the Economic Opportunity Act. Speaking at the signing ceremony in the White House rose garden, the President declared this nation's commitment to "eradicate poverty among its people." Armed with the metaphor, if not the money, of the military, the government inaugurated the "war on poverty." The enemy, poverty, would prove to be as elusive and difficult to define as the Vietcong, and the debate over strategies would be only slightly less furious than that over Southeast Asia. In the same year President Johnson signed the Civil Rights Act of 1964, widely regarded as the most significant step ever taken toward realization of the Fourteenth Amendment guarantee of "equal protection of the laws." Both civil-rights and poverty policies had thus been initiated in Washington, D.C., but both, especially the latter, have deeply implicated urban governments all over the nation. They are unquestionably the most controversial domestic policies enacted since the New Deal. Both are essentially *redistributive* policies, operating visibly to reallocate economic and political resources.[1] Re-distributive policies frequently set large social groupings against one another ("haves" versus "have nots," whites versus blacks) and engender maximum ideological conflict, partly because they both give *and* take away.

[1] Theodore J. Lowi, "American Business, Public Policy, Case-Studies, and Political Theory," *World Politics, 16* (July, 1964), 677–715, introduces the concept of redistributive policy.

## POVERTY: AMONG WHOM AND WHERE?

### Discovering poverty

It is an interesting question in the "sociology of knowledge" to ask when exactly Americans began to discover their poor. During the 1950s, both popular and scholarly writers discussed the "affluent society" and a "people of plenty" and debated the meaning of leisure time. Although economists like John Kenneth Galbraith emphasized the presence of pockets of poverty in an otherwise well-off society, their emphasis on affluence captured more attention in that comfortable Republican decade. In many ways, it was the 1963 publication of Michael Harrington's *The Other America* that brought home the persistence of poverty in the affluent society. President John F. Kennedy himself was influenced by Harrington's account of how the "other America" lived—the day after the assassination, an adviser found a dog-eared copy of the book in the White House Oval Room—and had proposed a major legislative program addressed to poverty just before his death. President Johnson made the program a major ingredient in his Great Society package of legislation, adopted by the Eighty-Sixth Congress. But before we embark upon a discussion of the war on poverty and urban policy, it may be useful to describe the nature and structure of American poverty, from both community and individual perspectives.

### Macro distribution of poverty

Sometimes we think of the poor as concentrated mainly in the racial ghettos of our biggest cities or in the most rural backwoods of Appalachia. The pattern, however, is somewhat more complex. Statistically speaking, there is *proportionately* more poverty in rural areas than in metropolitan areas, but, *in absolute terms,* there is more poverty in metropolitan than in rural areas, simply because such a large proportion of the nation's population (about two-thirds) lives in metropolitan areas. Moreover, there is proportionately less poverty in the largest than in the smallest cities. The percentage of poor people is, for example, twice as high in Bryan, Texas, as in Dallas; in East St. Louis, Illinois, as in Chicago; and in Newburgh, New York, as in New York City. But again, because so many more people live in large cities like Chicago, New York, and Dallas than in smaller ones, the absolute number—and the concentration—of poor people in major metropolitan areas is greater and offers greater challenges.

Within the metropolitan area itself, there are also important differences in the distribution of poverty. It is common to view metropolitan CCs as the havens of the poor and downtrodden and the suburbs as the homes of the white well-to-do. This image is, however, so oversimplified as to be seriously misleading. The size of the metropolitan area is a crucial variable in understanding the distribution of poverty within the metropolis (see Table 2.3). In the largest metropolitan areas, there is indeed a clear tendency for poorer people to reside in the central cities and wealthier ones to live in the suburbs, but this pattern reverses itself in the smaller metropolitan areas. In those with populations of less than 250,000, there are proportionately more poor people in the fringe areas than in the central cities. Within each central city, of course, there is a marked tendency for the poor to live in the oldest parts of town, where housing is cheapest. But the poor are not always separated by great physical distances from the wealthy. Some of the poorest neighborhoods in Washington, D.C., are within a short walk of affluent Georgetown. The socioeconomic distance between New York's Park Avenue and its slum dwellers is great, but the physical distance is surprisingly short.

## Micro distribution of poverty

Just as poverty is distributed on a macro scale, that is, among and within communities, it is also distributed on a micro scale. The probability of being poor varies from group to group and person to person. According to a recent study by the U.S. Census Bureau, a family of four needs an income of $3,553 a year to meet minimum nutrition, housing, and other essential needs. Certain types of families and individuals are especially likely to fall below this poverty line. Poverty is particularly concentrated among the aged, families headed by females, members of minority groups, and those with mental, emotional, physical, or occupational handicaps. In 1966 approximately 12 percent of all family units in the United States were classified by the government as poor, but, among the aged, the figure was twice as great.[2] Among other groups about 8 percent of white families lived below the poverty line, but a third of the nonwhite families were poor. The differences in the proportions of poor and others are greater between races than between the old and not old, suggesting that "being black" may be a more significant cause of poverty than "being old." These disadvantages appear to be cumulative, so that being both old and black significantly increases one's chances of being poor.

Several lingering myths about poverty ought to be dispelled forthwith:

[2] See Carolyn Jackson and Terri Velten, "Residence, Race, and Age of Poor Families in 1966," *Social Security Bulletin, 32* (June, 1969), 3–11.

1    *Most of the poor are unemployed.* Because most of the poor are, of
     course, either aged or under eighteen years of age, this statement is
     literally true. But the overwhelming majority of employable poor are in
     fact employed, though at wages so low as to keep them below the poverty
     line. Among "nonaged" families with male heads, nearly all the men
     work. The poor are no exception. Among the poor, 87 percent of white
     and 91 percent of black male family heads work.

2    *Most of the poor are on welfare.* In 1965 only 20 percent of poor people
     received public assistance and 82 percent of them were still poor (below
     the official poverty line) even with this assistance.

3    *Most of the poor are black.* Although a much larger *proportion* of blacks
     are poor than whites, a much larger *number* of whites are poor. In
     fact, two-thirds of the poor are white.

4    *Most of the poor live in large central cities.* Among blacks there is more
     poverty in the central cities, but many more white poor people live in
     the suburbs than in the central cities.

One curious aspect of the national attention recently devoted
to the poor is that interest in poverty has increased as the proportions
of poor people in the United States have declined. Whether we measure
the numbers of the poor by contemporary or by contemporaneous
standards, the percentage of the American population living below
some arbitrarily defined poverty line is decreasing.[3] Perhaps we can
now afford to take care of our poor. Or perhaps, since recent civil
disorders, we cannot afford *not* to take care of them.

Using adjusted statistics to account for changes in prices, economists counted about 40 million poor people in 1960, but in August,
1969, the Census Bureau counted only 25.4 million poor people, the
equivalent of 13 percent of the population. Perhaps the poverty problem is taking care of itself, and patience, rather than public policy,
is the most reasonable approach. There are, however, several difficulties
in any argument that assumes that poverty will simply "fade away"
over the years.

First, experience suggests that poverty is declining mainly in cases
where it is least acute. The groups that accounted for the largest proportion of the reduction during the 1960s were composed of non-
aged, white families with male heads. Surely, lifting this group up
from poverty is not the most difficult task facing the nation, for it is
the "hard core" cases who remain in poverty.

Second, there has been relatively little change in the gap between

[3] See Herman P. Miller, "Changes in the Number and Composition of the
Poor," in Margaret Gordon, ed., *Poverty in America* (San Francisco, Chandler, 1965),
pp. 81–101. Miller has drawn a distinction between contemporary and contemporaneous standards, emphasizing that, whether we apply today's higher living standard
or those of an earlier day, the incidence of poverty has still declined.

white and black incomes, despite the overall reduction in the number of the poor. If the cutting edge of the problem of race and poverty is the wide gap between economic gains by the two races, then almost no progress has been made over the past several decades.

Third, if we adopt the relativistic view based on *distribution* of income among the various groups in the population, then, in Downs' words, "there has been no decline in poverty whatsoever during the past twenty years."[4] In terms of money income, the poorest fifth of the population received 3.5 percent of national income in 1947 and 3.7 percent in 1966, whereas the corresponding figures for the wealthiest fifth of the population were 45.8 and 43.8 percent. From a strictly relative point of view, the poor are no better off, in comparison with the rest of us, than they were in 1947.

## Being poor

So far poverty has been treated as if it were entirely a matter of having a low income. Being poor, however, means much more than having too little money to buy what others consider essential. During the summer of 1969, several U.S. senators and their families simulated poverty for a week by living on a welfare-budget diet. The results, dutifully reported to the press, were persistent hunger, constant exhaustion, chronic irritability, and general malaise. However much this noble experiment dramatizes and "personalizes" poverty, it still fails to capture the multidimensional nature of "being poor," especially because the poor cannot look forward to the weekend.

Research has identified numerous variables on which the poor differ from the rest of the population.[5] Although a mere catalogue cannot do justice to the interrelated characteristics of the culture of poverty, it may illustrate the life style of the poor. They are more likely to be victims of crime. They also are more likely to be victims of disease, mental illness, and malnutrition. The psychological costs of being poor are indicated by the much larger proportions of poor people who report being generally "unhappy," by the higher incidence of mental illness among them, and by their feelings that they can do little to manipulate their own environment. This last feeling of social ineffectiveness is paralleled by a low sense of political efficacy and a

---

[4] Anthony Downs, *Who Are the Urban Poor?* (New York, Committee for Economic Development, 1968), p. 10.

[5] An excellent summary of this research is contained in the bibliographical essay by Zahava D. Blum and Peter H. Rossi, "Social Class Research and Images of the Poor: A Bibliographical Review," in Daniel P. Moynihan, ed., *On Understanding Poverty* (New York, Basic Books, 1969), pp. 343–398.

high sense of political futility. The poor see the political world as alien, complicated, distant, and impervious to them. Poor neighborhoods have very weak systems of social ties and organizations; most socializing takes place within the extended families and immediate neighborhoods. Very few poor neighborhoods have produced indigenous community or group leaders, which makes all efforts to organize the poor very difficult. Leaders claiming to represent the poor have usually gained their status by reference to race, rather than to poverty alone. Family life among the poor tends toward instability, sometimes fostered by welfare dependency. Family instability in turn produces higher levels of insecurity and occasionally deviant behavior among youth.[6]

Nonetheless, we should avoid the image of a nearly complete homogeneity of attitudes and behavior among the poor. No more than we would assume that every person whose income is over $10,000 thinks and behaves as does every other should we assume that all the poor are stamped from the same mold. Perhaps the most significant factor dividing the poor is race; conflict between whites and blacks overshadows whatever common interests are engendered by economic circumstances. The variety of belief and behavior patterns among the poor is particularly evident in political life. Political alienation, for example, is found more often among low-income groups than among the more affluent, but not all the poor are alienated. Even among the alienated, some express their hostility and isolation by withdrawal and nonparticipation, whereas others actively participate in ways that the middle class would call "deviant." The intensity of this "negative participation" may be expressed by voting "against" both incumbent officeholders and referenda propositions. For some black Americans participating in racial disorders is protest against the "system." Authoritarian political attitudes, characterized by intolerance of dissenting views and hostility toward "out-groups," also characterize many lower-class people, although the better educated among the poor are no more authoritarian than are other Americans. These observations on the political life of lower-class Americans suggest that, though some clear tendencies can be identified, the poor are certainly not a monolithic mass whose behavior can be perfectly predicted by their low incomes alone. But, even recognizing the variations among the poor, we may still agree with Harrington's political assessment:

[6] Notable for its emphasis upon the importance of family structure, especially among blacks, is the "Moynihan Report," reprinted in Lee Rainwater and William Yancey, eds., *The Moynihan Report and the Politics of Controversy* (Cambridge, Mass., M.I.T. Press, 1967).

*. . . the poor are politically invisible. It is one of the cruelest ironies of social life in advanced countries that the dispossessed at the bottom of society are unable to speak for themselves. The people of the other America do not, by far and large, belong to unions, to fraternal organizations, or to political parties. They are without lobbies of their own; they put forward no legislative program. As a group, they are atomized. They have no face; they have no voice.*[7]

## FIGHTING POVERTY: TWO STRATEGIES

### The welfare system

The traditional method for dealing with urban and rural poverty in the United States has been the public-welfare system. Public welfare is an administratively complex, even labyrinthine, set of specific programs, including (but not limited to)

*1*   old-age, survivors', disability, and health insurance;
*2*   aid to the blind, to the permanently and totally disabled, and to the aged;
*3*   vocational rehabilitation;
*4*   aid to families of dependent children;
*5*   workmen's compensation;
*6*   child-health and maternal services;
*7*   unemployment compensation;
*8*   mental-health services;
*9*   general relief.

Speaking broadly, welfare services may be classified as programs based on the social-insurance principle, for example, old-age, survivors', disability, and health insurance (commonly called "social security"); and those that provide such categorical assistance to the "deserving poor" as aid to families with dependent children. Welfare programs are a prototypical part of the cooperative federal system. They operate according to a maze of rules and regulations laid down by different governments, use multiple systems of support, and are administered by federal, state, and local agencies. About half the money for welfare programs comes from the federal government. The remainder is made up by combinations of state and local support that vary widely from state to state. But the day-to-day administration of the welfare system is usually decentralized among agencies of counties and other local governments, which employ thousands of social workers.

[7] Michael Harrington, *The Other America* (New York, Macmillan, 1963), p. 14.

The public-welfare system has always attracted ambiguous support and opposition among the public and among its clients. To the public, welfare has frequently symbolized social support for the indolent, paid for by taxing the hard-working. Although most people concede the necessity for helping the "deserving poor," particularly the very young, the old, and the disabled, there remains a nagging suspicion in the public mind that many people who prefer "doles" to work are being subsidized by the welfare system.[8] Social workers themselves have a different set of criticisms of the system, principally based on its incredible complexity and "red tape," its maze of rules and regulations, its arbitrary and differential support of various categories of "need," and its underfinancing of certain cases. Recently clients of welfare programs have also become increasingly vocal in their attacks on the welfare bureaucracy. Some of the bluntest charges have been leveled by the National Advisory Commission on Civil Disorders:

*The Commission believes that our present system of public assistance contributes materially to the tensions and social disorganization that have led to civil disorders. The failures of the system alienate the taxpayers who support it, the social workers who administer it, and the poor who depend upon it. As one critic told the commission, "The welfare system is designed to save money instead of people and tragically ends up doing neither."*[9]

Among specific criticisms of the welfare strategy of attacking poverty are, first, that it contains built-in discouragement to advancement. Until recently all payments received from work were deducted from welfare payments that the individual or family was otherwise entitled to. If the mother of dependent children undertook to improve her economic lot by working part time, she would thus lose an amount of welfare aid proportional to her wages. Under recent amendments, earnings of up to $30 a month will not be charged against welfare payments, but the discouragement is still apparent.

Second, the coverage of welfare programs is limited both in terms of money provided and of people included. The facts that only 20 percent of the poor received welfare payments and that 80 percent of those who did were still poor after receiving assistance suggest the limitations of traditional welfare programs.

Third, there is wide variation both among and within states.

[8] In an effort to dispel this suspicion, Senator Fred Harris of Oklahoma reported the results of an experiment conducted among Indians living on reservations. The Indians were permitted either to work or not to work but received the same money either way. The overwhelming majority chose to work.

[9] National Advisory Commission on Civil Disorders, *Report* (Washington, D.C., Government Printing Office, 1968), p. 252.

In one recent year the monthly payments under the Aid to Dependent Children (ADC) program varied from $62.55 in New York to $9.30 in Mississippi. The most important explanation for such variations is the variations in states' economic resources, and the poor in poor states are thus supported at low levels. That is, "the greater the need [for welfare], the less effort put out by the state to meet the need."[10] Moreover, local program administrators seem to have wide discretion in determining eligibility and payment levels, especially in the "general relief" program: People eligible in one jurisdiction may not be so in another.

Fourth, the public-welfare system is institutionalized charity and has the usual social stigma attached to such "doles." Because eligibility requirements are complex and usually rigid, there is considerable personal investigation and long-term surveillance of recipients. The most extreme form is the "midnight raid," in which a welfare agent checks to see if there is a man around the house of a mother receiving aid to dependent children.

Fifth, the relations between social-welfare workers and clients are commonly "abrasive" and "brittle," in the Kerner Commission's words. The case worker is forced into antagonistic relations with clients he is supposed to be assisting. Although the worker is supposed to establish a high level of personal rapport so that he may be able to influence client behavior, he also plays the antagonistic role of investigator and "snoop." Like the policeman, the welfare worker is a symbol of society and its authority, a society in which the clients have so visibly not "made it." And, in the client-caseworker relationship there is an element of paternalism, which is not lost on the welfare recipient.

Although we oversimplify somewhat, the common thread linking most of the criticisms of the welfare system is the assumption that poverty is primarily an individual phenomenon, the solution to which lies in the distribution of some cash and material benefits to families and individuals. The caseworker deals with individuals and families. His professional training—if he has had any—impels him toward individual "uplift." But, if the poor as a group lack the political and economic resources to demand what they need, critics say, a philosophy of individual change represents, at best, only a holding action against poverty. Many critics argue that the welfare system is based upon the theory that "defects in socialization" are the cause of poverty but

[10] Richard E. Dawson and James A. Robinson, "The Politics of Welfare," in Herbert Jacob and Kenneth N. Vines, eds., *Politics in the American States* (Boston, Little, Brown, 1965), p. 403.

that in fact the cause lies in the social system. This shift from a micro to a macro perspective on poverty characterizes the intellectual underpinnings of the war on poverty.

## Development of the economic opportunity program

If Harrington is right in claiming that the poor are invisible and "politically powerless," why then did the national government declare an "unconditional war on poverty" in 1964? Although it is not possible to answer that question fully, recent accounts of the origins of the Economic Opportunity Act of 1964 provide some useful insights.[11]

The beginnings of intellectual ferment over the problem of poverty during the Kennedy administration were influenced by two simultaneous developments: the Ford Foundation's Gray Areas Project and the deliberations of the President's Committee on Juvenile Delinquency. The Ford Foundation project was initially a reaction against the "bulldozer approach" to urban renewal, which wiped out entire neighborhoods and reconstituted them as tax-paying areas. Paul Ylvisaker, Ford's Director of Public Affairs, sought some alternative to such wholesale disruption of neighborhood life. Ylvisaker was also dissatisfied with the failure of existing social-welfare organizations to provide meaningful community organization and self-help to "gray areas." His proposed alternative was indigenous organization in such areas. In four cities and one state (Oakland, Philadelphia, New Haven, Washington, D.C., and North Carolina) the Ford Foundation helped to create community self-help organizations in poverty areas. It thus, in a sense, "invented" the Community Action Agency, which became the controversial cornerstone of the war on poverty.

The President's Committee on Juvenile Delinquency, established by President Kennedy in May, 1961, was given a modest mandate to coordinate various federal efforts to control delinquency. Under the stimulus of David Hackett, an intimate of Attorney General Robert F. Kennedy and chairman of the committee, the group interpreted its mandate broadly and argued for radical change in the conception of delinquency. Borrowing heavily from the theories of Richard A. Cloward and Lloyd E. Ohlin, the committee was persuaded that delinquency could not be explained either by innate character defects

---

[11] See, for example, Richard Blumenthal, "Antipoverty and the Community Action Program," in Allan P. Sindler, ed., *American Political Institutions and Public Policy* (Boston, Little, Brown, 1969), p. 180–229; John C. Donovan, *The Politics of Poverty* (New York, Pegasus, 1967); and Sar A. Levitan, *The Great Society's Poor Law* (Baltimore, Johns Hopkins, 1969). We have relied heavily on Blumenthal's brief but useful account.

or by inadequate socialization.[12] The problem was the gap between aspirations and opportunity. The socialization process worked, in fact, so well that middle-class aspirations were instilled, but the social structure—limited as it was by racial handicaps, poverty, and poor education—offered no legitimate opportunity to fulfill these aspirations. The solution the committee developed, which provided a working base for the Juvenile Delinquency and Youth Offenses Act of 1961, involved experimentation with *structural reform,* rather than *individual reform.* The public efforts of the juvenile-delinquency committee and the private efforts of the Ford Foundation intersected in New York City's Mobilization for Youth program, jointly funded by the foundation, the federal government, and the city. Formally established and inaugurated by a ceremony in the White House Rose Garden (the scene two years later of President Johnson's signing of the Economic Opportunity Act), MFY was supposed to demonstrate the potential for reducing the structural causes of delinquency through a root-and-branch program of community action. It was a trial run for the community-action agencies of the war on poverty.

Following the early efforts culminating in Mobilization for Youth, a group of Washington, D.C., bureaucrats, mostly in sub-Cabinet positions, came together informally to prepare legislation aimed at the broader problem of poverty in the United States. Although mem- they universally held to a structural, as opposed to an individualistic, bers of the group were divided among themselves on specific strategies, view of the causes of poverty. Such a perspective contained within it the seeds of a critique of traditional welfare policies, which they viewed as aimed at amelioration of individual problems rather than at institutional change. In the eyes of some members of the inner circle of poverty planners, public-welfare bureaucracies actually impeded antipoverty action, for they are more concerned with maintenance of their own organization than with major social change. In June, 1963, President Kennedy gave Walter Heller, who as chairman of the Council of Economic Advisers had been a major figure in the planning, his support for the antipoverty legislation. Those plans were nearly complete when Kennedy's death placed Lyndon Johnson in the White House.

Despite some planners' fears, Johnson evinced immediate interest in the legislation then being prepared for Congress: "That's my kind of program. It will help people. I want you to move full speed ahead," he told Heller. Once the commitment to "do something" had been made, jockeying for support among elements of the federal bureauc-

---

[12] Richard A. Cloward and Lloyd E. Ohlin, *Delinquency and Opportunity* (New York, Free Press, 1960).

racy followed. The Labor Department favored a major program of job retraining under its own administration. The Department of Health, Education, and Welfare favored major educational and health programs, though it was willing to provide some money to Labor for summer work programs. The Commerce Department favored loans to small entrepreneurs among the poor, whereas the Agriculture Department argued that there were surely as many poor farming entrepreneurs as there were poor businessmen. The Interior Department mentioned poverty among the Indians but did not formulate a program. These conflicts among the departments, as well as between the departments collectively and the Bureau of the Budget, became severe enough to threaten a delay in the legislative program. President Johnson appointed Sargent Shriver chairman of a task force to come up with a presentable program. After eight weeks of balancing, negotiating, and compromising, the task force drafted the legislation.

The result was a hastily forged compromise. The task force's most important contribution to the legislative package was the idea of an independent agency in the Executive Office of the President to administer the program. The Office of Economic Opportunity (OEO) thus became the nation's antipoverty agency. In both draft and final legislation the OEO was given the responsibility for administering several specific components of the war on poverty. The Job Corps was designed to provide education, vocational training, and work experience for youth. The Volunteers in Service to America (VISTA) program was envisioned as the domestic analogue of the Peace Corps, a group of volunteers who were to work in public projects or with community-action programs. The Head Start program, at once the most successful and the least controversial of the programs, was to provide preschool training for "disadvantaged" youngsters. The Neighborhood Youth Corps would provide work experience and vocational training for youths living at home. The OEO was also charged with administrative responsibility for community-action programs.

### The role of local government in the war on poverty

There was a general belief among the poverty planners that local choice and flexibility should be maximal. As the circumstances of poverty varied from community to community, it was necessary to include a "decentralizing element" in the legislation. The planners differed in their views about the Community Action Agency, but most favored its inclusion. The community-action program was modeled indirectly on the Ford gray-areas projects and, more directly, on the highly touted MFY program in New York City. The local agencies would be directed by boards broadly representative of the communities and would tailor specific projects to meet local needs, even though they would be funded mainly by the federal government.

Three little words, however—"maximum feasible participation"— threw the whole community-action concept into intense controversy once the warriors headed for the battlefield. The phrase appeared, innocently enough, in the definition of a community-action project in Title II, Section 202(b) of the Economic Opportunity Act. Specifically, a CAP was defined as an agency that (1) would mobilize community resources for an attack on poverty, (2) provide services to eliminate poverty by improving human performance and the like, and (3) would be "developed, conducted, and administered with the maximum feasible participation of residents of the areas and members of the groups served." Even participants in the original planning disagree about the source of the phrase, for at first no one paid much attention to it. In congressional hearings on the bill, only Robert F. Kennedy made even incidental reference to maximum feasible participation. Moynihan has claimed that the intent of the framers was merely to ensure that the poor were in fact the beneficiaries of the programs. If the poor, particularly blacks in the South, were "not sharing—that is, participating—in the benefits of the new program, Washington could intervene on the grounds that the requirements of the legislation were not being met."[13] In any event, no one, not even the most radical of the planners, intended the phrase to mean that the poor should be given control of the local programs. That some people, especially militant poverty workers, interpreted maximum feasible participation to mean policy control by the poor came to be the major political albatross of the war on poverty.

The draft legislation, maximum feasible participation and all, sailed through Congress with the minimum imaginable debate. Only a handful of changes were made in committee, and the bill passed both houses of Congress with comfortable majorities. Most of the opposition rhetoric was ideological, but even conservatives were cautious in their criticisms for fear of appearing to support poverty in an election year. Nearly all Democrats outside the South supported the legislation, and they were joined by most liberal Republicans. Opposition came mainly from southern Democrats and conservative Republicans, not an uncommon lineup against domestic social-welfare legislation.

Where had the poor been throughout that long process of planning, drafting, submitting, and passing antipoverty legislation? Plainly, they had not been standing outside the halls of Congress demanding action to alleviate their own plight, for the poor lacked

[13] Daniel P. Moynihan, *Maximum Feasible Misunderstanding* (New York, Free Press, 1969), p. 87.

the most basic of all political resources, motivation to act. The poverty planners were, rather, intellectuals: a handful of social scientists, career civil servants, and political "idea men." Moynihan, who later became Richard Nixon's White House "social scientist," was one of the original strategists of the OEO; he called his colleagues "professional reformers," men whose "profession might justifiably be described as knowing what ails societies and whose art is to get treatment under way before the patient is especially aware of anything noteworthy taking place." The war on poverty, he added, "was not declared at the behest of the poor: it was declared in their interest by persons confident of their own judgment in such matters."[14] The poor were later— much later—to march on Washington, D.C., but not until well after the poverty program was operational. In retrospect, it seems curious that a policy whose founders (at the national level) were professional, middle-class reformers had somehow unleashed programs in which (at the local level) the poor were expected by many to devise solutions to their own problems.

## ACTION AND REACTION IN COMMUNITY ACTION

By February, 1965, the Office of Economic Opportunity had published its *Community Action Program Guide,* containing "instructions for developing, conducting, and administering a community action program."[15] As the federal government was to fund up to 90 percent of a local agency's budget, local programs had to be approved by the OEO in Washington, D.C. The OEO's guide announced that

*The purpose of federal assistance to community action programs is to help urban and rural communities to mobilize their resources to combat poverty. Because community needs and resources differ widely, considerable latitude is allowed in the development and conduct of a community action program.*

The governing boards of the local CAAs were to consist of representation by three groups: public agencies, including the city government, school systems, and social-welfare agencies; private groups, including business, labor, and religious groups, and leaders of minority groups; and representatives of the areas to be served by the program. Representation of the poor on boards was thus considered one way to implement the maximum-feasible-participation clause. The guide also suggested

14 *Ibid.,* pp. 23, 25.
15 Office of Economic Opportunity, *Community Action Program Guide,* vol. 1, *Instructions for Applicants* (Washington, D.C., Government Printing Office, February, 1965), p. 7.

neighborhood meetings, surveys of the target areas, and employment of the poor in the CAA itself as ways to maximize participation. Local agencies could choose among a variety of programs authorized by the Economic Opportunity Act, including (1) such remedial or supplementary educational programs as preschool day-care centers; (2) employment development, job training, and counseling; (3) health and vocational-rehabilitation programs, like health examinations and family-planning advice; (4) home management and improvement; (5) improving welfare services; (6) consumer-information projects; (7) legal aid; (8) creation of neighborhood centers and organizations; (9) VISTA and Job Corps activities; and (10) encouraging resident participation in policy-making by both the CAA itself and by such other public and private institutions as the traditional welfare programs.

## Warring on poverty and the mayor: San Francisco

Just as planning for an antipoverty program at the federal level was not initiated "at the behest of the poor" but was originated by public officials, so the great majority of local community-action programs were initiated by public officials and established community organizations, rather than by the poor themselves. One Senate study of thirty-five poverty agencies found no instance of an indigenous group of the poor having initiated a program, although civil-rights groups had done so in eight cases.[16] San Francisco's community-action agency was thus typical in being introduced by the mayor, John F. Shelley.[17] The ink from the many pens President Johnson used to sign the Economic Opportunity Act was scarcely dry before Shelley, on September 2, 1964, set his program in motion. He created an Economic Opportunity Council (EOC), directed it to prepare a funding request for the OEO, and appointed its thirty-nine members. On October 23, the mayor's appointees, representing business, labor, social agencies, minority groups, and public agencies, met and chartered themselves as a nonprofit organization. There was an unspoken understanding in the mayor's office and on the EOC that the principal beneficiary of the program would be the black community. The mayor himself favored a broad-based coalition emphasizing business and labor groups, for he believed that jobs were the only real solution to poverty. One

[16] Howard W. Hallman, "The Community Action Program: An Interpretive Analysis," reprinted in Warner Bloomberg and Henry J. Schmandt, eds., *Power, Poverty and Urban Policy* (Beverly Hills, Calif., Sage, 1968), pp. 285–312.

[17] Our account of the San Francisco experience follows that in Richard Kraemer, *Participation of the Poor* (Englewood Cliffs, N.J., Prentice-Hall, 1969), pp. 25–67.

of the first actions of the EOC was the appointment of Everett Brandon, a young black stockbroker, as executive director. Brandon and the board designated four "target areas" for the antipoverty strategy: the neighborhoods of Western Addition, Hunter's Point, Mission, and Chinatown. (Later, a fifth neighborhood, the downtown Tenderloin, was added.) The EOC quickly devised a plan calling for each neighborhood to select its own advisory council. Each council was to assess neighborhood needs and contrive a plan to meet those needs, subject to final review by the EOC itself.

While Brandon and the board were formulating their plans for submission to the Washington OEO office, the Citizens United Against Poverty was created. It developed out of a meeting in the Macedonia Baptist Church on February 26, 1965, at which twenty-five ethnic, racial, and neighborhood organizations formed a loose coalition to challenge the mayor and his EOC, charging that the latter was not representative of the poor and that its programs would not be sufficiently "beneficial." Leaders of the new organization emphasized *maximum* participation of the poor, whereas the mayor wanted *feasible* participation. Specifically, CUAP demanded (1) the right of target-neighborhood residents to review and veto proposed programs, (2) employment practices in the community-action agency that would not discriminate against those without formal education or professional training, and (3) majority representation of the poor on the executive committee of the EOC. The protesters claimed that CUAP alone represented the poor and that the mayor's EOC violated the requirement of "maximum feasible participation."[18] The executive committee of EOC, though dominated by mayoral appointees, was willing to make some concessions, but the mayor himself denounced CUAP as a "self-appointed and self-annointed group engaged in a power grab." The most important resource of the protesters was the strategic advantage afforded by the OEO's adherence to the "participation" requirement. It seemed likely that, by claiming that the poor were being ignored, the CUAC could convince the OEO to reject the EOC program and budget. Finally, on May 20, Mayor Shelley verbally agreed to permit target areas to elect eight of the thirteen members of the central executive committee.

Soon thereafter, however, the mayor attended the annual meeting of the U.S. Conference of Mayors in St. Louis. He and Mayor Sam Yorty of Los Angeles jointly introduced a resolution denouncing

---

[18] Note, however, that in the legislation the word "poor" is not mentioned in connection with the "sticky" phrase. As at least one interpretation of the act was that it should coordinate existing agencies, it was sometimes argued that established community agencies should be the major participators.

the poverty program for "fostering class conflict" by insisting on control of each agency by the poor themselves. Claiming the support of both Vice-President Hubert H. Humphrey (the featured speaker at the conference) and the national office of OEO, Shelley returned to the West Coast in a less compromising mood. He announced his willingness to give the poor more representation by enlarging the executive committee but not to give them a majority. For seven weeks following Shelley's return, CUAP battled the mayor's office with mimeographed press releases. It accused the mayor of reneging on his promise of May 20; the mayor responded with his charge of a "power grab" in the name of the poor. Finally, following a bitter meeting of the EOC on August 31, at which "Mayor Shelley's name was hissed, jeered, and booed at every mention," the mayor admitted, in a masterly understatement, that "there seems to be a very strong feeling that control of the program should be with those who are involved in it."[19] The poor were given majority representation on the board, but Shelley's support and tolerance of the program thereafter waned.

The reconstituted EOC adopted a very decentralized administration, giving each of the original target areas broad powers to establish its own policies. Although a variety of projects were adopted by the various neighborhoods, all adopted "area-development programs." The term covered several schemes designed to organize the poor to exert pressure to change the policies of existing private and public agencies. Beyond this core program each neighborhood developed its own package. For example, "Western Addition, with a long tradition of Negro and civil rights activities, embarked upon a most extensive program of community organization, but was virtually consumed by factional conflict."[20] Chinatown, with a well-developed background of "traditional stewardship," developed a conservative program based upon coordination of established government, social, and educational agencies. There was little emphasis upon grass-roots organization of the poor. One of the Chinatown board members allowed that "the poor have enough troubles without having to go to endless meetings, too." The Hunter's Point program, in the most "ghettoized" of the four neighborhoods, was concentrated on tangible goals like housing renovation, devoting less attention than Western Addition to developing itself as a political force. The Mission district, the largest and most ethnically heterogeneous, had the only board made up entirely of the poor. Its program suffered from a series of rancorous conflicts over staff and planning, as each ethnic group and countless factions pushed their own demands for jobs and policy. On all four neighborhood

19 Kraemer, *op. cit.*, p. 33.
20 *Ibid.*, p. 34.

boards, there was considerable wrangling with the office of the parent EOC.

Richard Kraemer summed up the San Francisco experience: ". . . the fight for maximum feasible participation evolved from a contest between the mayor and minority group spokesmen for control of the program into a succession of power struggles within the target areas and between them and the central administration."[21] In time, the EOC and the neighborhood boards lost some of their enthusiasm for organizing the poor and instead devoted more serious attention to administering poverty programs. San Francisco's EOC became increasingly a program of the poor, for the poor, but no longer (if it ever really had been) by the poor.

### Competing conceptions of community action

We would be seriously remiss in portraying the San Francisco experience as typical of community-action programs. We have described it for two main reasons. First, it highlights, perhaps even caricatures, the types of conflict that in lesser degrees have plagued many local agencies. Second, and more important, many observers, including some journalists, a good many municipal officials, and not a few congressmen, *thought* that most CAAs were like San Francisco's EOC in their dogged dedication to redistribution of political power among the poor. Discovery that militant CAA employees have led a sit-in at a welfare office makes a livelier press report and a more dramatic congressional hearing than does the disclosure that half of all local expenditures go to Head Start and related educational and child-development programs. In fact, the breakdown of local expenditures in Table 9.1 suggests that the overwhelming proportion have gone to relatively uncontroversial programs related to neighborhood services, health, education, and the like. The only program clearly aimed at organizing the poor, "neighborhood organization," was a decidedly minor element in CAA budgets. A study of thirty-five local agencies concluded that the mobilization strategy was a relatively infrequent orientation among local CAAs. Howard Hallman has noted:

*Except for a very small number of communities, the community action program does not involve a predominant commitment to the strategy of giving power to the poor, or deliberate confrontation with established powers, of purposefully created conflict. . . . This approach is found only in San Francisco, Syracuse, and Newark of the thirty-five communities studied.*[22]

21 *Ibid.,* p. 66.
22 Hallman, *op. cit.,* p. 289.

Although fewer agencies have pursued a mobilization strategy than the newspapers have commonly assumed, there is nonetheless considerable variation in the dominant orientation of local CAAs. Most agencies have sets of core programs, which usually include educational programs like Head Start, neighborhood service centers, legal services, home-improvement assistance, and similar ventures. But beyond the core packages, CAAs differ in their choices both of programs and of strategies. A few have pursued the strategy of confrontation, following organizer Saul Alinsky and emphasizing solidarity among the poor and visible symbolic protests against established community agencies. The San Francisco and Syracuse CAAs have been perhaps the most publicized examples of this confrontation strategy. Many CAAs, especially those in which mayors and community agencies dominate the boards, have emphasized coordination of existing services and provision of some new ones to the poor. And some programs have stressed the quasi-activist strategy of neighborhood organization, though without marches on city halls and sit-ins in welfare offices.

Somewhere between the provocative programs of the poverty

**Table 9.1**  *Distribution of community-action agency expenditures through April 21, 1967*

| Major program components | Expenditures (in millions) |
|---|---|
| Child development, including Head Start | $ 393 |
| Education | 220 |
| Neighborhood centers, social service | 131 |
| Health | 41 |
| Employment | 40 |
| Neighborhood organization | 38 |
| Legal services | 36 |
| Homemaking, food, clothing | 26 |
| Cultural and recreational | 25 |
| Housing, community facilities | 20 |
| Economic development | 12 |
| Consumer services | · 4 |
| | $ 986 |
| Administration, evaluation, technical assistance, research, and the like | 207 |
| | $1193 |

SOURCE: Howard Hallman, "The Community Action Program: An Interpretive Analysis," in Warner Bloomberg and Henry J. Schmandt, eds., *Power, Poverty and Urban Policy* (Beverly Hills, Calif., Sage, 1968), p. 291.

planners and the antiseptic language of the antipoverty statute, the empty linguistic vessels "community action" and "maximum feasible participation" were filled with multiple meanings. Such a wide variety of interpretations was given to those phrases that Moynihan has flatly asserted that "the government did not know what it was doing." He detected four competing conceptions of "community action" held by one or more of the program's founders, including "organizing the power structure . . . confronting the power structure . . . expanding the power structure . . . and assisting the power structure."[23] The Bureau of the Budget preferred still another interpretation, emphasizing the coordination of varied services to the poor.

### Community commitment to the war on poverty

Some communities, like San Francisco, responded to the antipoverty legislation with quick action and managed to inaugurate major programs within short periods of time, whereas others pursued a slow-motion strategy. Some communities have well-developed and well-funded CAAs, whereas others devote only small proportions of their resources to organized antipoverty efforts.

A number of explanations may be offered for these variations in community commitment to the war on poverty, including the "public-regardingness" of community elites, the centralization of community decision-making structures, the perceived need for action indicated by the amounts of poverty and unemployment, and the level of citizen participation. In an effort to test several of these competing theories, Michael Aiken and Robert Alford have examined the expenditures of CAAs in 676 cities and related them to the socioeconomic and political characteristics of those cities.[24] Higher poverty expenditures were associated with

*1*  higher incidence of poverty, as measured by median family incomes and proportion of families earning less than $3,000 a year;
*2*  older cities;
*3*  larger cities;
*4*  higher unemployment rates in cities;
*5*  larger proportions of nonwhite population.

[23] Moynihan, *Maximum Feasible Misunderstanding,* p. 168.

[24] Michael Aiken and Robert Alford, "Community Structure and Mobilization: the Case of the War on Poverty" (Madison, Wisc., University of Wisconsin, Institute for Research on Poverty, discussion paper, October, 1968); see also J. David Greenstone and Paul E. Peterson, "Reformers, Machines, and the War on Poverty," in James Q. Wilson, ed., *City Politics and Public Policy* (New York, Wiley, 1968), pp. 262–292; and Andrew Cowart, "Anti-Poverty Expenditures in the American States," *Midwest Journal of Political Science, 13* (May, 1969), 219–236.

Aiken and Alford found little relation between the formal political structure of a city (form of government, types of elections, and types of constituencies) and the level of antipoverty expenditures. Despite an impressive list of socioeconomic and political characteristics, however, a large part of the variation in antipoverty expenditures is still unexplained. Factors unique to the community—the aggressiveness of a mayor, the poverty director's skills at obtaining grants, the connections of a congressman—may be particularly important in explaining the level of local antipoverty efforts. Still, as we have emphasized repeatedly, the expenditure of money alone is no guarantee that a program will accomplish its intended impact. It is to that more difficult question that we turn now.

## THE IMPACT OF THE ANTIPOVERTY PROGRAM

As no one was altogether certain what kind of antipoverty strategy was actually intended by the authors of the Economic Opportunity Act, there is necessarily uncertainty about how to measure its impact. The simplest indicator—counting the number of poor in the United States before the inception of the program and after several years of its operation—is grossly misleading, particularly because the proportion of the poor had been declining long before the dawn of antipoverty programs. Any thorough evaluation of the impact of the war on poverty would have to take account of both short-range, ameliorative goals and long-range goals like reduction in the probability of poverty over several generations. Against such benefits to be attributed to antipoverty efforts certain costs would have to be tallied. Perhaps, as both Shelley and Moynihan have feared, the class and racial antagonisms fostered by the antipoverty program constitute costs whose total cannot yet be measured. No public policy is devoid of spillover effects, and no discussion of policy impact can be complete without taking account of them. As measurement of those effects is difficult, if not impossible, we must emphasize that studies of the impact of the poverty program are both tentative and incomplete.

Nonetheless, one recent study does suggest a way to analyze impact. The National Opinion Research Center, using its Permanent Community Sample, studied fifty randomly selected communities and their CAAs.[25] Rather than attempting a complete analysis of program impact, the study took up a more modest and manageable goal: to

[25] James Vanecko, "Community Mobilization and Institutional Change: The Influence of the Community Action Program in Large Cities," *Social Science Quarterly*, 50 (December, 1969), 609–630.

determine which of four program orientations had been most effective in bringing about change in institutions serving the poor.

CAAs in the fifty cities were classified according to four predominant goal orientations: *education, social service, employment,* and *community organization and mobilization.* Eighteen measures of change in institutions serving the poor were used, including, for example, "increased numbers of people served by social welfare agencies," "increased number of graduates of vocational programs hired by employers," "increased participation of target area residents in school policy-making," and "increased participation in electoral politics by target area residents." Although not all the four strategies might be assumed to register on each indicator of change, it is reasonable to assume that agencies with an educational orientation should affect school policy, agencies with an employment strategy should affect hiring practices, and so on. The most significant finding was that *CAAs emphasizing community organization and mobilization have had the greatest impact in changing the policies of institutions serving the poor.* The most effective antipoverty agency in terms of impact is, according to Vanecko, the one that emphasizes organization of the poor and relies heavily upon the creation of strong neighborhood centers yet is not militant in its strategy.

Achieving impacts upon social institutions is only one potential goal of the war on poverty. Whether or not changes in institutions rebound in turn to improve the quality of life for the poor is still unknown. Until careful experimentation can determine the degree to which the poverty program contributes to an absolute reduction in the number of poor people or to improvement in the quality of their lives, any generalizations about its impact must be made with care.

### Constraints

The most significant constraint upon the ability of the war on poverty to ameliorate poverty is simply our limited understanding of poverty itself. In principle, it should be simple to eliminate poverty by redistributing income to the poor. One authority on urban poverty has estimated that $9.83 billion, less than the annual increase in the federal budget, could have (statistically at least) eliminated all poverty in 1966.[26] But because we know that poverty is more than a matter of having too little money, we recognize that no simple redistribution scheme could eliminate the psychological, social, political, and economic problem of poverty. The elimination of income disparities in statistical

---

[26] Downs, *op. cit.,* p. 12. Other estimates differ from this one, depending upon the assumptions made and the poverty lines established.

accounting is not the same thing as eliminating the factors that make and keep people poor.

A second constraint upon the war on poverty is its relatively limited financial base. Although the OEO budget for fiscal 1970 was the largest ever, about $1.7 billion, it was relatively small compared with the magnitude of the problem. A third constraint is that the spill-over effects of the poverty program—especially the creation of (or appearance of) support for militant activities that threaten the power of city officials and established agencies—have reduced support for community-action agencies.

### New directions in fighting poverty

The decade of the 1960s was marked by the transition from a micro to a macro strategy of fighting poverty. By the end of the decade the traditional welfare system was under fire from numerous quarters. President Nixon proposed a major overhaul of the welfare system that would establish a small minimum income for each family and require that all family heads either accept "suitable" jobs when offered them or enroll in job-training programs. A number of economists were proposing a "negative income tax" or a "guaranteed annual income." The OEO experimented with a guaranteed annual income for 1,359 families in New Jersey and Pennsylvania. Despite the fears of critics, virtually all the families with guaranteed incomes worked hard and even improved their employment circumstances. Earnings increased for 53 percent of the families receiving assistance and for 43 percent of a control group receiving no aid.[27] Whether or not the implications of such experiments will lay the foundation for public policy in the 1970s, however, time alone can tell.

## RACE, POVERTY, AND THE "CULTURE OF POVERTY"

Novelists like John Steinbeck, anthropologists like Elliot Liebow and Oscar Lewis, and social critics like Michael Harrington have all emphasized the *culture of poverty*, which tends to perpetuate poverty from generation to generation. The President's Council of Economic Advisers put this argument in the following terms:

*Poverty breeds poverty. A poor individual or family has a high probability of staying poor. Low incomes carry with them high risks of illness; limitations on mobility; limited access to education, information, and training. Poor par-*

[27] See the report of this experiment in Fred J. Cook, "When You Just Give Money to the Poor," *The New York Times Magazine*, May 3, 1970, pp. 23ff.

*ents cannot give their children the opportunity for better health and educa-
tion needed to improve their lot. Lack of motivation, hope, and incentive is
a more subtle but not less powerful barrier than lack of financial means. Thus
the cruel legacy of poverty is passed from parents to children.*[28]

Just as a child "inherits" his religious affiliation, his party identification, and his place of residence from his parents, so he "inherits" a
predisposition toward being poor or being rich. Stated simply, the
culture-of-poverty theory holds that people stay poor because they are
born that way.

One blunt fact, however, is that a majority of nonwhites are
poor, whereas a majority of whites are not. Nonwhites may be predominantly poor not because they "inherit" a predisposition toward
poverty but because they inherit a genetic, but socially conspicuous,
characteristic of skin color. The inheritance-of-poverty theory is that
"being born poor" keeps people poor, whereas the inheritance-of-race
theory is that "being born black" keeps blacks poor. The satisfactory
resolution of this conflict between theories would be most significant in
prescribing the content of any policy designed to eliminate poverty
among nonwhite groups.[29] If the former theory is correct, then antipoverty strategy should not differ according to the race of the clientele.
But if the latter theory better explains poverty among nonwhite groups,
a strategy intended to eliminate discrimination might seem more
likely to be effective than would one designed merely to break the
poverty cycle.

The most imaginative research into the issue of inheritance of
race versus inheritance of poverty has been conducted by Otis Dudley
Duncan.[30] In a national random sample of working Americans, Duncan identified an annual income differential between whites and blacks
of $3,790. What explains this income gap? Using statistical techniques
that permit apportionment of variation among specific factors, Duncan
concluded that $1,010 of the differential can be explained by family
characteristics (for example, father's education and occupation and
number of siblings in the family). The rest, however, is attributable
to differences in educational attainment ($520), to occupational dis-
crimination resulting from racial factors ($830), and to a residual
category that Duncan has called "income discrimination." Even when

[28] *1964 Economic Report of the President* (Washington, D.C., Government
Printing Office, 1964), pp. 69–70.

[29] Note that the existence of a culture of poverty is not being called into
question here. Rather, the issue is how important this culture is in explaining
black poverty, compared to the explanation of discrimination.

[30] Otis Dudley Duncan, "Inheritance of Race or Inheritance of Poverty?" in
Daniel P. Moynihan, ed., *On Understanding Poverty*, pp. 85–110.

family backgrounds and educational and occupational disadvantages suffered by blacks are accounted for, black men thus still receive considerably lower wages than do white men of comparable backgrounds, educations, and occupations. Although family-background factors are important, they are not nearly as important as are the collective effects of disadvantages of educational, job, and income discrimination. In Duncan's words,

> Negroes (that is, disproportionate numbers of them) are poor mainly because they are Negroes and are defined and treated as such by our society. . . . Their poverty stems largely not from the legacy of poverty, but from the legacy of race.[31]

This conclusion does not deny the existence of a poverty cycle, but it does suggest that for nonwhite Americans race is a more significant barrier to social mobility than are backgrounds of poverty. It directs our attention to public policies designed to eliminate racial discrimination.

## CIVIL RIGHTS AND URBAN POLICY

Most of the initiative for civil-rights legislation and policy has come from the federal government, and most of the federal initiative has been that of the Supreme Court or the executive rather than of Congress. The policies are not those of urban governments, although they affect urbanites. Many of these federal efforts are well known and need be only briefly mentioned here:

1    the 1954 Supreme Court decision (*Brown* v. *Board of Education of Topeka*) requiring desegregation of all public schools;
2    a succession of court decisions requiring equal access to public facilities like swimming pools;
3    the 1957 and 1960 Civil Rights Acts, which established a civil-rights section in the Department of Justice and authorized the U.S. Attorney General to sue to enjoin interference with voting rights in federal elections;
4    the Civil Rights Act of 1964, which forbade discrimination in public accommodations and in programs or facilities supported by federal funds, like public schools;
5    the Voting Rights Act of 1965, which sent federal registrars into several southern states to register voters;
6    the 1968 open-housing legislation, which forbade discrimination in the sale or rental of housing and, by January 1, 1970, covered nearly 80 percent of all housing units;

[31] *Ibid.*, p. 87.

7    the U.S. Supreme Court decision (*Jones* v. *Mayer*) in 1968 that held all
     discrimination in the sale or rental of public housing to violate section
     1982, Title 42, of the U.S. Civil Code.

Relatively few initiatives in civil-rights policy have come from
the states, although New York, New Jersey, and Connecticut were
early innovators in housing, employment, and public-accommodations
legislation. Even fewer initiatives have come from local governments.

## SUMMARY

We have described in this chapter two related policy areas involving expansion of citizens' opportunities—the war on poverty,
designed to broaden economic opportunities, and civil-rights legislation,
designed to expand political and legal opportunities. Only the poverty
program has been fought out on the terrain of local politics. Poverty,
of course, is a multifaceted problem, with economic, racial, psychological, political, and social dimensions. Poverty questions are especially
intertwined with issues of race. Although there is a "culture of poverty"
that perpetuates poverty over generations, a major barrier to blacks
is not this legacy alone but the effects of past and present racial discrimination.

Still, one of the principal myths about poverty is that it is
mainly a problem of minority groups packed in racial ghettos. Although poverty is disproportionately concentrated in minority groups,
a majority of the poor are white. Another myth is that most of the poor
are now being served by conventional welfare systems. The inade-
quacies of the welfare apparatus were one of many reasons for the
inauguration of the war on poverty. Since the passage of the Economic
Opportunity Act of 1964, hundreds of community-action agencies have
been operating a variety of programs to reduce the incidence of
poverty. The war on poverty, however, operates under severe environmental constraints. Some of them are political, occasioned by the
sometimes controversial nature of local agencies and by fears of "fostering class conflict." Another set of constraints—perhaps even more
restrictive—lies in our imperfect understanding of poverty. If poverty
were a matter only of having too little money, it could be eliminated
(at least statistically) with comparative ease. But the complexity of the
problem makes it resistant to solution by public policy. Whether or
not the war on poverty can register a significant impact on the lives
of the poor is a question that—though we have offered some fragmentary evidence—cannot now be determined.

# 10

# Managing urban growth: planning, housing, and redevelopment policies

As almost all population growth in the United States is concentrated in urban areas, there are some good reasons for keeping those areas habitable. Twenty years ago E. B. White concluded that "it's a miracle that New York works at all. The whole thing is implausible." There is, he said, "reason enough to abandon the island to the gods and the weevils."[1] Both the federal government and individual municipalities have, especially in the last decade, undertaken to make urban environments more hospitable.

Except for a very few cities that were actually *planned* by far-sighted founding fathers, most American cities have simply *grown*. Populations have swelled because of immigration, industrialization, and rural decline. Urban densities have increased and, then, with the rise of the automobile and the move to the urban fringe, decreased again. Little conscious public policy has directed this urbanization of the American population, however. Only in recent decades has the development of the city become a matter for public policy. In this chapter, we shall explore several policies, particularly those related to planning, housing, and redevelopment, whose intended impact is urban reconstruction or controlled urban growth.

[1] Quoted in *Newsweek*, August 18, 1969, p. 51.

## URBAN PLANNING

### Planners and their activities

If we take "planning" to mean identifying goals and the resources and constraints involved in attaining them, then it is clear that we all plan to some degree all the time. Much of such planning, however, covers only some of the available alternatives. The same is true of city politics, in which all actors (voters, mayors, agency heads, party leaders) attempt to match scarce resources to general goals. More narrowly, though somewhat tautologically, the term "city planning" refers to the activities undertaken by the city planning department and its professional staff.

Although most of the earliest city planners had been trained as engineers or architects, today the younger planners have been trained in university departments of city or regional planning. The graduate of an interdisciplinary curriculum that usually includes courses in architecture, design, engineering, public administration, the social sciences, and "planning" itself receives the degree of Master of City Planning (M.C.P). Most municipal planners are members of the American Institute of Planners (AIP), which has been concerned recently with securing public recognition of planning as a profession analogous to law and medicine. At the behest of Michigan's planners, for example, in 1966 the state legislature passed a law prescribing registration of planners, the passage of a professional examination, and fines and imprisonment for anyone calling himself a "community planner" without having met the law's registration requirements. Like city managers, planners are professional employees of the municipal government; in principle they are hired on the basis of their professional competence, rather than because of their personal contacts. Organizationally, the planning staff is a part either of a quasi-independent agency, usually called the planning commission, or of a staff agency assisting the mayor or city manager. Directors of most planning agencies are appointed by the chief executives, although a minority is still appointed by city councils or by the planning commissions themselves. Planners have debated for years the merits of insulating the planning agency from politics by placing it under a "nonpolitical" planning commission or of thrusting it farther into municipal politics by placing it under the chief executive. The trend is toward the latter, but there is little clear evidence to suggest that one form contributes more than does the other to the agency's influence.[2]

[2] Francine Rabinovitz, *City Politics and Planning* (New York, Atherton, 1969).

Regardless of the professional backgrounds or organizational milieus of planning agencies, several activities form a common denominator for almost all such staffs. All necessarily must *gather information* and *process data.* Although all municipal agencies gather and analyze data, cities with large and effective planning staffs are increasingly centralizing some of these activities in their planning departments. The information available to the planner is his most important resource. One of the most visible products of planning activities is the *land-use plan,* which reflects technical studies of existing land use, trends and projections of economic growth, municipal policies toward economic development, and planners' conceptions of community goals. Whatever the plan, once it is formulated the planner is usually involved in its implementation.

*Zoning,* the principal tool for enforcing use of private property as prescribed by the municipality, is designed to restrict what planners call "nonconforming uses," use of land in contradiction to the plans proposed by the professionals and adopted by the council. Ordinarily, after the adoption of a plan, nonconforming uses (for example, building a service station on a quiet residential street) may not be undertaken, and already existing ones may not be expanded. Land-use plans also include rules and regulations for subdivisions, specifying such details as sizes of lots, setbacks from streets, and sidewalk and street construction. Building codes containing standards for industrial, commercial, and residential construction are usually included in plans formulated and implemented by the planning office. Planners usually find it necessary to collaborate closely with such other municipal agencies as housing and renewal authorities, model-cities boards, airport boards, highway departments, and utilities departments, as well as with private groups and federal and state agencies.

## Planners' orientations and roles

THE PLANNING MOVEMENT   Their education, their occupational milieu, and the intellectual origins of the planning movement itself incline planners toward the view that physical and spatial relations strongly determine social interaction. David C. Ranney has described this attitude as a philosophy of "environmental determinism."[3] For planners, land and its uses, spatial relations, and aesthetics are critical components in any formula for the good life.

Environmental determinism is rooted in the origins of the planning movement. One of the founding fathers of city planning was

[3] David C. Ranney, *Planning and Politics in the Metropolis* (Columbus, Charles E. Merrill, 1969), p. 20.

Ebenezer Howard, whose book *Tomorrow*[4] stressed that most urban problems arise from the sheer size and density of the urban population.[5] Howard argued that smaller, less dense settlements would solve the social and economic ills of the cities and advocated the creation of "new towns" of limited size (32,000) and severely limited density. Altering people's spatial relations, he argued, could alter the social and economic problems attributable to high densities for the better. Although "new towns" have been developed extensively in Great Britain and Europe and advocated vigorously in the United States, there are few important examples on this side of the Atlantic. Reston, Virginia, and Greenbelt and Columbia, Maryland, are perhaps the most important.

The urban-planning movement began with the reformism of the Progressive era, with which it shares an important affinity. Like the reformers, planners are interested in the "community as a whole," which they believe transcends narrow and private-regarding interests of community segments. Accordingly, the "public interest" appears to them both different from and morally superior to transitory individual and group interests. "The view," according to Alan Altshuler, "that clashes of interest are only apparent has always appealed to one element of the American intellect. It is assumed by most conservative defenders of the status quo no less than by progressive attackers of 'politics.' "[6]

The planner shares with both the Progressives and the contemporary reform groups a bias against things political. Ranney has suggested that "planners have traditionally distrusted local government, viewing it as the pawn of special interest groups. This distrust is at least partly the result of the relationship between the planning movement and the municipal reform movement."[7] Rightly or wrongly, many planners see the municipal political process as sacrificing "community-regarding" goals in favor of rewards to self-seeking individuals and groups. Politicians, as we saw in Chapter 5, cannot often claim to behave rationally because of the myriad constraints upon rational choice. Planners, however, are likely to believe that rational choice, though never easy, is in principle an attainable goal.

TECHNICIANS, BROKERS, MOBILIZERS, AND ADVOCATES    Planners, as other decision-makers, can choose among several roles in the performance of

---

[4] Ebenezer Howard, *Garden Cities of Tomorrow* (Cambridge, Mass., M.I.T. Press, 1965; first published as *Tomorrow* in 1898).

[5] The "optimum size of cities" is still a lively question among social scientists. For an excellent discussion, see Robert A. Dahl, "The City in the Future of Democracy," *American Political Science Review, 61* (December, 1967), 953–970.

[6] Alan Altshuler, *The City Planning Process* (Ithaca, N.Y., Cornell University Press, 1965), p. 315.

[7] Ranney, *op. cit.*, pp. 28–35.

their activities.[8] Planners' suspicion of politicians and politics leads many of them to a kind of political asceticism and withdrawal from controversy. This professional role has been described as that of "technician," for they try never to allow considerations of political feasibility to interfere with their work. They see themselves as specialists working for municipal governments, developing plans strictly on the basis of planning theory and avoiding "entangling alliances" with politicians or groups. The technician's principal resources are his expertise and his information. This role may or may not enhance the effectiveness of planning, depending upon the specific community politics.[9] Where there is relative consensus in the power structure, taking the technician's role may enhance the planner's influence over public policy, assuming, of course, that the power structure is committed to planning values and policies. If, on the other hand, the monolithic elite is unsympathetic to the planners and their "Christmas lists" of proposals, the technician's role may be the least effective one the planner can choose. In Altshuler's words, "the professional whose claims to expertness are generally accepted rules supreme within his sphere."[10] Conversely, technicians who lack support from the power structure can have little impact upon public policy.

Other planners see their role as that of "broker." The broker's role is often assumed in communities where the power structure is competitive rather than monolithic. Instead of putting himself forth as a technician or "neutral expert," the planner stresses his position as confidential adviser to the policy-makers. He may thus permit considerations of political "marketability" to affect his recommendations and plans. His "constituency" is the mayor (or manager), rather than the planning profession or the community as a whole. The broker casts his lot with the politicians in power and serves as adviser, confidant, and technical assistant to the chief executive.

The planner as "mobilizer," who goes outside city hall to obtain support for his plans and programs from "influentials" in the community at large, is more likely to be found in a system of fluid multi-factionalism. One planning specialist has observed that planners

*usually find it easier to get public support for the planning program if they first enlist the interest and secure the backing of established civic, business, and professional organizations, including such groups as service clubs, real estate boards, engineering and landscape societies, and labor organizations.*[11]

8This discussion of planners' roles relies heavily on Rabinovitz, *op. cit.*, chap. 4.
9 *Ibid.*, p. 81.
10 Altshuler, *op. cit.*, p. 335.
11 Donald Webster, *Urban Planning and Municipal Public Policy* (New York, Harper & Row, 1958), p. 308.

Some of these groups, particularly the civic, professional, and business organizations, are the natural allies of planners, partly because they share a reformist orientation toward city politics (including the predilection for rational decision-making, aversion to politics, and desire to produce economic growth and development). The planner as mobilizer gambles his own job security in an unstable political environment in efforts to generate support for his programs. Regardless of the type of political system, the mobilizer is always less secure than is either the technician or the broker because he is willing to enter the fray of politics, sacrificing (to some degree at least) the "Olympian neutrality" of the disinterested professional expert.

One variant of the mobilizer's role is what Paul Davidoff has called the "advocate planner."[12] The planner as advocate proceeds from the assumption that planners cannot be neutral technicians but must constantly choose among competing interests and groups. Davidoff has emphasized that, whereas our conception of rational decision-making involves selecting from among alternative strategies to procure a desired end, traditional planning theory has assumed that a single agency should develop a single plan or a single set of alternatives. This "unitary" philosophy produces, he has argued, a partial, shallow, and incomplete analysis. Advocacy planning rests upon the "pluralistic" assumption that competing interests have stakes in the formation of plans and that these alternative perspectives ought to be cultivated and deliberately put forward. Planners should, then, function as advocates for various groups; an analogy is the public-defender system designed to provide counsel for all defendants in legal cases. Davidoff has urged planners to take special care to articulate the views of traditionally unrepresented groups, like the poor and racial minorities. The advocate planner is thus a mobilizer par excellence, as deeply involved in the political process as the technician planner is alienated from it. As Lisa Peattie has put it:

> The advocate planners in effect reject both the notion of a single "best" solution, and the notion of a general welfare which such a solution might serve. They take the view that any plan is the embodiment of particular group interests, and they therefore see it as important that any group which has interests at stake in the planning process should have those interests articulated in the form of a plan. Planning in this view becomes pluralistic, and partisan, in a word, overtly political.[13]

In addition to deliberately "politicizing" the planning profession, advocate planners urge attention to the social as well as the physical

---

[12] Paul Davidoff, "Advocacy and Pluralism in Planning," *Journal of the American Institute of Planners, 31* (December, 1965), 331–338.

[13] Lisa Peattie, "Reflections of an Advocate Planner," *Journal of the American Institute of Planners, 34* (March, 1968), 81.

aspects of the city. Davidoff has observed sardonically that planners "cope with the problems of the alienated man with a recommendation for reducing the journey to work."[14] An advocate planner emphasizes planning for people instead of places.

Most planners today are not comfortable with the implications of the advocate's role. Many are relatively content with the technician's role, even though it may limit their influence over policy. But, as the education and social concerns of younger planners operate to leaven thinking in the planning profession, planners are likely to become more politically sophisticated and to relinquish to some extent the technician's role.

### The master plan

The most ambitious activity undertaken by planners in city government is what is called "master planning" or "comprehensive planning." A master plan, according to Banfield and Wilson,

*is a set of maps and policy statements that describe in general terms the present intention of the authorities respecting actions they may take over the long run and that may affect the physical development of the city.*[15]

The emphasis is on physical, rather than social, phenomena. An ideal master plan would guide specific land-use decisions in both the public and private sectors. A question of use for any parcel of land could be determined simply by matching up the plan's prescriptions with the proposed use. Just as the late Justice Owen Roberts once defined the task of the Supreme Court as putting the particular law in one hand and the relevant part of the Constitution in the other and seeing that they are squared, so the planning agency would need only to evaluate each proposed change in land use as it conformed with the master plan. Indeed, Charles M. Haar, a specialist in planning law, once called the master plan the "impermanent constitution" of a city.

The layman may think that the formulation of a realistic master plan for a city of thousands of people, a complex social and economic structure, and infinitely varied preferences about the role of government would be impossible to achieve—and he would not be all wrong, for few master plans can be both comprehensive and detailed enough to guide decisions. Nearly every city has developed, under the spur of federal legislation, some type of master plan, and many of these plans have been condemned as "ninety-day wonders." Because master plan-

14 Davidoff, *op. cit.,* p. 337.

15 Edward C. Banfield and James Q. Wilson, *City Politics* (Cambridge, Mass., Harvard University Press, 1963), pp. 188–189.

ning is in principle a rational process—general goals are stated, and the most efficient means to attain those goals are incorporated—we can gain some insights into the constraints upon master planners by reformulating our discussion of rational decision-making (see pp. 179–185) in terms of planning.

When the planner attempts to identify the abstract goals of a city before formulating them in a specific master plan, he is inevitably struck by their abstractness and their contradictions. Various groups in the community have different stakes and interests in public and private policy, and the common denominator of agreement may permit the planner to state his goals only in terms so abstract as to be vacuous. The goal of the St. Paul land-use plan, for example, was stated as the "evolution of St. Paul as a better place to live and work." Surely only a misanthrope would dissent from such a goal!

A second barrier to comprehensive planning is the sheer complexity of predicting changes in the environment. The urban system is an open one, with both external and internal forces shaping changes. Predicting changes within the community is difficult enough, but predicting changes in external forces is nearly impossible. Although planners have developed sophisticated models of systems analysis, cost-benefit theories, and computerized simulations of urban change, prediction accurate enough to use in prescribing policy for future decades remains an ephemeral goal. The impossibility of accurate prediction has led some advocates of master planning to call for "plasticity," or "flexibility," in plans, in order to permit adaptation to environmental change. (This call is reminiscent of Senator Everett Dirksen's dictum that "I am a man of principle and my first principle is flexibility.") "Flexibility," however, undercuts a strictly rational approach to planning and is, moreover, difficult to use as an operational guide.

A third barrier to rational planning lies in the nature of politics. In Banfield's blunt words,

*The important questions are settled ultimately by elected officials (politicians) whose decisions are normally mere by-products of their competitive struggle to get and keep office. No competent politician will sacrifice votes that may be needed in the next election for gains, however large, that may accrue to the public 10, 20, or 30 years hence.*[16]

Given the limited information available to most voters, the immediate costs of any proposal must be weighted more heavily than the long-term gains. Politics, according to Lowi, "works in the short run," but

16 Edward C. Banfield, "The Uses and Limitations of Comprehensive Planning in Massachusetts," in H. Wentworth Eldridge, ed., *Taming Megalopolis*, (Garden City, N.Y., Doubleday Anchor, 1967), vol. 2, p. 713.

comprehensive planning emphasizes the long run. (John Maynard Keynes's observation that "in the long run we are all dead" strikes a deeper chord in the politician and the public than in the planner.) Given all these constraints upon comprehensive planning, we might expect it to be most successful when (1) planners' information is at a maximum, (2) articulated goals are congruent with those of politically influential groups in the community, and (3) politicians and voters are willing to sacrifice short-term for long-term satisfactions. This set of requirements for successful comprehensive planning is stringent indeed.

## The impact of planning

ZONING    Probably the greatest single impact of planning upon the socioeconomic environment of American cities has been through zoning policy. The typical regulations, which consist of the zoning ordinance itself, subdivision regulations, and building codes, divide the city's space into various categories. The most common classifications are industrial, commercial, and residential, although each may contain gradations within. The residential category, for example, may be further divided into land for single-family dwellings and multiple-family dwellings. In the industrial classification distinctions may be made between areas for industries with noxious effects (smoke, noise, congestion) and those without. Requests to alter the zoning classification of a particular piece of property are usually considered by the municipal planning commission, whose decisions are ordinarily subject to review by the city council. Some planning commissions take a jaundiced view of any modifications in a zoning classification laid down in the ordinance and reject all requests for change. Others are sometimes eager to permit numerous exceptions in the form of "spot zoning," granting exceptions for a few pieces of property in a larger area of homogeneous land use. Zoning ordinances, housing codes, and subdivision regulations typically prescribe land use and other matters as well. For residential areas, minimum lot sizes, the buildings' distance from streets, and certain other regulations may be invoked. Requirements also may be established for commercial and industrial property. The latter may also be regulated to minimize smoke, pollution, and noise.

As zoning represents a government's efforts to control the uses of private property, the rights of municipalities to enact and enforce zoning have been repeatedly challenged in the courts. But, despite arguments that zoning is "socialistic" and an infringement on private property rights, the late Justice George Sutherland, usually considered a very conservative member of the Supreme Court, wrote a crucial opinion supporting zoning, in *Village of Euclid* v. *Ambler Realty Co.*[17]

Zoning is both more popular and more effective in newer suburbs than in older central cities. The reasons why are not obscure. As the physical development of older cities took place before zoning had been developed to a fine art, land use there has been determined by the often haphazard decisions of the marketplace. Today nearly all major cities have zoning ordinances (Houston, Texas, is the only significant exception). In most, however, zoning affects choices only at the margins. Most land-use decisions are already "given" by market considerations. But many suburbs, whose development has postdated the "zoning revolution," began their growth with rigid land-use restrictions already in force. Zoning has quite literally shaped those communities. One disgruntled property owner in Greenwich, Connecticut, has grumbled that "in Greenwich, no one can get elected unless he swears on the Bible, under a tree at midnight, and with a blood oath, to uphold zoning."[18]

The importance of zoning in suburbia, of course, is that it permits a community to manipulate its social and economic environment through sophisticated land-use policy. Wood, in his study of the New York metropolitan region's 1,400 governments, noted that

*planning, zoning, and promotion . . . represent ways by which all local units of general jurisdiction can keep "undesirables" out and encourage "desirables" to come in, if they choose. And, of course, the definition of desirables and undesirables varies from place to place.*[19]

The kind of zoning undertaken to encourage or prevent certain land uses necessarily depends upon the strength of various interests in the community.

FISCAL ZONING AND PROMOTION    Zoning alone does not lead to the kind of economic development that residents desire. It merely classifies land for use. If industry is wanted, a hospitable zoning policy must be combined with the willingness of city planners to gather data for prospective firms, with special promotional efforts, and, in many communities, with tax incentives. Where the desire to keep taxes low is a major objective, communities usually try to attract industry. Industries, it is widely believed, are generous taxpayers. Moreover, their operations spill over into the macro and micro sectors of the local economy. Yet industries are not only taxpayers but also very heavy service con-

17 272 U.S. 36 (1927).

18 *The New York Times*, May 29, 1967, p. 13.

19 Robert C. Wood, *1400 Governments* (Cambridge, Mass., Harvard University Press, 1961), p. 79.

sumers. In the Philadelphia region, for example, the highest municipal expenditures were found in the industrial suburbs, largely because of service consumption by industries.[20] Industries also bring workers and managers who consume municipal services, particularly education. Some industries impose higher service costs than they contribute in taxes to the public coffers. The trick is thus to secure industries whose input into the public and private sectors is high and whose "outtake" from the public sector is low. Firms specializing in "research and development" employ highly trained and well-paid personnel and are preferred to noisy, sooty factories that contribute to congestion. The problem is that there are not enough "R & D" firms and their equivalents to go around.

Municipalities are thus compelled to play a "fiscal zoning game" in an effort to attract—or pirate—industries that pay more in taxes than they consume in municipal services.[21] The nature of communities will restrict strategies in the fiscal zoning game. Although some residents may settle for any industry that pays its way, others draw the line at noisy ones, smoky ones, or ones that bring congestion. Whatever the limitations, most communities, large and small, play the game through promotional policies, free or inexpensive services to new business, and favorable land-use policies.

SOCIAL ZONING   Some communities want no part of zoning and related policies to attract industry. These communities are typically high-income, upper-class residential suburbs, which prefer to accept the increasing costs of local government in order to retain the pristine character of a residential greenbelt. These cities play the game of "social zoning" rather than fiscal zoning. Zoning industry out is easy enough; all land can be reserved for residential and retail development. It is more challenging to manipulate land-use regulation to secure a particular class (and, by accident or design, racial) composition. It may be accomplished by requiring, for example, minimum lot sizes from half an acre to four acres or by establishing such stringent building-code requirements that housing costs become prohibitive except for the wealthy. Greenwich, Connecticut, and Scarsdale, New York, both upper-middle-class communities, have used tight zoning restrictions to maintain homogeneous residential communities amid creeping industrialization. Such practices, when carried to extremes, produce what Whitney Young has called "gilded ghettos." Restrictive covenants, devices by which deed restrictions are used to prevent the sale of

[20] Oliver P. Williams *et al.*, *Suburban Differences and Metropolitan Policies* (Philadelphia, University of Pennsylvania Press, 1965), pp. 91ff.
[21] Alan K. Campbell and Seymour Sacks, "The Fiscal Zoning Game," *Municipal Finance*, 65 (1964), 140–149.

housing to members of minority groups, were declared unenforceable by the Supreme Court in 1948,[22] and Congress has forbidden racial discrimination in the sale or rental of housing since 1968. But zoning policies that substitute class for racial premises may have consequences similar to racial ones.

### Correlates of planning expenditures

Throughout our chapters on policy in the urban setting we have attempted to identify the primary socioeconomic and political correlates of policy levels. With respect to planning, a number of hypotheses might be developed to explain why some communities spend more (or less) on planning activities than others do. Given the intimate associations between planning and the reform ethos, it might be assumed that reformed government structures would be associated with higher planning expenditures. Or, in light of the preference of middle- and upper-class groups for ordered and planned communities, it might be assumed that the social-class composition of the population is associated with planning expenditures or that planning is a function of community need, as measured by such factors as growth rate or the incidence of poverty.

Whatever our hypotheses about the correlates of planning expenditures, however, they appear to be disproved by the data in Table 10.1, which indicate that none of twenty-four political and socioeconomic characteristics of cities is very strongly associated with planning expenditures. Perhaps we should not make too much of negative findings, but it is interesting to note that other characteristics—taxation and expenditure levels, desegregation rates, school programs, and others—are moderately or strongly associated with factors in the community environment. Perhaps these negative findings point up the political distance between local planning agencies and the sociopolitical structures of municipalities. If planners are not well integrated into the larger community and do not draw power from their contacts there, then their impact may be blunted. Although certain elements of planners' activities—social and fiscal zoning, for example—may have considerable impact on the community, others may not be so effective. One planning activity that is frequently ineffective is metropolitan planning.

### Metropolitan planning

The problem of metropolitan planning, or the lack of it, is an indirect by-product of the success that local governments have enjoyed in play-

[22] *Shelley* v. *Kraemer*, 334 U.S. 24 (1948).

**Table 10.1** *Simple correlations between 24 variables and planning expenditures in 190 American cities over 50,000 population in 1960*

| Variable | $r$ |
| --- | --- |
| Manufacturing ratio | .042 |
| Private-school attendance | —.237 |
| Owner occupancy | —.152 |
| Bureaucratization | .056 |
| Party strength | .147 |
| Electoral turnout | —.137 |
| Percentage Roman Catholic | —.083 |
| Reformism score | —.018 |
| Population size | —.075 |
| Density | —.096 |
| Population change, 1950–1960 | —.155 |
| Percentage black | —.063 |
| Median age | —.165 |
| Ethnic character | .002 |
| Percentage incomes under $3,000 | —.046 |
| Percentage incomes over $10,000 | .120 |
| Median family income | —.086 |
| Median education in years | .094 |
| Percentage college educated | —.003 |
| Mobility | .080 |
| Percentage white-collar | .203 |
| Percentage housing units standard | .036 |
| County Republican vote, 1960 | .109 |
| City noneducational expenditures | —.166 |

SOURCE: Robert L. Lineberry, "Community Structure and Planning Commitment: A Note on the Correlates of Agency Expenditures," *Social Science Quarterly*, *58* (December, 1969), 727, Table 1. More detailed descriptions of the measures can be found in the original article.

ing the "fiscal zoning" and "social zoning" games. When each of the discrete units of a metropolis shapes its own environment, all the other units bear some of the consequences. These consequences are the "externalities" of metropolitan fragmentation we described in Chapter 4 (see pp. 137–139).

Robert Lineberry has argued that cities within the metropolis are locked into a "prisoner's dilemma" in which independent choices preclude optimal growth for the whole metropolitan area.[23] When

[23] Robert L. Lineberry, "Reforming Metropolitan Governance: Requiem or Reality?" *Georgetown Law Journal*, *58* (March–May, 1970), 675–718. The "prisoner's dilemma" represents a situation in which individual players (municipalities) play rational strategies, but the group as a whole (the metropolitan area) receives less than optimal payoffs.

communities successfully play the zoning games, costs and benefits result—costs, they hope, to other communities and benefits to their own. The Advisory Commission on Intergovernmental Relations has argued that "under present zoning law, the affluent suburbs are able to exclude low income families and minimize tax burdens which are then transferred to the overburdened central city."[24] Some New Jersey communities have adopted zoning ordinances that encourage industrial development and tax advantages but discourage workers from living there. Wood has called such decisions "beggar-thy-neighbor" policies.[25] Competitive zoning within metropolitan areas can have uneconomic spillovers, because space that could best support residential or commercial development may be used for industrial development. Viewed from the perspective of a single city, this result may be desirable. Alternatively, viewed from a metropolitan perspective, the impact may be a spiraling series of inefficient land-use decisions. The result of uncoordinated metropolitan planning policies is less than optimal economic and social growth.

It is by no means clear that, left to their own devices, fragmented local governments would develop a metropolitan planning structure. Metropolitan planning agencies were created mainly under the impetus of federal legislation. The federal carrot-and-stick approach began with financial assistance to metropolitan (and other state and local) planning agencies in Section 701 of the Housing Act of 1954. In fiscal 1969 nearly $44 million was provided through the Department of Housing and Urban Development for "701" planning grants, a large portion of which went to metropolitan agencies. The federal "stick" was a series of acts requiring review of local grant and loan requests by metropolitan-level agencies. In the Demonstration Cities and Metropolitan Development Act of 1966, Congress provided that all applications for federal aid in ten functional areas must be reviewed by an area-wide agency, which was, "to the greatest extent practicable," to be composed of or responsible to elected officials of governments in the metropolis. Many of the metropolitan planning agencies have been reconstituted as councils of government (COGs), the planning-agency staffs serving as the staff of the reorganized COGs. (For further discussion of COGs and their limited powers, see pp. 143–144.) Metropolitan planning is now a reality, but most of the key decisions of metropolitan growth are still made in the private sector, and most of the power to regulate decisions in the marketplace remains with local governments in the fragmented metropolis. The extension of federal programs requiring metropolitan planning as a condition for aid has increased

24 Advisory Commission on Intergovernmental Relations, *Metropolitan Fiscal Disparities* (Washington, D.C., Government Printing Office, 1967), p. 44.
25 Wood, *op. cit.*, p. 85.

the formulation of plans, but whether or not it will stimulate the effectiveness of plans in prescribing growth patterns is still uncertain.


## THE HOUSING PROBLEM

There is broad agreement among citizens and public officials that the urban physical environment, though perhaps more hospitable than it once was, is less satisfactory than it might be. We shall be concerned with two related policies in the remainder of this chapter. The first is directed at urban "blight," or "decay," produced by the natural effects of aging, weathering, and deterioration and by the social effects of residential and commercial mobility. The second is the problem of housing and urban population, a policy area complicated by the dilemma of race.


### Urban "blight"

Decentralization of production and population is the fundamental feature of metropolitan America. Millions of urbanites, mostly white and middle-class, have moved to the suburbs. As most young suburbanites have never lived in any other kind of community, it is becoming dated to speak of the "suburban migration." Industries, department stores, and commercial establishments have also found their places in the suburbs. On almost every indicator of economic activity, central cities have experienced a relative decline in comparison with fringe areas, and some central cities have experienced absolute declines as well.[26] The cost of relocation within the central city may be many times greater than a move to the suburbs. The same economic patterns appear to affect both families and firms: The most prosperous of both are the most mobile, with the result that the poor, whether firms or families, are left behind to add to the human and economic problems in the central city. At the very time when the greatest demands are being placed upon city governments, those best able to pay for services have departed for the hinterlands. In the decade 1950–1960, 14,000 jobs and $78 million in taxable assessments disappeared from Boston. The flight of economic resources is thus paralleled by an intensification of service needs in the central city. This is another example of the irony of urban wealth.

Logically, three alternatives are available to deal with the deterioration of American central cities: Accelerate it, ignore it, or impede it. Whatever alternative is preferred, the basic socioeconomic forces—the

[26] Raymond Vernon, *The Changing Economic Function of the Central City* (New York, Committee for Economic Development, 1959).

cost of land, the "transportation revolution," the impact of technology, and the immigration from rural areas—may be beyond the reach of public policy in a democracy. But decisions to accelerate or ignore these forces are not lightly undertaken, for then at least three considerations must be dismissed:

1   Millions of Americans live now in those central cities, and more will arrive because of the low cost of deteriorated housing.
2   Minority groups, particularly blacks and Spanish-speaking Americans, whose fate is a matter of policy concern, are heavily concentrated in central cities.
3   The central city continues to perform important social and economic functions, particularly with respect to the production of culture and the financial and commercial operations of the economic system.

## Housing urban Americans

That poverty and substandard housing are related is a truism, but whether or not this fact means any more than that poor people live in the poorest housing is not clear. Plainly, people are not poor merely because they live in inadequate houses. But still it is possible that the quality of housing itself has something to do with the behavioral, economic, and psychological syndrome we call poverty. One view, that poverty has little to do with housing, is argued cogently by the sociologist John Dean, in a somewhat dated but still excellent critique of the traditional notion of slums and poverty. The simple-minded implication of many housing reformers, he has argued, is

*"Remove the slums and you remove the social ills!" . . . but it would be just as illogical to say that the ills of slum areas are caused not by substandard housing conditions, but by the absence of telephone service, which also correlates with indexes of social disorder.*[27]

Dean has emphasized that a correlation between slum housing and the incidence of social problems must not be interpreted as establishing a causal relation. Alvin Schorr, on the other hand, thinks that such a causal link between poor housing and poverty can be demonstrated. Poor housing may lead, he has argued, to

*. . . a perception of one's self that leads to pessimism and passivity, stress to which the individual cannot adapt, poor health, and a state of dissatisfaction; pleasure in company but not in solitude, cynicism about people and organizations, a high degree of sexual stimulation without legitimate outlet, and*

27 John P. Dean, "The Myths of Housing Reform," *American Sociological Review, 14* (April, 1949), 283.

**Table 10.2**  *Housing conditions, 1950 and 1960*

|  | 1950 | | 1960 | |
|---|---|---|---|---|
|  | *Number (in 1,000s)* | *Per-centage* | *Number (in 1,000s)* | *Per-centage* |
| Total units | 46,137 | 100.0 | 58,468 | 100.0 |
| Dilapidated | 4,503 | 9.8 | 4,002 | 6.8 |
| Lacking hot water or other plumbing facilities | 12,504 | 27.1 | 7,406 | 12.7 |
| Not dilapidated, with all plumbing facilities; "standard" | 29,130 | 63.1 | 47,060 | 80.5 |

SOURCE: U.S. Bureau of the Census, *1960 Census of Housing*, (Washington, D.C., Government Printing Office, 1960), vol. 1, Table 1.

*difficulty in household management and child rearing; and relationships that tend to spread out into the neighborhood rather than deeply into the family.*[28]

According to Schorr, the effects of inadequate housing are no less significant for their obviousness. Inadequate space for sleeping means that less sleeping is done; the lack of privacy for schoolwork means that schoolwork is done in the midst of turmoil or not at all; excessive cold or heat means discomfort; cramped quarters send children into the streets, which means that they escape parental supervision younger than do well-housed children. Dean and Schorr do not agree fully about the precise effects of housing conditions, but both acknowledge that poor housing creates real problems.

There is ample evidence to suggest that the American housing situation has improved significantly since Franklin D. Roosevelt announced that "one-third of a nation [is] . . . ill-housed, ill-clad, ill-nourished" in his 1937 inaugural address. The data in Table 10.2 detail the current housing picture in the United States and clearly suggest that the overwhelming majority of housing units are structurally sound and sanitary. Most of the inadequate housing is found in rural areas, rather than in cities. At least half the substandard housing units in the United States are in rural areas, and fewer than a quarter are in large cities. Still, most middle-class Americans would not consider only such facilities as hot and cold running water and private baths to be very reliable criteria of creature comforts. The higher one's standards for "good" housing, the larger is the number of units that must be described as substandard.

[28] Alvin Schorr, *Slums and Social Insecurity* (London Thomas Nelson and Sons, 1964), pp. 20–21.

Were inadequate housing units scattered about the city randomly, they would probably be of little moment for politics and policy, but substandard housing is not randomly distributed. It tends, rather, to cluster in certain areas. There are five significant consequences of this clustering of substandard housing ("slums").

First, such housing tends to be occupied by the poor and minority groups because of economy and the tendency to associate with peers. People select houses for numerous reasons, but their incomes limit their choices: Their home sites are near their places of work, their information on alternatives is limited, and racial discrimination limits the alternatives themselves. Lower-class groups face common constraints and end up living next to one another. An important social consequence is that *they reinforce one another's behavoir and value patterns.* This reinforcement may, of course, be good or bad, depending upon one's evaluations of the patterns, but it does reduce the exposure of one class to another's beliefs, behavior, and preferences.

Second, because schools in America have historically been tied to neighborhoods for reasons originally related to transportation technology, the poor tend to attend the same schools, which produces a high degree of class and racial segregation. A child's peers in school are thus other poor children, who reinforce the common set of norms and behaviors. Teachers in such schools commonly tend to be the least experienced or the least dedicated of the city's teachers.

Third, because there is so much mutual reinforcement of lower-class value and behavior patterns in slums—and because the concentration reinforces the middle-class stereotype of slum dwellers—upward mobility is more difficult than it would otherwise be.

The fourth and fifth consequences of residential segregation by race and class are political. In cities that use ward elections, the poor are likely to have at least one councilman of their own, unless gerrymandering chops up the slum area. Finally, the fact that the poor are concentrated in specific areas tends to enhance their effectiveness as an organized group. Communication is facilitated, leadership is easier to exercise, and a sense of community can be developed. Residential dispersion of the poor, without other changes in their condition, would condemn the poor to being a permanent minority throughout the city. A concentration of the poor in a few areas at least guarantees them majorities in those areas. These last two consequences of the concentration of substandard housing and of the poor suggest that neighborhood segregation is a mixed blessing. The social and economic disadvantages of neighborhood concentration are thus to some degree offset by the political advantages. Black Power advocates have increasingly come to recognize that, *for political purposes,* the ghetto may be preferable to integration.

**Table 10.3**  *Average values of indexes of residential segregation for regions, 1940, 1950, 1960*

| Region | 1940 | 1950 | 1960 |
|---|---|---|---|
| Northeast | 83.2 | 83.6 | 78.9 |
| North Central | 88.4 | 89.9 | 88.4 |
| West | 82.7 | 82.9 | 76.4 |
| South | 84.9 | 88.5 | 90.7 |
| Total | 85.2 | 87.3 | 86.1 |

SOURCE: Reprinted from Karl E. and Alma F. Taeuber, *Negroes in Cities* (Chicago, Aldine, 1965); copyright © 1965 by Karl E. and Alma F. Taeuber.

## Housing and race

The overwhelming majority of whites, regardless of income, live in white neighborhoods, and the overwhelming majority of blacks live in black neighborhoods—in central cities and suburbs, small cities and large ones, the North and the South. Moreover, black areas are almost universally poor, whereas white areas are usually not poor. In 1960, only 12 percent of whites with incomes above the poverty level were living in poverty areas, but fully two-thirds of blacks with comparable incomes were living in poor neighborhoods. By far the most extensive research on race and residential segregation has been undertaken by Karl and Alma Taeuber.[29] They have developed a "segregation index," which varies from 100 (complete segregation with no whites in black areas and no blacks in white areas) to 0 (random distribution by race). Table 10.3 demonstrates the average segregation scores for 109 American cities in 1940, 1950, and 1960. The national pattern, reflecting only slight regional variations, is compellingly simple: The overwhelming majority of American cities are very highly residentially segregated by race.

What are the causes of this residential segregation? Karl Taeuber has cited Gunnar Myrdal, the distinguished Swedish economist and student of the American race problem, who has offered three hypotheses to explain housing segregation. First, it may result from deliberate preference for living among members of one's own race. Second, it may result from poverty. Because the income levels of whites and blacks differ markedly, blacks may simply be unable to afford homes

[29] Karl E. and Alma F. Taeuber, *Negroes in Cities* (Chicago, Aldine, 1965); and Karl E. Taeuber, "Residential Segregation," *Scientific American, 213* (August, 1965), 12–19.

anywhere but in the poorest neighborhoods. Housing segregation would thus be a matter of class, rather than of race. Third, it may be the result of discrimination.

There is no doubt some merit in each of these explanations. Surely deliberate choice is involved in residential location, but Myrdal and the Taeubers all have noted that "choice" is not altogether "free" when made in a society in which racial discrimination and prejudice are widespread. The more probable explanations for segregated housing patterns are thus the income and discrimination theories.

Some data on the relative validity of these two theories are contained in Figure 10.1. Statistically, the figure demonstrates the degree of "expected segregation" there would be if the amount paid for housing were the only factor in housing choice and compares this figure with the actual amount of segregation for each city. It is apparent from the graph that the economic factor explains only a small fraction of existing segregation. Karl Taeuber has concluded that

*Negroes are excluded from many residential areas in which their economic status could allow them to live. . . . Discrimination is the principal cause of Negro residential segregation, and there is no basis for anticipating major changes in the segregated character of American cities until patterns of housing discrimination can be altered.*[30]


## PUBLIC HOUSING AND URBAN RENEWAL

### Housing and public policy

The preceding discussion of the physical environments of American cities offers a backdrop for a description of public policies to restructure the cities. In recent years, the principal policy responses have taken the form of urban renewal and public housing.

There are at least four possible government responses to the housing problem. First, government can do nothing at all. It can assume that the private sector will handle the problem,[31] that its own efforts would be ineffective, or that the spillover costs would outweigh the benefits. Second, government can adopt an indirect strategy of general assistance to the poor but not for housing per se. The underlying

[30] Taeuber, "Residential Segregation," p. 19.

[31] Martin Anderson has argued that "there is not a physical shortage of decent housing units. The real problem is that there is a certain group of people who either cannot or will not spend enough money to rent or buy this housing." Martin Anderson, *The Federal Bulldozer* (Cambridge, Mass., M.I.T. Press, 1964), p. 200.

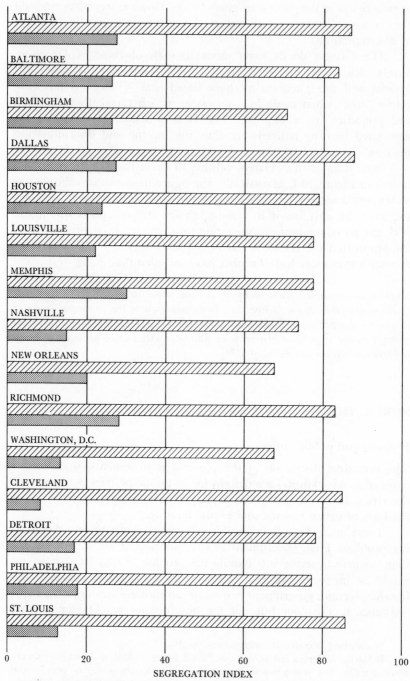

SEGREGATION INDEX

SOURCE: Reprinted by permission from Karl E. Taeuber, "Residential Segregation," *Scientific American, 213* (August, 1965), 18.

**Figure** 10.1 *(opposite) Residential segregation indexes for fifteen cities. Actual and expected segregation indexes are shown for these cities on the basis of 1960 census-tract data. The comparison relates to the argument that the poverty of Negroes is the sole cause of residential segregation. The "expected" indexes* (lower bars) *show how much racial segregation there would be if the amount paid for housing were the only cause of segregation. Actual segregation indexes* (top bars) *are much higher, indicating that factors other than poverty are involved in the determination of Negro housing patterns.*

premise of this strategy is that poor housing is merely symptomatic of deeper and more pervasive poverty, which should be attacked through welfare payments or a form of guaranteed annual income. Third, the government can, in Lawrence Friedman's words, "attempt to get rid of bad housing by forbidding it."[32] This approach includes enforcing housing codes for new construction and maintenance codes to which landlords must conform. Fourth, the government can try to provide good housing. In practice, of course, these four strategies are not mutually exclusive, and federal and city governments actually use combinations of them.

The problem of inadequate housing did not begin with the Depression of the 1930s, but the first significant housing legislation was the National Housing Act of 1934, which recognized housing as a subject of national concern and created the still-thriving Federal Housing Administration. The FHA's principal activity through the years has been to guarantee home mortgages. In the third of a century of its existence, it has insured billions of dollars of single-family housing. The FHA, however, has consistently benefited families with medium incomes, rather than the poor.

Another Depression agency, the Public Works Administration, undertook some slum clearance during the 1930s and constructed a few units of public housing, but it was the Housing Act of 1937 that laid the real basis for public housing, slum clearance, and later urban renewal. That act created the U.S. Housing Agency, funded it with a half-billion dollars, and authorized it to lend money to local public-housing authorities to clear slum land and provide public housing. Once minimum federal standards had been met and the loan provided, a local public agency (LPA) was responsible for land acquisition, clearance, planning, construction, and operation.

The Housing Act of 1937 was the first in a series of laws tying public housing to slum clearance, but with the Housing Act of 1949, and especially its 1954 amendments, public housing began to take a back seat to "urban renewal." Title I of the 1949 act authorized the

32 Lawrence M. Friedman, *Government and Slum Housing* (Skokie, Ill., Rand McNally, 1968), pp. 22–23.

purchase of slum land by local public authorities. The land would then be sold to private developers, who in turn were required to use the land for "predominantly residential" construction. Local housing or redevelopment authorities could use the power of eminent domain to acquire land and sell it to private development corporations.[33] The difference between the high price paid for the land and the lower price received for it would be made up largely by federal grants. The federal government would absorb two-thirds (in certain cases, three-fourths) of the "net project cost," that is, the difference between purchase and sale prices. The local government was required to make up the other one-third (or one-fourth) in cash, kind, or services. Not surprisingly, some groups, real-estate interests, for example, which had vocally opposed public-housing legislation gave wholehearted support to Title I.

The 1949 act applied the concept of urban redevelopment to public housing. The public-housing provisions of the act were not popular with either Congress or business interests, but federal sub-sidizing of land transfers was attractive to city officials and commercial interests. Cities could shore up sagging tax bases with revenues from more valuable property, and developers could enjoy federal subsidies instead of small profits and possible losses. Urban renewal thus became a popular vehicle for redressing the urban financial imbalance, while public housing continued to eke out narrow victories or heavy losses. New York City alone has built 145,000 public housing units, one-fourth of the national total but less than five percent of the total housing in the city. It has been estimated that 2 million people lived in public housing in 1968 but that another 8.5 million families were eligible under current requirements.[34]

Some of the sluggish growth of public housing has resulted from the rude facts of political power. Such housing has its proponents, but it also has a formidable array of opponents, including the National Association of Real Estate Boards, the construction industry, banks, and savings-and-loan institutions.[35] Public housing has also challenged some fundamental precepts of American ideology, including laissez-

[33] Eminent domain is the power of government to take possession of property for public purposes, paying just compensation to the owner. There was little doubt of the constitutionality of slum clearance in its earlier form, in which property was taken and *retained* by local housing authorities. The constitutionality of the 1949 Title I provisions, which permitted local authorities to use eminent domain to obtain land and then *sell it to private developers* was a more serious question. The Supreme Court, however, upheld Title I in *Berman* v. *Parker*, 348 U.S. 26 (1954).

[34] Ira S. Lowry, "Housing," in Anthony H. Pascal, ed., *Cities in Trouble: An Agenda for Urban Research* (Santa Monica, Calif., RAND, 1968), p. 6.

[35] For an analysis of group politics and public housing, see Leonard Freedman, *Public Housing* (New York, Holt, Rinehart & Winston, 1969), chap. 2.

faire and faith in private ownership. To conservatives, the program smacks of socialism because it rewards those who are least "deserving." One congressman, in debate on New Deal housing legislation, declared that "the poor are living in shacks and hovels because God made them unable to earn more."[36] Recently public housing has suffered a further challenge, which Friedman has called the *"disillusionment* of the experts." "The cause of public housing," he has written, "has been psychologically abandoned by many of its former supporters. In the past ten years, assessment of public housing has been more and more negative."[37] Catherine Bauer has claimed that the program has reached a "dreary deadlock," that it is strong enough to survive in the incremental budgeting process but too weak to counter emasculation by its critics.

As with other urban problems, public housing has been complicated by the dilemma of race. Housing projects can be located either in the heart of the ghetto, thus promoting segregation, or in mixed neighborhoods, thus facilitating integration. The former is objectionable to civil-rights leaders, and the latter upsets whites because of what they regard as encroachments upon their life styles or property values. Even sympathetic councilmen are reluctant to locate "black" housing projects in their wards.[38] In Chicago and perhaps in other cities councilmen seek to punish their enemies by voting to locate housing projects in their constituencies.[39]

Much of the disillusionment among the experts results from the sterility of the projects themselves. Cost of land in the central city makes "high-rises" imperative, and housing projects of twenty stories are not uncommon in the larger cities. The interiors of the buildings are often drab; social interaction is minimal; crime in hallways and elevators is high; racial conflict is sometimes intense; the stigma of "charity" is pervasive; and parental supervision is simply impossible from ten stories up. There is little encouragement for either community or individuality. Many of the residents have been relocated from neighborhoods bulldozed for highways or urban renewal. They exhibit sustained grief and frustration.[40]

Public housing suffers the further disability of aiding only a

[36] Quoted in Jewell Bellush and Murray Hausknecht, "Urban Renewal: A Historical Overview," in Bellush and Hausknecht, eds., *Urban Renewal: People, Politics and Planning* (Garden City, N.Y., Doubleday Anchor, 1967), p. 9.

[37] Friedman, *op. cit.,* p. 141.

[38] Although only a minority of the poor are black, a majority of public-housing residents are black. See Freedman, *op. cit.,* pp. 140–144.

[39] Martin Meyerson and Edward C. Banfield, *Politics, Planning, and the Public Interest* (New York, Free press, 1955), p. 121.

[40] Marc Fried, "Grieving for a Lost Home: Psychological Costs of Relocation," in Leonard J. Duhl, ed., *The Urban Condition* (New York, Basic Books, 1965), p. 151.

limited segment of the poor. It aids neither the poorest nor those just below the poverty line. Projects must be financially self-sustaining. A local agency must cover operating costs from rents, and it cannot, therefore, accommodate many of those who can afford only token payments. At the other extreme, there are income limits upon eligibility. A family that earns more may be evicted to make room for the more "deserving." The policy also operates to discourage people from seeking better jobs because the price of a wage increase may be the need to seek housing in the private market, where rents are often much higher. Moreover,

[the departure of those] who did increase their incomes and who went out into the private housing market . . . represented a serious loss to the quality of life in the projects, for they tended to be the more energetic, ambitious, and "responsible" tenants. . . . Those left behind were, to a large extent, families who would never be successful by the usual tests of achievement in America.[41]

No one is better aware of the dilemmas and spillover effects of housing policy than are housing administrators. But they are locked into dilemmas by the compelling realities of financial necessity, political considerations, and the ingrained American suspicion of "socialism."

## Urban renewal

THE BEGINNINGS   Urban renewal, as we have seen, was originally tied to public housing in the 1949 and 1954 housing acts. The 1949 legislation established the principle of federal subsidies for land sold to private developers through the slum-clearance program. Between 1934 and 1954, slum clearance in its various forms eliminated an estimated 400,000 substandard housing units, but they constituted only 7 percent of the 5.6 million substandard units counted in the 1950 Census. There was no net increase in the availability of low-cost housing; in fact, more slum dwellings were demolished than public-housing units were constructed. Moreover, there was an inevitable lag between demolition and construction, and, as long as the program continued to expand, more units were taken out of the market than were replaced. The 1954 Housing Act was partly designed to rectify these flaws, by providing what some called "an alternative to the bulldozer." The 1954 provisions, which added the term "urban renewal" to our vocabulary, emphasized rehabilitation rather than demolition and wholesale reconstruction of an area. Structures that are deteriorating but salvageable can be "renewed" rather than demolished. The act also broke earlier precedents

41 Freedman, op. cit., p. 108.

that had insisted upon the "predominantly residential" requirement for all new construction. It permitted 10 percent of federal grants to be used for nonresidential construction, a figure that was increased to 20 percent in 1959 and to 30 percent in 1961. Urban renewal became, through a series of incremental changes, more and more remote from the notion of improved housing. Increasingly it became a program to revitalize the private marketplace and the city treasury. To city officials faced with crushing demands for services and limited resources, urban renewal was a blessing in disguise. The disguise was public housing.

URBAN RENEWAL IN OPERATION    Like the social-security system and the interstate-highway program, urban renewal is an example of cooperative federalism. The key ingredients are congressional definition of standards and sharing of costs and administrative responsibilities by federal and local agencies. The program is administered through the Department of Housing and Urban Development, while operation at the local level is the responsibility of local public authorities.

The national administration of the housing and urban-renewal programs has undergone a series of reorganizations, and today programs are headed by the Assistant Secretary of Housing and Urban Development for Renewal and Housing Assistance. Under him are two deputy assistant secretaries, one running the Housing Assistance Administration and the other the Renewal Assistance Administration. These agencies are responsible for carrying out the intent of the housing acts by laying down standards for local programs, approving or rejecting local applications, and disbursing grants and loans. Participation by local governments in both housing and urban renewal must be authorized by state enabling legislation, which specifies the form and structure of the "local public authority."

By December 31, 1968, the Renewal Assistance Administration had approved 2,525 urban-renewal projects in 1,022 communities. A total of $7.3 billion had been authorized for these projects, although only $2.7 billion worth of projects had actually been completed.[42] The financial picture, or "budget," of a fairly typical urban-renewal project is given in Table 10.4. The figures in this table do not represent average costs but are used rather for simplicity of calculation and presentation. Assuming that total or "gross" cost of the project is $10 million and that proceeds from the sale of land are $4 million, there is a deficit, or "net project cost," of $6 million. Two-thirds (or three-fourths) of this sum is supplied by federal grants and one-third (or one-fourth) by local contributions in cash, kind, or services.

[42] These data are from U.S. Department of Housing and Urban Development, *Urban Renewal Directory* (Washington, D.C., Government Printing Office, 1968).

**Table 10.4**   *A sample urban-renewal project: the financial structure*

| | |
|---|---:|
| Gross project cost | |
|    Land acquisition | $ 8 million |
|    Demolition, relocation | 1 million |
|    Provision of public facilities by city | 1 million |
|     Total | $10 million |
| Proceeds from sale of land | $ 4 million |
| Net project cost: gross cost less proceeds from land | $ 6 million |
| Grants | |
|    Federal grant for ⅔ (sometimes ¾) net project cost | $ 4 million |
|    Local grant of cash, kind, or services | 2 million |
|     Total | $ 6 million |

VARIATION IN HOUSING AND URBAN-RENEWAL EXPENDITURES   The urban-renewal and public-housing programs have received varying support from American cities. Several scholars have examined the correlates of community commitment to the two programs.[43] Among the major variables associated with per capita support for the two programs are the following:

1    Communities with high incidences of poverty spend more heavily upon both programs.
2    The more pluralistic and decentralized the decision-making structure, the higher is the level of spending.[44]
3    Larger and older cities spend more money on both programs.
4    Governmental reformism is not strongly related to urban-renewal and housing commitments, but the direction of the relationship is negative; that is, cities with manager governments, nonpartisan elections, and elections at large have smaller urban-renewal and housing programs.
5    Although the evidence is mixed, some studies have concluded that heavily ethnic or Roman Catholic cities have higher per capita urban-renewal expenditures.

[43] George S. Duggar, "The Relation of Local Government Structure to Urban Renewal," *Law and Contemporary Problems, 26* (1961), 49–69; Amos H. Hawley, "Community Power and Urban Renewal Success," *American Journal of Sociology, 68* (January, 1963), 422–431; Terry N. Clark, "Community Structure, Decision-Making, Budget Expenditures, and Urban Renewal in 51 American Communities," *American Sociological Review, 33* (August, 1968), 576–593; and Michael Aiken and Robert R. Alford, "Community Structure and Innovation: The Case of Urban Renewal," *American Sociological Review, 35,* (August, 1970), 650–664.

[44] Hawley, *op. cit.,* found that more centralized power structures had higher urban-renewal activity, but later evidence from both Clark, *op. cit.,* and Aiken and Alford, *op. cit.,* suggests that decentralization is associated with higher urban-renewal expenditures.

None of these correlations or even their combined effect is so strongly associated with variations in urban-renewal and public-housing expenditures that spending levels can safely be predicted from macro characteristics alone. There are a number of micro characteristics in each community that explain its commitment to both programs. The dedication of a mayor, the effectiveness of an urban-renewal entrepreneur, the political clout of a city's congressman, and other unique factors cannot be discounted. To gain additional perspective on these features, we shall now move from a macro to a micro level of analysis, examining urban-renewal policy in two cities, Newark and New York.

## Case study: the NHA

Two communities whose commitments to urban renewal are rarely exceeded are Newark, New Jersey, and New York City. New York City alone has accounted for almost one-third of all new construction under urban renewal.

Newark is an extreme example of the physical deterioration of large American cities, the suburbanization of the middle classes, and the residual human and economic problems. Newark's class and racial structure was "inverted" during the 1960s, as a result of long-term population shifts. From 1960 to 1967, the city lost a total of 70,000 white residents, mostly to nearby suburbs. The composition of the population changed from 65 percent white to 52 percent black and 10 percent Cuban and Puerto Rican.

The emigration of commerce and industry and massive social problems were a constant drain on the city's treasury. Property taxes soared to such staggering heights—$661.70 on a $10,000 house in 1967—that those who were able moved to the suburbs. One-third of the land within the city was occupied by the Newark airport and thus unavailable for taxation. In Harold Kaplan's view,

*the single most significant characteristic of Newark's politics in the last quarter-century has been the alienation of the city's business and professional groups. Throughout the 1940's the city's corporation executives, lawyers, realtors, and educators fled Newark for suburban residence.*[45]

The economic, social, and political milieu of Newark made it a tinderbox, and on June 20, 1967, a race riot erupted during which twenty-three people were killed. One of the major background issues in that disorder, incidentally, was the urban-renewal project in the Central

[45] Harold Kaplan, *Urban Renewal Politics* (New York, Columbia University Press, 1963), p. 61. Our case study of the Newark Housing Authority is based upon Kaplan's excellent treatment of the Newark experience.

Ward, which involved a proposal to devote 150 acres of ghetto land to a state medical college.

Newark's renewal program was one of the first to be authorized and funded.[46] Its first project was announced less than eighteen months after the passage of the Housing Act of 1949. Much of the credit for the brisk start belongs to Louis Danzig, the executive director of the Newark Housing Authority. The NHA had been established in 1938 to provide low-rent public housing under the provisions of the Housing Act of 1937. Danzig, who had taken over direction of the NHA in 1948, was as far removed from the image of the pencil-chewing, paper-pushing bureaucrat as could be imagined. Like Edward Logue of New Haven and Boston and Robert Moses of New York, Danzig was an urban-renewal entrepreneur.[47] Jewell Bellush and Murray Hausknecht have described the three interlocking elements of the entrepreneurial role, comparing the public entrepreneur to the early capitalist. First, the entrepreneur supplies money—not his own, of course; he is a master of applying for grants. Second, he is a manager and a technocrat, whose efficiency is measured quantitatively—in number of acres cleared, value of construction completed, and number of families relocated. Third, the modern entrepreneur is a major link between the public and private sectors. The urban-renewal program provides the opportunity for the public sector to alter the physical character of the private sector, and the renewal entrepreneur's goal is maximum impact. Danzig was such an entrepreneur.

The effectiveness of Danzig's entrepreneurial skills was maximized by the decentralized and permissive character of Newark politics. In urban-renewal and housing decisions, the NHA was very nearly autonomous. Its unchallenged power was apparent in both its relations with the successive mayors and councils of the city and its dealings with grassroots groups. At the outset, Danzig secured a commitment of noninterference in his program from city hall. The NHA never informed the council or the mayor of its plans until a public announcement was being prepared, and the council and mayor never failed to assent. They trusted Danzig as an efficient administrator to have already considered all possible problems. One way in which he retained the support of successive council majorities was to permit councilmen some intervention in selection of tenants for public housing. Such matters were unimportant to the "bricks and mortar" of the project, but they were of political interest to councilmen.

46 *Ibid.*, pp. 10–12.

47 Jewell Bellush and Murray Hausknecht, "Entrepreneurs and Urban Renewal: The New Men of Power," *Journal of the American Institute of Planners, 32* (September, 1966), 289–297.

Nor did the NHA ever encounter much resistance from neighborhood groups in areas to be renewed. Neighborhood committees of incensed owners or renters in areas scheduled for the bulldozers and the cranes sometimes organized but never obtained many concessions from NHA. Other actors did not lack the power to thwart the NHA—councilmen and mayors could have balked at appropriating funds, neighborhood groups could have protested seriously, as did New York's Greenwich Villagers, the NHA directors could have examined instead of merely accepting Danzig's proposals. But none of these potential obstacles developed.

The urban-renewal system in Newark was quite unlike the model of the monolithic power structure that we described in Chapter 5. No covert, behind-the-scenes group made Newark's urban-renewal policy. But, on the other hand, renewal decision-making did not reflect the pluralist model either. In Kaplan's words, "the model of alert interests, strongly committed to their goals and prepared to press these goals at every occasion, does not apply to Newark renewal."[48] This permitted the NHA to exercise considerable influence over renewal policies.

### Case study: the West Villagers

It is just a short distance across the Hudson River from Newark to Greenwich Village in New York City. Over the years the Village has developed a reputation as a habitat for Bohemians, beatniks, and itinerant artists and intellectuals, but actually it is an enormously heterogeneous neighborhood, a microcosm of New York City. Many middle-class professionals live in the Village, as do many Italians, Puerto Ricans, and other recent immigrants. Although opinions differ on whether the neighborhood is "blighted" or simply "old," the 1960 Census identified 42 percent of the housing units in the area as deteriorating or dilapidated.

In November, 1960, sensing both a need for and neighborhood sentiment favoring additional housing in the Village, the city's Housing and Redevelopment Board selected a site in the West Village to study as a renewal and middle-income housing area.[49] In February, 1961, the board announced its plan and submitted a request for planning funds to the New York City Board of Estimate, the budgeting unit of the New York City Council. The Housing and Redevelopment

---

[48] Kaplan, op. cit., p. 177.

[49] James Clarence Davies III, Neighborhood Groups and Urban Renewal (New York, Columbia University Press, 1966). Our discussion of the Villagers and their battle is based upon Davies' Chapter 4.

Board took pains to indicate that it was not proposing a "bulldozer approach" to urban renewal and favored instead a program emphasizing preservation and rehabilitation. The city council took the proposal under advisement.

Then Villager Jane Jacobs, mother of three and assistant editor of *Architectural Forum,* entered the scene. Mrs. Jacobs is also the author of *The Death and Life of Great American Cities,*[50] a scathing critique of contemporary planners and urban renewers and, particularly, their knack of destroying socially integrated neighborhoods and building homogenized, ultramodern, antiseptic and "high-rise" neighborhoods. In her view, Greenwich Village was the quintessence of the desirable neighborhood and did not need urban renewal. The city had assumed that neighborhood sentiment in the Village favored new housing, but it had not taken into account Mrs. Jacobs and her Committee to Save the West Village (CSWV), a group of residents and sympathizers devoted to killing the entire renewal project. The committee, a masterpiece of political organization, had a solid base of support not only among the upper-middle-class professionals in the Village but among the Italian, Irish, and Puerto Rican minorities as well.

Complicating the conflict over the Village proposal was a broader political conflict related to the New York City elections of 1961. The incumbent mayor, Robert F. Wagner, was renouncing his long allegiance to Tammany Hall, the Democratic organization, and was trying to build support among the Reform Democrats. The Mayor and his loyal Borough President of Manhattan, Edward Dudley, tended to favor renewal projects in principle, but they hesitated to antagonize constituents in an election year. Pressuring the Mayor thus became an important tactic in the Villagers' campaign to avert renewal. Finally, on April 27, 1961, the Board of Estimate met and faced a hostile assortment of residents from the CSWV. Following a bitter exchange between Deputy Mayor Paul R. Screvane and the Villagers, the Board of Estimate decided to avoid conflict by sending the proposal back to the City Planning Commission for further study. On June 7, in a meeting that lasted from 4:00 P.M. to 4:00 A.M., the planning board heard testimony from the Villagers, who had a solidly crafted political strategy: Three lawyers discussed the illegality of the city's moves, an acoustical engineer presented data to demonstrate that the Village was quieter than the rest of the city, a resident provided statistics from the city's air-pollution department to show that the air was cleaner in the Village, and a Puerto Rican resident argued that the area was

---

[50] Jane Jacobs, *The Death and Life of Great American Cities* (New York, Random House, 1961).

happily integrated. In another demonstration of conflict avoidance, the City Planning Commission delayed its decision on the project. This delay gave Mrs. Jacobs and her committee even more time to drum up support through press releases, meetings, and letters to politicians.

On October 18, the Planning Commission met and declared the West Village area "blighted," an official designation required before planning for a renewal project could proceed. Some Villagers responded with a sit-in at the commission's meeting room and were ejected by the police. Finally, a week later, the Housing and Redevelopment Board announced that it was scrapping the West Village project. The Villagers remained adamant, however, in their efforts to have the "blighted" label removed from their area. Upon his reelection, Mayor Wagner prevailed upon the Planning Commission to remove the "blighted" designation from the West Village. The Villagers had routed the redevelopers.

One difference between the unusually successful Newark program and the defeat of the Housing and Redevelopment Board over the West Village project was the characteristics of the neighborhoods in question. Both cases suggest that the most significant opposition to urban-renewal programs comes not from the hard-core slums but from those neighborhoods composed of relatively stable populations with middle-class components.[51] The Village is an extreme example of the kind of neighborhood where citizen protest is both most intense and most likely to be successful. Most of the areas chosen for renewal in Newark, on the other hand, were lower-class neighborhoods, where social organizations that might provide the basis for opposition to renewal were minimal. Urban-renewal legislation requires that a "workable program" for renewal include citizen participation. Yet Wilson has noted that this requirement usually means that "middle-class persons who are beneficiaries of rehabilitation will be planned with; lower-class persons who are disadvantaged by rehabilitation are likely to be planned *without*."[52]

### The impact of urban renewal

We tread on difficult terrain when we attempt to assess the impact of urban-renewal programs. Many of their most important dimensions are not susceptible to measurement. Although several excellent studies have attempted to apply cost-benefit analysis to urban renewal, many

---

[51] Kaplan, *op. cit.*, p. 136; and Davies, *op. cit.*, p. 153.

[52] James Q. Wilson, "Planning and Politics: Citizen Participation in Urban Renewal," in James Q. Wilson, ed., *Urban Renewal* (Cambridge, M.I.T. Press, 1966), p. 418.

variables have had to be either measured indirectly or ignored altogether.[53] The costs and benefits of a project, from the perspective of the municipal budget, are relatively easy to measure, but the costs and benefits to those relocated cannot be measured without making some capricious assumptions.

## The economic and fiscal impact

RENEWAL AND TAX BASES   The most universally accepted claim for urban renewal, and probably the most valid one, is that it has expanded the tax base and improved the economic vitality of the city. William L. Slayton, for many years the director of the Urban Renewal Administration, presented to Congress the "before" and "after" tax effects of renewal.[54] For 185 projects on which land acquisition had been completed, the estimated increase in property values was from $168 million to $694 million, or 312 percent; from this increase the cities could reap generous tax revenues. The twenty-seven renewal projects in Chicago increased relevant land values from approximately $2.3 million to an estimated $4.8 million. Norfolk's downtown renewal project was estimated to have raised land values from $165,000 to $375,000. In economic terms, each of these projects also had a potential "multiplier effect," stimulating more jobs and production in service industries. Given evidence of this sort, it is small wonder that some city officials have considered renewal a godsend. Nevertheless, Martin Anderson has cautioned that such lavish assessments of the economic productivity of renewal projects should be discounted somewhat.[55] He has noted that (1) some of the new construction would have been undertaken in any case; (2) cities lose tax revenues between the times when structures are demolished and new construction is completed—often a period of five to ten years; and (3), even without renewal projects, land would increase somewhat in value over the years. Anderson investigated the tax gains from Boston's West End project and concluded that it would not begin to "break even" and make up the revenues lost after demolition until 1980 or later, even though the city had taken title to the land as early as 1958. Although Anderson's case may be overstated,[56] it is

---

[53] Stanley Rothenberg, *Economic Evaluation of Urban Renewal* (Washington, D.C., Brookings Institution, 1967).

[54] Wilson, ed., *op. cit.*, pp. 223, 516.

[55] Anderson, *op. cit.*, chap. 10.

[56] See the critique of his book in Robert Groberg, "Urban Renewal Realistically Reappraised," *Law and Contemporary Problems*, 30 (Winter, 1965), 212–229. Groberg has noted that bankers, never noted as big risk takers, have often purchased bonds whose interest is to be paid out of increased revenues derived from urban-renewal programs.

a useful corrective to unqualified enthusiasm over renewal's contribution to city tax coffers. On balance, and despite Anderson's reservations, most of the evidence from specific cities indicates that both direct and multiplier effects enhance municipal revenues and stimulate economic growth.

PROFIT MOTIVES    The success of renewal in raising municipal tax receipts has led to the somewhat paradoxical pattern of a public project that must turn a "profit" in order to be "successful." The necessity for profit from urban renewal is registered in two ways. In the private sector each project must be profitable enough to attract private developers to whom land can be sold. In the public sector, the city government seeks "profit" for its own treasury from increased tax receipts. The former requirement is obvious enough. The first renewal project undertaken by the NHA in the North Ward was stalled for several years while the agency tried to find a private redeveloper to purchase the site. The NHA soon remodeled its redevelopment schemes on the principle "Find a redeveloper first, and then see what interests him."[57] The responsibility for site selection, planning, and decisions about land reuse is thus defined in terms of profit for the redeveloper, as well as of professional criteria.

Renewal must also be attractive to city government. Its net effect should be to produce, rather than to consume, tax revenues. What kinds of projects are likely to be profitable to both developers and city governments?

A negative answer is easiest. The least profitable use of cleared land is for public housing, simply because the latter yields neither city taxes nor private profit. Perhaps the next least profitable use is low-cost private housing, for it produces relatively little in taxes and attracts people with low incomes, who have minimum "multiplier effects" upon the economy. The most productive residential use, of course, is for middle- or high-income housing. Equally productive— sometimes more productive, depending upon the kind of business attracted—is commercial or industrial use. In some respects, the net effect of urban renewal is thus to *redistribute land to higher- and higher-cost enterprises.* Newark is again a case in point. As one Newark redevelopment official said, NHA's goal was "middle income housing on cleared slum sites."[58] Because of the profit incentive in urban renewal, the initial choice of land for clearance is important. The key questions become whether or not the private redeveloper can make a profit from middle-income housing (or other justifiable use under the law) and

57 Kaplan, *op. cit.,* p. 24.
58 *Ibid.,* p. 15.

**Table 10.5**  *Land use and urban renewal: previous use and proposed new use of project land*

| | Previous use | |
|---|---|---|
| | Blighted residential (N=769) | Other[a] (N=364) |
| Proposed new use | | |
| Exclusively residential | 13% (101) | 7% (24) |
| Residential and nonresidential | 61 (470) | 48 (171) |
| Exclusively nonresidential | 26 (198) | 44 (169) |
| | 100% (769) | 100% (364) |

[a] Includes "other blighted areas," mainly open land, disaster areas, and university or college land.

SOURCE: Computed from Department of Housing and Urban Development, *Urban Renewal Project Characteristics*, December 31, 1965, Table 4.

whether or not the city can improve its fiscal situation. The local renewal authorities and prospective redevelopers thus "tend to pick the best possible area that could still be justified as a slum to meet the requirements of the Title I law."[59] In Newark, at least, there seemed to be "an inverse correlation between the degree of blight in the area and its acceptability to [federal renewal officials] and the redevelopers."[60] The upshot of the public and private "profit" requirements is that the very worst slums rarely are renewed.

The 1949 renewal law requires that renewal land be used for "predominantly residential" purposes. The term "predominantly" was usually interpreted to mean that "over half" of new land use would be residential. In a succession of amendments, however, the requirement that all federal funds must be expended on residential reuse has been progressively relaxed. A 1961 amendment permitted up to 30 percent of funds to be devoted to purposes other than residential redevelopment. Table 10.5 provides data, by project, on the differences between former use and proposed new use of renewal land. These data suggest that the renewal program also redistributes land from residential to nonresidential use.[61] Of the 769 projects in which former land use was described as "blighted residential," only 13 percent were exclusively residential, and twice as many were exclusively nonresi-

59 Davies, *op. cit.*, p. 15.
60 Kaplan, *op. cit.*, p. 16.
61 It should be noted, however, that these data are related characteristics of *projects*. They do not offer information on the relative numbers of units available before and after renewal. In most projects, however, the numbers of housing units available to the poor are lower than before renewal.

dential. The renewal program has therefore meant a major change in land-use patterns in American cities.

The economic effects of urban renewal are not limited to land use and financial gains to real-estate interests and municipal governments. Charles Abrams has described "some blessings of urban renewal":

1  increased capacity of cities to attract and maintain industries and commercial establishments;
2  ability of universities, hospitals, and other public institutions to expand facilities;
3  impetus to cultural "improvements" like New York City's Lincoln Center;
4  expanded middle-income housing;
5  revitalization of downtown and central-city areas;
6  greater aesthetic appeal.[62]

THE SPILLOVER EFFECTS  We have emphasized that all public policies have *spillover effects,* or *latent impacts,* the unintended by-products of the manifest (or intended) impacts of the policies. Perhaps the spillover effects of no other public policy have been so much investigated as have those of urban renewal; perhaps these impacts have been decried by critics more loudly than have those of any other policy. Many, though not all, of the spillover effects of urban renewal are related to relocation and displacement of people.

Since the passage of the New Deal public-housing acts and the urban-renewal provisions of the 1949 and 1954 acts, hundreds of thousands of Americans have received letters similar to the following:

*The building in which you now live is located in an area which has been taken by the Boston Redevelopment Authority according to law as part of the Government Center Project. The buildings will be demolished after the families have been relocated and the land will be sold to developers for public and commercial uses, according to the Land Assembly and Redevelopment Plan presently being prepared.[63]*

By March, 1963, it was estimated that 153,000 families and a number of unattached individuals had received such notices.[64] A congressional study estimated that, between 1964 and 1972, no fewer than 825,000 families and 136,000 businesses would be required to vacate their present structures because of urban-renewal and federal

[62] Charles Abrams, *The City Is the Frontier* (New York, Harper & Row, 1965), chap. 9.

[63] Anderson, *op. cit.,* p. 1. The quotation is from a letter sent on October 25, 1961, to residents of a Boston area slated for renewal.

[64] *Ibid.,* p. 54.

highway programs.[65] If we estimate that each of these families has three people (possibly an underestimation), then in eight years about 2.5 million people, equivalent to the population of Los Angeles, would be displaced. Some people have moved into areas slated for later clearance, thus becoming "two-time losers."

Needless to say, the vast majority of families and individuals who have to relocate are the poor and the nearly poor. More than 60 percent of the displaced are nonwhite, leading to charges that the urban-renewal program is really "Negro removal." Many families and unrelated individuals in renewal areas are elderly, both white and black.

The Renewal Assistance Administration has estimated that 54 percent of the families displaced are eligible for public housing, in which they are given priority. According to the RAA, however, only 20 percent of the dislocated families actually move into public housing. There are four principal reasons:

1    Public housing is simply unavailable for many who would take it. The urban-renewal program, as we have explained, has been more dedicated to construction of middle-income units than public housing. Moreover, as long as the urban-renewal program continues to expand, more housing units are being taken out of the market than are being made available for families.

2    For many families, public housing has a social stigma attached to it.

3    Many uprooted families have incomes *too low* for public housing. As housing authorities must meet fixed costs (paying off bonds, operation, maintenance, salaries), they can accept only a certain proportion of very low-income tenants, whose payments on the sliding scale of rents will be too low to cover the costs of their own housing.

4    Finally, many people find the sterile, tightly regulated, spartan accommodations of the high-rise public-housing project distinctly distasteful.

Urban-renewal legislation requires authorities to establish that adequate housing is available for all people to be displaced by renewal projects. They are also required to assist in relocation and to provide relocation payments, but the average relocation payment per family is less than $100, principally for moving expenses. Most critics and many supporters of urban renewal consider the relocation problem its most serious defect. The critics doubt that local authorities can in practice guarantee suitable accommodations at reasonable costs to the displaced. They argue, reasonably enough, that, if suitable housing were available at rents that the relocated could afford, they would be living there already, instead of in slums. Urban-renewal officials claim that more than

65 Cited in Advisory Commission on Intergovernmental Relations, *Metropolitan America: Challenge to Federalism* (Washington, D.C., Government Printing Office, 1966), p. 57.

90 percent of relocated families have moved to standard housing, but most private studies dispute such claims.[66] Anderson concluded that

*privately sponsored studies generally indicate that the people displaced by urban renewal tend to move into housing of approximately the same quality as the housing they moved from, and, in addition, they pay higher monthly rentals.*[67]

Few are able to return to the neighborhoods that they have left, as the median monthly rentals (and, of course, the quality of housing) have skyrocketed. The national median monthly rental of housing units erected on renewed land in 1962 was $192.[68] Such sums were neither within the reach nor even the imagination of the former residents, 80 percent of whom had annual incomes below $6,000. To some degree, then, urban renewal merely reshuffles slums, rather than eliminating them.

Small businessmen are especially vulnerable to relocation. Most businesses in renewal areas are small, employing only handfuls of people and depending upon carefully nurtured neighborhood clienteles. A Boston study indicated that almost 40 percent of the businessmen who were forced to evacuate renewal areas went out of business,[69] and the Renewal Assistance Administration's own national studies indicate that about a third of dislocated businesses have discontinued operations altogether.[70] The disappearance of the small businessman, partly because he seems an anachronism in our age of mass production and mass marketing, is particularly likely to be a spillover effect of urban renewal.

Finally, relocation has exacted a psychological cost as well. People's reactions differ, of course, when they are displaced from their homes and forced to seek other habitation, but for a good many, according to Marc Fried, "it seems quite precise to speak of their reactions as grief."[71] Some of the relocated from Boston's West End, whom Fried studied, expressed intense emotion at separation from the old neighborhood social patterns: "I felt like my heart was taken out of me"; "What's the use of thinking about it?"; "Even now I feel like crying

66 See, for example, Chester Hartman, "The Housing of Relocated Families," *Journal of the American Institute of Planners, 30* (November, 1964), 266–286.

67 Anderson, *op. cit.*, p. 62.

68 Herbert Gans, "The Failure of Urban Renewal," *Commentary* (April, 1965), pp. 29–37.

69 Basil G. Zimmer, "The Small Businessman and Relocation," in Wilson, *Urban Renewal,* p. 382.

70 Cited in Advisory Commission on Intergovernmental Relations, *Metropolitan America,* p. 69.

71 Fried, *op. cit.*, p. 151.

when I pass by." To middle-class Americans, these strong emotional responses may be surprising. But the social networks and spatial relations within a neighborhood are much more salient to lower-class than to middle- and upper-class people because almost all the socializing of lower-class Americans takes place in the immediate neighborhood, whereas middle-class contacts and interactions are much wider.[72] For this reason, the disruption of neighborhood social ties can foster deep feelings of alienation and frustration among low-income residents.

SUMMING UP THE IMPACT   The multidimensional impact of a public policy involving a dozen legislative acts, years of development, and billions of dollars does not lend itself to hasty summary. Although significant public resources have been provided to cities, the overwhelming majority of decisions about land use, housing, and industrial location are still made in the private sector. The $7 billion previously committed to urban renewal by the federal government represents only a fraction of the estimated $26 billion spent annually on residential construction alone. The major constraint upon the renewal program's goal of restructuring the urban environment is the hundreds of thousands of private decisions made by families, commercial establishments, and industrial corporations. Similarly, the public-housing units constructed since the Depression represent only a fraction of the total number of existing housing units. Decay, obsolescence, and mobility may have been slowed by renewal and housing programs, but they have not been halted. And, as with all public policies, even the gains have not been won without spillover costs.

## MODEL CITIES

The "model-cities" program is the latest in the arsenal of weapons to restructure the urban environment. This highly touted program was created by the Demonstration Cities and Metropolitan Development Act of 1966. (For fear that the title might imply a reward to "demonstrations" by "rioters," the program came to be called "model" rather than "demonstration" cities.) The city applying for a grant must develop a comprehensive program to improve the quality of life in a given neighborhood, through education, housing, municipal services, crime and delinquency control, health services, economic development, and transportation plans. Model-cities grants take three principal forms.

[72] Donald E. Muir and Eugene A. Weinstein, "The Social Debt: An Investigation of Lower Class and Middle Class Norms of Social Obligation," *American Sociological Review,* 27 (August, 1962), 532–539.

A planning grant covers a year of planning, during which time government officials, private groups, and neighborhood residents establish priorities and prepare a request for additional funds, which are available to those cities whose plans are approved. They can be used for various purposes consonant with the approved plans but are directed primarily at those parts of the program for which conventional grants are not available. Urban-renewal grants cover redevelopment activities within the "model neighborhoods."

Local officials have been enthusiastic about the model-cities program. From their perspective, it introduces considerable flexibility into federal aid to urban areas. In principle, everything from sewers to schools may be included in the program. Moreover, model cities, though not guaranteed assistance under related federal programs, are given priority. The program also appeals to local officials because they have the final say about each component of the total package. In model-city plans city hall has a veto over any particular item, in contrast to both the urban-renewal and antipoverty programs, where quasi-governmental agencies have had considerable autonomy. City councils are also comforted by the predominantly "bricks and mortar" orientation of this program. In contrast to the war on poverty and its community-action agencies, model neighborhoods are to be improved mainly through upgrading facilities and services, in contrast to the poverty program, which often seeks to improve the lot of the poor by "politicizing" them.

Yet the enabling legislation for model cities does require "widespread citizen participation" in both planning and execution. (Note that this phrase is milder than the "maximum feasible participation" of the Economic Opportunity Act.) Neighborhood groups, often through organizations developed under the poverty programs, have, in many cities, succeeded in winning concessions from city hall. In the final analysis, neighborhood groups cannot be ignored, simply because the city must convince the federal government that citizen-participation requirements are being met. A city government that rides roughshod over neighborhood groups will have difficulty defending itself against the charge of ignoring neighborhood sentiments. The planning stage in some model cities has been marked by continual skirmishing between neighborhoods and city halls, whereas the traditional public and private bureaucracies (for urban renewal, social welfare, and school systems) have played relatively small roles.[73]

The model-cities program is designed to provide "models" for comprehensive and coordinated development of "disadvantaged" neigh-

[73] Roland L. Warren, "Model Cities First Round: Politics, Planning, and Participation," *Journal of the American Institute of Planners, 34* (July, 1969), 245–253.

borhoods. Such models are to be major social experiments, to be used by other cities. The degree to which this goal is met will depend in part upon the funding. Under the original proposal, a handful of cities (a commonly mentioned figure was six) were to receive generous aid for major innovations. Programs providing benefits to few constituencies, however, are not popular in Congress, and the number was increased, first to 63 and later to 150 model cities. In the first three years of the program (1966–1969), Congress provided about $1 billion ($23 million for planning grants, $572.5 for supplemental grants, and $412.5 for urban-renewal grants in model neighborhoods). But model cities were major victims of federal economy in the fall of 1969, when President Nixon ordered a 42 percent decrease in the proposed budget. A major dilemma may be inherent in the program: On one hand, spreading $1 billion among 150 cities may not permit any city to fund a major innovation, yet, on the other, if genuine "models" do develop, other cities may still lack the resources to emulate them.

## SUMMARY

Planning, urban renewal, public housing, and model cities are all designed to manage urban growth. Changes in the urban environment—weathering, deterioration, population and production mobility —all produce demands on decision-makers to reverse, accelerate, or manipulate what Banfield has called the "logic of metropolitan growth." According to Banfield,

*Much of what has happened—as well as of what is happening—in the typical city or metropolitan area can be understood in terms of three imperatives. The first is demographic: if the population of a city increases, the city must expand in one direction or another—up, down, or from the center outward. The second is technological: if it is feasible to transport large numbers of people outward (by train, bus, and automobile) but not upward or downward (by elevator), the city must expand outward. The third is economic: if the distribution of wealth and income is such that some can afford new housing and the time and money to commute considerable distances to work while others cannot, the expanding periphery of the city must be occupied by the first group (the "well-off") while the older, inner parts of the city, where most of the jobs are, must be occupied by the second group (the "not well-off").[74]*

Whether these factors are "imperatives" or merely tendencies is debatable, but they accurately characterize the patterns of growth in the

[74] Edward C. Banfield, *The Unheavenly City* (Boston, Little, Brown, 1970), p. 23.

American metropolis. The policies described in this chapter represent government efforts to cope with these changes. Through planning, zoning, and related policies, urban governments can attempt to secure particular kinds of environment. Through sophisticated use of planning and zoning, it may be possible to create an environment uniquely satisfying to the community or to important groups within it. These strategies, however, typically involve spillover costs to other communities within the metropolis.

Redevelopment and public-housing policies are also intended to have impacts on the urban physical environment. Although the two were originally coupled, urban renewal has been effectively divorced from public housing and has been more favored by municipal officials —partly because it can compensate somewhat for the loss of tax revenues resulting from commercial and personal emigration. Renewal programs also have significant unintended impacts, particularly those arising from the dislocation of families and businesses in areas slated for the bulldozer. Public housing has not been able to accommodate more than a fraction of those displaced by urban renewal; indeed, over the years, public housing has been a source of consternation to both its friends and its enemies. The former have managed to save the housing program but have expressed some disillusionment over its effects, and its enemies oppose it as a "socialist" infringement on the private-enterprise system. "Model cities" is the latest in the arsenal of redevelopment policies. Although its effects are not yet fully apparent, it is designed to create models for managing urban growth. But, as with the other policies examined here, it suffers significant constraints. The most significant is what Banfield has called the "logic of metropolitan growth": The character of the metropolis is shaped by powerful socioeconomic forces that are not easily deflected by public policy.

# epilogue
## The urban crisis and political science

"Local politics" is no longer one of the dustbins of political science. Urban affairs present some of the most dynamic and controversial issues in contemporary society, and social scientists are using tools of increasing sophistication in order to comprehend urban phenomena. They are also turning to a wider range of sources as the "need to know" grows. Political scientists, for example, make use of materials produced by sociologists, psychologists, economists, geographers, and ecologists to comprehend the human and physical dimensions of urban affairs and offer in turn their own insights about the dynamics of urban politics and the policies produced by urban political systems.

In this text we have presented the best of the material about urban politics in a framework emphasizing the policy-making process. We have considered a number of elements that shape the policies of urban areas, the major policies offered in several fields of service, and—as far as possible—the effects of environment and policy feedback on the decisions of public officials. In this epilogue we shall take an overview of urban problems and deal with two evaluations of urban life: one negative, one positive. We shall also look closely at some newly developed tools of political science. By themselves, these tools will not solve any problems of urban life or even prescribe solutions for the policy-makers. Yet they can help policy-makers define the magnitude of the social and economic problems that occur in their communities and may help them define a set of policies that are feasible for local conditions.

## THE URBAN CRISIS: THE NEGATIVE VIEW

The urban crisis has many aspects. At the very least, it represents a sharp divergence between aspirations and achievements in personal income, employment opportunity, racial segregation, education, housing, health, crime, and pollution. At worst, it represents failure in all these areas, failure that may—if not remedied—destroy our culture. Some critics see the various components of the urban crisis as fitting together in an interrelated whole. To us, however, the picture is less one of an integrated whole than of various pieces that may or may not be related to one another in various communities.

One element in the urban crisis is economic. The poor in the central cities have little immediate hope of rising out of their poverty. The most visible feature associated with poverty is race. Many whites live in cities, but it is the poor blacks who present the most serious concentrations of poverty and who suffer numerous other social dislocations that seem based upon—and to feed—their poverty. Blacks show the highest rates of unemployment and underemployment; they are segregated in primary and secondary schools that are said to be "holding pens," rather than educational institutions whose graduates are fit for productive lives; their crime and disease rates are the highest in any city; and they have meager opportunities for decent housing and public recreation.

Although blacks in central cities face an array of obstacles to the "good life" that seem nearly insurmountable, the parameters defining the crisis affect all city dwellers. Among these parameters the following are the most significant:

1   growing central-city concentrations of the poor, uneducated, and black;
2   the segregation of blacks in central-city neighborhood schools;
3   educational programs and teachers who are unresponsive to the social and linguistic problems of the urban poor and unable to provide the training necessary to maximize their economic potential;
4   unemployment concentrations among males eighteen to twenty-five years old with little education, which makes them highly visible and susceptible recruits for civil disorder;
5   periodic social conflagrations far beyond the capacities of local police to control;
6   dispersion of industrial and commercial jobs to the suburbs, beyond easy commuting range of the central-city labor pool;
7   failure of mass transit to meet the needs of low-income communities for cheap home-to-job transportation;
8   poor diets resulting in low stamina for school and job performance;
9   high rates of infant mortality and mental retardation, traceable partly to inadequate prenatal care and infant diets;

10    high rates of venereal disease and illegitimacy, with attendant problems
      of fatherless homes and delinquency passing through the generations;
11    substandard housing, plus social and economic barriers against the dis-
      persion of low-income, especially black, populations to better neighbor-
      hoods;
12    high crime rates in poor neighborhoods, which reflect social dislocations
      and add to the burdens carried by neighborhood residents.

The city dweller's emotional response to these features of the urban
crisis is heightened by his view of government as incapable of cor-
recting them. It is said that local governments lack the commitment or
ability to deal with such problems and that state and federal governments fail to provide the incentives and resources necessary to deal with
them. In fact, some pessimists argue that federal policies serve to aggra-
vate rather than to alleviate urban problems.

As we have seen, urban areas contain the greatest concentrations
of wealth in our society, but many governments compete for this
wealth. The state and national governments soak up huge amounts
of resources through their income and sales taxes, and a plethora of
local governments divide the funds available from taxes on real property. The cities are thus left with the least popular and least flexible
sources of revenue. Moreover, city governments are most vulnerable
to tax competition. Industrial and commercial taxpayers have numerous
options among the jurisdictions of a metropolitan area, and local
officials are susceptible to the argument that high taxes will keep
away—or drive away—property owners who would otherwise make substantial contributions to the local economy.

Large cities also find themselves left with the legacy of their historic wealth in the form of requirements that they contribute to state
and federal coffers so that "poorer" rural areas may receive intergovernmental assistance. Undoubtedly the urban areas will have to continue
acting as fiscal crutches for the hinterlands. Yet many anachronistic formulas of state and federal aid provide greater benefits to wealthy suburbs
than to struggling central cities. As the cities are caught between the
migration of big taxpayers to the suburbs and the competition from
state and federal tax systems that do not return fair shares to the cities,
their schools and other social services seem totally inadequate in the
face of demands from populations beset by problems.

The disparities in the federal government's housing programs for
the urban poor and the middle- and upper-income suburbanites provide
just one example of the policy inequities that seem destined to aggra-
vate the cities' problems. For the home-owning member of the middle-
and upper-income brackets the federal government provides mortgage
subsidies under the programs of the Veterans Administration and the

Federal Housing Administration, plus further subsidies in the form of tax deductibility of interest and property-tax payments. For the urban poor there are meager funds for low-rent public housing. In 1968 the President's Commission on Civil Disorders asked for 6 million low- and moderate-income housing units over a five-year period. Between 1966 and 1968, the average annual number of public-assisted housing "starts" was only 71,000 units.[1] One study found that federal programs to subsidize housing for the *poorest* fifth of the population cost $820 million in 1962, whereas federal subsidies (like interest write-offs on income tax) of housing for the *wealthiest* fifth of the population cost $1.7 billion.[2]

At one time the inequitable representation of central-city residents in state legislatures and Congress was said to be responsible for the meager response to urban needs. Now that we are almost a decade into the era of reapportionment this political reform seems to be less rewarding than had been expected. Suburbs have gained more representation than central cities have, and the new urban legislators are frequently unable to agree on policies to try to persuade state and national governments to adopt. Urban representatives reflect the divisions in social backgrounds, political parties, and philosophies that mark the populations living in metropolitan areas, with the result that there may be little change in the benefits coming to central cities. In most states the central cities seem destined for minority status in the electorate. Any "goodies" they extract from the states will have to come on the same old basis of persuasion and not from any newly acquired political clout.[3]

Even recent awareness of environmental pollution presents problems for urban politics. Among middle-class college students, the environment ranks as a unifying issue. They all favor clean air and water. Yet, to one perceptive segment of black urban leadership, the ecology issue represents a diversion of both funds and interest from the blacks' basic needs for jobs, housing, and education. They regard cutbacks on urban industrial development just when blacks seem on the verge of getting their share of the "action" as one more instance of the double racial standard in American life.

[1] Alan K. Campbell and Donna E. Shalala, "Problems Unsolved, Solutions Untried: The Urban Crisis," in Campbell, ed., *The States and the Urban Crisis* (Englewood Cliffs, N.J., Prentice-Hall, 1970), pp. 14–15.

[2] Alvin Schorr, "National Community and Housing Policy," *The Social Service Review, 39* (December, 1965), quoted in Campbell and Shalala, *op. cit.*, pp. 13–14.

[3] A. James Reichley. "The Political Containment of the Cities," in Alan K. Campbell, ed., *The States and the Urban Crisis* (Englewood Cliffs, N.J., Prentice-Hall, 1970), pp. 169–195.

## THE URBAN CRISIS: A BRIGHTER VIEW

Banfield is one of the most vocal proponents of the view that things are not as bad as they seem, that, in fact, they are better than ever before:

*The plain fact is that the overwhelming majority of city dwellers live more comfortably and conveniently than ever before. They have more and better housing, more and better schools, more and better transportation, and so on. By any conceivable measure of material welfare the present generation of urban Americans is, on the whole, better off than any other large group of people has ever been anywhere. What is more, there is every reason to expect that the general level of comfort and convenience will continue to rise at an even more rapid rate through the foreseeable future.*[4]

In *The Unheavenly City,* Banfield has not disputed the existence of an urban crisis, but he has defined it in terms of frustrated expectations rather than of objective deprivation. According to him, the problems of poverty, ignorance, disease, poor housing, and crime affect "only a rather small minority of the whole urban population."[5] Moreover, some of the "problems" are necessary accompaniments of the attractions of urban society. Congestion will not go away as long as many people find great benefits in living close to many other people and the jobs and commercial and cultural oportunities that exist in urban areas. Traffic snarls will remain as long as people resist staggered employment hours.

Banfield has not denied the presence of segregation, inadequate housing, and poverty in urban areas, but he has claimed that conditions are better than in poor rural areas. The vast majority of inadequate housing exists *outside* large cities and metropolitan areas. Education levels are, to be sure, lower in central cities than in the suburbs, but they are lower in rural areas than in central cities. The urban police may be intemperate in their dealings with blacks and other ethnic minorities, but not to the extent of rural southern sheriffs.

Banfield has found some of the alleged problems in urban areas grossly exaggerated. Population growth in low-income neighborhoods was greater in earlier decades of urban history because of immigration of the European poor, he has said, and to those who argue that vast numbers of poor blacks will overburden the cities' capacity for economic and social accommodation, he has replied that earlier decades of peasant immigration placed larger numerical strains on urban political systems.

[4] Edward C. Banfield, *The Unheavenly City* (Boston, Little, Brown, 1970), pp. 3–4.
[5] *Ibid.,* p. 11.

There are urban problems that do concern Banfield. One is the unprecedented concentration in cities of urban blacks whose psychological alienation from the dominant society may be far greater than suggested by indexes of material deprivation. Young, unemployed black males have especially bleak economic prospects, and, though their condition may be no worse economically—and may even be better— than that of their rural forebears, their concentration in urban ghettos provides the human masses that can explode and threaten our basic social fabric. Second, there is a gap between anticipated social and economic gains and the benefits actually achieved. As long as aspirations rise faster than do accomplishments, this gap will continue to widen; no matter how much social progress is achieved, the tinder for a social revolution will remain. Third, government programs that are unable to solve basic social and personal problems nevertheless sometimes help to increase aspirations and thus pave the way for increased frustrations:

To a large extent . . . our urban problems are like the mechanical rabbit at the racetrack, which is set to keep just ahead of the dogs no matter how fast they may run. Our performance is better and better, but because we set our standards and expectations to keep ahead of performance, the problems are never any nearer to solution. . . .

The effect of too-high standards cannot be to spur us on to reach the prescribed level of performance sooner than we otherwise would, for that level is by definition impossible of attainment. At the same time, these standards may cause us to adopt measures that are wasteful and injurious and, in the long run, to conclude from the inevitable failure of these measures that there is something fundamentally wrong with our society.[6]

There is merit in both the negative view of the urban situation and in Banfield's brighter assessment of it. Banfield seems right in his claim that things have never been better, yet he concedes that achievements have not caught up with aspirations and may even be falling farther behind. Social progress is not measured only by what is but also by what could be.

Our concern here is less to identify and to prescribe cures for urban problems than to introduce a set of analytic techniques that political scientists (and other social scientists) can use to improve our information about the problems and opportunities that face urban policymakers. We offer not solutions but means of understanding. As intellectuals, we must claim that understanding is the first step toward solution. Yet perfect understanding is not much easier to obtain than are perfect solutions when we are dealing with complex problems that

6 *Ibid.,* pp. 21–22.

so far have proved intractable. Through such procedures, policy analysts can learn much that is useful but not everything they should know. As we have noted before (see Chapter 6, pp. 203–204), policy-makers cannot wait until all the information is in before they make decisions. But it is to be hoped that they are always open to new information and will take cognizance of it at some point in the endless cycle of policy formulation, implementation, and reformulation.

## BASIC RESEARCH IN THE POLICY PROCESS: COMPARATIVE POLICY ANALYSIS

In recent years academic political scientists and economists have shown considerable interest in the analysis of public policy. This interest is wide-ranging and includes oratory in behalf of certain favored policies, case studies designed to flesh out elaborate models of the policy-making process, sophisticated commentaries at high levels of abstraction on the ways policies are chosen, academic adaptations of benefit-cost analysis, and elaborate comparisons of the policies offered by different governments.[7]

Our concern is with comparative studies that pursue a consciously scientific course in measuring policies in several jurisdictions quantitatively and qualitatively and defining their statistical relations with various features in their environment. Although much of the literature concerns policy processes of state governments, a good deal is also relevant to local political systems.[8] Even what is almost exclusively

[7] See, for example, Michael Lipsky, *Protest in City Politics: Rent Strikes, Housing and the Power of the Poor* (Skokie, Ill., Rand McNally, 1970); Graham T. Allison, "Conceptual Models and the Cuban Missile Crisis," *American Political Science Review, 63* (September, 1969), 689–718; Yehezkel Dror, *Public Policymaking Reexamined* (San Francisco, Chandler, 1968); Charles E. Lindblom, *The Policy-Making Process* (Englewood Cliffs, N.J., Prentice-Hall, 1968); Bruce M. Russett, "Who Pays for Defense?" *American Political Science Review, 63* (June, 1969), 412–426; and W. Lee Hansen and Burton A. Weisbrod, *Benefits, Costs, and Finance of Public Higher Education* (Chicago, Markham, 1969).

[8] Some representative pieces include Thomas R. Dye, *Politics, Economics and the Public: Policy Outcomes in the American States* (Skokie, Ill., Rand McNally, 1966); Thomas R. Dye, "Income Inequality and American State Politics," *American Political Science Review, 63* (March, 1969), 157–162; Bryan Fry and Richard Winters, "The Politics of Redistribution," *American Political Science Review, 64* (June, 1970), pp. 508–522; Charles Cnudde and Donald McCrone, "Party Competition and Welfare Policies in the United States," *American Political Science Review, 63* (September, 1969), 858–866; Robert L. Lineberry and Edmund P. Fowler, "Reformism and Public Policies in American Cities." *American Political Science Review, 61* (September, 1967), 701–716; Allen Pulsipher and James L. Weatherby, Jr., "Malap-

oriented to the state level suggests modes of analysis that are relevant to local politics. The concern is not simply with how policies differ from one jurisdiction to another but also with the *salient,* or distinctive, differences in policies and the elements related to the distinctions. Some scholars are interested in explaining the policy differences that exist; they look at certain policies as "dependent variables" and consider their relations with the economic, social, or political characteristics that seem likely to have shaped them. Others are interested in explaining the effects of different policies; they look at certain policies as "independent variables" and consider their relations with the economic, social, and political characteristics that may be affected by them.[9]

The comparative analysis of state or local policies shares certain traits with PPB (planning-programming-budgeting, see pp. 201–203), but comparative analysis also shows important differences. Both favor

---

portionment, Party Competition, and the Functional Distribution of Government Expenditures," *American Political Science Review, 62* (December, 1968), 1207–1219; Robert E. Crew, Jr., "Dimensions of Public Policy: A Factor Analysis of State Expenditures," *Social Science Quarterly, 50* (September, 1969), 381–388; Ira Sharkansky and Richard I. Hofferbert, "Dimensions of State Politics, Economics and Public Policy," *American Political Science Review, 63* (September, 1969), 867–879; and Alan K. Campbell and Seymour Sacks, *Metropolitan America* (New York, Free Press, 1967).

[9] Strictly speaking, it is inaccurate to say that current research identifies the *influence* of certain elements over policies or the changes that policies *cause* in their economic, social, or political surroundings. The closest approach to causation is the discovery of relations that are consistent with causal patterns. Starting with the hypothesis that element A brings about policy B we can infer support for that hypothesis if we find element A and policy B typically associated in the same time and place. Of course, we must determine if the coexistence of A and B result from the common trait C. That is, we must "control" the relationship between A and B to discover if it is not simply a product of C. One hypothesis, for example, is that high levels of political participation bring about high levels of public service. If we find that cities with high citizen participation also have high levels of public service, we have superficial support for the hypothesis. But we must check other explanations of the findings. It may be that the general level of economic well-being influences both political participation and the availability of public services. We know that people who are wealthy and well educated show more than the average interest in politics, and we know that wealth has something to do with the resources necessary to support public services. The amount of economic wealth in a city may thus cause both its high (or low) levels of political participation and public services. On the other hand, it is possible that the political cultures in certain cities lead their citizens to participate more (or less) actively than would be expected on the basis of wealth, or lead their government officials to greater (or lesser) levels of commitment in offering public services. At this point, it appears that participation has an "independent" relationship with certain kinds of state polices: those that are "politicized" and the subjects of intense public dispute. See Sharkansky and Hofferbert, *op. cit.*

the most rigorous qualitative or quantitative measurement feasible, and both are self-conscious in their choice of the statistical procedures appropriate for each problem. There are differences, however, in techniques and in the kinds of information produced. Specifically, comparative policy analysis operates at a higher level of abstraction than does PPB. The concern of comparative policy analysis is with aggregate indicators of policies within several different jurisdictions, rather than with alternative proposals for certain aspects of one jurisdiction's program. Comparative policy analysis is concerned less with the costs of program elements than with the magnitudes of overall program "outputs" and with the environmental features that accompany them. Comparative policy analysis is less directly useful to the policy-maker than is PPB. At its present stage of development it is more clearly "basic research" than is PPB. Its findings provide useful information to the policy-maker—as we shall demonstrate—but the policy-maker must add important elements in "translating" the results of comparative policy analysis to his own needs. He can determine where his own jurisdiction stands in comparison to others on certain aggregate measures of performance, and he can estimate the chances (given environmental features) of his jurisdiction's making certain changes in performance. At the present stage of comparative policy analysis, however, the policy-maker must still provide much from his own insight into local conditions in judging "what it would take" in proposals and strategies to produce desired changes in performance. Comparative policy analysis also offers a valuable perspective to a policy-maker. It can broaden his horizons and familiarize him with the programs and problems of other judisdictions. As does PPB, it may provide a useful training exercise even if it does not "pay off" as its most optimistic promoters hope it will.

Generally speaking, comparative policy analysis is more concerned with description and explanation than with prescription, yet it does not totally lack interest for the proper forms of policy. Indeed, interest in the environmental features that may influence policy and in the influence that policy may exert on the environment leads to the use of social science to produce better information about the policy process. Social science can tell the policy-maker and the student of public policy what features of the environment are—and are not—likely to constrain major changes in policy, how strong the constraints are likely to be, and how much difference a certain policy change is likely to make in certain features of the environment.

## Selected findings of comparative policy analysis

In order to grasp the possibilities and limitations of comparative policy analysis, it is necessary to look at some representative findings.

Some early research produced surprising refutations of widely accepted propositions. For example, the equality of state legislative apportionment typically received high priority in the desires of urban reformers. With greater urban-rural equality in legislative districting, state governments were expected to become more responsive to the interests of urban citizens. Yet a sizable body of scholarship found no substantial differences between the states that were well and poorly apportioned in policies on taxation, welfare, education, health, highways, and natural resources.[10] Similarly, many people assume that competition among political parties is a "good thing" and should make itself felt in the policies offered by state and local governments. In their quest for popular support, competitive parties should "bid up" the nature of services offered. But here, too, there is contrary evidence. Taking account of the economic differences among the states, early research found no substantial policy differences between those states with competitive parties and those dominated by single parties. Since the first wave of "revisionist" scholarship, some later research has specified certain conditions that determine the salience of legislative apportionment or competition among political parties for policy-makers. The relations with policy are not as strong as suggested by reformers or casual observers, but neither are they as weak as suggested by the early "revisionists."[11]

ECONOMIC DEVELOPMENT AND PUBLIC POLICY    One line of research that seems especially fruitful in identifying constraints and resources for the policy-maker involves the level of economic development within a jurisdiction. The model used to guide this research is simple. It merely posits that economic features of a jurisdiction have something to do with the nature of public policy. This model is used most often as part of a systems framework that treats the economy as providing the inputs of resources, demands, and supports for a conversion process in which other inputs from politics may affect the relations between the economy and policy.[12] Some regard the economic-policy model as too simple because it leaves out many specific features of the policy-making process. It does, but its simplicity also offers several benefits: a demonstrated capacity to support empirical research and to produce a series of propositions about the conditions that create more or less powerful

10 Dye, *Politics, Economics and the Public.*
11 Pulsipher and Weatherby, *op. cit.;* Sharkansky and Hofferbert, *op. cit.;* and Cnudde and McCrone, *op. cit.*
12 See Dye, *Politics, Economics and the Public;* Glenn W. Fisher, "Interstate Variation in State and Local Government Expenditures," *National Tax Journal, 17* (March, 1964), 57–73; and much of the literature cited there.

relationships between various features of the economy and various features of public policy. The practitioners of comparative policy analysis append various additional aspects of the policy-making process to this basic model and consider several kinds of economic traits as correlates of public policy. It is appropriate for us to concentrate on the economic-policy links, for the literature provides us with richer information about them than about other features of the policy process and there are many allegations that the most pervasive influences on public policy come from the economy. Many of these allegations are misleading or exaggerated. By reviewing the findings available to date, we can assess the strength of the economic-policy links and how much latitude for policy innovation is permitted by economic constraints.

According to much of the current literature, the nature of a jurisdiction's economy limits the magnitude and quality of the jurisdiction's "policy outputs." Limiting the resources available is said to limit an official's capacity for current performance and innovation. It is important to understand which limitations may be placed on the policy-maker by economics and under what conditions they are likely to inhibit innovation. The first wave of research into economic-policy links tended to exaggerate the strength of economic influence over policy and to neglect findings that provided clues to policy arenas that are relatively free from economic influence. Dye has made the strongest argument that the level of economic development within a state imposes severe limits on the nature of policy outputs. High levels of economic development (measured by such variables as percentage of a state's population that is urban, per capita personal income, median education level, and industrial employment) are generally associated with high levels of expenditure and service outputs in education, welfare, and health. These service outputs are measured by teachers' salaries, rates of attendance in schools, success on national examinations, average welfare benefits, and incidence of medical facilities. Economic development may provide the wherewithal to purchase these services or may increase the demand for them among client groups.

It is true that economic development and policies generally stand in these mutual relations. Yet the relations are not so strong as to preclude noneconomic factors from having crucial impacts on public policy. Thomas Dye has reported 456 coefficients of simple correlations between policy measures and his four economic measures of income, urbanism, industrialization, and education, but only 16 (4 percent) are strong enough to indicate that an economic measure accounts for at least 50 percent of the interstate statistical variation on a policy measure. He also reports 54 coefficients of determination that show the combined strength of his four economic measures with policy. Only 19 (35 percent) indicate that all economic measures together account for 50 percent of the interstate variation in policy.[13] There are economic constraints upon public policy, but they are not immutable. There is no "iron law" of economics that establishes the level and content of public policy. Rather, the economy varies in its influence over policy. This variation can occur between different levels of government, different periods of time, different kinds of public service, and at difference levels of affluence. Some of the comparative findings on state and community policy indicate these kinds of variations in economic influence over policy.

Economic influences appear to be strongest in local policy processes and weakest in those of state and federal governments. Explanations cite differences in economic resources and fiscal opportunities. Most local governments must draw upon limited geographical areas for resources and are confined to one major revenue source (property taxes). State governments, in contrast, can draw upon their larger jurisdictions and can transfer resources from "have" to "have-not" communities. State officials also have wider revenue options, including taxes on income and retail sales. State income and sales taxes appear to be less upsetting politically and less vulnerable to economic downturns than do local property taxes. As a result, state officials can escape many of the constraints on policy that seem to originate in the economic sector and that limit the policy discretion of local government officials. Federal officials can also escape economic constraints, partly because of their ability to tax resources of wealthy areas throughout the country and partly because of their power to borrow to meet current deficits in the balance between taxing and spending. Indeed, the federal government operates numerous programs to control levels of employment, interest, and wages and may be as much the master as the subordinate of the economy. Moreover, not all local governments are equally influenced by the nature of local economies. Where the municipality has adopted "reformed" government structures there is less of an economic-policy link than where it has an unreformed structure (see Chapter 7, pp. 222–225). The principal features of a reformed local government structure are a professional city manager, nonpartisan elections for local offices, and a council selected at large rather than by wards. These features seem to "depoliticize" the social and economic cleavages within a community and to permit local officials to make their policy decisions with relatively little concern for the demands of different economic factions.[14]

[13] Dye, *Politics, Economics and the Public.*
[14] Lineberry and Fowler, *op. cit.*

There are also variations in economic influences on policy over time. There is some evidence that the influence of economic conditions on state and local government policies is diminishing. Alan K. Campbell and Seymour Sacks, for example, found a decreasing correlation (from .920 to .558) between state and local expenditures and income levels in 1903–1965.[15] Although the influence of economic elements still appears quite important, policy-makers may now have greater independence from their economic environment. Some of this increased flexibility may reflect changes in federal aid. The federal government is able to tax multiple sources of wealth and to make up for some of the differentials between states. Also state and local governments now have somewhat more flexible tax structures than in the past.

Economic conditions exert less constraint on some kinds of policy than on others. The political salience of a policy is one of the factors that can lessen the influence of economics. To the extent that programs are the subject of prominent disputes among individual candidates and political parties, they can attract the use of substantially more resources than are normally associated with the jurisdiction's level of wealth. Officials "try harder" under the impetus of public demand. Under other conditions—when public demand runs counter to a program—performance is less than would be expected on the basis of economic conditions. There are also differences between policies supported by "earmarked" revenues and those that compete in each budget cycle for their share of "general funds." Funds for highways and natural resources generally come from taxes or license fees specified for those purposes by state statutes or constitutions. Whatever each year's economic activity produces through those taxes and fees goes to those activities. Only occasionally does a legislature grant a change in such allotments or a special appropriation. In the case of most states' welfare and education programs, however, officials in the executive and legislative branches make funding decisions during each budget cycle. There is a much greater chance for political or program considerations to produce higher—or lower—education and welfare budgets than would be expected on the basis of economic indicators.[16]

The economic-policy relationship can also vary with the level of affluence shown by a jurisdiction. One study found that relations between welfare policies and economic conditions are strongest among those states at the highest and lowest levels of wealth and income. In the middle range of states (and, by implication, municipalities) there

[15] Campbell and Sacks, op. cit., p. 57.
[16] Cnudde and McCrone, op. cit.; and Sharkansky and Hofferbert, op. cit.

are many cases of both higher and lower levels of service than would be expected on the basis of economic conditions. [17]

INCREMENTALISM AND INFORMATION    Analysis of comparative policy-making studies indicates the strong, but variable role that economic factors play. But the variability of the economic-policy relationship does not mean that policy innovation comes easy. Incremental decision-making is another significant constraint upon policy change and may stifle innovation. Even in those areas in which economy seems to have little influence over policy-making, officials may be bound tightly by the inhibitions of their own decision routines. Studies of national, state, and local budgeting illustrate the pervasiveness of incremental decision-making.[18]

Incrementalism points to a feature of the policy-making process that is of primary importance: its conservatism, except under unusual circumstances that provoke rare departures from previous levels of activity. Ralph K. Huitt, commenting on the difficulty of innovation in an incremental system, has written:

*Paradoxically, it is politically attractive to tout a proposal as "new" so long as it is generally recognized that it is not new at all, but a variation on a familiar theme. . . .*

*It follows that what is most feasible is what is incremental, what can be made to seem a comfortable next step under a program that has already received the good-conduct medal. Nothing is better than an amendment.*[19]

The unavailability or high cost of information, both political and technical, encourages decision-makers to rely upon incrementalism. Participation in urban politics is low, and what there is is filtered through input channels that may obscure interests, rather than clarify them. Elections are relatively ineffective in presenting clear alternatives to the voters, and their results are ambiguous guides to policy. Reformed institutions, including manager governments, nonpartisan elections, and constituencies at large may bring greater efficiency to municipal services, but they may also impede the identifica-

17 John G. Grumm, "Structural Determinants of Legislative Outputs" (Paper delivered at the Conference on the Measurement of Public Policies in the States, Inter-University Consortium for Political Research, Ann Arbor, Michigan, 1968).

18 Otto Davis, M. A. H. Dempster, and Aaron Wildavsky, "A Theory of the Budgetary Process," *American Political Science Review, 60* (September, 1966), 529–547; John P. Crecine, *Government Problem Solving: A Computer Simulation of Municipal Budgeting* (Skokie, Ill., Rand McNally, 1968); and Ira Sharkansky, *The Politics of Taxing and Spending* (Indianapolis, Bobbs-Merrill, 1969).

19 Ralph K. Huitt, "Political Feasibility," in Austin Ranney, ed., *Political Science and Public Policy* (Chicago, Markham, 1968), p. 274.

tion of interests. In light of multiple interests and the limited economic and informational resources available to them, decision-makers often take the incremental path of least resistance.

As we have said before, urban governments are short on technical information. Although civil engineering has progressed to remarkable levels, social engineering is still in its infancy and represents—to some —a disquieting idea in any case. Civil-engineering projects usually "work." Bridges rarely collapse; highways seldom crumble. But we never know whether or not social engineering might have its intended impact. Comparative policy analysis helps explain why some city governments "outspend" others, but it has yet to enlighten us on the actual impacts of public policies on the resources of communities and individuals. Moynihan observed of the war on poverty that "the government did not know what it was doing," and we suspect that this observation is equally applicable to other policy areas.[20] The lack of technical knowledge about policy supports the concerted search for the determinants of policy outputs. It also emphasizes the need for greater knowledge of such dimensions of the policy process as "performance," "use," "distribution," and "impact."[21] The dearth of information both on human wants and needs and on the impacts of policy on them impedes responsible urban policy-making. The blame for imperfect information must be shared alike by citizens, policy-makers, and social scientists.

## COMPARATIVE POLICY ANALYSIS AND THE URBAN CRISIS

What does all this discussion mean for the urban policy-maker who must toil in the midst of alleged or genuine crisis? In all likelihood, there will be continuing tension between the roles of academics and practicing policy-makers. Nevertheless, some academic techniques of comparative policy analysis and research findings will aid the specific concerns of some policy-makers. Given the policy-makers' greater familiarity with their own needs for information, however, it may be their task—rather than that of the academicians—to learn just which techniques and findings are useful in the policy process. As academi-

---

[20] Daniel P. Moynihan, *Maximum Feasible Misunderstanding* (New York, Free Press, 1969), p. 170.

[21] Ira Sharkansky, *Policy Analysis in Political Science* (Chicago, Markham, 1970), chap. 4, 6; and Edwin Olson, "Research in the Library Service Process," in Irene A. Braden and Alice S. Clark, eds., *Quantitative Methods in Librarianship: Standards, Research, Management* (Columbus, Ohio State University Press, 1970).

cians, we may be able to offer no better general recommendation for the practitioner than that he acquire sophisticated training in comparative policy analysis and reflect upon academicians' work.

Some findings in the available basic research can help the policy-maker by telling him how policies are generally related to levels of economic activity, how "general" the relations are, and what conditions are associated with relative freedom from economic influence. The analysis of individual cases and general tendencies can indicate where the policies of a particular jurisdiction stand in relation to others of comparable environmental characteristics. For the policy-maker who wants to innovate, this information may specify the fields of policy where his current performance is at—or below—par for his level of economic resources.

Several of the findings we have reported are not self-evident and would not be within the ken of policy-makers lacking empirical research. They include the evidence that many economy-policy links are weak in statistical power. We therefore know there are many jurisdictions—especially state governments—that surpass the expenditures and policy benefits "usually associated" with their levels of economic development. "We can't afford it" and "The voters won't stand for it" should not excuse state officials from promoting improvements in public services. Many populations pay unusually high bills for public services. Even where taxes are already highest, comparative analysis may reveal policy outputs that are markedly lower than comparable ones in other states. It may take an investment in public relations to convince one's own population that an increase in its tax bill is feasible and worthwhile. But then the problem becomes a selling game and not an encounter with immovable economic barriers. We do not know how many public officials can "sell" their way out of a revenue-service bind. For some, at least, the payoff in better services would be worth the risk.

Another untrivial finding is that state and federal governments are less vulnerable to economic constraints than are local governments. This finding suggests the arenas most likely to bear policy fruit. All taxpayers sound loud shouts of pain, but the local property taxpayer seems to present the most serious challenge to the policy-makers of his jurisdiction. During wartime, no level of government is rich in domestic resources,[22] so we should not be surprised by the recent lack of federal money for many domestic programs. With the hoped-for relaxation of international tensions a concerted push for program development at the federal and state levels, especially in middle- and lower-income states, may become advisable. There the

---

[22] Sharkansky, *Taxing and Spending*, chap. 5; Russett, *op. cit.*

local governments are weakest, and public services depend most on
federal and state help.


## A PERSONAL POSTSCRIPT

We wish we could end this book with a definitive statement about
the urban future. In this volatile urban age, however, all predictions
are hazardous.[23] Whether or not the urban system is in crisis may
be open to debate, but it is irrefutable that the cities do face a
massive array of problems. Many of these problems may be ultimately
beyond the reach of public policy in a democracy. Some of them—crime,
congestion, decay—may be inherent aspects of the urban condition
and simply irremediable. Others—pollution, for example—are the
almost inevitable by-products of the forces that produce urban
wealth. In many cases, a solution to one problem will exacerbate
another. The pollution of land, air, and water, for instance, cannot
be solved without partially dismantling the economic system, which
in turn would make the fight against poverty even more difficult.
Moreover, some public policies may, as conservatives and radicals both
argue, do more harm than good.

We part company with those conservatives, however, who believe
that urban problems are absolutely unyielding to public policy. We
also part company with those radicals who deny that real reform of
urban government is possible and demand radical or revolutionary
change. We believe that urban governments have massive human and
economic resources that are available to policy-makers in principle
but inaccessible in fact, and we believe that this situation is exacerbated
by severe service needs, prevailing philosophies of incrementalism
rather than innovation, substitution of rhetoric for responsibility, and
policies constructed upon fragmentary information.

---

[23] For two attempts, however, see the computerized futurism of Herman
Kahn and Anthony Wiener, *Toward the Year 2000* (New York, Macmillan, 1967);
and of Jay W. Forrester, *Urban Dynamics* (Cambridge, Mass., M.I.T. Press, 1969).

# index

Roberts, Congressman, 276
Robinson, James A., 6
Rochester, Mich., 73
Routines, 185
Rural areas, 22
Rustin, Bayard, 104

Sacks, Seymour, 358
St. Louis, 25, 140, 163, 166
  blacks voting in, 93
  labor in, 67
  political participation in, 59
Sait, Edward M., 80
Sales taxes, 39, 209
Salisbury, Robert, 192
San Antonio, Tex., 13
San Francisco, Calif., 143
  antipoverty program in, 292–295
  mass transit system in, 273
Sayre, Wallace S., 15, 176, 177, 179
Scarsdale, N.Y., 314
Schnore, Leo F., 33
School boards, 257–258
School superintendent, 258
Schorr, Alvin, 319
Scoble, Harry, 59
Screvane, Paul R., 334
Seattle, Wash., 25, 73
Segregation, 262–265, 350
  correlates of, 264
  degree of, 262
  residential, 321, 322
  See also Desegregation
Service charges, 209
Sexton, Patricia C., 197, 266
Shared taxes, 132
Sharkansky, Ira, 224
Shelley, John F., 292
Sherrill, Kenneth S., 85
Shippers, 42
Shopping centers, 40
Sick Cities, 3
Silverman, Arnold R., 98
Slayton, William L., 336
Sloan, Lee, 164
Slums, 321
  See also Housing
Social indicators, 203
Social structure, and poltical partici-
  pation, 56
Social worker, 285, 286
Sorensen, Theodore, 157
Spangler, Richard, 220
Special district, 47
Spillover effects, 198
Stakes, 14–15
  and political participation, 59

Standard Metropolitan Statistical
  Area (SMSA), blacks in, 92
central-city–outside-central-city
  disparities (CC-OCC), 28–32, 48
decentralization in, 318–319
defined, 1
distribution of poverty in, 280
economic resources of, 19–25
  unequal distribution of, 43–50
education in, 22
fragmentation of government in, 25
income in, 22
migration in, 25–28
population growth in, 21–22, 26
  See also Fragmentation of
  government; Metropolitan reform
State constitution, 114, 231
State control over local government,
  46, 49, 109, 113, 115, 162,
  209–210, 224, 231, 348
State government, 48, 125, 348, 352
  aid to cities by, 132–136, 207, 208,
  217, 222–224
State legislatures, 49, 349
State-local centralization, and city
  expenditures, 222–223
  See also State government
Steinbeck, John, 300
Stokes, Carl, 171
Stone, Harold, 74
Stouffer, Samuel A., 150
Strange, John H., 94
Structure of government, 123
Suburbanization, 32
  consequences of, 34–35
Suburbs, 25, 30, 31, 32–35, 74, 111, 222
  migration to, 25–28
  population growth in, 26
  types of, 33–34
  See also Central city-outside
  central city (CC-OCC); Stand-
  ard Metropolitan Statistical
  Area (SMSA)
Supreme Court (U.S.), 252
Sutherland, George, 312
Sventig, Charles, 101
Swanson, Bert E., 74, 156, 162
Syracuse, N.Y., 25
  police in, 245

Taeuber, Alma F., 322
Taeuber, Karl E., 322, 323
Tax concessions, 42

71 72 73 74   7 6 5 4 3 2